PARENTING IN THE 90s

JANE B. BROOKS

KAISER MEDICAL CENTER

Mayfield Publishing Company

Mountain View, California

Toronto • London

To my grandparents and parents,
my children and their children

Library of Congress Cataloging-in-Publication Data

Brooks, Jane B.
    Parenting in the 90s / Jane Brooks.
        p.   cm.
    Includes bibliographical references and index.
    ISBN 1-55934-251-X
    1. Parenting. 2. Child rearing. 3. Parent and child. I. Title.
  II. Title: Parenting in the nineties.
  HQ751.8.B76 1994   93-32036
                                 CIP

Manufactured in the United States of America
10 9 8 7 6 5 4 3 2

Mayfield Publishing Company
1280 Villa Street
Mountain View, CA 94041

Sponsoring editor, Franklin C. Graham; production editor, Sharon Montooth; manuscript editor,
Ruth Letner; text designer, Diane Beasley; cover designer, Susan Breitbard; manufacturing manager,
Martha Branch. The text was set in 10½/12 Berkeley Oldstyle by TBH/Typecast, Inc. and printed on
50# Ecolocote by Malloy Lithographing, Inc.

Photo Credits: pg. 5, © Ulrike Welsch/PhotoEdit; pg. 14, © Elizabeth Crews/The Image Works;
pg. 44, © H. Armstrong Roberts; pg. 47, © Erika Stone; pg. 64, © Joel Gordon 1993; pg. 76,
© Elizabeth Crews; pg. 96, © Shirley Zerberg; pg. 100, © Elizabeth Crews; pg. 126, © Erika Stone;
pg. 145, © Elizabeth Crews; pg. 173, © Elizabeth Crews; pg. 182, © David M. Grossman/Photo
Researchers, Inc.; pg. 194, © Elizabeth Crews, pg. 207, © Bob Daemmrich/The Image Works;
pg. 244, © Elizabeth Crews; pg. 247, © Phiz Mezey; pg. 264, © Elizabeth Crews; pg. 283,
© Mark Richards/PhotoEdit; pg. 300, © Bill Bachmann/The Image Works; pg. 303, © Alan Carey/
The Image Works

Text Credit: pg. 51 through pg. 54, from *Between Generations: The Six Stages of Parenthood* by
Ellen Galinsky. Copyright © 1981 by Ellen Galinsky. Reprinted by permission of Times Books,
a division of Random House, Inc.

 This book is printed on recycled paper.

PARENTING IN THE 90s

Books are †

t,

04

]4

CONTENTS

CHAPTER 6

THE ELEMENTARY SCHOOL YEARS 158

CHAPTER 7

ADOLESCENCE   190

CHAPTER 8

PARENTING/WORKING   223

CHAPTER 9

PARENTING AT TIMES OF CHANGE AND TRAUMA 254

CHAPTER 10

SUPPORTS FOR PARENTS AND CHILDREN 294

PREFACE

Most Americans say they find their greatest satisfaction and meaning in life in their relationships within the family. It is a source of satisfaction that can last a lifetime. Although family is most significant in our lives, it also is most demanding. Caring for an infant or child requires more commitment, patience, control, and persistence than anything else we will ever do.

We receive little, if any, training or practice in parenting—or for that matter in living within the family unit. Trimming someone's nails for pay or driving a car requires a license to demonstrate the ability to perform the task to some standard. High schools now offer driver-training and vocational classes, yet they seldom provide the parent education that may matter most. Perhaps in the future, as the long-term significance of family relationships and the value of being trained for the parenting task is realized, a course in parenting may become part of the standard high school curriculum.

This book attempts to fill the present gap in our education by examining the tasks parents carry out as they raise children from birth through adolescence. It focuses on the core components of parenting, paying particular attention to rearing children who are comfortable with and able to express their feelings appropriately and who enjoy other people and are able to attend to others' needs and concerns as well as their own. The development of responsibility, self-esteem, and optimism receives special attention.

This book focuses on two basic tasks of parenting—creating closer emotional relationships with children and establishing effective limits for children. It shows how parents carry out these tasks with children of different ages and with changing life circumstances, for example, when both parents work outside the home or when divorce or trauma occur.

In addition to describing what parents do, the book describes how parents feel as they raise children. Stages of parenthood are identified, and interviews with parents provide information about what people wish they had known about parenting before they became parents. In 1948 Arthur Jersild said that most of the interest in parenting was focused on the problems parents experienced, and little attention was given to "the cheerful side of the ledger." This book addresses that imbalance and emphasizes the joys that parents experience.

Parenting in the 90s also describes how much has changed over time in response to changing social and economic needs. It examines the stresses that contemporary life places on parents and children alike and identifies supports that can enable parents and children to flourish when we as a society direct our efforts in the cooperative venture of rearing the next generation.

I write this book from the point of view of a parent, a clinician, a researcher, a teacher of parenting. I have the firm conviction that anyone who wishes to invest attention and effort in becoming a competent, caring parent can do so in his or her own way. The single prerequisite is the desire to succeed along with the willingness to invest time and energy, and the results are well worth the effort. My experience as a clinician has shown me that children face many difficult situations; with a loving, supportive caretaker, children can live life fully and happily even if temporarily engulfed by trauma.

Children are not the only ones enriched by adults' efforts to be effective parents. Helping children grow is an intense, exciting experience that brings special meaning for parents. Our physical stamina, agility, and speed increase as we care for infants and toddlers. Our emotional stamina grows as we deal with our own intense feelings with our children and help children learn to express and modulate their feelings. Our intellectual skills grow as we answer young children's questions and later, help them master school subjects. In helping new life grow, we gain for ourselves an inner vitality and richness that affects all our relationships.

ACKNOWLEDGMENTS

Writing the acknowledgments is one of the pleasures of completing a book; and as one reads galleys and page proofs, there are constant reminders of all the people who have helped make the book a reality.

I thank all the clinicians and researchers who gave generously of their time not only for the interviews themselves but also for their additional time reviewing the excerpts and clarifying points. They are: Jay Belsky, Elaine Blechman, Judy Dunn, Susan Harter, Arlie Hochschild, Barbara Keogh, Jacqueline Lerner, Richard Lerner, Susan McHale, Paul Mussen, Arlene Skolnick, Jill Waterman, Emmy Werner, and Steven Wolin.

Special appreciation goes to Dr. Robert Kremers, Chief of the Department of Pediatrics of Kaiser Medical Center, for his willingness to give questionnaires about the joys of parenting to parents in the waiting rooms. I thank the many anonymous parents who completed them there and in parenting classes. Most particularly, I express my gratitude to all those parents I interviewed about the joys of parenting and the ways they changed and grew through the experience. I gained valuable insights about the process of parenting, and their comments enliven the book immeasurably. These parents are: Wendy Clinton, Mark Clinton, Judy Davis, Robert Rosenbaum, Linda Dobson, Douglas Dobson, Jill Fernald, Charles Levine, Otie Gould, Warren Gould, Caryn Gregg, Robert Gregg, Jennifer Lillard, Michael Hoyt, Henrietta Krueger, Richard Kreuger, Patricia Landman, Steven Tulkin, Chris McArtor, Robert McArtor,

Kathy Malone, Jean Oakley, Susan Opsvig, Paul Opsvig, Sherry Proctor, Stewart Proctor, Iris Yotvat-Talmon, Moshe Talmon, Raymond Terwilleger, Patricia Toney, Anthony Toney, Barbara Woolmington-Smith, Craig Woolmington-Smith.

I'd also like to thank the following reviewers: Dr. Don Bower, University of Georgia; David S. Duerden, Director, Ricks College Child Labs; Jeannette D. Wilson, Ph.D., Central Michigan University; Ellen L. Wray, M.S.E., Hutchinson Community College; and Kristin A. Zink, Cuyamaca College.

Coworkers at Kaiser Medical Center at Hayward were supportive and helpful throughout. Marsha Mielke, the medical librarian, obtained all the books and articles I requested. Pediatricians and pediatric advice nurses have provided helpful information about parents' concerns. I am most appreciative of the leadership at Kaiser. Dr. Paul Jewett, the Physician-in-Chief, Dr. Norman Weinstein, the former chief of psychiatry, and Dr. Jerome Rauch, the current chief, all promote an atmosphere in which creativity flourishes.

I also thank Paul Mussen for his suggestions and interest in my writing over the years. He recommended using comments from researchers to make material more vivid for students. His concern with the social forces impinging on parenting has continued to influence my thinking.

The staff at Mayfield Publishing Company deserve special appreciation for the care and diligence they exercised in transforming the manuscript into a book. Franklin Graham, the sponsoring editor, has brought his enthusiasm and critical skill to the task of producing a book students will enjoy and use. His interest and knowledge of the area are invaluable. Andrea Sarros, his assistant, has been a helpful supporter, organizing survey data for my use and solving many practical problems. Sharon Montooth, production coordinator, has worked quietly and efficiently to move the manuscript, seemingly magically, to book form. Ruth Letner, copy editor, has improved the manuscript with her writing and editing, always keeping the reader very much in mind; I appreciate her enthusiasm and support for the book.

Finally, I wish to thank my family and friends for their thoughtfulness and their company. I thank my patients for sharing their lives and experiences with me. I hope they have learned as much about life from me as I have learned from them. Finally, I want to thank my children who are now grown and live away from home. They are very much in my mind as I write and as I relive experiences with them in the different developmental periods. I find that I have learned the most important truths of parenting from our interactions. I believe that when I have paid attention, they have been my best teachers.

PARENTING IS A COOPERATIVE VENTURE

CHAPTER 1

When you first realize that you are about to become a parent, a whole new role begins to take shape in your mind. What does parenting really mean? Is parenting like learning to ride a bike—a process everyone must go through to gain the new skill, responsibility, and freedom? Do most parents plan on becoming parents, or does it just happen to them? If one does plan for parenthood, are there advantages to early timing and later timing of births? How have family structure and childrearing practices evolved throughout the 1900s? As we explore the cooperative venture of parenting, these issues will be examined.

Four million babies are born in the United States each year.[1] The challenge, for parents and for society, is to rear children to realize their full potential in adulthood. This book describes how parents help children grow to their full capacity. It shows how parents adapt broad guidelines to the age and temperament of a particular child and to the different life circumstances each family encounters. The book also describes the vital role society plays in providing resources and supports to parents as they go about the important task of rearing the next generation.

WHAT IS PARENTING?

The American Heritage Dictionary of the English Language[2] defines a parent in several ways—as a mother or father; as an organism that generates new life; and as a guardian or protector. Combining these definitions, one can define a parent as a person who fosters all facets of a child's growth—nourishing, protecting, guiding new life through the course of development.

The words *protecting* and *guiding* are vague. What do they mean in day-to-day life interactions? Saul Brown presents four main tasks of a family: (1) establishing *basic commitments* to family members, (2) providing *warmth and nurturance* for all members, (3) providing *opportunities* and encouraging the development of individuality, and (4) *facilitating ego mastery* and *competence*.[3] When these four tasks are related to the process of rearing children, we can describe the parents' main tasks

1

as establishing warm, nurturant emotional relationships with children and providing opportunities for the development of competence and individuality. Several studies have found that a child's effectiveness is related to a strong emotional tie with a caretaker who stimulates a positive approach to other people and the world and to a consistent set of reasonable limits within which the child is free to explore and to develop skills. The challenge of parenting, then, is to relate to children in ways that stimulate their potentialities for growth and provide appropriate opportunities for experiences that develop these potentialities.

These are researchers' definitions of family and its tasks. What do contemporary Americans think? In a recent survey,[4] 74 percent of adults define family broadly, as "a group of people who love and care for each other." They most value the emotional qualities of family life—the emotional support they get in families, the communication of feelings, the respect family members have for each other, and the responsibility individuals assume for their actions—just the qualities studies find important.

The relationship between parent and child is special, complex, and unique to each parent-child pair. Yet many factors influence the ways in which this highly personal, private relationship develops. A parent brings to the relationship all his or her experiences as a child and an adult as well as hopes and expectations for satisfaction in the relationship. The child, even when only hours old, brings to the relationship inborn characteristics, ways of reacting to the world, that will mold interactions with parents. The parent-child relationship is embedded in a specific family with other members of different ages, and the family lives in a social and cultural milieu that in turn exerts an influence on the family. The parent-child dyad is thus nested in a social group that expands as the child grows and comes into contact with school and other community activities.

THE PROCESS OF BECOMING PARENTS

Each individual who becomes a parent does so within unique circumstances. Some plan enthusiastically; others become parents without deciding to. Factors including the parent's age, career and social status, economic situation, extended family and community support system make the process of anticipating, having, and raising a child special for each.

Reasons for Having Children

Erik Erikson, a clinician and theorist who has described lifetime psychological development, believes adults have a basic need to create and nourish new life.[5] If they do not care for someone or something outside themselves, they become stagnant and unproductive. In the past, men gratified generative needs by working and women by raising children. With changes in men's and women's roles, both sexes are free to express creative energies in work and at home with children.

A large 1979 survey reported the most frequent reasons for having children cited by men and women of all ethnic backgrounds, parents and nonparents alike, was a desire for love, interpersonal satisfactions, and close ties to others.[6] A couple who have a child become a family unit, which is seen as a defense against loneliness, isolation, and anonymity in our society. For women, particularly, children may be primary providers of affection and warmth. Children may be seen as compensation for difficulties between the parents and for lack of affection in the marriage.

The second most frequent set of reasons was desire for stimulation, the novelty children bring to marriage. Children are lively and they keep parents young; it is exciting to see them grow and change. In addition, children may help to keep a balanced perspective in a home because they impose a routine on family life and help parents to forget outside troubles.

A third common reason focused on parenting as a way of developing the self, linking oneself with the community. Rearing children stimulates the development of personal characteristics such as selflessness, responsibility, and sensitivity. In addition, as parents care for children, they express previously untapped talents and develop new abilities. Parents become skilled storytellers, superb negotiators, and spontaneous teachers. Parenthood also expands self-concept by linking the parent to other people in a close family setting and in the larger social community. It is sometimes only because of children that adults take active roles in community activities. Children are also a link with generations yet unseen, and for some parents they provide a sense of immortality.

A fourth reason cited in the survey was to establish that they are stable adults. More than work or marriage, parenthood is regarded as "proof" that an individual is a mature person. Parents, relatives, and friends expect that children will follow marriage, and adults oblige to meet social expectations.

A fifth reason was that children give parents a sense of creativity and achievement. Helping children grow, seeing them surmount the hurdles of childhood, gives parents a sense of accomplishment and competence.

A sixth group of reasons centered on parenthood as an expression of religious and moral beliefs. Many people equate motherhood with virtue and fatherhood with respect and authority. Children are viewed as manifestations of God's blessing and God's will. Individuals not connected with any formal church may consider having children a sign that they are more altruistic, less selfish, and less egocentric than those who remain childless.

A final reason for having children was economic utility. In the past, especially in agrarian societies, children were valued as laborers who contributed to the family's productivity. More recently, grown children have been the caretakers of aged parents and less fortunate relatives, but today these responsibilities are beginning to be assumed by governmental agencies. And now that the cost of raising a child through age eighteen is about $125,000 for a middle-class family in San Francisco,[7] children are an economic burden rather than a utility.

In addition to the reasons cited in the survey, in some countries and in some North American subcultures, children bring power to the parent, particularly to the mother. Mothers who have been subservient in the marriage relationship may, at times, have the courage to make demands for their children. Both mothers and fathers may derive a sense of power from being responsible for their children. Some adults have few opportunities to achieve power; control over children may give them their only experience of it.

◆
BOX 1-1
PARENTS' REASONS FOR WANTING CHILDREN*

1. Love and satisfying, close relationship with others
2. Stimulation and excitement of watching children grow
3. Means of self-development—becoming more responsible, more sensitive, more skilled in relationships
4. Way of achieving adult status—parenthood is "proof" of being mature
5. Sense of creativity and achievement in helping child grow
6. Expression of moral, religious belief
7. Utility—belief that children will care for parents when parents are older

*Adapted from: Lois Wladis Hoffman and Jean Denby Manis, "The Value of Children in the United States: A New Approach to the Study of Fertility," *Journal of Marriage and Family 41* (1979): 583–596.

As children grow, their achievements are sources of pride and can be compared with the achievements of friends' and relatives' children. If children are valued only because of their objective achievements, they feel unimportant as individuals and the parent-child relationship is disrupted. Some children are pushed to live out the fantasies of their parents. The parent whose child does not comply with such wishes is disappointed with his own life and compounds his disappointment by diminishing the parent-child relationship.

If any of these reasons carry too heavy a weight in the decision to have children, difficulty in the parent-child relationship can occur. Yet all these motives are probably present, in varying degrees, in each family.

Decision to Parent

Knowing the reasons for having children does not tell us about *the process* whereby parents decide to have a child. Caroline Cowan and Philip Cowan conducted an extensive study of couples as they became or did not become parents. They conclude:

> Much of what happens after the birth of the baby is shaped by what is happening in couples' lives before the baby comes along. And one of the most important things that happens in the prebaby period is the way the couple goes about deciding whether to become parents in the first place.[8]

They identified four decision-making patterns. *Planners* (52%) discussed the question and made a definite decision to have or not to have a child. *Acceptance of fate* couples (14% of those expecting) had unplanned pregnancies that they accepted either quietly or, in many cases, enthusiastically. *Ambivalent* couples (about 26%) expressed both positive and negative feelings about being parents with one parent

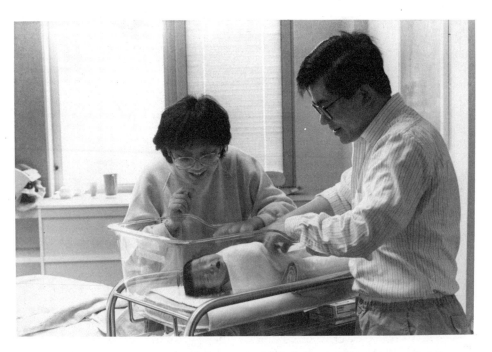

Becoming a parent gives meaning and purpose to life and is a defense against loneliness.

leaning in one direction and the other parent leaning in the other direction. *Yes-No* couples (about 10%) were in marked conflict about having or not having a child.

The couples' decision-making process regarding pregnancy was related to their problem-solving skills in other areas.[9] *Yes-No* couples were less effective in solving everyday problems, just as they were less effective in deciding about the pregnancy. The decision-making process regarding pregnancy was also related to marital satisfaction over time. When couples plan the decision, regardless of whether they do or do not have a child, their marital satisfaction remains high following the birth or equivalent time period. Couples who accept an unplanned pregnancy have a drop in marital satisfaction, but their initial level is so high that they are still as high as the parents who plan the decision.

Marital dissatisfaction is most marked among couples who are ambivalent or in conflict, and still have a baby. *Ambivalent* couples are not as satisfied as the other couples in their initial levels and drop down. *Ambivalent* couples who do not have a child remain high in satisfaction level. The *yes-no* couples have least satisfaction. Of nine *yes-no* couples who had a child, seven divorced by the time the child entered kindergarten. In all seven cases, the husband did not want a child. The two women who did not want to have children seemed better able to adjust, and their marriages continued.

Since planning and acceptance of children are important determiners of later marital satisfaction, and in turn, to adjustment to the baby, what can parents do if

THE JOYS OF FAMILY GENERATIONS

"My mother died when my daughter was about two. My mother had saved my clothes from when I was a child, so it's fun for me to pass these things on to her and have her wear them and enjoy them. It was particularly nice to have the things because of my mother's death. It was a very great sadness not to have her here." MOTHER

"One of the nice things also, is being a part of the family, bringing her into the family and seeing all the grandparents and great-grandparents and the fuss they make over her." FATHER

"Carrying on tradition is something I like to do. My mother sewed my Halloween costumes for me and I do that for my daughter. I keep her costumes, and she talks about maybe her child wearing her costume. These are small things, but they give her a sense of tradition." MOTHER

"At her christening party, we had a tape recorder, and each guest taped a little message into the recorder. When she began to sing, she would sing into the recorder, and when her grandmother was alive, she sang the old Norwegian songs into the recorder so we have that on tape. And every year at various times, at birthdays or holidays, we would all talk into the tape recorder about what our lives had been like and what had gone on since the last time we did it. We have her singing 'Silent Night' with all the words wrong, and that has been a real thread. We have a sort of oral history, and it's a real pleasure for us." MOTHER

"Thomas Wolfe wrote *You Can't Go Home Again,* but James Agee said you do go home again in the lives of your children. It is a sort of reexperiencing what you experienced when you grew up—they're reading the same books you read, the conflicts they have are the ones you remember having with your parents, or issues

one or both are uncertain about whether to have a child? Several books are available to help them make the decision. Judith Blackfield Cohen has written *Parenthood After Thirty? A Guide to Personal Choice,* including questionnaires and exercises to help parents focus their thinking and arrive at a decision about children.[10]

Ellen Peck and William Granzig are authors of *The Parent Test: How to Measure and Develop Your Talent for Parenthood.*[11] They believe that our culture glamorizes parenting and that many people have children without really understanding what they are undertaking. So, in addition to reviewing reasons for wanting children, they present the problems of rearing children—the financial strains, the time pressures, the psychological stresses. These authors explore the resources, skills, interests, and motivations required for parenting, and they urge prospective parents to examine themselves to determine if they possess these qualities. If they do not have these qualities, are they willing to develop them?

Peck and Granzig have suggestions about ways to develop interests and qualities related to successful parenting. Parents can develop knowledge and interest in that mattered to you as a child are issues for them. When you have time to reflect on them, they bring you back over and over again to issues in your own childhood that I guess you have a second opportunity to resolve. You have a different perspective on them than you did before." FATHER

"One of the interesting things was when we took our children back to Ohio, and before she could crawl, one used to scoot around on her rear end and tuck one knee under the other, and she wore out all the seats of her pants. Her great-grandmother was alive then and said, 'Oh, that is just the way her grandfather did it.' We never knew that and it was just amazing. One of our girls is so like her great-aunt who never had any children of her own and was such a lovely woman. It would have pleased her so much to see my daughter grow up. Our son looks like my father and is so much like him in every way. He has his build. My father always had a joke at dinner every night and our son has always loved jokes. As soon as he could read, he had joke book and was always telling us jokes at dinner. Our other son looks just exactly like his father and his grandfather." MOTHER

"One of my great joys was the first time my parents came to visit us, very proudly handing my son to my father and saying, 'Here's my boy!' That was a real highlight, a great thrill. I get choked up saying it now." FATHER

"I like having my family around. For the first time in my life, I want my mother to be here. There is a basic need to have your family around you. My husband's family and cousins are here, and I have a really strong urge to have everyone around. I was not really prepared for that." MOTHER

"Being a parent has helped me to see into myself. It's very illuminating in a personal way. It brings back a lot of memories, good and bad." FATHER

children by babysitting with the children of friends, by volunteering time to recreational projects for children, by joining Big Brothers or Big Sisters, or by becoming foster parents. A couple can begin to create a lifestyle that would enhance the lives of children, perhaps by moving to an area where they would like to raise children and by saving money. All these activities would help a couple see whether parenthood would be an enjoyable activity even if their scores on the tests were low. In fact, with these life changes, the scores would change, too.

Elizabeth Whelan suggests guidelines similar to those of Peck and Granzig for making the decision to parent or not to parent.[12] Whelan, however, stresses the very personal nature of the decision. She encourages parents to talk to older parents with similar interests, to determine their satisfactions with having children. She suggests that this should be a personal decision, rather than one based on test scores. While it is important to be aware of the problems children bring, couples must also think of the pleasures, which cannot be experienced in advance as easily as the limitations. The cuddling, hugging, loving; the warm sense of community with other people and other families; the pleasure and closeness that comes with watching children grow; the possibility of mastering upsetting experiences of our own—all these sensations are hard to duplicate in experiences with other people's children.

Despite all the discussion and planning and despite all the advances in contraceptive methods, many babies are unplanned—35% in one study,[13] 39% in another.[14] In the latter study, however, only 5% of couples found themselves unexpectedly pregnant with a second child. Most couples who had an unplanned child felt the nine months of pregnancy gave them an opportunity to come to terms with the baby and accept the child at birth.

Although most unplanned children are welcomed by the time of birth, actively unwanted children may have a more difficult time. Children whose mothers had twice requested abortions to terminate that particular pregnancy had significantly more problems and less enjoyment in life than children whose parents wanted them.[15] The unwanted children, seen in elementary school, had fewer friends, more behavior problems, and poorer school performance even though they had equally high intelligence.

In adolescence, the difference between the two groups widened. In young adulthood, individuals unwanted before birth were less happy with their jobs and their marriages. They had more conflict with coworkers and supervisors and less satisfaction with friends. They were discouraged about themselves and their lives, but many took the positive step of getting help for their problems. So, being definitely unwanted during gestation is related to fewer satisfactions in work, friendships, and marital relationships in adulthood.

Thus agreement on having children is not only helpful to the couple and their relationship but helps the long-term well-being of the child.

The Timing of Children

Does it matter when parents have children? Is it better to be younger or older? Pamela Daniels and Kathy Weingarten[16] compared parents who had their children *early* (when they were an average 20.5 years old) and those who had children *later* (when they averaged 30.5). They found that although the number of problems parents experienced was about the same in early and late timing births, the content of the problems differed for the two groups. Those parents who had children quickly in their early twenties found themselves rearing children before they themselves had firm identities. They were less established in work roles and were generally less experienced out in the world. The partners had not had time to become thoroughly acquainted with each other and settled as a couple. This group was nurturing children before they felt mature; it had, however, less difficulty adjusting to the wife's role as mother and caregiver.

Late-timing couples had established themselves as individuals out in the world. They had work they enjoyed. They had time to focus on their relationship, to learn about each other's reactions, to establish routines of working together and accomplishing tasks. When the baby came, late-timing couples were ready to nourish new life, but they had difficulty with the disruption of their intimate connection and established ways of doing things.

Many of the early-timing parents, if they had it to do all over again, would have postponed having children, whereas none of the late-timing parents would have had children earlier. Parents' individual "readiness" to be parents is the critical factor. When individuals have a clear sense of who they are, what they like, how they relate to other people, when they can care for themselves and have established patterns of intimacy with the other parent, then they are ready to nourish new life.

Over-35 Parents

A still older group is the *over-35* parents who have increased dramatically since 1970. In 1988, 310,000 babies were born to women over thirty-five.[17] Feminism, general postponement of child-bearing, the large number of baby-boomer mothers who are now in that child-bearing age, advanced contraception, better health for women, and advances in obstetrical care account for these growing numbers. While there have always been women over 35 having children, in the past these older mothers were having the *last* of several children. Now many are mothers for the *first* time.

Older mothers, as already noted, have many advantages—higher education, higher status jobs, and, as a result, higher incomes with more spent on child-related items like child-care.[18]

Further, these families have a lower divorce rate, are more stable, and are frequently more attentive and sensitive parents. Yet parents' work and community responsibilities may make it more difficult for them to incorporate an unpredictable, time-consuming young child into their lives.

Andrew Yarrow wonders what it is like for children to have older parents.[19] He obtained a volunteer sample of adults who described their experiences growing up with older parents. Many reported appreciating older parents' greater patience, broader outlook on life, and the more comfortable, settled life style. Many, however, had numerous worries about parents' possible illness and death, feelings of being isolated from a larger family network as grandparents were often dead, feelings of being isolated from peers whose parents were younger, more playful and physically active with them. Some felt they were cheated of childhood and had to grow up too fast as they were around adults so much. Further they had to assume responsibilities for aging parents just as they were entering young adulthood. (Note: today, children with older parents may not have the same experiences because society is more accepting of the older parent.)

Older parents can become sensitive to their children's feelings. See Box 1-2. Children will then be able to enjoy the benefits of older parents with a minimum of the problems.

Teenage Parents

While older parents are viewed positively, teenage parents are often viewed negatively. Certainly teenage mothers face many problems, but the authors of a seventeen-year study in Baltimore write that *diversity of outcome* was their most striking finding. Many adolescent mothers overcome the problems.

BOX 1-2
GUIDELINES FOR OLDER PARENTS*

1. Be open with children about your age and reasons for postponing children. Lying and avoiding the issue give children a sense of shame or embarrassment about parents' age.
2. Make a special effort to understand your children's world as it may seem very different from the one in which you grew up.
3. Connect your children to extended family members. If this is not possible, then there should be an extended support network of friends who serve as uncles, aunts, grandparents.
4. Stay physically fit and energetic so you can share physical activities like hiking, camping with your children. If you can not participate, then see that children join with friends and other adults in these activities.
5. Most important, balance the time you spend on work and non-family commitments with your family's needs so children feel they are important parts of your lives.

*Adapted from Andrew Yarrow, *Latecomers* (New York: Free Press, 1991).

The invidious stereotype of the adolescent childbearer underestimates young mothers' chances of recovery . . . Ironically, part of the handicap of being a teenage mother may come from a widespread perception that failure is virtually inevitable—a belief that may become a self-fulfilling prophecy.[20]

In 1988, teenage mothers had about 500,000 babies.[21] Approximately 60 percent of these children are born to unwed mothers—a dramatic increase from the comparable figure of 15 percent in 1960.[22] The large majority of these births are unplanned and unwanted. Further, a pattern of generational continuity is developing in which a significant percentage of teenage mothers are themselves products of teenage pregnancies.

Teenage mothers become parents under difficult conditions. Because they frequently do not get good prenatal care and are physically less mature, teenage mothers suffer more pregnancy complications and more often have babies with problems. Prematurity and low birth weight—which increase the likelihood of cerebral palsy, mental retardation, and epilepsy—occur most frequently in the babies of teenage mothers.

In addition, because teenage mothers frequently do not complete their education, they have limited job opportunities. As a result, a large percentage live in poverty. Further, the life circumstances of the families include many changes—changes in residences, changes in childcare figures, and changes in male support.[23]

The psychological immaturity of these mothers poorly prepares them to care for young children. Observers find that when their children are infants, young mothers prematurely foster independence, pushing children to hold their own bottles, sit up too early, and scramble for toys before they really can get them.[24] These mothers often tease their children as well. As infants become toddlers, however, these mothers reverse their behavior and try to control children, not letting them explore freely, not giving them choices in activities and toys. Children of teenage mothers have a greater likelihood of school problems, school failure, and behavior problems.

So these are the problems. But these mothers are committed to their children, and many raise them successfully. Unfortunately, we pay less attention to the successes. For example, 75 percent of the mothers in the Baltimore study were employed and not involved with social services; yet, we focus on the 25 percent who are getting social services.[25]

Who are the successful mothers? They are women who use birth control and limit their fertility. They stay in school or return to school and complete their education. They maintain a high level of motivation and high educational goals for themselves. The most successful entered stable marriages with men who provided support and help.

The children may have strengths that buffer them in the situation—intelligence, adaptive temperamental qualities, the ability to cooperate with the parent easily, the ability to soothe themselves. And the mothers may find strengths that help them become good parents—emotional availability and responsivity to the child, the ability to form goals for the future and to use community resources to obtain goals.

Two kinds of programs attack the problems of teenage pregnancies: (1) those that postpone the birth of the first child by means of effective education and birth control and (2) those that help mothers once they have had children. Both programs emphasize effective birth control at the same time that teens are encouraged to develop a sense of confidence about their ability to make and carry out future goals for themselves.

Nonparents

Some couples actively decide not to have children. Some women know from an early age that they do not want children, but most report going through a sequence similar to the following four-step sequence: (1) postponing children for a definite period, (2) postponing children for an indefinite period, (3) considering the possibility of not having children, and (4) making a definite decision not to have children.[26]

Some couples want children very much and can not have them. Do they feel frustrated and unhappy? Involuntarily childless wives are more likely than mothers or voluntarily childless wives to report feeling a lack of fulfillment and purpose in life, but they report especially close and supportive relationships with their husbands and their families. As a result, overall sense of well-being is the same as that of mothers and voluntarily childless women.[27] Marital happiness and overall well-being are related to the quality of adult relationships, and one can be happy with a husband and extended family whether one does or does not have children.

FAMILY LIFE IN A CHANGING SOCIETY

Parents rear children in families, but our understanding of what families are and what they do has changed dramatically in the last fifty years. To get a sense of the momentous changes that have occurred in the North American family, let us look back a hundred years.

Families in the Past

Nineteenth century families lived primarily on farms and in rural settings. Although the lifespan then was shorter than it is today, marriages occurred later and family size was large. In the early nineteenth century, mothers had an average of eight children. Both men and women spent most of their adult lives as active parents. Families also lived more settled lives. All family members worked together as economic producers, and children often followed in the occupational footsteps of parents. There was less geographical mobility than today, so many relatives lived close together and served as additional role models for children growing up. Parents had a clear sense of the lives they were preparing their children to live as adults and a solid core of values that were supported by the community at large.

Life was not necessarily easy in nineteenth-century North America. Since life expectancy was shorter, parenting years longer, and loss of the mother in childbirth more frequent than today, many families were disrupted by the death of a spouse. Epidemic and unpreventable illness, economic hardship, and discrimination against minorities also took their toll. Family members, however, retained strong feelings of closeness, belonging, and interdependence that provided strength and comfort at times of trouble.

Following the Industrial Revolution, as families moved to urban settings, fathers left their families to go to work, and women's and children's economic labor decreased. In the Early Twentieth Century, it was a sign of father's success that the mother could stay at home and focus on childrearing. Wives of blue-collar workers often continued to work for financial reasons. Women worked in large numbers during the Depression of the 1930s and World War II, but their labor force participation was the temporary result of hard times and not a socially approved ideal.

The **post–World War II** days brought the flowering of what we think of as the **nuclear family**: Men were employed in a booming economy; women remained at home, rearing three or more children. Families tended to be child-centered and the principal source of warmth and affection for their members. Sex role attitudes were fixed—men were economic providers, competent and skilled in the world of work outside the home. Women were the heart of the family, nourishing children, supporting their husbands in their careers.

The 1960s were a decade of turbulence and change that disrupted this view of the family. Disagreement with government policy in many areas, the violence reflected in assassinations and war, led to wide-scale social protest. Rebellion initiated by younger people drove a wedge between youth and older adults, and families were sometimes split on issues of values and goals in life.

Summarizing polls conducted in the 1970s, Daniel Yankelovich described attitude changes from the 1950s to 1980 in *New Rules: Searching for Self-Fulfillment in a World Turned Upside Down*.[28] Individuals in the 1970s, certain of the successful economy in the 1960s, became bored with hard work as the driving force in life. Young people felt they had more options than their parents, and they wanted greater meaning in

life, more opportunities for self-expression. Men no longer had to be the sole providers for their families. They endorsed sharing in a more equal division of responsibilities at work with women. They also endorsed women's greater freedom to choose
what they wanted.

As these new generations of North American adults searched for self-fulfillment,
they had less interest in sacrificing for their children. Nearly two-thirds of parents
rejected the idea that parents should stay together for the children if the parents were
unhappy with each other. Two-thirds felt that parents should be free to live their own
lives even if it meant spending less time with children, and about two-thirds of parents endorsed the view that they had the right to live well now even if it meant leaving less to children. But likewise, parents did not expect children in turn to sacrifice
for them or take on burdens for them in the future.

Accompanying the search for self-fulfillment are undercurrents of traditional values. Two-thirds of people sampled favored traditional standards of family life and
responsibilities. Both in 1970 and in 1980 96 percent of those surveyed sought the
traditional ideal of two people sharing their lives with each other.

Statistics since 1980 suggest the rates of marriages, births, and divorces have stabi-
lized. The contemporary family is now dealing with all the changes that occurred
before 1980.

Contemporary Families

Poppy

Families today are more varied than ever before. There are families in which the
father works and the mother stays home to raise children; there are families in which
the mother works outside the home and the father stays home and cares for children;
there are families in which both parents work, sometimes split shifts, and
both care for the children. There are single parent families headed by women, and
single parent families headed by men. There are stepfamilies that include children
by previous marriages with children of that marriage. There are families in which
grandparents raise their grandchildren. There are families in which both parents are
of the same sex.

Contemporary families are small. About half the families have no children living
in them—either children are not yet born or they have grown and left the home.[29]
Most of the 49 percent of families with children under age 18 have only one or two
children. Only 10 percent of all families in the United States have three or more children. Some ethnic groups, for example the Hispanic-American group, have a higher
percentage (18 percent) of families with three or more children. Even so, their family
size average is 3.76 compared to the 3.11 for the whole population.[30]

In 1990, 74 percent of children lived with two parents and 26 percent lived
with a single parent. Most often this single parent is the mother (21%), but a growing number of children live with single fathers (5%).[31] Though single mothers are
most often separated or divorced, a growing number of single mothers have never
married. This group includes teenage girls who can not or do not want to marry
the fathers, older women who fear they will not marry in time to have children so
they choose to conceive a child, and lesbian couples who have children by artificial
insemination.

Single divorced fathers increasingly are rearing their young children alone.

A growing number of Americans live alone. In 1989, 23 million people lived alone, a 25 percent increase from 1980, and a 68 percent increase from 1960.[32]

Let us look at the social factors influencing contemporary family life.

Women's work participation increased as child-bearing took up less time in the adult life span, and as women became aware of satisfactions attainable in the world outside the home. Women not only joined the labor force in increasing numbers, but they also sought higher-status occupations in business and the professions.

When these women married and had children, they stayed at work, and the work force today includes many mothers of young children. Fifty-five percent of women with children under a year work, and about two-thirds of women with children older than a year have employment outside the home.[33] Employment figures for single mothers are even higher. So the mother is no longer full-time caregiver of children, and families have adapted to her transformed role in a variety of ways.

Fred + Ginger?

The increasing divorce rate has had a profound effect on both adults and children. Though parents are divorcing, they are marrying again, blending families in a variety of ways. Children become part of a larger network of stepparents, half-siblings, step-siblings, and stepgrandparents. Thus, the family unit, as well as the number of role models, has been greatly expanded for children.[34]

New values are incorporated in our society as we include different *ethnic groups*. Because of immigration and a higher reproductive rate in some groups, the proportion of ethnic group members is increasing. By the term *ethnic* we refer to groups of people who share a sense of communality with regard to religious, racial, national, or cultural traditions passed from one generation to another. *Ethnic* is a broader term than race, religion or place of national origin.

The United States is the most culturally diverse country in the world; we consider our society a "melting pot" that blends everyone into a cohesive group with one set of values. There is evidence, however, that people retain ethnic traditions for generations, and we are now beginning to think of our country as a "tossed salad" with separate ingredients making up the whole. Different traditions bring richness to our society.

The main ethnic groups in this country now are Euro-Americans, Afro-Americans, Hispanic-Americans, Asian-Americans, and American Indians. Just as Euro-Americans trace their origins to different cultures in Europe, so other ethnic groups consist of several subgroups, each with its own set of values. For example, Hispanic-Americans from Mexico differ from Hispanic-Americans from Cuba. Asian-Americans from Vietnam have different traditions from Asian-Americans from China.

We use the term **predominant culture** or **majority culture** to refer to that set of beliefs emphasizing initiative, independence, achievement, individualism, ownership of material goods, mastery, and planning. The ease with which any new ethnic group fits in with the predominant culture depends on many factors—the circumstances of the arrival in this country as well as similarity in characteristics such as color, language, and values to the majority culture. Each subgroup will have its own individual experience with the majority culture.

Nevertheless, reviews of the literature describing the attitudes and *values of minority families* reveal they use common strategies, though in differing degrees and combinations, to survive and flourish in the majority culture. Relying on the extended family, becoming bicultural (functioning well in more than one culture and using whatever behavior is adaptive to the situation), developing role flexibility, and drawing strength from ancestral or spiritual world views are ways to adapt traditions to a majority culture that stresses competitive individualism.[35]

Though the majority culture sometimes assumes that differences in family life mean deficiencies, Diana Baumrind points out in a discussion of cultural variations in social competence that the continued survival of Afro-American and Hispanic-American families in our highly industrialized society is "proof of their outstanding and durable competence."[36] As we move toward a new century, we do not know what qualities will be most adaptive. We may need different values and find ourselves drawing on the strengths of our minority cultures—for example, by incorporating the more cooperative approaches these groups favor.

As we shall see when we examine resources and strengths for individuals in times of trouble, the values of the extended family, role flexibility, and a spiritual orientation all promote resilience in people. Recent work suggests that the most understanding and perceptive parents are those who go through the process of integrating two cultures into a meaningful whole. Mexican-American mothers who are attached equally to their Mexican heritage and to the American culture have a broader, more understanding view of their children's development than do mothers attached to only one culture, be it Mexican or American.[37]

Poverty affects an increasing number of children who are then at risk for chronic problems like malnutrition, poor health, and school failure. The poverty rate in 1987 was 20 percent for all children, but it was higher for children of certain ethnic groups. For white children it was 15 percent, but for Afro-American children it was 45 percent, and for Hispanic-American children, 39 percent.[38]

Even more disturbing are figures showing that Afro-American children experience more persistent poverty. Longitudinal data from 1968 to 1982 reveal that 24 percent of Afro-American children were poor for at least ten years of the fifteen-year period, and 5 percent were poor for the entire time. Less than 1 percent of non-Afro-American children were poor for ten years and none was poor for fifteen years.[39]

Poverty has increased with the rise in single-parent households. In 1989, the median family income for married couples with children under eighteen was $38,664, and for single female heads of household $17,383. For single male householders the median income was $30,336.[40] Poverty is also related to other economic changes like the decline in higher-paying manufacturing jobs, the rise in lower-paying service jobs, and changing governmental policies that have taxed low-income families more and provided fewer supportive programs.

Economic hardship affects parenting. Vonnie McLoyd developed a model of how poverty affects parents, and, in turn, children.[41] Rand Conger and his coworkers have demonstrated a similar process in rural families with low incomes.[42]

Financial pressures create day-to-day problems, and cause parents to experience increased irritability, depression, and demoralization. McLoyd found that the pressures followed the poverty, not vice versa. Parents under stress are less likely to support each other, are more irritable with children, and give them less affection. As a result, children suffer more emotional problems. Conger and his associates found that both parents' reactions had impact on children's behavior.

Violence is very much a part of children's lives so childhood is no longer a time of safety. A recent news article began,

> Take 10 inner-city children in a large metropolis. By the time they're 18 years old, five of them will know someone who has been murdered and five will know someone who has been the victim of armed robbery. Two will have witnessed a murder and four a shooting. One of them will have been assaulted with a weapon, one raped and two had their lives threatened.[43]

Middle-class children are at risk as well. People with guns invade schools and shoot students and teachers. Since children are kidnapped, a child can not be allowed to play alone in front of his or her home. Young children can not go alone to the store. Even if middle class children are not as often the victims of crime as

---

BOX 1-3
TRENDS IN FAMILY VALUES IN LAST FIFTY YEARS*

Traditional Familism (mid-1940s to mid-1960s)

1. dominance of couples with children
2. high birth rates
3. low divorce rates
4. high degree of marital stability
5. economic factors affecting family include strong economy with high standard of living and expanding middle class
6. cultural values emphasized conformity to social norms, different sex roles for men and women, and idealization of family life

Period of Individualism (mid-1960s to mid-1980s)

1. greater diversity in population
2. creation of single life style
3. postponement of marriage
4. declining birth rate
5. rising divorce rate
6. economic factors affecting family include women's increasing participation at work and idealization of work
7. cultural values emphasized self-expression as the source of meaning in life and a decline in definite sex roles for men and women

New Familism (mid-1980s to present)

1. increase in birth rate
2. leveling off of divorce rate
3. economic factors affecting family include leveling off of women's participation in work force but a decrease in the number of adequate paying jobs
4. cultural values include a shift from self-expression to greater attachment to family but with less conformity than in the traditional period

*Adapted from: Barbara Dafoe Whitehead, "The New Family Values," *Utne Reader,* May/June 1993.

---

inner-city children, the signs of possible crime are all about. For example, in 1992 the Solano County fair, presumably a safe place, installed metal detectors so officials could remove all weapons prior to entrance. It is hard to feel safe. All children must learn to cope with violence in whatever form they encounter it.

Americans are puzzled, confused, and angry because they do not understand why the government and institutions are not working better, why poverty and violence are increasing, why the country seems on the wrong track. Pollster Daniel Yankelovich describes the present American mood as one of a "deepening sense of frustration."[44] He sees this as a sharp shift from the euphoria of the 1980s. He concludes, however, that Americans are activists, and now that they are becoming aware of very real societal problems, they will seek strategies to address and solve these problems.

Box 1-3 summarizes many of these changes.

Children Today

Social scientists, too, worry about the quality of children's lives and make a strong case for more social supports for families. In *Today's Children,* David Hamburg, a psychiatrist and president of the Carnegie Corporation, writes that problems such as poverty, adult drug and alcohol abuse, failing education, poor health care, increased violence, and less parental attention put children at risk.[45]

These problems affect poor children to a greater degree; affluent children face other problems such as too much planned activity. Psychologist Edward Zigler worries:

> Children aren't having the kinds of fun they once did because of all this over-programming. The idea that kids could lie on their backsides and look at a passing cloud—we don't let children do that anymore. We used to form our own neighborhood baseball teams and play in the local sandlot. Now you go to Little League. I worry about the pleasures of childhood, which seem to keep vanishing.[46]

He believes that parents are under stress from work and that, while they love their children, they often substitute expensive activities or material things for time together.

Critics of the family blame the problems on the decline of the nuclear family, women's increasing participation in the labor force, day care, divorce, and poverty. But, Arlene Skolnick, author of *Embattled Paradise: The American Family in an Age of Uncertainty,*[47] argues that economic factors are the major sources of children's difficulties. These are controllable when society views the family as fragile and provides support, as European countries do, in the form of allowances for children and for housing, benefits for working parents such as parental leave, childcare, flexible work schedules.

Numerous programs exist to support families, teach new skills, and provide hope that problems are solvable. David Hamburg believes we must go beyond the stated purposes of institutions like schools, churches, community organizations, to provide basic human supports to children when parents and extended family members can not. Sensitive, caring adults in these settings can give children feelings of being protected, guided, stimulated, and nurtured. It is these feelings of being attached, nurtured, and important that are the most significant feelings in childhood. Investments in these programs, Hamburg writes,

> . . . have to be seen for what they are—a responsibility of the entire society. Not just of the federal government, but of other levels of government; not just of business, but of labor; not just of light-skinned peoples, but of dark-skinned as well; not just of the rich, but of the middle class and the poor. We are all in this huge leaking boat together. We will all have to pay and reason and care and work together.[48]

Parents Today

Family life is the center of our life satisfactions. A 1990 *Los Angeles Times* survey finds that 80 percent of 1,000 men and women say that family and children, marriage and love, and financial security are more important than work, career, or leisure time.[49] Two-thirds describe the family and their love life as the most satisfying aspects of their lives.

While they value children and family, men and women say they have too little time and do not live up to their own standards. Over half the mothers (55 percent) and fathers (57 percent) believe they spend too little time with their children. Forty percent of fathers and 80 percent of mothers would quit their jobs to raise their children full time if they could afford to.

Too little time results in parents not doing what they want with children. For example, 95 percent of parents believe they should talk to children about school and activities, yet only 75 percent do. Eighty-six percent believe it is important to eat dinner together, but only 66 percent do so regularly.

Box 1-4 summarizes responses of a sample of San Francisco-Bay Area parents to questions about raising children.[50]

Supports for Parents

Structural changes in the workplace and in governmental policy—subsidized day care, improved sick leave policies that include absence because of a child's illness, paternity leave, job sharing, and flexible hours—can support parents.

While programmatic supports are necessary, Carolyn Cowan and Philip Cowan make a plea for giving parents psychological support in the form of couples groups.[51] When new parents met together with a couple who were counselors and discussed their feelings around the transition to parenthood, these couples could discuss their feelings and were more supportive and understanding of each other. Three years later, all the couples who had met in groups were still together whereas 15 percent of those who did not have this opportunity had divorced.

Couples groups at times of transition in rearing children can help parents move through these periods more easily because the couples are able to talk to other couples about areas of conflict and get emotional support from other parents.

Societal changes are necessary to support parents; the changes include organized ways to create feelings of nurturance, attachment, and warmth in children and parents. The interview with Arlene Skolnick on pages 22–23 discusses this issue.

THE JOYS OF PARENTING

We have discussed the strains and changes that parenting creates but have made little mention of the many joys that children bring to their parents' lives. In a remarkable study forty years ago, Jersild and his co-workers interviewed 544 parents about the joys and problems of childrearing. They introduced the book with the following comments:

> There has been relatively little systematic study of the cheerful side of the ledger of childrearing. Studies of characteristics that bring headaches to a parent have not been matched by surveys of characteristics that warm a parent's heart. . . . The fact that the emphasis has been so much on the negative side is perhaps no more than one should expect. Behavior that is disturbing to the parent or to others usually calls for action or for a solution of some sort, and as such it also attracts the research worker. On the other hand, what is pleasant can be enjoyed without further ado.[52]

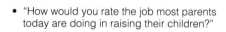

BOX 1-4
CHRONICLE POLL ON PARENTING*

- "Do you think raising children today is easier, more difficult or about the same as when your parents were raising you?"

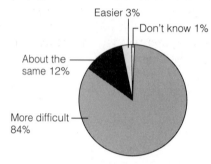

Easier 3%
Don't know 1%
About the same 12%
More difficult 84%

- "How would you rate the job most parents today are doing in raising their children?"

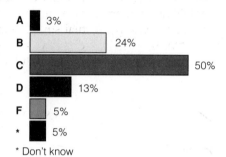

A 3%
B 24%
C 50%
D 13%
F 5%
* 5%

* Don't know

- "How satisfied are you with the amount of time you are spending with your children?"

	Parents	Fathers	Mothers
Very satisfied	46%	39%	54%
Somewhat satisfied	34	38	30
Dissatisfied	20	23	16

- "Would you sacrifice your career goals, such as turning down a new job with higher pay or a promotion to a higher position, for the sake of spending more time with your children?

	Parents	Fathers	Mothers
Yes	77%	74%	79%
No	21	23	19
Don't know	2	3	2

- "What do you think is the biggest problem for parents who are raising children in your city (or community) today?"

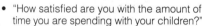

Drugs, alcohol	31%
Lack of money	9%
Lack of time	9%
Child's boredom	8%
Poor schools	6%
Discipline, morals	6%
Crime, gangs	6%
Peer groups	5%
TV, rock, movies	2%
Divorce	1%
Sex, teen pregnancy	1%
Other	9%
Nothing	7%

- "As far as your current experiences with raising children, in what area are you most in need of help?"

	Parents	Fathers	Mothers
Child care	27%	31%	23%
Financial help	24	23	25
Household chores	18	13	24
Emotional support	9	7	11
Child-rearing advice	7	4	9
Other	2	4	0
None	12	18	7
Don't know	1	0	1

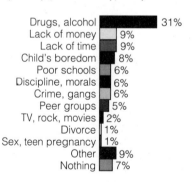

The Chronicle Poll was conducted by Mark Baldassare and Associates. The telephone survey of 600 Bay Area Adult residents was conducted August 22–25 on weekday nights and weekend days using a computer-generated random sample of listed and unlisted phone numbers. The margin of error is plus or minus 4 percent.

Torri Minton, "Bay Area Parents Feeling Frustrated," *San Francisco Chronicle,* October 1, 1991.

What did Jersild and his group find when they talked to parents? They learned that by and large parents experienced many more joys than difficulties, though the latter certainly existed. They found that children bring what parents hope they will—affection, companionship, enjoyment of the child as a special person, and delight in development and increasing competence. Jersild et al. conclude about parenthood, "Perhaps no other circumstance in life offers so many challenges to an individual's powers, so great an array of opportunities for appreciation, such a varied emotional and intellectual stimulation."[53]

In this book we will describe the many joys parents report with children of different ages, emphasizing the "cheerful side of the ledger."

MAJOR POINTS OF CHAPTER I

Parenting is:

- nourishing, guiding, protecting children as they grow
- a process of interaction between parent and child
- a role with two major tasks of establishing warm relationships and providing limits
- an activity usually occurring in family settings

People's reasons for wanting children include:

- love and affection
- stimulation
- creative outlet
- proof of adulthood
- sense of achievement
- proof of moral behavior
- economic utility
- power

Decision for parenthood involves:

- planning child
- accepting child if unplanned
- resolving ambivalence so child is wanted member and not rejected
- assessing parental readiness in terms of time, money, and psychological resources

Timing of children:

- is best when parents are personally ready to take on responsibilities of care for child

INTERVIEW
with Arlene Skolnick

Dr. Arlene Skolnick is a research psychologist at the University of California Berkeley. She is the author of The Intimate Environment: Exploring Marriage and the Family *and* Embattled Paradise: The American Family in an Age of Uncertainty.

You have studied and written about the family. If the government offered you unlimited amounts of money to design programs to support the family, what would you suggest are important ways to help families?

I think there are lots of things you can do to support families. You have to think not just of helping families directly but of improving the context in which families live.

One of the biggest profamily programs is getting the economy straightened out. We not only have high unemployment, but we have a scarcity of jobs that enable one person to support a family so both parents have to work. Sometimes it is even hard to find two jobs that support a family.

Many people believe that if you just fix families, many social problems will go away. But the causal arrow goes both ways. The state of the economy has many effects on families. Unemployment is correlated with increasing rates of alcoholism, spousal and child abuse, marital breakups. This isn't to say that every time father gets unemployed he is going to turn into an alcoholic and child abuser, but it is well established that these things increase as unemployment rates go up.

Other supports include health services broadly defined to include psychological well-being. I don't just mean psychological counseling when people need it, though that is certainly important, but conditions of life that support psychological well-being.

One thing that people complain about is the sense of isolation of families from each other and the community they live in. We need family-friendly cities, family-friendly urban environments, and gathering places where people can go. People have written about the decline of "third places" like cafes, parks, downtown areas, and public spaces where people can gather. Some architects and city planners are re-creating little towns with central gathering places, building houses close together, emphasizing walking to stores and workplaces, and integrating home and workplaces. That is not going to solve everyone's problem, but it is a direction to go in for the long run.

In addition to jobs, health care, and restoring communities, we have to have a strategy for dealing with points in the family life cycle that are particularly stressful and difficult. Clearly a crunch time is the transition to parenthood. We need to think about the whole period of infancy and how to support families when children are little, how you make it possible for mothers and fathers to stay home if they want to without losing months of income and their position in the work world. That is also a time when the connection between health and the rest of family life is important. In some countries they have visiting nurse services that can help parents deal with the child, that can help with problems that come up, teach them how to care for little children. Also they can notice any strains in the family and be a resource for them.

Another crisis period in the family is adolescence. Again, we have to put the troubles into historical perspective. In the past there were no adolescent problems because children were working when they were teenagers. They worked in the family economy, on the family farm or in the family business or they were off working as someone else's apprentice or hired hand. The whole concept of adolescence as a major life stage did not develop until the end of the 19th century. Adolescents are home and more emotionally involved with their parents now. They are more dependent than they used to be so they have to struggle for independence. During the era when children were working at this age, you didn't have the psychological issues you have now. Then you did not have to search for your identity because it was given to you. There wasn't a focus on the emotional relationship between the parent and the child so you didn't have to cultivate a good relationship with this teenager who was going through all these struggles to find him or herself.

In thinking about interventions, we must realize that we have had an incredible amount of change in a short time, and it has been very uneven. Women have changed the most, and men have changed some. The rest of society has changed very little and assumes that life is what it was in the 1950s with a mother at home and available all day, not just to children but to the repair person. Corporate attitudes are changing; some are becoming family-friendly work places. But until recently the attitude has been, "You want a job, be here from 9 to 5 or 9 to 9; but if you want to have children, they are your problem." That is beginning to change around the edges, but it is still true of many places.

The fact is, we already know what we can do. Berry Brazelton and others have written about what is needed and what works, and we just do not fund it enough. For example, Head Start for all who are eligible, immunizations for children, adequate nutrition are effective programs, but not well enough funded. Americans have to realize how unusual we are in comparison to other countries in our lack of support for families and in our lack of a national family policy. In other countries—our competitors—manage to have elaborate systems of family support. They realistically think of families and children as vital economic resources. The money spent on programs that favor children and families is not throwing money down a rat trap but an investment in the future.

We don't seem able to think that way in this country even when it is so obvious that a little bit of investment in prevention saves enormous money later on. We have large numbers of people who do not receive prenatal care, and so we have premature, low birth-weight babies who require enormous expense for premature care.

Do we have the will to make the changes needed to support families?

I think we are ready to deal pragmatically with problems that families face and stop thinking that we can roll back the changes. We are in a period of what some call "a new familism" or "new traditionalism." I don't think it's a "new traditionalism" so much as a New Tradition. People are trying to keep what is good about the family in the past yet adapt to the new roles for women and men.

- is best when parents are in agreement
- does not depend on age of parent but on psychological qualities of parents
- has effect on child's later adjustment—if parents are not mature, child may develop later problems
- has impact on other people—negative stereotypes of teenage mother and positive view of older mother

Nonparents:

- usually decide in stages not to have children
- are as happy as couples who have children

Family life in the past:

- involved both men and women as active economic producers in the family
- included extended family that provided additional role models for children
- involved a clear view of children's future so parents knew what they were preparing children for
- was often disrupted by death

Contemporary families are:

- smaller
- more varied in composition
- involved with many important figures outside the family—day care providers, teachers

Social changes affecting family settings are:

- more effective contraception, leading to later marriage
- population control, leading to smaller families
- women's increasing commitment to work, leading to new roles for mothers and new adults in child's life
- rise of divorce and remarriage, leading to changes in family living and new adults
- rise in ethnic population, leading to greater diversity in family traditions and values
- rise in poverty and violence, leading to more stressful lives for children

Children today:

- are more at risk because of poor health care, increased poverty and violence, poorer school programs, and less attention from adults

- stimulate adults to become involved in community activities
- require support from governmental programs that bolster family functioning

Parents today:
- love children and want to be with them
- feel they don't have enough time
- feel they don't live up to their own standards
- feel they are only doing an average job as parents
- feel they need additional financial supports

Joys of parenting are:
- available to all parents regardless of experience with own parents
- in large part what parents hoped they would be

EXERCISES

1. Take the year in which you were born and trace the social influences acting on your parents as they raised you. For example, for the 1970s, influences might have been women's greater participation in work force, rising divorce rate, remarriage, economic recession. Show the effects of social change on your daily life and the ways in which your parents cared for you—mother's working resulted in specific day care, divorce led to being in two homes, remarriage led to more adults in your life, increased violence led to greater restrictiveness.

2. Think about why, when you want children. List factors influencing your decisions—school, work considerations. Will it be harder for you to be a parent than it was for your parents?

3. Imagine you are a fifteen-year-old girl who becomes pregnant and wants to keep the child. Investigate the resources in your community to enable you to keep your child, remain in school, get a job. Are services adequate?

4. Read the newspaper for one week and cut out all the articles that are of interest to parents, including news and feature articles, and describe what these articles tell you about parenting experience in the 1990s. The articles might focus on solving certain kinds of behavior problems or providing opportunities for children's optimal development (certain play or educational activities), or they might consider laws relating to parents' employment benefits and rights of parents and children in courts at times of special circumstances.

5. In California, a surrogate mother petitioned the court for the baby she bore even though the child was not genetically related to her. Who are the parents of the child—the genetic parents or the parent who carried the child in utero?

ADDITIONAL READINGS

Brazelton, T. Berry. *Families: Crisis and Caring.* New York: Ballantine, 1989.

Cowan, Caroline Pape and Cowan, Philip. *When Partners Become Parents.* United States: Basic Books, 1992.

Hamburg, David A. *Today's Children.* New York: Times Books, 1992.

Skolnick, Arlene. *Embattled Paradise: The American Family in an Age of Uncertainty.* United States: Basic Books, 1991.

Yarrow, Andrew. *Latecomers.* New York: Free Press, 1991.

Notes

1. U.S. Bureau of the Census, *Statistical Abstract of the United States: 1991.* 111th ed. (Washington, D.C.: U.S. Government Printing Office, 1991).
2. William Morris, ed. *The American Heritage Dictionary of the English Language* (Boston: American Heritage Publishing and Houghton Mifflin, 1969).
3. Saul L. Brown, "Functions, Tasks and Stresses of Parenting: Implications for Guidance," in *Helping Parents Help Their Children,* ed. L. Eugene Arnold (New York: Brunner/Mazel, 1978), pp. 22–34.
4. Lee Salk, *Familyhood* (New York: Simon & Schuster, 1992).
5. Erik H. Erikson, *Childhood and Society,* 2nd ed. (New York: W. W. Norton, 1963).
6. Lois Wladis Hoffman and Jean Denby Manis, "The Value of Children in the United States: A New Approach to the Study of Fertility," *Journal of Marriage and the Family* 41 (1979): 583–596.
7. F. Philip Rice, *Intimate Relationships, Marriages, and Families* (Mountain View: Mayfield, 1993).
8. Caroline Pape Cowan and Philip Cowan, *When Partners Become Parents* (United States: Basic Books, 1992), p. 32.
9. Ibid.
10. Judith Blackfield Cohen, *Parenthood After 30? A Guide to Personal Choice* (Lexington, Mass.: D. C. Heath, 1985).
11. Ellen Peck and William Granzig, *The Parent Test: How to Measure and Develop Your Talent for Parenthood* (New York: G. P. Putnam's Sons, 1978).
12. Elizabeth M. Whelan, *A Baby? . . . Maybe* (New York: Bobbs-Merrill, 1975).
13. Cowan and Cowan, *When Partners Become Parents.*

14. Pamela Daniels and Kathy Weingarten, *Sooner or Later: The Timing of Parenthood in Adult Lives* (New York: W. W. Norton, 1983).
15. Henry P. David, "Developmental Effects of Compulsory Pregnancy," *The Child, Youth and Family Services Quarterly,* Spring 1992.
16. Daniels and Weingarten, *Sooner or Later.*
17. U.S. Bureau of the Census, *Statistical Abstract of the United States: 1991.*
18. Andrew Yarrow, *Latecomers: Children of Parents Over 35* (New York: Free Press, 1991).
19. Ibid.
20. Frank F. Furstenberg, J. Brooks-Gunn, and S. Philip Morgan, *Adolescent Mothers in Later Life* (Cambridge: Cambridge University Press, 1990), pp. 145–146.
21. U.S. Bureau of the Census, *Statistical Abstract of the United States: 1991.*
22. Joy D. Osofsky, "Risk and Protective Factors for Teenage Mothers and Their Infants," *Newsletter of the Society for Research in Child Development,* Winter 1990.
23. Ibid.
24. Ibid.
25. Furstenberg, Brooks-Gunn, and Morgan, *Adolescent Mothers in Later Life.*
26. Jean E. Veevers, "Voluntarily Childless Wives: An Exploratory Study," *Mental Health Digest* 5 (1973): 8–11.
27. Victor J. Callan, "The Personal and Marital Adjustment of Mothers and of Voluntarily and Involuntarily Childless Wives," *Journal of Marriage and the Family* 49 (1987): 847–856.
28. Daniel Yankelovich, *New Rules: Searching for Self-Fulfillment in a World Turned Upside Down* (New York: Random House, 1981).
29. U.S. Bureau of the Census, *Statistical Abstract of the United States: 1991.*
30. Ibid.

31. Ibid.
32. Ibid.
33. Ibid.
34. Ibid.
35. Algea O. Harrison et al. "Family Ecologies of Ethnic Minority Children," *Child Development 61* (1990): 347–362.
36. Diana Baumrind, "Subcultural Variations in Values Defining Social Competence," Society for Research in Child Development, *Papers presented at Western Regional Conference,* April 1976, p. 26.
37. Jeannie Gutierrez and Arnold Sameroff, "Determinants of Complexity in Mexican-American and Anglo-American Mothers' Conceptions of Child Development," *Child Development 61* (1990): 384–394.
38. "Child Poverty 'Tragedy' for U.S.," *San Francisco Chronicle,* April 27, 1990.
39. Vonnie C. McLoyd, "The Impact of Economic Hardship on Black Families and Children: Psychological Distress, Parenting, and Socioemotional Development," *Child Development 61* (1990): 311–346.
40. U.S. Bureau of the Census, *Statistical Abstract of the United States: 1991.*
41. McLoyd, "The Impact of Economic Hardship on Black Families and Children."
42. Rand D. Conger et al., "A Family Process Model of Economic Hardship and Adjustment of Early Adolescent Boys," *Child Development 63* (1992): 526-541.
43. "City Kids Face More Violence," *San Francisco Chronicle,* August 11, 1992.
44. Daniel Yankelovich, "At a Crossroads: American Attitudes and U.S.-Japan Economic Relations," *Japan Society Newsletter,* April 1991.
45. David A. Hamburg, *Today's Children* (New York: Times Books, 1992).
46. Marlene Cimons, "The End of Kids' Endless Summer," *San Francisco Chronicle,* July 23, 1992.
47. Arlene Skolnick, *Embattled Paradise: The American Family in an Age of Uncertainty* (United States: Basic Books, 1991).
48. Hamburg, *Today's Children,* p. 328.
49. Lynn Smith and Bob Sipchen, "Workers Crave Time with Kids," *San Francisco Chronicle,* August 13, 1990.
50. Torri Minton, "Bay Area Parents Feeling Frustrated," *San Francisco Chronicle,* October 1, 1991.
51. Cowan and Cowan, *When Partners Become Parents.*
52. Arthur T. Jersild, Ella S. Woodyard, and Charlotte del Solar, in collaboration with Ernest G. Osborne and Robert C. Challman, *Joys and Problems of Child Rearing* (New York: Bureau of Publications, Teachers College, Columbia University, 1949), pp. 1–2.
53. Ibid., p. 122.

ENCOURAGING CHILDREN'S POSITIVE BEHAVIOR

C H A P T E R 2

Whether you plan or happen to become a parent, you'll face the awesome responsibility of promoting your child's healthy growth. You've landed the big job—to provide the loving care and the opportunities that will lead your child to competence and self-esteem—but you're handed no job description. Will your duties come naturally or must they be learned? What makes one an effective parent? What qualities do children attribute to "good" parents? That parents are important in their children's lives seems obvious, but just how important? If parents change children, do children change parents? Parents go through their own stages while children experience stages of development, making the task of encouraging positive behavior a difficult and ever-changing one.

Parents create the environment in which children grow. They organize the daily routines that govern children's lives. This chapter describes what we know about the environments and experiences that help children develop positive qualities and how parents create these environments. Let us first look at what parents' role has traditionally been with children.

THE ROLE OF PARENTS

The role and function of a parent has changed from one generation to the next.[1] Understanding the changes serves as a starting point for understanding the role of parent in our society today. In Europe there was no concept of childhood until about the seventeenth century. If children survived infancy, they were treated as adults. They wore adult clothes, played adult games, and went off to work when they reached the age of seven or eight. Apprenticeship was the only form of schooling. Sometime in the seventeenth century there was a change, perhaps because of a decline in infant mortality, and families became closer and more concerned about the welfare of the children.

Until late in the nineteenth century, parents were most concerned about the physical survival of their children rather than about effective parenting. And even children who survived infancy could still succumb to disease at any time. Because of their precarious hold on physical life, there was great concern about the moral state of the infant and child. The doctrine of original sin suggested an evil nature that had to be subdued quickly. Parents were strict and punished the child for his or her own good.

During the early years of the twentieth century, this notion of an evil child was changed by the early behaviorists, particularly *John B. Watson,* a psychologist of the 1920s. He believed, as did many psychologists, that children are "blank slates" who need to learn good habits. The behaviorists stressed the importance of parenting in determining how children would develop emotionally and intellectually. Watson wrote:

> There is a sensible way of treating children. Treat them as though they were young adults. Dress them, bathe them with care and circumspection. Let your behavior always be objective and kindly firm. Never hug and kiss them, never let them sit on your lap. If you must, kiss them once on the forehead when they say good night. Shake hands with them in the morning. Give them a pat on the head if they have made an extraordinarily good job of a difficult task. Try it out. In a week's time you will find how easy it is to be perfectly objective with your child and at the same time kindly. You will be utterly ashamed of the mawkish, sentimental way you have been handling it.[2]

In the 1930s and 1940s, two trends led away from such strict habit training. Drawing on Freud's insights, psychologists began to urge parents to relax and permit children to grow without frustrations and repression of impulses. Parents were encouraged to be lenient and understanding so that internal conflicts and neurotic symptoms would not develop. At the same time pediatrician Arnold Gesell observed the growth of healthy, upper middle-class children and concluded that the patterns for healthy growth were within the child and that, if the parents would relax, growth would occur naturally. Both Freud and Gesell stressed the importance of the natural child with natural impulses, a child who needed to be understood and gratified in certain ways. These views, in contrast with the rigid habit training of Watson, provided a welcome emphasis on the needs of the child.

Three current developments in psychology have again altered our view of the nature of the child and the role of the parents. *Jean Piaget,* a Swiss psychologist, describes the many differences between a child's thinking and an adult's logic.[3] He emphasizes that children construct a view of the world based on their own experience with people and objects in the environment. Children must act in order to develop. Piaget asserts that children proceed through a predictable series of stages of cognitive development. Parents can provide experiences and opportunities that will enable children to develop a complex view of the world.

The *ethological* perspective in psychology has also become an important influence in the past twenty years. Ethologists study human behavior in terms of its adaptive qualities. They are concerned with behaviors that may be built into the organism but that require environmental stimulation to develop fully. Critical periods of growth are studied to determine what happens if the environment does not permit behavior to develop. Ethologists believe that children have enormous potential and that a stimulating environment is needed if children's capacities and abilities are to develop. That environment must include people who provide the emotional bonds and the environmental experiences that trigger and nourish the child's growth.

The most recent perspective is the *interactional* model of growth. It emphasizes that development results from the interplay between the child and the environment. The interaction changes both contributors, resulting in turn in a new form of behavior. The environment includes not only people like parents, but other features as well. It includes geographic location. City and rural children grow up differently. The environment includes the social status of the family—the amount of money available, the physical living conditions, the values parents have. It includes ethnic background. For some children, the ethnic cultural background of their parents and grandparents has little impact on everyday life; for others, it is an important feature. Children who look different or whose behavior is different from the norm may be treated differently. The child's environment also includes school. Children spend approximately 1,000 hours a year in school once they go into first grade. The friends they meet there and the teachers they have are strong influences not only on academic learning, but also on their feelings of confidence and self-esteem. Television, a powerful agent in a child's life, makes its first appearance early in infancy and toddlerhood and is present for several hours a day thereafter.

Finally, the environment includes what we might term the "accidents" of life, events that have a strong impact on a person's life but are not under anyone's control. Natural events such as hurricanes, earthquakes, and floods can change a child's way of life overnight. Illness—of the child or other family member—changes everyone involved. Economic hardship, whether experienced on a personal level or on a broad scale, has profound effects.

In describing a process model of parenting, Jay Belsky lists three major influences on parenting: (1) the child's characteristics and individuality, (2) the parents' personal history and psychological resources, and (3) the context of stresses and supports in the parents' lives.[4] The child comes with his or her own temperament, patterns of growth, birth order position, and sexual gender. Parents bring all these qualities plus a complex history of experience in the world and a complicated pattern of daily life. We have already touched on some of the stresses. Supports for parenting include the marriage, support from family and friends, and a nourishing community.

Goodness of Fit

Figure 2-1 shows the relationships Richard Lerner describes between the child, parent, social networks, larger community, society, and culture.[5] The arrows show how people and institutions influence each other. The child lives in a social context that makes demands on him or her and, at the same time, reacts to the child's behavior and is changed by it.

Parents and social institutions, like schools, have values and shape the child's behavior to fit these values. If the child's temperamental qualities do not fit the demands of the parents or school, then there is not a good fit between the child's individuality and the context the child lives in.

FIGURE 2-1
A dynamic, interactional model of child and parent development

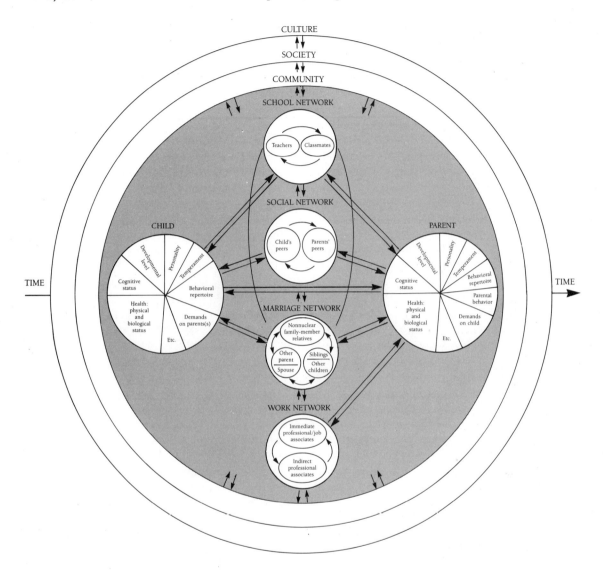

From R. Lerner, *On the Nature of Human Plasticity* (New York: Cambridge University Press, 1984), p. 144.

Adaptive behavior does not depend on the child's characteristics or on the environment's demands, but on the match between the two. A highly active child who lives on a farm where he works with the animals before and after school and walks a mile to the bus stop may be highly valued at home because of his great energy. He may have little trouble meeting the teacher's expectations for quietness and sitting still in school because so much of his out-of-class time is active. The social context of his daily life fits very well with his temperament.

Contrast this situation with that of an equally active child who lives in a small apartment and whose parents both work. Before and after school, he goes to the babysitter's, where he gets little outdoor time and little exercise. Instead, he watches TV. He squirms in school and gets out of his seat a lot. At home, he nags his parents to let him go out to play; but there is no supervised play space for him, and they are reluctant to let him play on the sidewalk unsupervised. His parents are irritated by his demands and the teacher's complaints about his behavior. There is not a good fit between what parents and social networks ask of the child and the child's individuality. Consequently, the child is labeled a problem at school and at home.

Parental expectations create standards that can help or block children's development, and so parents need to develop reasonable and sensitive expectations of their children.

Though we know parents' role is to interact with children and be responsive to their needs and behavior, that does not tell us specifically how parents are to interact or what they must do to respond. Let us look at more detailed theories that describe children's development and parents' role in promoting it.

DEVELOPMENT OF THE INDIVIDUAL

As children grow, they pass through identifiable stages. Parents must be aware of these transitions and prepared to respond to children in new ways appropriate to their changed needs.

Eight Stages of Growth

Erik Erikson,[6] a Freudian psychoanalyst with a strong interest in cross-cultural research and the social and cultural determiners of personality, has created a scheme for understanding life-span psychological development. He has worked on long-term studies of healthy children and adults. In the development of the eight stages of life, he has used his clinical experiences with patients, his knowledge of healthy growth and development, and his cross-cultural research.

Erikson describes growth as a series of stages (see Figure 2.2). In each stage, the individual has specific physical and psychological needs. Each stage has a developmental crisis that must be met and resolved. People have positive and negative experiences in satisfying needs, and both kinds of experiences are important for optimal development. If you have only positive gratifications, you never learn how to cope with difficulties. However, for healthy growth the balance should be on the positive side. When this occurs, a strength or virtue[7] develops.

Erikson does not believe that you solve each crisis once and for all. Later experiences can change earlier resolutions, for better or for worse. For example, stress during adulthood can disrupt mature ways of coping, so that for a brief period the individual may seem immature. Positive experiences in adulthood can reverse mistrust or doubt developed in childhood.

FIGURE 2-2
Erikson's Eight Stages of Growth

1.	2.	3.	4.	5.	6.	7.	8.
							Integrity vs. Despair (Wisdom)
						Generativity vs. Stagnation (Care)	
					Intimacy vs. Isolation (Love)		
				Identity vs. Identity diffusion (Fidelity)			
			Industry vs. Inferiority (Competence)				
		Initiative vs. Guilt (Purpose)					
	Autonomy vs. Shame, doubt (Will)						
Trust vs. Mistrust (Hope)							
1. 0–1	2. 1–3	3. 3–5	4. 5–12	5. 12–19	6. 19–	7.	8.

Years

Adapted from Erik H. Erikson, *Childhood and Society*, 2nd ed. with the permission of W. W. Norton. Copyright 1950, © 1963 by W. W. Norton & Co., Inc.

Let's look at each of the stages in Figure 2.2. In the first stage, which lasts for about the first year of life, the child is dependent on a caregiver for food, clothing, warmth, and cuddling. Infants can cry and draw attention to their needs, but those needs must be met by others. If the caregivers are reliable, the baby develops trust and feels good about herself as a person deserving care. Of course, caregivers cannot always be prompt and satisfying, and all babies will have experiences that lead to feelings of mistrust. When most experiences are positive and basic trust develops, children develop the strength or virtue of hope—the enduring belief that even though things are dark and gloomy, wishes and desires can be achieved.

The second of Erikson's stages takes place in the second and third years of life. Children have matured physically and have learned to walk and climb. They begin to express their basic sense of self in their verbal "No's" and "Do it myself." The child wants to do things by herself—to go where she wants, eat what she wants, get what she wants, and influence other people. If parents encourage this behavior and provide opportunities for self-direction, children develop a sense of autonomy, of being able to act independently. Failures occur, and parents are not always supportive and patient as children go at their own pace and do what they want. If failure and frustration occur often, children develop a sense of shame and doubt about themselves and their abilities. If most experiences are positive, children develop strength of will, the resolution to make free choices and to act with self-control.

In the third stage, usually in the fourth and fifth years, children have gained control over their bodies, have language, and can plan and direct self-initiated activity. Their language skills are well developed, and they explore the world with questions.

This is the period of the Oedipal and Electra complexes. A boy experiences a romantic attachment to the mother, and a girl, a romantic attachment to the father. Children give up these romantic fantasies about the opposite-sex parent because of fear of punishment and abandonment by the parents. As children accept the command of parents and society, the superego or conscience develops and becomes an integral part of the child's personality. If parents criticize children's activities, ridicule their fantasies, and refuse to answer questions, children develop guilt and feel that what they make and what they do is bad. If most experiences at this stage are positive, children develop strength of purpose, the ability to set and pursue goals, free of fears of failure, punishment, or criticism.

In the fourth stage, from five or six to eleven or twelve years, children's skills and abilities increase. They go off to school, learn to read and write, take up hobbies, start lessons, and join groups. They are industrious and experience pleasure in what they can do and produce. If they have few experiences of success and accomplishment, they develop a sense of inferiority; they feel their efforts are doomed to failure and that they are useless. If the balance of experiences is positive, children develop a sense of competence—the feeling one can use one's skills and abilities to accomplish goals, free of feelings of inferiority.

Children must now incorporate sexuality into the evolving sense of self. This is the task of the adolescent years—to integrate all previous experiences with a blossoming sexuality and increased intellectual competence, to form a psychosocial identity that will permit the individual to meet the tasks of adulthood. Erikson uses the word "identity" to refer to a sense of sameness and continuity of the self—the real inner me who thinks, feels, and experiences life in an active, vital way. In addition to sexual and intellectual influences, Erikson emphasizes that we incorporate social values in our individual identities. For example, we all incorporate, in our individual ways, society's views of what men are, what women are, what members of our race and religion are.

Individuals need to have their identities validated and confirmed by their parents and society. If teenagers are unable to integrate previous life experiences with their emerging capacities and obtain confirmation from others that they are who they think they are, role confusion results. They remain uncertain of who they are and where they are heading.

When life events and family members have not been supportive, an individual may develop a negative identity. He or she may become a delinquent, a dropout, a person who feels unable to do anything positive. When the balance of the experiences is on the positive side and a sense of identity is formed, the virtue that develops is fidelity—what Erikson describes as faithfulness and loyalty to one's choices, whether they are persons, goals, or ideals.

In the first five stages, children grow from dependence on others into individuals able to trust themselves to get around independently in the world, able to initiate and sustain activities and to form a stable, realistic identity. The first stage of adulthood is the establishment of intimate personal ties. Once individuals know who they are, they can enter into relationships that are freely chosen. Erikson talks in greatest detail about intimacy in heterosexual relationships, but he also speaks of intimacy with co-workers and friends. He uses the marital ties to illustrate the important processes of intimate relationships—the mutuality and surrender of the self to the other person and the relationship. Without a stable sense of identity, the individual has nothing to surrender. The ability to be close to other people leads to love—sharing of identities between friends and partners. This is a freely chosen, active love and involves transferring the love experienced in the developing years of childhood to adult relationships that are actively sought and of mutual concern to the two partners.

The second stage of adulthood is the initiation of generativity, or the creation of new life. In the past this has, for women, most often occurred in the family setting, and, for men, in their work, where they create new products and new ideas. However, now parenting and work are significant activities for both sexes. Generativity includes caring for the children and work that have been created. The virtue that develops in this period is care—concern and attention to what has been created, even if this requires sacrifice. If you do not learn to care for people or to work outside yourself, Erikson believes you then become a pet, or a child, to yourself.

In these first two stages of adulthood, the emphasis is on integration of the self with others—with intimate peers and children—and with social and economic activities. In the eighth stage of life, the focus is on the individual and the development of a sense of ego integrity. Individuals must come to terms with their lives and be satisfied with who and what they are and what they have done. If people cannot accept their own life experiences as important and meaningful, they suffer from despair because there is not time to start again. The virtue or strength that develops during this period is wisdom, deep understanding of life that is enriched by coming to terms with the prospect of one's own death. Erikson points out that children will be able to face life if elders can face death.

Erikson links the experience from youth to old age with the word *care:* "In youth you find out what you care to do and who you care to be—even in changing roles. In young adulthood you learn who you care to be with—at work and in private life, not only exchanging intimacies but sharing intimacy. In adulthood, however, you learn to know what and whom you can take care of."[8]

Examining the ego qualities and the virtues of each stage, we can see that Erikson describes the growth of active, adaptive individuals who are independent, giving, and concerned with other people and the world around them. Erikson believes children grow best when they experience reliable, trustworthy caregiving, opportunities for self-directed activity, and parental and social confirmation that what they make and do is valuable.

Stages of Intellectual Growth

Jean Piaget, a Swiss psychologist, has deepened our understanding of how children's minds grow and develop. According to Piaget, the child *acts* on the world and builds up ideas from his or her own actions and the actions of others. Knowledge of the world is not a gradual accumulation of fact after fact. Rather, growth occurs in stages, and each stage is qualitatively different from the others. Thus, babies do not respond and organize the world in the same way that toddlers or older children do, and older children differ from adolescents and adults. Piaget's work has made fundamental contributions to our knowledge of children's intellectual growth and is a tremendous aid to parents in understanding their children's reasoning and intellectual abilities.

Piaget believes intelligence involves the individual's adaptation to the world in such a way that the person interacts effectively with the environment.[9]

Children construct knowledge of the world through their interactions with people and objects in the world. Piaget believes two processes are at work in constructing a view of the world—*assimilation* and *accommodation*. Children take in or assimilate information as they act in the world. They form internal structures of the general behavior patterns they observe. These internal structures are termed *schemes*. In infancy schemes consist primarily of actions such as grasping, mouthing. Older children have schemes of mental behaviors such as naming, grouping, classifying.

As children continue assimilating information, they find their internal schemes are inadequate for representing what is new. They must modify or change their schemes to fit new information. This process of modifying internal schemes is termed *accommodation*. For example, the toddler who has a scheme of four-legged animals with tails as cats calls all four-legged animals "cats." When she meets a dog, she initially calls it a cat, but her scheme does not fit the world. She has to form a new scheme of four-legged animals with tails as dogs and note the differences between the two kinds of animals carefully so she can name them correctly. She has to note, for example, that dogs do not meow or climb trees, but instead bark and chase cats.

Intellectual growth is a constant interplay of taking in new information (assimilation) and modifying it (accommodation) to achieve balance or equilibrium between the individual's structure of the world and the world itself. *Equilibration* is the active process by which the individual achieves this effective balance.

Piaget believes intellectual growth is not just a matter of adding more and more refined schemes. Growth also results from new ways of responding to experience and organizing it. Paiget describes intellectual growth in four major periods which

TABLE 2-1
JEAN PIAGET'S PERIODS AND STAGES OF INTELLECTUAL DEVELOPMENT IN CHILDHOOD

	Ages	Behaviors
Sensorimotor period	0–2 years	Child perceives, then acts.
Reflexive stage	0–1 month	Baby practices built-in reflexes like sucking.
Primary circular reaction stage	1–4 months	Baby repeats acts like opening and closing hands. Baby often uses two senses at same time; e.g., seeing and hearing.
Secondary circular reaction stage	4–8 months	Baby repeats acts to see change in the environment; e.g., kicks mobile to make it go.
Coordination of secondary stage	8–12 months	Child uses responses to solve problem; e.g., child removes wrapping to get toy.
Tertiary circular reaction stage	12–18 months	Child is interested in properties of objects themselves, how they work. Can imitate more accurately.
Beginning of thought	18–24 months	Child begins to use language and symbolic mental representations.
Preoperational period	2–7 years	Child learns to represent objects, persons, and perceptions with symbols (e.g., language); can reason intuitively but not with a set of verbalized principles.
Preconceptual stage	2–4 years	Child can represent mentally what is seen or heard with language; child is more imaginative in play.
Intuitive stage	4–7 years	Child is able to reason intuitively, but pays attention to appearances of objects; e.g. believes taller, thinner glass holds more than short, fat glass.
Concrete operations period	7–11, 12 years	Child can think more logically and is not bound by appearances. Child can grasp relations between objects and easily arranges a series of sticks in terms of length.
Formal operations period	12 through adulthood	Child thinks logically and abstractly, thinks about possible alternative situations, imagines future.

Adapted from Herbert Ginsburg and Sylvia Opper, *Piaget's Theory of Intellectual Development* (Englewood Cliffs, N.J.: Prentice-Hall, 1969).

include substages. Table 2-1 describes changes in the way the child structures knowledge. In the first two years, perceptions and motor activity are the sources of knowledge, and schemes consist of action patterns. In the preconceptual period, symbols such as language and imitative play lead to knowledge. The child reasons intuitively but not logically. In the period of concrete operations, the child structures knowledge symbolically and logically but is limited to concrete objects and events that are present and seen and manipulable. In the last stage, the individual reasons logically and is able to go beyond what is present to consider hypothetical and abstract situations.

Piaget describes intellectual growth as an active process of constructing knowledge based on experience and maturing capacities to react to the experience. He says little about the role of other people in generating knowledge.

While Piaget emphasizes individual action and maturing capacities, Russian psychologist Lev Vygotsky emphasizes the social aspect of intellectual growth.[10] Born in the same year as Piaget, Vygotsky died at the early age of 38 from tuberculosis. Psychologists are turning to his work now to increase our understanding of children's intellectual growth. He believes knowledge, thought, and mental processes such as memory and attention all rest on social interactions.

Whatever the child learns has first been experienced at the social level in a social interaction with someone and then is internalized at the individual psychological level. Look, for example, at the infant who watches how an adult shakes a rattle or plays with a toy, then carries out the same action. Later the child independently carries out the activity. The adult or more experienced person leads the way for the child, and gradually the child develops similar capacities.

Social interactions rest on the organization of the individual's culture and society. Every culture has a view of the world and the way to solve problems. Language, writing, art, methods of problem-solving all reflect this social world view. Adults use these societal forms in interacting with children, and children internalize them.

Social interaction conveys not only societal knowledge of the world; it plays an important role in stimulating children to master that knowledge. Vygotsky describes a unique concept called "the zone of proximal development." There is a range of behavior a child can perform alone, demonstrating a capacity that is clearly internal. This is what most of us would consider the child's level of ability. But Vygotsky points out that the child's behavior in this area can improve. When a more experienced person guides or prompts the child with questions, hints, or demonstrations, the child can respond at a more mature level not achieved when the child acts alone. So, the child has potential that emerges in social interaction. For example, a child who is mastering language may use a certain number of words spontaneously. That would be the child's verbal ability. A mother, however, might increase the number of words by prompting the child to remember what she called an item when she used it or increase the number of words put together by waiting for the child to add an action to an object he just identified, saying, "The doggie?" then adding "runs" or "goes bow-wow."

This zone of behavior, extending from what the child can do alone to what the child has the potential to do when guided, is the zone of proximal development. Vygotsky's interest goes beyond what the child can do to what the child's learning potential is. Teaching has the greatest impact, he believes, when it is directed to the child's potential at the high end of the zone of proximal development. The experienced person helps the child do alone what he or she can initially do only with guidance.

Like Piaget, Vygotsky believes the child is an active learner, but he focuses on the strategies children use to master material and to learn more efficiently. Teaching encourages children to develop and use strategies to master a task. For example, children can use strategies to remember material, and part of teaching involves helping them develop and use these strategies.

Language plays a significant role in mental development. Language develops from social interaction and contact, and initially is a means of influencing others. Adults talk to children, influencing their reactions or behavior. Children initally guide their own behavior with external language similar to that already heard. They talk to themselves as others have and guide their behavior with their speech. Many a young toddler will say, "No, no" to herself as a way of stopping forbidden action with varying degrees of success. As the child matures, the speech that guides behavior becomes internal or inner speech. Such inner speech becomes thought in the older child.

Just as Piaget believes intellectual development hinges on action in the world, Vygotsky believes it hinges on social interaction. The most complete view of intellectual development includes both points of view and sees mental processes as developing from social interactions and individual action on the world. These theories suggest that parents' role is (1) to interact with children, serving as a model and guide in the world, helping them reach their potential and (2) to provide opportunities for independent investigation and action in the world.

The Growth of the Self

We have looked at children's development from three theoretical perspectives that taken together emphasize children's needs for independent action in an atmosphere of close, guiding relationships with adults. Let us look briefly at development from the individual's point of view. What qualities do people value in themselves and what experiences lead to these qualities? Understanding how a sense of self and self-esteem develop gives us this information.

Michael Lewis and his co-workers[11] have studied the burgeoning sense of self in infancy and conclude: "By the end of the second year of life children have developed an elaborate self system."[12] Children have a sense of being separate individuals who can act on their own, but as yet they have only limited self-awareness in the sense of understanding the ways others regard them. In other words, they have a clear sense of an active "I," but a less well developed sense of the "me" others react to.

Susan Harter and her co-workers describe an extended series of studies mapping the development of the self-concept and feelings of global self-worth or self-esteem from early childhood (beginning at age 3) through adulthood.[13] Table 2-2 describes the domains of the self-concept at each stage of development. Across the life-span, the self-concept becomes increasingly differentiated though the basic dimensions remain surprisingly similar. Young children do not verbalize global feelings of self-worth, but they do express them in behavior that has been studied as well.

Global feelings of self-worth are related to two independent factors—one's feelings of competence in domains of importance and the amount of social support one receives from others. Those highest in self-worth feel good about the abilities they value and also feel that others support and accept them. Those lowest in global self-worth feel they lack competence in domains deemed important and report that they

TABLE 2-2
DOMAINS OF THE SELF-CONCEPT AT EACH PERIOD OF THE LIFE SPAN*

Early Childhood	Middle/Late Childhood	Adolescence	College	Adult
Cognitive competence	Scholastic competence	Scholastic competence	Scholastic competence	
			Intellectual ability Creativity	Intelligence
		Job competence	Job competence	Job competence
Physical competence	Athletic competence	Athletic competence	Athletic competence	Athletic competence
	Physical appearance	Physical appearance	Physical appearance	Physical appearance
Peer acceptance	Peer acceptance	Peer acceptance	Peer acceptance	Sociability
		Close friendship	Close friendship	Close friendship
		Romantic relationships	Romantic relationships	Intimate relationships
			Relationships with parents	
Behavioral conduct	Behavioral conduct	Conduct/ morality	Morality	Morality
			Sense of humor	Sense of humor
				Nurturance
				Household management
				Adequacy as a provider
	Global self-worth	Global self-worth	Global self-worth	Global self-worth

*Susan Harter, "Causes, Correlates, and the Functional Role of Global Self-Worth: A Life-Span Perspective," in *Perceptions of Competence and Incompetence Across the Life-Span,* eds. J. Kolligian and Robert Sternberg (New Haven: Yale University Press, 1990), p. 73.

receive little social support. Harter notes that no amount of social support can directly counteract one's perception of incompetence, and conversely, no amount of competence can completely overcome feelings of lack of social support. So, to increase self-esteem, one has to increase both feelings of competence in valued domains and social support.

High self-esteem children, aged three to seven, had two qualities—confidence in approaching situations and resilience when frustrated or upset.[14] These are also the qualities of children securely attached to their caregivers. Parental experiences that foster secure attachment are most likely those that help develop high self-esteem. Parental support, then, is a more important determiner of early self-esteem than competence per se. In later childhood, both support and feelings of competence are important in determining self-worth.

INTERVIEW
with Susan Harter

Dr. Susan Harter is professor of psychology at the University of Denver. She has spent twenty years studying the development of the self and self-esteem and has written numerous articles and chapters on the subject.

You have done a great deal of research on self-esteem. More than any other quality, I would say, parents hope to help children develop self-esteem. What can they do to promote it in their children?

We have identified two broad themes that impact children's self-esteem. First, the unconditional support and positive regard of parents and others in the child's world are particularly critical during the early years. What do we mean by support? It is communicating to children that you like them as people for who or what they are.

That sounds relatively easy but is in fact extremely difficult. Most of us as parents are far more skilled at providing conditional regard or support for children even though we are unaware we are doing it. We approve of our child if he cleans up his room or shares or doesn't hit his brother. So our support is conditional on their conduct. However, it isn't perceived by children as supportive at all. Basically it specifies how the child can please the parents. That does not feel good to children.

Unconditional regard validates children as worthy people and lets them know they are appreciated for who they are, for their strengths and weaknesses. It also involves listening to them which is very validating to children as well as adults. So many well-meaning parents, and I make the same mistake, preach at their kids because we think we have a lot to say. We think we're teaching when we are really preaching. We don't refrain from talking; we don't shut up, listen well, and take the child's point of view seriously.

With unconditional support early on, children internalize positive regard so that when they are older, they can approve of themselves, pat themselves on the back, give themselves psychological hugs—all of which contribute to high self-esteem.

Another major part of self-esteem, beginning at about age eight, is feeling competent and adequate across the various domains of life. One does not have to feel competent in every domain in order to experience high self-esteem. Rather one needs to feel competent in those domains that he/she judges to be *important*. Two children's profiles of competence in the different areas of athletic, social, and intellectual competence can look very similar, but one can have high self-esteem while the other can have low self-esteem. They both can feel competent in the same areas and feel inadequate in the same other areas. What distinguishes the *low* self-esteem child is the fact that areas of incompetence are very important to one's feeling of being worthwhile, thus the child doesn't feel good about himself or herself. The *high* self-esteem child feels the low areas are very unimportant so still feels good about himself or herself.

You wrote that the one domain which contributes most highly to children's, adolescents' and adults' self-esteem is physical appearance. Unfortunately, this domain seems to be somewhat out of one's control. What can parents do to help a child in these areas?

continued

INTERVIEW with Susan Harter   *continued*

There are two approaches to the problem that one's self-esteem is so highly linked to physical appearance. You can take the route of improving appearance by going to the beauty parlor, having a weight loss program if needed, doing things that make a difference, physically.

The other route is to try to convince the child that other things matter, that physical appearance is not the measure of one's worth as a person. That is extremely difficult since our society places so much emphasis on appearance. The role models present punishing standards of appearance that are impossible for most, and it is therefore devastating for children who do not measure up.

There is an intimate relationship between our inner selves and our outer selves. I think most parents are benevolent about their child's appearance even if the child is not striking looking. But other people react to a child's appearance and right from day one we are being bombarded with messages about our looks. "You are cute," or "You are handsome."

Our appearance is so salient, constantly on display. Other domains are not always on display. Scholastic competence or athletic competence come and go in their contexts. But your physical self is always there for other people to observe and react to. Thus, even though benevolent parents react positively to their child who may not be highly attractive by societal standards, that child will have trouble once he or she hits the social world of peers. Peers perpetuate these standards and react to other children accordingly.

I have a diagram showing the high relationship between physical appearance and self-esteem. These data were collected across many samples. In the third grade, males and females do not differ in their perceptions of their appearance, they each feel they look relatively good. Then with each passing grade, averages for the girls systematically decline, whereas boys' averages stay constant. Since males continue to approve of their appearance, they continue to feel good about themselves, to have reasonably high self-esteem. This is speculation, but if males have power and status, if they are perceived as athletic, they are perceived as better looking than they might be if you looked objectively at their features and their physique. Because more males are in positions of power, others' perceptions of their appearance are affected; thus more males think they look just fine.

For females, there is less latitude for what constitutes good looks; standards are much narrower. Just look at the magazines. There is a difficult message in them for girls. It requires many, many "takes" to get that one photograph of the model that lands on the cover, but we pick up the magazine and say, "Why don't I look like that?" The models don't look like that most of the time either. In addition, our society promotes the notion that a girl's self-esteem depends on her appearance. How you feel about your inner self depends upon whether your outer self conforms to society's standards for beauty. I think it's absolutely amazing that any teenager has the courage to adopt the opposite, healthier orientation—namely, that how I feel about myself determines how I feel about my physical appearance.

Our own findings reveal that we need to shift people to the orientation that how we feel about our inner selves is the most critical factor. Let children know that other things besides looks should be important in determining their worth as a person, such as being caring, honest people. You want them to know that, even if society emphasizes looks, you like them for their inner qualities, not just their outward appearance.

The other factor that is an important determiner of self-esteem is being approved of by peers and parents, but some children are temperamentally shyer and less confident.

We have approached the issue of social approval in the same way that we have dealt with physical appearance. We ask kids, "Is it that your worth as a person depends on how much others accept you or is it that if you first like yourself as a person, others will like or accept you too?" If they endorse the view that self-esteem depends on the opinions of others, we speculate that early in life they did not get the kind of unconditional support that validated them as people, and thus they have not internalized a sense of self-acceptance. So these kids are buffeted about by the squints, glares, and party invitations of others. Actually, such children have lower ratings of approval and self-esteem than those who believe that self-esteem leads to social approval.

We recently conducted a study with young children ages four to seven, and demonstrated that parent approval is the most important contributor to self-esteem. If children never receive such early support, they do not have approval to internalize. I think we are beginning to understand that neglect or failure to build in positive self-feelings is a powerful force. Self-esteem all harks back to being validated as a person—being listened to and having your feelings as a person accepted.

More from Susan Harter in Chapter 7.

The specific areas of competence that contribute most to feelings of self-worth are physical appearance and social acceptance by others, namely parents and peers. Surprisingly, physical appearance and support continue to be salient across the life-span for individuals from eight to fifty-five years of age.

Which comes first—do children and adolescents base their self-esteem on others' social approval and others' perceptions of their attractiveness or do children and adolescents high in self-esteem feel others like them and find them attractive?[15] Questionnaire responses indicate about 60 percent of children and adolescents fall in the category saying their self-esteem depends on others' views of them and about 40 percent say they like themselves and feel others approve of them. Those in the first category have lower self-esteem because they are dependent on the shifting regard of others. Those who like themselves and assume others do too have higher self-esteem that is more stable because it is an internal quality.

Though self-esteem depends on early positive regard of parents and caregivers, self-esteem is not a fixed quality for life. Levels of self-esteem can increase over time as individuals become more competent in areas of importance to them or as they receive increased support from others. Self-esteem decreases under the reverse conditions.

Times of change and transitions—entrance to kindergarten, junior high school, college, moves to new schools or new neighborhoods—can trigger changes in self-esteem. New skills to master, new reference groups for comparison, new social groups for support provide the stimulus for change. People maintain self-esteem most successfully when they join or create positive social support or when they increase in competence.

Children need the unconditional positive regard of parents as a basis for feeling good about themselves.

Harter's work on the development of the self-concept and self-esteem reinforces the conclusions of theoretical positions which emphasize the importance of children's experiencing both social support and opportunities for competent behavior.

Let us look at what research on parent-child relationships tells us about developing positive behaviors.

GUIDELINES FROM RESEARCH AND CHILDREN

Many studies of infant behavior reveal that "attentive, warm, stimulating, responsive, and nonrestrictive caregiving" promote healthy socioemotional and cognitive development.[16]

A critical ingredient is *involvement* with the child. What does involvement mean? It means having conversations with children, knowing what they are doing, who their friends are, where they are going, considering their opinions. Summarizing research with two longitudinal studies, Dr. Jack Block wrote:

In order for a child to become appropriately controlled, someone has to invest time and trouble. The responsibilities of parenthood take much effort and, perhaps more crucial, the proper timing of the effort. It is so often the case that when the child requires a parental response, the parent would much rather be doing something other than being a parent. The test of the good parent is that she (or he) functions parentally even when she (or he) could gain more immediate pleasures elsewhere.[17]

Children who grow up in homes with parental involvement become responsible, competent, achievement-oriented adults who are appropriately controlled and happy. Children growing up in homes where parents are self-focused and uninvolved tend to be impulsive, moody adults who find it difficult to control aggression.

Beyond parent involvement, what else is important?

Diana Baumrind has conducted careful research on the effects of parents' child-rearing practices on children's behavior.[18] The findings suggest that parents who are accepting and who also provide structure and limits have the most competent children. Baumrind identified three patterns of childrearing: (1) authoritative, (2) authoritarian, and (3) permissive.

Authoritative parents exercise firm control of the child's behavior but also emphasize the independence and individuality in the child. Although the parents have a clear notion of present and future standards of behavior for the child, they are rational, flexible, and attentive to the needs and preferences of the child. "Authoritative parents . . . balanced what they offered with what they demanded. They balanced high control with high independence-granting, high standards for maturity with much support and nurturance."[19] Their children are self-reliant and self-confident and explore their worlds with excitement and pleasure.

Authoritarian parents employ a similar firm control, but use it in an arbitrary, power-oriented way without regard for the child's individuality. They emphasize control, without nurturance or support to achieve it. Baumrind writes, "The authoritarian parent values obedience as a virtue and believes in restricting the child's autonomy. This parent values the preservation of order and traditional structure as an end in itself. He or she does not encourage verbal give and take, believing that the child should accept the parent's word for what is right."[20] Children of authoritarian parents, relative to other groups of children, are unhappy, withdrawn, inhibited, and distrustful.

Permissive parents set few limits on the child. They are accepting of the child's impulses, giving as much freedom as is possible while still maintaining physical safety. They appear cool and uninvolved. Permissive parents sometimes allow behavior that angers them, but they do not feel sufficiently comfortable with their own anger to express it. As a result, the anger builds up to unmanageable proportions. They then lash out and are likely to hurt the child more than they want to. Their children are the least independent and self-controlled and could be best classified as immature.

Extensive studies of self-esteem and the family and school behaviors related to it reveal that self-esteem is an important ingredient in effective functioning. The childrearing practices that enhance the development of self-esteem resemble those used by Baumrind's authoritative parent, who uses warm acceptance, attention to individuality with definite limits, and high but reasonable expectations. Stanley Coopersmith, who has studied the development of self-esteem, describes a stimulating family atmosphere as follows:

> The treatment associated with the formation of high self-esteem is much more vigorous, active, and contentious than is the case in families that produce children with low self-esteem. Rather than being a paradigm of tranquility, harmony and open-mindedness, we find that the high self-esteem family is notable for the high level of activity of the individual members, strong-minded parents dealing with independent, assertive children, stricter enforcement of more stringent demands, and greater possibilities for open dissent and disagreement.[21]

Studies of families rearing competent children have found that members care about each other;[22] they reach out to each other, and reach out with the expectation that interaction will be positive. They love and respect each other, but all are individuals and all are free to be open and honest. They value individual differences and consider many options when solving problems. Members of healthy families are active in meeting problems and show initiative. Often they are involved in community activities. Parents respect each other as individuals and present models of leadership to children. Power structure is clear, but parents negotiate problems when they arise. Family members are close, but all are encouraged to be individuals who accept responsibility for their acts. They are accurate in understanding each other, in part because they are able to communicate feelings and ideas. Healthy families are made up of individuals who share differing ideas and opinions in an accepting atmosphere. Disagreements occur, but they serve primarily to broaden points of view rather than stimulate conflict. Parents are supportive of each other; family members are involved in activities, connected to community groups. They have positive attitudes toward themselves and other people.

Prosocial children who help and share with others come from homes where parents model considerate, caring behavior and explain their values to their children. They draw their children's attention to the needs and feelings of others and encourage kind, thoughtful actions. Such parents discipline children gently, avoiding harsh punishment and instead using reason to stimulate behavior change. In the disciplinary process, they remain sensitive to the child's feelings while still maintaining high standards. Further, they treat all the children in the family in this way and do not single children out for preferential treatment.[23]

We must be cautious in generalizing the results of these studies to all ethnic groups, for they were carried out primarily on white, middle-class families and children. Baumrind, for example, found that the authoritarian parenting style linked with withdrawn, inhibited behavior in white girls, led to competent, mature behavior in her small sample of Afro-American girls.[24] In the Afro-American culture, strict control seemed to be interpreted as a sign of caring and involvement rather than a sign of the cold rejection it seems to be in the white culture.

We must not assume ethnic differences in parental attitudes, values, or behavior unless recent, well-controlled research documents them. We come upon too many surprises in well-done studies for us to make assumptions—for example, one surprise was the finding that Chinese parents value the open expression of affection as much as Anglo-Americans do.[25]

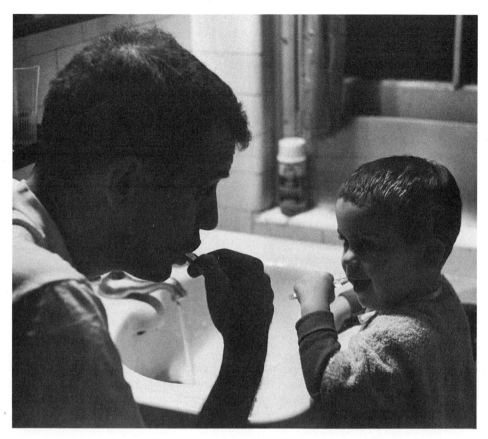

Because children observe, imitate, and model the behavior of their parents, parents have the opportunity to exert both positive and negative influences over their children.

We must be cautious in interpreting research because in too many instances differences attributed to ethnic values are a matter of educational or social differences. Luis Laosa found that Mexican-American mothers used more modeling and visual cues to direct children in making a toy whereas Anglo-American mothers used questioning and praise. The ethnic differences disappeared when he had groups of mothers with equal amounts of schooling.[26]

Childrearing activities of different ethnic groups have to be understood in terms of the traditional values of the culture of origin as well as the values of the culture to which the group is adapting. When, for example, the childrearing attitudes of Chinese immigrant parents in this country are compared with the attitudes of Anglo-American parents, the Chinese immigrant parents are more controlling, more achievement-oriented, and more encouraging of independence than are Anglo-American parents. You might think they have not adapted to this country at all. Yet when the attitudes of immigrant Chinese parents are compared to those of Chinese parents on Taiwan, they are less controlling, less achievement-oriented, and less encouraging of independence. The immigrant parents have moved in the direction of absorbing the values of the majority culture. It is of interest that the Chinese seem able to encourage both strong family interdependence and individual independence. Also note that the three groups did not differ on open expression of affection.[27]

Within the limited scope of this book we cannot enumerate the characteristics of major ethnic groups and still be sensitive to social and educational differences within each group, so we shall focus on general characteristics associated with many ethnic groups. All parents use similar techniques for socializing their children—modeling, reinforcement, identification—but they use the techniques to pass on different values, different ways of doing things.[28]

The values of many ethnic minority parents frequently center on giving children a positive view of their own group so that they will develop a bicultural vision and carry on their own cultural traditions. Children learn that their obligations to the family and the group are of first importance. They are taught that cooperation, sharing, and reciprocating favors are primary values. Interdependence is more important than competitive individualism. As a result of learning two sets of values, minority children can become more flexible and broader in outlook.

We have looked at what researchers think is effective. But what do children want in their parents?

Interestingly, children value these same qualities of involvement and limit-setting in parents.[29] Preschoolers interviewed about the qualities of a good mommy and daddy and a bad mommy and daddy believe that good parents are physically affectionate and nurturant, especially in the area of providing food for children. In addition, good parents like to play games with their children and read to them, and they discipline them—that is, they keep children from doing things they should not, but they do not spank or slap in the face. Bad parents have the opposite qualities. They don't hug or kiss, don't fix food, don't play games. They hit and don't let you go outside. Bad parents are also described as generally irresponsible—they go through red lights, throw chairs at people, don't read the newspaper.

As children grow older, they continue to value nurturance and affection, but they also appreciate qualities reflecting psychological nurturance. Mothers' good qualities include "understanding feelings and moods," "being there when I need her," "sticking up for me." Children continue to emphasize the limit-setting behaviors in a good mother—"she makes us eat fruit and vegetables," "she yells at me when I need it"—but they want their mother to consider their needs and wishes in setting the rules. Older children still enjoy mutual recreational time—playing, joking, building things together. Finally, as children get older they appreciate the teaching activities of the good mother.[30]

So research and children, too, tell us that, first, healthy parents have close emotional relationships with their children, regard their children positively, and give them opportunities to develop and express their own thoughts and feelings. Second, parents modify children's behavior with reasonable, firm limits that are consistently enforced. Thus, they provide structure within which the child is independent and free to initiate activities. Chapters 3 and 4 discuss these two tasks of parenting in greater detail.

PARENTAL COMPETENCE, CHILD COMPETENCE

Jay Belsky, Elliot Robins, and Wendy Gamble point to parental patience, endurance, and commitment as the important qualities underlying parental sensitivity and involvement.[31] Patience enables parents to control their feelings and impulses so they can be sensitive to the needs of the child. Endurance gives parents the energy to persist and carry out all their activities and still remain involved. Finally, commitment to children insures that parents will use patience and endurance to meet the child's needs.

Parental resources, social supports, and the child's own characteristics are the three basic factors determining the probability of child competence. When all factors are supportive, then the probability of child competence is high. When two of the three factors are supportive, there is still a good probability of child competence. For example, if a child develops a chronic illness like diabetes, but parents' personal resources are strong and the family has many relatives who provide practical help and emotional support, then the probability of child competence is high.

Conversely even when the child has many skills and positive qualities, but there is little social support and the parent is not involved, then the probability of child competence is lower. Belsky et al. believe that all can go wrong, but if the parent brings his or her personal resources to bear in behalf of the child, then there is a good chance of average child competence.

A vicious cycle sometimes occurs when, for example, a child's temperamental characteristic—high activity level, for example—can exhaust the parent's capacity for support and alienate possible social supports. Intervention can occur at any point in the cycle, however, and effect change.

THE IMPORTANCE OF PARENTS AND EARLY EXPERIENCE

In contemporary developmental psychology, two contradictory sets of beliefs about the nature of parent/family influence on children's development are prominent. On the one hand, Jerome Kagan, and more recently Sandra Scarr, point to the importance of individuals' qualities in determining development. In his 1984 book, *The Nature of the Child,* Kagan insists that early experience has little long-term impact on the individual's development.[32] Development, he believes, is a series of loosely connected stages triggered by the child's maturing capacities and by information the child garners from life events and interactions with people. Early experience ceases to be important when the child moves to the next stage of development. Though parents and family are important influences, they can neither destroy nor insure a happy future. He understands that such a view violates a strongly held belief in the importance of parents and early experience, but he believes it important to emphasize the power of the individual's own unfolding capacities.

More recently, Sandra Scarr points to the importance of a child's genetic makeup as determiner of development, given the sufficiently supportive environment most parents provide. "Being reared in one family rather than another, within the range of families sampled, makes few differences in children's personality and intellectual development."[33]

On the other hand, clinicians have emphasized the long-term consequences of certain kinds of early experiences, and now researchers are identifying certain behavioral styles that are transmitted across two or three generations of a family. Gerald Patterson and his co-workers show how patterns are transmitted from grandparents to parents to children.[34] Grandparents who are abusive and irritable individuals whose disciplinary techniques involve explosive behavior are more likely to rear anti-social, impulsive children. When such children grow up, they have less education, get lower-paying jobs, and experience more life stress due to unemployment and divorce. When they become parents, they are less effective disciplinarians and poorer monitors of children's behavior so their children have problems as well. Such problems are reversible when parents use more effective discipline and more consistent monitoring of children.

Jay Belsky, Laurence Steinberg, and Patricia Draper also describe the transmission of behaviors, both positive and negative, from one generation to another.[35] They see evidence that children whose parents are sensitive, responsive, authoritative caretakers develop competence and trust in themselves and others. When they grow up, they have mutually satisfying, long-term relationships with partners and have energy free for investing in parenting. Conversely, children raised with harsh, rejecting parents who use inconsistent discipline develop negative social behaviors that lead to greater difficulty in forming relationships. When they grow up, they tend to have a series of brief relationships that are often negative in tone. They have little energy available for parenting.

Within the childhood period, early positive attachments with parents may pave the way for later positive interactions with others.[36] In a sample of poor families, children with positive attachments to mother in the infant/toddler years showed better adaptation in the elementary school years than those who had insecure attachments even though both groups of children had had problems in the preschool period. The early positive experience may have given the children a later advantage by providing early internal models of care and self-worth that stimulate these children to seek out similar experiences in the elementary school years.

As in so many areas, the broad view encompassing both these points of view appears most accurate. Individuals have strong drives to development, and no one event dooms an individual to a life of difficulty. But it also appears clear that parents and social supports can help individuals maximize their potential. Further, very effective and very ineffective styles of approaching and reacting to people and events can be transmitted across generations.

Parents may worry if they read statements connecting childhood experiences with later adult parenting. Most parents want a fresh start with their children. They do not want to feel doomed to poor parenting by events of their own past lives. And, in fact, they are not doomed to poor parenting. Recent research reveals that parents who come to terms with their own negative childhood experiences do not repeat the unhappy interactions with their children.[37] Mothers and fathers who understand and accept their feelings that their own parents could not give them what they wanted are able to create new kinds of relationships with their sons and daughters. Parents who describe difficult times but deny any emotional reaction like anger, sadness, or frustration in response to their parents are those most likely to carry over negative patterns in their day-to-day contact because they have not worked through their feelings about their childhood.

When parents have strong feelings of dislike about some feature of their childhood and find themselves acting the same as their parents did or having trouble in the same area, they can take action. Talking to friends or relatives who also have children and know the parents' children can give a fresh view on what is happening. Sometimes just the opportunity to air feelings makes a parent feel better and return to deal with the problem more effectively. Joining a parent group, hearing the problems and views of others, can give a more balanced perspective on childrearing issues. It also helps to know that other parents have similar concerns.

As parents become more aware of childhood experiences that were full of conflict, they can take action to change the relationships. In *Making Peace with Your Own Parents,* psychiatrist Harold Bloomfield and psychologist Leonard Felder describe a variety of techniques they present in workshops.[38] Exercises and personal growth skills help individuals master the conflicted feelings and create satisfying relationships with parents. The exercises focus on becoming aware of hidden feelings, particularly buried resentments, and then learning to heal the hurts. People learn to forgive their parents for not being what they wanted them to be. Adults are then free to discover and appreciate their parents' unique qualities. Increasing communication skills makes possible a more satisfying give-and-take in current relationships with parents.

Bloomfield and Felder emphasize that creating new relationships with parents requires self-observation, awareness of others' behavior, and much practice in changing behavior patterns. Changes in parenting require the same persistence and effort as that required to master a new sport, and the effort is worth it. People who are distant and alienated from their own parents are more likely to take on their parents' negative qualities and hence are more likely to repeat the behavior they so disliked.[39]

HOW PARENTS CHANGE

Parents and psychologists have begun to look at the parenting experience in terms of its effects on parents. How do parents change as a result of having children? Ellen Galinsky found herself changing after her children were born. Curious about the meaning of her feelings, she found little written on the subject. She began to run groups for parents of young children then interviewed 228 parents who represented a broad cross-section of the population but not a statistically random one.

Galinsky divided parenthood into six stages in which parents focus their emotional and intellectual energy on the task of that period.[40] Parenting stages are different from most other stages because a parent can be in more than one stage at a time with children of different ages. The first stage, occurring in pregnancy, she terms the *image-making* stage. It is a time when parents prepare for changes in themselves and in their relationships to others. The second *nurturing* stage goes from birth

THE JOYS OF BEING A PARENT

In what way would you say being a parent has changed you as a person?

"It has changed my priorities, my perspective. I am much more protective. If I see someone driving like an idiot, I get much more upset. I feel more like a regular person, more grown up." FATHER OF TODDLER

"Now I'm officially grown up. It's kind of funny because I am a forty-year-old person who is just feeling grown up. For me, it's being less caught up in myself, more unselfish. I don't do everything I want to do all the time, and that's changing and it's okay. I used to resent that. I am less self-centered, less concerned with myself and how I'm doing, how I'm feeling, what's up. Now I am thinking more about him. For both my husband and me, I don't know whether this is going to change, but we are more oriented toward the future. We have to plan for his college, plan for our retirement; all of a sudden, it's not just living in the present; the future is there. We spend less time thinking about the past, but now we are more caught up in what is coming. That's different. We are going to be retiring when he goes off to school, and how are we going to handle all these expenses?" MOTHER OF TODDLER

"My own personal sense of the meaningfulness of life, in all aspects, has really gone through a dramatic change. It's just been so gratifying and meaningful and important to have this other little life, in a sense, in my hands, to be responsible for it. It's just been one of the best things I could have done. I am always looking forward to going home to see him. My attitude about things has changed. I'm more patient, even when I'm on my own, say, in a traffic jam, when I used to get irritable. Somehow I'm happy enough and satisfied enough with the rest of my life that it doesn't have the same effect on me. It doesn't matter." MOTHER OF TODDLER

"It has changed my sense of the past. I appreciate more of what my parents must have gone through for me. No matter what their problems or shortcomings, gee, they had to do all this for me; my mother changed all the diapers, she must have, someone did. My father was exactly the same age when I was born that I was when my son was born, so I have a sense of what it was like for him to be a certain age and be a father, even though he had an older son too. All the existential issues are taken care of." FATHER OF TODDLER

to the time when the child starts to say "no," about eighteen to twenty-four months. As parents become attached to the new baby, they arrange their lives to be caregivers, balancing their own and their child's needs, setting priorities. The third *authoritative* stage lasts from the time the child is two to four or five. Parents become rulegivers and enforcers as they learn that love for children goes hand in hand with structure and order. From the child's preschool years through adolescence, parents are in the *interpretive* stage. Children are more skilled and independent, and parents establish

"It's that overused word, maturity. It happened for both of us, my husband and me. We look back on how our lives were before our son and afterwards. We were well-established adults, older, we had resolved all our career issues, we had nice incomes, and we were in love. Our whole lives were what we wanted every hour of every day. Along came the baby and, by choice, there was a reverse, almost 100 percent. We don't get to go out like we used to. We don't get to go on vacations or go to meetings with the same abandon that we used to; our budget is much tighter; our daily life with our son in it is much more decided by him, at times I think to a fault. We talk about problems that come up and grapple with them. It seems like an agony sometimes, but we are growing as a couple and as a family. It's very enriching." MOTHER OF TODDLER

"It has changed me for the better. It matured me, really at the core. I am much more responsible because I want to be a good example for them, provide stability for them. It has helped me to see into myself. I recall things I did as a child, and I understand better what was happening then. It has changed the kinds of things I think of as fun. I never would have found sailing on my own, and I like it a lot because he made me try it. It has changed my finances for the worse, but I can't think of a better use for the money. It has changed my whole outlook. It has made me better at my work because I understand people better." FATHER OF ELEMEN-TARY SCHOOL CHILD AND EARLY ADOLESCENT

"I wish I could say it has made me more patient, but it has intensified my emotions; and if something really difficult has happened, as it did today when she destroyed something I took a lot of time to make for her, because she didn't follow a simple rule, then I am amazed at how furious I feel. I almost never felt that angry at anyone before I had children. Yet a little while later, the great love I have for her makes forgiveness easy, and I sat down and started to make the whole thing over. So now I have extremes of feeling from great love to great anger." MOTHER OF ELEMENTARY SCHOOL CHILD AND EARLY ADOLESCENT

"Having children makes you more patient, more humble, better able to roll with the punches because life is not so black and white. You can't just base your life on platitudes. You have the experience of having things go, not the way you would have them go, having your children do things you would not have them do; and you have to roll with that. You learn; it either kills you or you go on, and you have a different view of life. You become more patient and, I think, more kind." MOTHER OF EARLY AND LATE ADOLESCENTS

a way of life for them. They interpret outside authorities such as teachers to children. Parents teach values and morals. In brief, they teach children what life is all about.

When their children are adolescents, parents enter the *interdependent* stage. They form new relationships with children and, though they are still authorities, their power becomes shared with children in ways it was not in past years. In the sixth *departure* stage, parents evaluate themselves as their children prepare to leave home. They see where they have succeeded and where they might have acted differently.

Galinsky summarized her views of how parenthood changes adults:

Taking care of a small, dependent, growing person is transforming, because it brings us in touch with our baser side, it exposes our vulnerabilities as well as our nobility. We lose our sense of self, only to find it and have it change again and again. We learn to nurture and care. We struggle through defining our own rules and our own brand of being an authority. We figure out how we want to interpret the wider world, and we learn to interact with all those who affect our children. When our children are teenagers, we redefine our relationships, and then we launch them into life.

Often our fantasies are laid bare, our dreams are in a constant tug-of-war with realities. And perhaps we grow. In the end, we have learned more about ourselves, about the cycles of life, and humanity itself. Most parents describe themselves as more responsible, more accepting, more generous than before they had children.[41]

MAJOR POINTS OF CHAPTER 2

The parenting process involves:

- a balance in the roles of disciplinarian and nurturer
- an interaction between the child, the parents, and the environment
- an environment that provides both stresses and supports
  - stresses are negative events such as economic hardship, experiencing discrimination
  - supports are positive factors such as work, marriage, extended family, friends
- a child who brings:
  - sexual gender
  - temperament
  - birth order
  - own growth patterns
- parents who bring:
  - sexual gender, birth order, temperament
  - experience with own parents
  - satisfactions/frustrations in other areas of life—marriage, work
  - expectations of themselves and their children

Goodness of fit means:

- a good match between the child's qualities and what parents and the environment demand
- parents' expectations are reasonable for this child

Erikson's theory emphasizes parents' role as:

- reliable, trustworthy caregiver
- provider of opportunities for independence

- validator of child's identity and worth
- source of individual growth for parent

Theories of intellectual development emphasize that children:

- organize experience differently from adults
- need stimulating people to interact with them and help them maximize their potential
- require opportunities for action so they can construct knowledge of the world
- use language as a forerunner of thought

People evaluate themselves in terms of:

- physical appearance and ability
- social acceptability
- intellectual competence
- behavioral/moral conduct

Self-esteem is based on:

- getting early unconditional support
- getting ongoing support from family and friends
- achieving competence in areas of importance to the individual

Research guidelines for parenting emphasize importance of:

- attentive, warm, stimulating caregiving in infancy
- parental involvement
- balancing parental control and demand for high standards of maturity with parental support, nurturance, and granting of independence
- becoming a model of kind, compassionate behavior with others
- encouraging and respecting the expression of the child's thoughts and feelings
- considering many options for action when differences occur
- taking account of cultural and ethnic differences in parents' values

Child competence depends on:

- social support system, child's characteristics, and parental resources
- intervening to stop any vicious cycle of negative behavior that occurs

Parents:

- help children maximize innate capacities

• transmit to children, and sometimes grandchildren, styles of behavioral approach to situations and people
• can change negative ways of relating to children with motivation, self-searching, and effort

As they raise children, **parents go through the stages of:**

• image making
• nurturing
• being authorities
• interpreting the world to children
• being interdependent with children
• departure

EXERCISES

1. Review Erikson's theory of life-span development and look at your own life in terms of positive qualities and strengths as Erikson discusses. What positive qualities have you developed? What virtues or strengths? Can you describe the kinds of family experiences that led to your positive qualities?

2. Rate yourself on the dimensions Susan Harter says college students use to describe themselves. (See Table 2-2.) For each dimension, rate yourself on a seven-point scale (1 = low; 7 = high) in terms of where you want to be on these dimensions and where you think you are. Note your areas of strong feelings of competence. Also rate yourself on global self-worth on a seven-point scale. What dimensions seem to be most strongly related to your feelings of global self-worth?

3. Describe how you think you and your siblings have changed your parents as individuals. If possible, interview your parents about how they changed in the course of rearing you and your brothers and sisters.

4. To get an idea of the range of values in rearing children, interview a classmate or interview parents of different ethnic groups in the community to determine their values in childrearing: (a) What kind of child do they want to raise? (b) How much help do they anticipate from family and friends? (c) Will caregivers outside the family be used? (d) How much contact will there be with different generations? (e) What disciplinary techniques do they think they will use? (f) Do they have very different expectations about raising boys and girls? (g) How much independence will they encourage in their children?

5. Interview your classmates or children in a preschool or elementary school and ask them to describe the qualities of a good mother, a good father, a bad mother, and a bad father. Is there general agreement among you and your classmates? Among schoolchildren?

ADDITIONAL READINGS

Bloomfield, Harold, with Felder, Leonard. *Making Peace with Your Parents.* New York: Random House, 1983.

Erikson, Eric H. *Childhood and Society.* 2nd ed. New York: Norton, 1963.

Galinsky, Ellen. *The Six Stages of Parenthood.* Reading, Mass.: Addison-Wesley, 1987.

Greene, Bob. *Good Morning, Merry Sunshine: A Father's Personal Journal of His Child's First Year.* New York: Penguin, 1985.

Guarendi, Ray with Eich, David. *Back to the Family.* New York: Simon & Schuster, 1991.

Notes

1. John Newson and Elizabeth Newson, "Cultural Aspects of Child Rearing in the English-Speaking World," in *The Integration of a Child into a Social World,* ed. Martin M. P. Richards (London: Cambridge University Press, 1974), pp. 53–82.

2. John B. Watson, *Psychological Care of Infant and Child* (New York: W. W. Norton, 1928), pp. 81–82.

3. Herbert Ginsburg and Sylvia Opper, *Piaget's Theory of Intellectual Development* (Englewood Cliffs, N.J.: Prentice-Hall, 1969).

4. Jay Belsky, "The Determinants of Parenting: A Process Model," *Child Development* 55 (1984): 83–96.

5. Richard M. Lerner, *On the Nature of Human Plasticity* (New York: Cambridge University Press, 1984); Richard M. Lerner and Jacqueline V. Lerner, "Children in Their Contexts: A Goodness of Fit Model," in *Parenting Across the Life Span: Biosocial Dimensions,* ed. Jane B. Lancaster, Jeanne Altmann, Alice S. Rossi, and Lonnie R. Sherrod (New York: Aldine de Gruyter, 1987), pp. 377–404.

6. Erik H. Erikson, *Childhood and Society* 2nd ed. (New York: Norton, 1963).

7. Erik H. Erikson, "Human Strength and the Cycle of Generations," in *Insight and Responsibility,* ed. Erik Erikson (New York: Norton, 1964), pp. 109–157.

8. Erik H. Erikson, *Dimensions of a New Identity* (New York: Norton, 1974), p. 124.

9. Jean Piaget and Barbel Inhelder, *The Psychology of the Child* (New York: Basic Books, 1969); Ginsberg and Opper, *Piaget's Theory of Intellectual Development.*

10. John M. Belmont, "Cognitive Strategies and Strategic Learning," *American Psychologist* 44 (1989): 142–148; Laboratory of Comparative Human Cognition, "Culture and Cognitive Development," in *Handbook of Child Psychology: Volume 1 History, Theory, and Methods,* ed. William Kessen (New York: John Wiley, 1982), pp. 295–356; James V. Wertsch and Peeter Tulviste, "L. S. Vygotsky and Contemporary Developmental Psychology," *Developmental Psychology* 28 (1992): 548–557.

11. Michael Lewis, *Shame: The Exposed Self* (New York: The Free Press, 1992).

12. Ibid., p. 58.

13. Susan Harter, "Causes, Correlates, and the Functional Role of Global Self-Worth: A Life-Span Perspective," in *Perceptions of Competence and Incompetence Across the Life-Span,* ed. J. Kolligian and Robert Sternberg (New Haven: Yale University Press, 1990), pp. 67–97.

14. Ibid.

15. Susan Harter, "Visions of Self: Beyond the Me in the Mirror," University Lecture, University of Denver, 1990.

16. Jay Belsky, Elliot Robins, and Wendy Gamble, "The Determinants of Parental Competence: Toward a Contextual Theory," in *Beyond The Dyad,* ed. Michael Lewis (New York: Plenum, 1984), pp. 251–280.

17. Jack Block, *Lives Through Time* (Berkeley, Calif.: Bancroft Books, 1971), p. 263.

18. Diana Baumrind, "The Development of Instrumental Competence Through Socialization," in *Minnesota Symposia on Child Psychology,* vol. 7, ed. Ann D. Pick (Minneapolis: University of Minnesota Press, 1973), pp. 3–46.

19. Ibid., p. 21.

20. Ibid., p. 13.

21. Stanley Coopersmith, *The Antecedents of Self-Esteem* (San Francisco: W. H. Freeman, 1967), pp. 252–253.

22. Jerry M. Lewis, W. Robert Beavers, John T. Gossett, and Virginia Phillips, *No Single Thread* (New York: Brunner/Mazel, 1976).

23. William Damon, *The Moral Child* (New York: The Free Press, 1988); Nancy Eisenberg, *The Caring Child* (Cambridge, Mass.: Harvard University Press, 1992).

24. Baumrind, "The Development of Instrumental Competence."

25. Chin-Yau Cindy Lin and Victoria R. Fu, "A Comparison of Child-rearing Practices among Chinese, Immigrant Chinese, and Caucasian-American Parents," *Child Development* 61 (1990): 429–433.

26. Luis M. Laosa, "Maternal Teaching Strategies in Chicano and Anglo American Families: The Influence of Culture and Education on Maternal Behavior," *Child Development* 61 (1990): 759–765.

27. Lin and Fu, "A Comparison of Child-rearing Practices among Chinese, Immigrant Chinese, and Caucasian-American Parents."

28. Algea O. Harrison, et al., "Family Ecologies of Ethnic Minority Children," *Child Development* 61 (1990): 347–362.

29. Jay D. Schaneveldt, Marguerite Fryer, and Renee Ostler, "Concepts of 'Badness' and 'Goodness' of Parents as Perceived by Nursery School Children," *The Family Coordinator* 19 (1970): 98–103.

30. John R. Weisz, "Autonomy, Control and Other Reasons Why 'Mom Is the Greatest': A Content Analysis of Children's Mother's Day Letters," *Child Development* 51 (1980): 801–807.

31. Belsky, Robins, and Gamble, "The Determinants of Parental Competence: Toward a Contextual Theory."

32. Jerome Kagan, *The Nature of the Child* (New York: Basic Books, 1984).

33. Sandra Scarr, "Developmental Theories for the 1990s: Development and Individual Differences," *Child Development* 63 (1992): p. 3.

34. G. R. Patterson and D. M. Capaldi, "Antisocial Parents: Unskilled and Vulnerable," in *Family Transitions,* ed. Philip A. Cowan and Mavis Hetherington (Hillsdale, N.J.: Lawrence Erlbaum Associates, 1991), pp. 195–218.

35. Jay Belsky, Laurence Steinberg, and Patricia Draper, "Childhood Experience, Interpersonal Development, and Reproductive Strategy: An Evolutionary Theory of Socialization," *Child Development* 62 (1991): 647–670.

36. L. Alan Sroufe, Byron Egeland, and Terri Kreutzer, "The Fate of Early Experience Following Developmental Change: Longitudinal Approaches to Individual Adaptation in Childhood," *Child Development* 61 (1990): 1363–1373.

37. Mary Main, Nancy Kaplan, and Jude Cassidy, "Security in Infancy, Childhood and Adulthood: A Move to the Level of Representation," in *Growing Points of Attachment Theory and Research,* ed. Inge Bretherton and Everett Waters. Monographs of the Society for Research in Child Development, no. 50 (1985), serial no. 209, pp. 66–104; Margaret Ricks, "The Social Transmission of Parental Behavior: Attachment Across Generations," in *Growing Points of Attachment Theory and Research,* eds. Bretherton and Waters, pp. 211–227.

38. Harold Bloomfield with Leonard Felder, *Making Peace with Your Own Parents* (New York: Random House, 1983).

39. John A. Clausen, Paul H. Mussen, and Joseph Kuypers, "Involvement, Warmth, and Parent-Child Resemblance in Three Generations," in *Present and Past in Middle Life,* ed. Dorothy H. Eichorn et al. (New York: Academic Press, 1981), pp. 299–319.

40. Ellen Galinsky, *Between Generations: The Six Stages of Parenthood* (New York: Times Books, 1981).

41. Ibid., p. 317.

Establishing Close Emotional Relationships with Children

The first parenting task—to establish a close emotional relationship with your child—sounds easy enough. But what happens if the child is unwanted? Not the preferred sex? What happens when the baby won't stop crying? The toddler misbehaves? How can you create and maintain warm, close ties with your child when you feel angry? When you experience the distance between yourself and your child that naturally occurs from time to time? There's no foolproof recipe for a good parent/child relationship since the essential ingredients and environmental conditions are unique and unpredictable. Fortunately, experts on parenting do offer methods to enhance communication and strengthen the bond between parent and child.

PARENTING EXPERTS REVIEWED

This book identifies basic strategies of parenting drawn from the work of Haim Ginott, Thomas Gordon, Dorothy Briggs, Rudolf Dreikurs, and the behaviorists. Ginott, Gordon, and Briggs focus on feelings. Clinical psychologist Haim Ginott conducted parent groups in the 1960s and wrote two best-selling parenting books, *Between Parent and Child*[1] and *Between Parent and Teenager.*[2] The application of Ginott's method in day-to-day life is chronicled in *Liberated Parents/Liberated Children*[3] and *How to Talk So Kids Will Listen So Kids Will Talk,*[4] by Adele Faber and Elaine Mazlish, two mothers who participated in discussion groups with Ginott for over five years. Thomas Gordon, also a psychologist, organized his principles into Parent Effectiveness Training (PET) programs given around the country. His major books are *P.E.T. Parent Effectiveness Training,*[5] *P.E.T. in Action,*[6] written with his daughter Judith Sands, and *Teaching Children Self-Discipline.*[7] Dorothy Briggs is also a psychologist and marriage, family, and child counselor who has led many parent education groups. Her book, *Your Child's Self-Esteem,*[8] focuses on how parents can help children to develop the quality that forms the basis of psychological health.

Rudolf Dreikurs, a Chicago psychiatrist, had an early interest in promoting healthy family functioning. He held groups for couples to improve their marriages

TABLE 3-1
COMPARISON OF STRATEGIES

Specific Aspect	Ginott	Gordon	Briggs	Dreikurs	Becker	Eimers & Aitchison
Goal of responsibility	•	•	•	•	•	•
Parent as model	•	•	•	•	•	•
Child's ability to learn	•	•	•	•	•	•
Respect for child	•	•	•	•	•	•
Communication of feelings	•	•	•	•	•	•
No ridicule or shaming	•	•	•	•	•	
Importance of time, attention	•	•	•	•		•
Criticize idea love is enough	•	•	•	•	•	•
Use of praise	•	•	•	•	•	•
Democratic living	•	•	•	•		
Impersonal statement of rules	•		•	•	•	•
Consistency	•		•	•	•	•
Needs of parents	•	•	•	•		
Use of specified rewards					•	•
Use of specified punishment					•	•
Positive image of child	•	•	•	•		
Use of choice	•		•	•		•
Parents express anger		•			•	•
Distinguish deed and doer	•		•	•		
Uniqueness of child			•	•		
Preventive measures		•				•

and for mothers to improve their parenting skills. His major books are *The Challenge of Parenthood*[9] and, with Vicki Soltz, *Children: The Challenge.*[10]

The behaviorists use principles of experimental learning studies to modify children's behavior. Those behaviorists whose work will be cited here include Gerald Patterson, who worked with aggressive children and wrote *Families*[11] and *Living with Children;*[12] Wesley Becker, who wrote *Parents Are Teachers;*[13] Robert Eimers and Robert Aitchison, who wrote *Effective Parents/Responsible Children;*[14] and Helen and John Krumboltz, who wrote *Changing Children's Behavior.*[15]

Table 3-1 summarizes the similarities among the strategies. The major goal of parenting, the importance of modeling, communication of positive feelings, respect for children, importance of praise, avoidance of ridicule and shaming, criticism of the idea that love is enough—these are features of all the methods. Making impersonal statements of rules, offering choices to children, being consistent in demands, emphasizing the needs of parents, and viewing the child in a positive light are agreed on by most of these strategists. The main disagreements are in the use of external rewards and punishments, parents' expression of their anger at children, differing emphases on the uniqueness of the child, and the use of preventive statements to ward off trouble.

Do all these strategies share some deficiencies? Yes. The effects of sex differences on parents' behaviors or on forms of intervention are not discussed in detail. Parents need to be aware of the subtle differences in the ways mothers and fathers interact with children and of the different effects interventions may have, depending on the sex of the child. As we apply parenting strategies, we need to be alert to differences in results stemming from the child's sex.

Another deficiency is the tendency to minimize the effects of age on the application of the methods. Each strategy tends to separate the problems of children in early and middle childhood from the problems of adolescence. But that is often the extent of the concern with age of the child in relation to parenting behavior. Yet parents need to have greater awareness of the effects of age and level of development on parents' application of these methods. There is also little guidance on how to help children develop optimal levels of functioning in intellectual and creative activities.

This book distills and synthesizes these strategies and shows how they are applied to the problems children experience at different ages. We have included ideas about how to facilitate children's development as well.

CLOSE EMOTIONAL RELATIONSHIPS

Parents want children, they say in surveys, so they can have close emotional relationships with them. These warm, intimate ties not only bring parents pleasure, but they also stimulate the infant's and child's healthy psychological growth.

Parents begin to form the relationship when they love the child as a special, unique person. The *American Heritage Dictionary* first defines *love* as "an intense affection for or attachment to another based on familial or personal ties," and "a strong affection for or attachment to another person based on regard or shared experiences or interests."[16] Other definitions refer to sexual attraction and passion, brotherly love, and enthusiasms—for example, love of language or love of science. Synonyms for love are devotion, affection, and infatuation, but love implies a more intense, less consciously controlled feeling than its synonyms.

When parents talk about loving their children, it is in terms of the first definition—having a strong affection for and attachment to the child. The attachment may grow slowly or may appear in full strength at birth. Parents are often surprised at the intensity of their attachment to their child. They are unprepared for how engrossing children are.

Love and caring grow as children stretch their parents' capacities to give, asking for more time, more attention, more interest. Parents express their love in many ways. Physical affection—hugs, kisses, pats—conveys love. How much physical affection parents gives depends on their own personalities and the personalities of their children. Some parents do not feel comfortable with many physical gestures. But since

CHAPTER 3
Establishing
Close
Emotional
Relationships
with Children

the average child enjoys being touched, physically reserved parents can sometimes unlearn old habits of restraint with their children. It is wise to give some physical demonstrations of love, even if just a friendly pat or tussle of the hair, but it is unwise for parents to force themselves too much. Some children enjoy hugs and cuddles; still others prefer playful wrestling or being thrown up in the air. These differences are explored in Chapter 5.

Parents reveal their love in other ways. With young children, parents reveal their caring as they go about their daily routines. Recall that in the last chapter preschoolers defined the good parent—and, presumably, the loving one—as someone who plays with children, hugs, cuddles them, looks after their needs, and protects them. As children grow older, parents reveal love in their understanding of the child, their support, their availability. A loving parent is one who is there for children and who continues to protect children and guide them to learn new behaviors. When we examine the nature of love, in fact, we find it a given factor in all interactions with children—in routine care, in physical affection, in play, and in parental understanding and support.

Parents become aware of their child's unique qualities through listening to the child's thoughts and feelings, observing the child's interests and behavior, and responding to the child with an open and appropriate expression of parental feeling. This may seem impossible with a baby, but as we will see in Chapter 5, it is not. Understanding and expressing feelings are at the center of intimate relationships from the start.

COMMUNICATING FEELINGS

Ginott describes emotions as follows:

> Emotions are part of our genetic heritage. Fish swim, birds fly, and people feel. Sometimes we are happy, sometimes we are not; but sometimes in our life we are sure to feel anger and fear, sadness and joy, greed and guilt, lust and scorn, delight and disgust. While we are not free to choose the emotions that arise in us, we are free to choose how and when to express them, provided we know what they are. That is the crux of the problem. Many people have been educated out of knowing what their feelings are. When they hated, they were told it was only dislike. When they were afraid, they were told there was nothing to be afraid of. When they felt pain, they were advised to be brave and smile. Many of our popular songs tell us "Pretend you are happy when you are not."
>
> What is suggested in place of this pretense? Truth. Emotional education can help children to know what they feel. It is more important for a child to know what he feels than why he feels it. When he knows clearly what his feelings are, he is less likely to feel "all mixed up" inside.
>
> How can we help a child to know his feelings? We can do so by serving as a mirror to his emotions. A child learns about his physical likeness by seeing his image in a mirror. He learns about his emotional likeness by hearing his feelings reflected by us.[17]

Babies come into the world with emotions and feelings that serve as the primary signals to others of what the infant experiences and needs. Long before they have language, children express surprise, joy, fear, anger, pain, and distress by their smiles, laughs, cries, and frowns. They not only express feelings, but they are also very reactive to the feelings of those around them. A child as young as three months old ceases to play when his mother appears depressed, even if the depression is just part of a laboratory experiment. So children express and react to feelings long before they have the intellectual understanding of what different feeling states are and what events cause certain emotional states.

Infants and toddlers are eager observers, however, and even young toddlers begin to learn words for emotions and to develop surprisingly accurate ideas as to why people feel a certain way. Nevertheless, they do misunderstand and sometimes make faulty connections, so they do need parents to feed back feelings and clarify what events produce what feelings. For example, as we'll see later in the chapter, little children often believe they are the cause of family members' anger even when adults are angry at something else; children need information from parents about the source of their irritation.

When parents feed back children's feelings, children feel understood, important, and valuable as individuals. As their responses receive attention, their self-esteem grows. How do you go about feeding back feelings? First, pay attention and listen to hear what the feelings are, then restate what you perceive in simple language.

Active Listening

Active listening is Gordon's term for what parents do when they reflect their children's feelings. Parents listen to children's statements, pay careful attention to the feelings expressed, then make a response similar to the child's statement. If a child says she feels too dumb to learn a school subject, the parent feeds back that she feels she is not smart enough. Ginott might feed back a response about the child's fear, worry, or frustration. Gordon gives examples of feeding back responses about deeper feelings, so the difference between the two strategies is minimal. Following are Gordon's examples of active listening.

CHILD: I don't want to go to Bobby's birthday party tomorrow.
PARENT: Sounds like you and Bobby have had a problem maybe.
CHILD: I hate him, that's what. He's not fair.
PARENT: You really hate him because you feel he's been unfair somehow.
CHILD: Yeah. He never plays what I want to play.

CHILD: (Crying) I fell down on the sidewalk and scraped my knee. Oh, it's bleeding a lot! Look at it!
PARENT: You're really scared seeing all that blood.[18]

If the parent's response accurately reflects the child's feeling, the child confirms the feedback with a positive response. If the parent's interpretation is wrong, the child indicates that and has a chance to correct the misinterpretation by expanding on feelings. The parent can continue active listening and gain greater understanding of what is happening to the child.

64

CHAPTER 3
Establishing
Close
Emotional
Relationships
with Children

Listening to children's feelings brings family members closer together.

Active listening has many advantages. First, it helps children express feelings in a direct, effective way. As feelings are expressed and parents accept them, children learn they are like everyone else, and they need not fear what they feel. In the process of being understood, children gain a feeling of being loved and cherished. When parents talk about feelings and help their children pay attention to others' feelings, their children understand and get along better with people.[19]

Second, as feelings are expressed, parents and children together learn that the obvious problem is not necessarily the real or basic problem. Like the rest of us, children use defenses and sometimes start by blaming a friend, a parent, or circumstances for what they are feeling. Sometimes they deny, at first, that they are upset. As parents focus on the feelings, children gradually come to identify the underlying problem and discover what they can do about it.

Gordon tells of a teenager who insisted she did not want any dinner. When her father used active listening to get at her feelings, she revealed she did not want to eat because her stomach was in knots. She was worried and frightened that her boyfriend was going to leave her for another girl. She felt the other girl was more popular and successful with boys. She wanted to be that comfortable with boys but was afraid of making a fool of herself. After describing her feelings, she decided she would take a few chances and speak up. The father's active listening moved the conversation from a refusal to eat dinner to the daughter's statement of a serious problem and how she might handle it. As children feel understood, they feel increasingly competent and become responsible problem solvers. A positive cycle is set up, in which parents are accepting of children and trust them to behave responsibly, and children become separate persons who act independently, thus reinforcing the parents' beliefs.

A third advantage is that listening to children's feelings sometimes resolves the problem. Often when we are upset, frustrated, sad, or angry, we simply want to express the feeling and have someone respond, "Yes, that's frustrating," or "It is really painful when a friend walks off with someone else and leaves you behind." The response validates the feeling as being justified and important, and frequently that is all we want.

What qualities must parents have to do active listening? At first active listening involves more work and time than the characteristic responses of advice, criticism, or instruction. When a child says, "Oh, I'm furious at Margie!" it's easier to advise getting a new friend than to engage in a conversation about feelings. Gordon warns parents not to attempt active listening when they are hurried or when they are preoccupied. It takes time and effort to determine whether a joking comment covers up a wealth of sadness over some disappointment, whether a cutting, critical remark hides a feeling of hurt from rejection, or whether a casual remark about a success covers real pleasure at a difficult achievement. Parents need to think carefully, to phrase and time their words with sensitivity, to make the comment that will move the dialogue along and facilitate expression of true feelings.

Active listening requires persistence, patience, and a strong commitment. Be aware of both the child's words and the behavioral clues that accompany what is said. Is the child's attitude casual, or do you sense an emotional intensity that is inconsistent with the words? Is the child fidgety, uncomfortable, withdrawn, silent, or distracted and thinking about something else? When you begin to use active listening, conversations may seem unnatural, stilted, even contrived. But you will improve with practice—and you can use active listening with your mate and friends as well as with children.

Active listening is a helpful method when it is appropriate. But there are times when it is not. If a child asks for information, give the information. If a child does not want to talk about feelings, respect the child's privacy and do not probe. Similarly, if you have been using active listening and the dialogue has gone as far as the child is willing to go, then you need to recognize that it is time to stop. And finally, don't begin an active listening conversation if you are too busy or too preoccupied to stay with it and really hear and respond to the child's feelings.

One of the mothers in Ginott's groups raised the question of reflecting back feelings of great sadness over a loss.[20] Is this wise? Does it help children? Might not such feelings overwhelm them? Ginott responded that parents must learn that suffering can strengthen a child's character. When a child is sad in response to a real loss, a parent need only sympathize, "You are sad. I understand." The child learns that the parent is a person who understands and sympathizes.

I-messages

When a parent is angry, frustrated, and irritated with a child, the parent communicates his or her feelings with an **I-message.** The I-message contains three parts: (1) a

CHAPTER 3
Establishing
Close
Emotional
Relationships
with Children

clear statement of how the parent feels, (2) a statement of the behavior that has caused the parent to feel that way, and (3) a statement describing why the behavior is upsetting to the parent. For example, a parent who is frustrated with a teenager's messy room might say, "I feel upset and frustrated when I look at your messy room because the family works hard to make the house look clean and neat, and your room spoils our efforts."

An I-message is a very effective means of communication, but one that is not, in the beginning, easy to use. You will find that you have to concentrate and practice to develop skill with I-messages. But when you are comfortable with them and they come easily, I-messages facilitate communication. I-messages help children to understand their parents as individuals. When parents use I-messages and feel free to express their individuality, they serve as models that encourage children to react openly, too.

Parents may look at their feelings and at children's behavior and discover that, after all, the behavior has no effect on them. When this happens, the reasonable parent decides there is no need to ask the child to change the behavior. For example, many parents have been concerned about the style of their child's hair. But since this has no direct effect on them, parents do not discuss their dislike of the hairstyle and do not ask the child to change it.

Parents need to spend time analyzing their feelings and becoming more aware of exactly how they feel. Gordon points out that, often, when a parent communicates anger at a child, the parent may actually be feeling disappointment, fear, frustration, or hurt. When a child comes home an hour late, the parent may burst out in a tirade. The worry that grew into fear during the hour of waiting is transformed into relief that the child is safe, and that relief is then translated into angry words intended to prevent a recurrence of this disturbing behavior. Similarly, a parent may complain about a child's behavior when, in reality, what is disturbing the parent is a problem at work. The parent who has learned to use accurate I-messages is less likely to misplace anger and use a child or mate as a scapegoat.

What should you do if a child pays no attention to your I-messages? First, be sure you have the child's attention when you send the I-message. Don't try to communicate your feelings when the child is getting ready to rush out of the house or is already deeply immersed in some other activity. If your I-message is then ignored, send another, more forceful message. And be sure that the feeling tone matches your feelings.

I-messages have several benefits. First, when parents use I-messages, they begin to take their own needs seriously. This process benefits all family relationships because parents feel freer—more themselves—in all areas of life. Second, children learn about the parents' reaction, which they may not have understood until the I-message. Third, children have an opportunity to engage in problem solving in response to I-messages. Even very young toddlers and preschoolers have ideas, not only for themselves but also for others. Siblings often have good ideas about what may be bothering another child in the family. They think of things that might have escaped the attention of parents.

Sometimes a child responds to an I-message with an I-message. For example, when a parent describes upset and distress because the lawn is not mowed, the daughter may reply that she feels annoyed because mowing interferes with her after-school activities. At that point, the parent must "shift gears," as Gordon terms it, and reflect back the child's frustration by using active listening.

Appreciative I-messages Gordon's techniques can be used for family interactions that do not involve conflict. He suggests that parents send appreciative I-messages. These statements consist of three parts: how the parent feels, what the child did to make the parent feel that way, and the specific effect of the behavior on the parent. For example, "When you let me know where you are, I feel relieved, because I don't have to worry about you." Appreciative I-messages can improve the quality of family life. One mother commented that she never realized how much time she spent sending I-messages of irritation, in contrast to appreciative I-messages, until one evening when her son reported that he had cleaned up a huge mess made by the dog. Often when the dog had an accident, it went unattended until the mother came home from work. She would complain about how upset she was and how it delayed her getting dinner. She later realized that, in contrast to the long period spent expressing irritation, she spent only a few seconds saying "Thank you" and expressing her appreciation. As a result she resolved in the future to be more attentive to helpful behaviors and more verbal in expressing her thanks.

Preventive I-messages Preventive I-messages are useful in heading off problems and in helping children to see that parents are fallible, too. These messages express parents' future wants or needs and give children an opportunity to respond positively. For example, if you say "I got very little sleep last night and want quiet so I can take a nap," you make it possible for them to help you. Preventive messages can be especially practical before an unusual event that may place a special strain on family members. One mother reported that within an hour after the family started out on a long driving trip, the two children, ten and thirteen, began bickering in the back seat. She stopped the car and explained they would be driving for several days, and she needed cooperation. She realized that it would be hard to be cooped up in the car, but it would be easier for everyone if they did not fight. Miraculously, she said, in five days there was hardly a single fight, and the whole family had a good time.

A parent's acceptance of the child, responsiveness to his or her needs, willingness to express positive and negative feelings, along with willingness to listen to the child's feelings—all these behaviors build more harmonious relationships among family members because individuals' feelings are respected and validated.

PROVIDING OPPORTUNITIES FOR SELF-EXPRESSION

Family relationships are most harmonious when children and parents alike have outlets for expressing feelings. Activities such as daily physical exercise, opportunities to draw, model clay, paint, and cook all serve as outlets to drain off tensions and irritations and provide individuals with additional sources of pleasure and feelings of competence. Parents are wise to see that children have a variety of outlets so that they develop many skills. Research indicates that childhood leisure activities,

68

CHAPTER 3
Establishing
Close
Emotional
Relationships
with Children

especially a wide variety—such as painting, reading, athletics—are more predictive of psychological health in adulthood than the child's own personality characteristics in childhood. These activities develop confidence and self-esteem that increase psychological health.[21]

Negative feelings like anger and irritation get in the way of happy relationships. In addition to the psychological ways of dealing with anger just described, parents can also provide special activities to discharge these feelings directly. Young children can divert their energy to physical play. Preadolescents and teenagers can learn the value of physical work and exercise to drain away frustration. Cleaning a room or scrubbing a floor discharge feelings and also provide the pleasure of accomplishment. Helping children learn these techniques strengthens them as individuals and gives them resources in times of trouble.

Parents help children express themselves when they make time for conversation about school, friends, activities of the day and convey to children that their reactions are important. When children are skilled at verbalizing their everyday experiences, they will be better able to talk about their feelings and frustrations at times of stress. They can learn the power of words to tell other people exactly how they feel and to resolve difficulties in an equitable way.

THE CHILD'S BASIC COMPETENCE

There are other ways to build close emotional ties with children: by expressing respect for the child's competence and by giving the child opportunities to participate in the family group as a contributing member. Dreikurs believes that children have built-in capacities to develop in healthy, effective ways.[22] Because they have a push to be active and competent, a parent's main task is to provide an environment that permits this development to occur. The child's strongest desire is to belong to a group, and from infancy the child seeks acceptance and importance within the family. The deepest fear of childhood is fear of rejection. Each child develops a unique path to family acceptance. The child accomplishes this task by using innate abilities and environmental forces to shape dynamic relationships with other family members.

Do parents usually help children discover their own strengths and abilities? No, says Dreikurs. Most often we tear down their confidence with such comments as "What a mess you make," or "I can do it for you faster," or "You are too little to set the table." Dreikurs recommends that parents use encouragement to help children develop their abilities. He defines encouragement as a "continuous process aimed at giving the child a sense of self-respect and a sense of accomplishment."[23] Encouragement is expressed by word and deed.

A parent's facial expression, tone of voice, gesture, and posture all tell children how the parent feels about them. In many different ways—warm cuddling, active play, gentle nurturing—a parent can communicate that children are worthwhile and capable of participating in social living. How does a parent provide encouragement for development? First, by respecting the child and, from infancy, permitting self-sufficiency in all possible situations. Babies, for example, are encouraged to entertain themselves; they are left alone at times to explore their fingers and toes, play with toys, and examine their surroundings. As soon as possible, they feed themselves. Very young children of one or two are included in family chores and responsibilities as soon as they show any interest in helping. Even a toddler can empty a wastebasket and carry small nonbreakable items to the dinner table. Second, by giving verbal encouragement, telling children specifically what they do well: "I like your painting with all the bright colors," "You certainly picked up all your toys quickly and that helps Daddy when he vacuums."

Parents offer encouragement when they teach children to ask for what they want. Children need to learn that parents cannot read their minds and that they must take an active role in saying what they want. As children try out new activities, parents wait until children ask for help before giving it. If children ask for help, parents can start off with aid at the beginning or request that children begin and say they will be available when children cannot proceed. When parents give encouragement, they call attention to the challenge of the task—"It's hard practicing now, but you'll master the keys and really enjoy playing the piano as you get more experience." Finally, parents emphasize children's gains. They show children how far they have come since starting the activity. Encouraging comments often refer to the completed task. But children soon learn that enjoyment comes from the process as well as from final success.

DEMOCRATIC FAMILY LIVING

Thomas Gordon and Rudolf Dreikurs both emphasize the importance of a democratic atmosphere, but each gives a slightly different meaning to the word.

In his recent book, *Teaching Children Self-Discipline,* Thomas Gordon describes his great concern about authoritarian families in which parents control children through rewards and punishments.[24] He is highly critical of parents who manipulate children in order to change them into what powerful parents think is desirable. He dislikes the concept of praise because it implies the parent judges and evaluates the child in terms of some external standard. He disapproves of punishment because it allows a powerful person to take advantage of a less powerful person, and he especially condemns physical punishment for children because it belittles them, makes them angry and fearful of the parent, and does not work.

Gordon also criticizes a permissive atmosphere of chaos and disorganization. He encourages a democratic atmosphere in which children are accepted as they are, with important needs and wishes that at times conflict with others' needs. When there is a problem, parents send I-messages, reflecting their own thoughts and feelings, and do active listening to get the child's point of view. If a solution does not arise, then parents and children engage in the mutual problem solving described in the next chapter.

Parents never dictate solutions but work cooperatively with children to form a plan that meets everyone's needs. Working together this way frees children from feeling judged, evaluated, or manipulated. Children and parents become partners in solving the hassles of life.

Dreikurs, too, believes that democratic family living provides an encouraging atmosphere in which the needs of children and parents are given equal respect and

CHAPTER 3
Establishing
Close
Emotional
Relationships
with Children

consideration. Everyone, however, has responsibilities as well. Parents provide food, shelter, clothes, and recreation for children. Children, in turn, must contribute to family functioning by doing chores and errands. Material rewards are not given for doing a particular number of chores. When mutual respect among equal individuals is the rule in a family, members work together to do the jobs that are necessary for the welfare of all. To deny children the opportunity to do their share is to deny them an essential satisfaction in life. Democratic living ensures freedom for family members but does not imply an absence of rules. Dreikurs strongly favors structure in family life and believes it provides boundaries that give a child a feeling of security.

To help children follow routines, parents serve as models. They also teach children how to do routine tasks. Parents often expect that children will be able to master self-care and household chores without any instruction, and they do not spend the time needed to teach children. How many parents have taught a child, step by step, how to make a bed or how to get dressed, then observed as the child increased in skill, giving added coaching as needed? An encouraging parent helps children to be both self-sufficient and involved with other people.

Even in ideal family conditions, children make mistakes. Parents must accept mistakes without dwelling on them. Dreikurs describes parents' tendencies to overemphasize the errors children make. We want so much for children to grow up and do well that sometimes we trot at their heels, pointing out every minor mistake, telling them what they must do to improve. Under such a regime children may feel they have to be perfect to be accepted. That fear may immobilize the child. Dreikurs writes,

> We all make mistakes. Very few are disastrous. Many times we won't even know that a given action is a mistake until after it is done and we see the results! Sometimes we even have to make the mistake in order to find out that it is a mistake. *We must have the courage to be imperfect*—and to allow our children also to be imperfect. Only in this way can we function, progress, and grow. Our children will maintain their courage and learn more readily if we minimize the mistakes and direct their attention toward the positive. "What is to be done now that the mistake is made" leads to progress forward and stimulates courage. Making a mistake is not nearly as important as what we do about it afterward.[25]

Parents separate the deed from the doer when responding to mistakes and make clear that the child is not a failure but unskilled, in need of teaching. In coping with a mistake, parents stay problem-oriented—look at the situation, see what needs to be done, and help the child function well by giving encouragement and guidance. When a junior high school student gets a poor school grade, the parent sits down with the child and helps figure out what the trouble is and how the child might improve. Perhaps more studying, more careful attention to deadlines for papers, or greater participation in class will result in better grades. Parents guide the child to select the actions that will bring improvements.

Mistakes are a natural part of life and need not have lasting ill effects. When children learn a healthy attitude towards mistakes early, they are freer to explore and act, and as a result they learn and accomplish more. A healthy attitude consists of believing mistakes are an expected part of life; they are often accidental but they do have causes and can be prevented. So children and parents can learn to look at mistakes carefully and find out what to do differently the next time. Mistakes are proofs the child is trying to do something, but may not be quite ready to achieve the goal. Mistakes are incompletions, not failures. The child can take more time learning the activity or perhaps take more time practicing to achieve the goal.

Mistakes are unfortunate in the sense that they take up time and sometimes money, but they are rarely disastrous or damaging. To the contrary, they are very often valuable experiences because a child learns what is not effective. In addition, many warm family memories center on mistakes that were made and survived.

Research supports Dreikurs' advice on handling mistakes and documents the power parents' explanatory style has in shaping children's ways of thinking about themselves and their abilities.[26] Some children, at a very early age, show vulnerability to criticism. After receiving criticism about a single mistake, they generalize the criticism to their overall ability and feel helpless and inadequate. Vulnerable children five to six years of age who lack a clear concept of ability interpret the criticism as a comment on their goodness or badness as a person. When children feel helpless and inadequate, they give up and find it very hard to improve. Sensitive children are more likely than confident children to report that parents make critical comments about their mistakes. The sad fact appears that even young children internalize these comments and feel helpless and inadequate when they make a mistake.

Martin Seligman,[27] who has studied the widespread effects of optimistic and pessimistic attitudes towards adversity, advises parents to teach children how to dispute global, pessimistic beliefs or interpretations of mistakes and difficulties.

Parents must teach children that a negative event has many causes, some beyond their control. For example, a student may get a poor grade on a test because she did not study enough, the test was unusually hard, the class has many bright students and grading was on the curve, the teacher came late and allowed less time for the exam, she was nervous and could not organize her answers as well. The student might blame herself, saying she is stupid, is going to fail the class and won't be able to take more courses in that area. She is "latching onto the worst of these possible causes—the most permanent, pervasive, and personal one."[28]

Parents teach their children to dispute pessimistic interpretations with questions like, "What is the evidence for my belief?" "What are other, less destructive ways to look at this?" "What is the usefulness of this belief?" Seligman advises, "Focus on the changeable (not enough time spent studying), the specific (this particular exam was uncharacteristically hard), and the nonpersonal (the professor graded unfairly) causes."[29] Then parents and children generate alternative explanations and future actions. Seligman calls his method the ABCDE (Adversity; Belief (usually negative); Consequence (usually negative); Dispute; Energize) method illustrated in Box 3-1.

MISBEHAVIOR: MISTAKEN GOALS

When children feel discouraged and unable to make positive contributions to the social group, they seek other ways to feel important and competent. Misbehavior results from the pursuit of goals that give feelings of importance instead of feelings of self-sufficiency and social integration. Dreikurs identifies four goals of behavior and calls them "mistaken" goals because they do not bring genuine feelings of competence and participation. These goals are attention, power, revenge, and inadequacy.

72

CHAPTER 3
Establishing
Close
Emotional
Relationships
with Children

BOX 3-1
DEALING WITH ADVERSITY*

Adversity: My teacher, Mr. Minner, yelled at me in front of the whole class, and everybody laughed.

Belief: He hates me and now the whole class thinks I'm a jerk.

Consequences: I felt really sad and I wished that I could just disappear under my desk.

Disputation: Just because Mr. Minner yelled at me, it doesn't mean he hates me. Mr. Minner yells at just about everybody, and he told our class we were his favorite class. I guess I was goofing around a little, so I don't blame him for getting mad. Everyone in the class, well everyone except for maybe Linda but she's a goody-goody, but everyone else has been yelled at by Mr. Minner at *least* once, so I doubt they think I'm a jerk.

Energization: I still feel a little sad about being yelled at, but not nearly as much, and I didn't feel like disappearing under my desk anymore.

*Reprinted from Martin E. P. Seligman, *Learned Optimism,* p. 241 (New York: Pocket Books, 1990).

The parent's task is (1) to understand which of the four mistaken goals is motivating the child's behavior and (2) to act so that the purpose is no longer achieved. Thus, the parent must understand the child's underlying feelings, but instead of reflecting back feelings, Dreikurs advises action to modify the child's behavior.

A child is seeking mistaken goals when the behavior conflicts with the needs of the situation. For example, a child may seek attention by being talkative and charming. This behavior is pleasant and endearing rather than annoying. When such behavior prevents others from talking, however, it becomes misbehavior. A child may ask his mother to play a game with him—a reasonable request. But when he insists on this attention when the mother is preparing dinner, she can assume he wants attention rather than to play a game. Where there are several children in a family, they may band together and seek attention by bickering.

When attention is denied, a child may hunt for an issue to use in the struggle for power. A three-year-old may insist she does not have to go to bed at 7:30 p.m. If she persists, running around the house and causing the mother to spend a lot of time in the chase, the child is struggling for power. Sometimes parents find it hard to tell whether a child is seeking attention or power. Dreikurs points out that children usually stop the mistaken behavior after the first request if they are seeking attention, but not if what they want is power. Attempts to stop the behavior only aggravate children, who will try all the harder for power.

When problems continue, children may intensify the power struggle and seek revenge and retaliation. Here children have lost hope of getting approval through positive behavior and feel there is nothing to lose, so revenge is sought as a means of feeling important. Children are determined to feel important even if they have to hurt others physically.

Dreikurs remarks that this form of misbehavior is particularly sad because children who need the most encouragement are the ones most likely to be punished. Parents need to offer warm understanding and sympathetic acceptance so that children can release their own positive qualities. Unfortunately, punishment intensifies anger and guilt, leads to further attempts to provoke the parents, and sets up a vicious cycle.

Children who claim inadequacy to explain poor performance in some activity also pursue a mistaken goal. Dreikurs gives the example of an eight-year-old boy who was having school difficulties. The teacher told the mother he was a poor reader, was slow in all subjects, and showed no improvement despite the teacher's extra efforts. She asked the mother what he did at home. The mother replied that he did not like chores and did them so poorly that she had stopped asking him. The child had developed a low opinion of his abilities over a period of time and found it easiest to claim incompetence. Feelings of helplessness exaggerate any real or imagined problem. In such a situation, a parent can demonstrate the chores and work with children until they feel competent to function alone. Encouragement helps children persist until they are able to finish a job independently.

The behaviorists write less about relationships than other strategists. When children's behavior meets parents' and other authorities' standards, children receive rewards in the form of approval and positive social attention. Parents feel pleased with children and the children enjoy the attention. Thus, positive family relationships flourish when parents teach children approved behaviors without scolding, blaming, or judging. Using appropriate rewards or punishments, parents have no need to resort to uncontrolled yelling, screaming, or threatening behavior.

Behaviorists also pay much less attention than the other strategists to the feelings of children and parents. They assume that positive emotional and attitudinal changes will occur as behavior changes. Behaviorists, however, do inquire into feelings to determine the most appropriate rewards and punishments. For example, they need to know children's likes and dislikes to select the most effective reinforcements for behavior. They need to know when children are fearful so they can teach new responses to the stimuli that trigger fears. They urge parents to be warm and nurturing so that their rewards will have great impact. As children grow, parental warmth, attention, approval, and praise are more powerful reinforcers than any material rewards. In the behaviorist approach, however, feelings are considered primarily as a basis for determining how to change the child's behavior. The effects of rewards and punishments depend, in part, on the characteristics of the individual who is learning. What is a reward for Suzy is not a reward for Mary; what helps Johnny learn to read does not help Jimmy. Thus, behaviorists are interested in the unique characteristics of each child.

FAMILY ANGER

We have long known that physical violence in families damages children and all participants. Children who are physically abused or witness the physical abuse of others in the family tend to become depressed, more aggressive, and prone to repeat the

CHAPTER 3
Establishing
Close
Emotional
Relationships
with Children

pattern as adults. We are not so aware that ordinary yelling and the angry outbursts of everyday life have destructive effects on children as well.

Mark Cummings and his co-workers have carried out a series of studies, assessing the responses of children two to nine years old when they are exposed to different forms of anger. Children respond with emotional arousal that changes heart rate and blood pressure[30] as well as the production of hormones.[31] Whether the angry interaction is actually observed or only heard from another room, or only angry silence is observed, young children react in a variety of ways.

A majority of children show signs of anger, concern, sadness, and general distress that can disrupt play, lead to increased aggressiveness, or result in attempts to end the conflict or comfort the participant. By the preschool period, definite styles of responding to anger are identifiable.[32] Some children, almost half, primarily feel distress with a strong desire to end the fights. Other children, slightly over a third, are ambivalent, revealing both high emotional arousal and upset, but at the same time reporting that they are happy. A small percentage (15 percent) give no response. The ambivalent child is the one who becomes more aggressive in behavior.

Children who are exposed to parents' fighting at home have strong physiological and social reactions to anger.[33] They are more likely to comfort the mother if she is involved in an angry exchange in a laboratory setting. The exposure to marital conflict changes the way young children relate to their own friends. Characteristically they play at a less involved level; and when anger occurs with friends, they find it very hard to handle.

Does this mean that parents are never to fight or disagree in front of children? No. Conflict is a natural part of life when people live closely together, and observing how conflicts are settled may be necessary for children to learn these skills themselves. Children need to see adults arrive at fair compromises. In Cummings and his co-workers' study, children who viewed angry adults finding a compromise to the situation had emotional reactions that were indistinguishable from their responses when viewing friendly interactions.[34] They had the most negative reactions to continued fighting and the silent treatment. Their responses to submissions or to changing the topic indicated they did not consider the situation resolved. So, what is most important to children is whether adults achieve a fair compromise to settle conflicts after they erupt.

Even when there is no particular distress, family members, both parents and children ages five to fifteen, see themselves as a major cause of angry feelings in others.[35] Fathers (for whom there is limited information since they were not questioned in as much detail) and children of all ages see themselves as the major cause of mothers' anger. Although mothers cited more general reasons like violence and poverty, when they were asked to keep diaries of what made them angry on a daily basis, they most often cited the noncompliance, destructiveness, and demanding nature of children. Thus, the children's perceptions appeared more accurate.

Children cited the family as the major source of their own anger and saw their happiness as coming from experiences outside the home with friends and personal accomplishments. In contrast, mothers thought children's happiness came from the family and their anger from other experiences. This is how mothers attribute their

---

BOX 3-2
EIGHT WAYS TO DEAL WITH PARENTAL ANGER*

1. Exit or wait—taking time out is a way of maintaining and modeling self-control
2. "I," not "You" statements help the child understand your point of view
3. Stay in the present—avoid talking about the past or future
4. Avoid physical force and threats
5. Stay short and to the point
6. Put it in writing—a note or letter is a way of expressing your feelings in a way that the person can understand
7. Focus on the essential—ask yourself whether what you are arguing about is really important and worth the energy involved
8. Restore good feelings—talk over what happened calmly or give hugs or other indications that the fight is over

*Adapted from Nancy Samalin with Catherine Whitney, *Love and Anger: The Parental Dilemma* (New York: Penguin Books, 1992).

---

own feelings—the family providing major positive feelings and other experiences providing anger—and they assume children view life in the same way.

Equally important, all family members believe they can change other members' feelings even when anger is involved. The majority of children believe they can alter their mothers' feelings—68 percent say they can make happy mothers angry, 68 percent said they can make sad mothers happy, and 63 percent said they could make angry mothers happy. Here there is agreement. Mothers say children can change their feelings dramatically, but also believe that they can alter children's feelings as well. Behavioral and verbal strategies were most frequently used by adults and children, but children also included material reward strategies.

So all family members see anger as very much a part of family life. Children appear more accurate in seeing their behavior as a major cause of family anger—though on any given occasion they may be mistaken—and the family routines and demands as the major source of their own irritations.

This study supports the active listening and I-message techniques of Ginott, Gordon, and Briggs, which alter misperceptions and give accurate information so that problems are solved. When parents listen to children's complaints and underlying feelings, they learn exactly how children view situations—how angry they feel sometimes, how responsible. When parents send I-messages effectively, children learn they are not the only source of problems in their parents' lives and, indeed, are a major source of happiness and pleasure to parents. The youngest children know their positive contribution to family life, but this awareness fades as children grow older, and so parents need to help children retain their feeling of importance with I-messages to that effect. When parents use problem-solving techniques to negotiate differences leading to anger, children are less upset at the anger because it is resolved.[36]

76

CHAPTER 3
Establishing
Close
Emotional
Relationships
with Children

When children are happy, they are more concerned about the needs and perspectives of others. Thus, well-being in families increases. Close relationships also serve to promote positive qualities in children.

THE POWER OF POSITIVE FEELINGS

Just as there has been increased attention to the destructive aspects of ordinary angry exchanges, so there has been increased attention to the power of good feelings to make changes in both current behavior and future well-being.

A primary protective factor at times of risk is a secure emotional relationship. Close emotional relationships bring pleasure to all family members and contribute to everyone's well-being. When people are happy, research shows, they are more concerned about others' needs.[37] Pregnant mothers who experienced warm relationships with their own parents look forward with confidence to their own mothering, and the prophecy comes true. Their babies flourish. Husbands and wives who are happily married are more effective parents. Infants with strong attachments to mothers become competent, effective toddlers and preschoolers. As we will see in Chapter 4, older children with strong attachments to a parent are more likely to internalize and obey social rules.

Although closeness is enjoyable and helpful to children, some parents may not feel good about themselves or some of their own qualities, causing them to wonder if their children might not be better off remaining distant from them. They fear their children will pick up their bad qualities. Research on close and nonclose relationships among adolescents and their parents revealed that children who feel close to their parents are less likely to take on the parents' negative qualities than children who feel distant. Negative parental qualities are more potent influences on children when parents and children are not close.[38]

We can speculate that when children feel close to a parent and have some understanding of the parent as a person, they look at the undesirable quality more objectively and reject it as undesirable for themselves. When children are distant from a parent, perhaps feeling rejected by the parent, they may have less understanding of the parent and the negative behavior, causing the children to imitate it. It can also be that imitating the parent's behavior may represent a thwarted attempt to be close to that parent.

Thus, even when parents have many self-doubts and self-criticisms, closeness with them and all their failings is still a positive experience for their children.

Good feelings come from one's own actions and successes as well as from relationships. Kirk Felsman and George Vaillant, following the development of a sample of men from early adolescence to late middle life, identify boyhood competence as an important forerunner of adult mental health. Boyhood competence—a summary measure of having part-time work, having household chores, participating in extracurricular activities, getting school grades commensurate with IQ, participating in school activities, and learning to make plans—all bring good feelings of effectiveness. Felsman and Vaillant write, "Perhaps what is most encouraging in the collective portrait of these men's lives is their enormous capacity for recovery—evidence that the things that go right in our lives do predict future successes and the events that go wrong in our lives do not forever damn us."[39]

We do not always have a recent accomplishment to treasure, but studies reveal that if a child just thinks of some pleasant event for a short time, even as short a period as 30 seconds, then performance improves and behavior becomes more friendly, responsive, and responsible. Children resist temptation more successfully and they respond to unfair treatment with fairness and generosity.[40]

Happy feelings serve as an inoculation against the effects of negative events. These good feelings are not just fleetingly helpful. Longitudinal research shows that how one spends leisure time, how one has fun in childhood, is more predictive of later psychological health than the presence or absence of problems in childhood.[41] So parents are wise when they follow Dreikurs' advice to remind children of their progress and accomplishments and to build recreational activities into children's everyday lives.

78

CHAPTER 3
Establishing
Close
Emotional
Relationships
with Children

EMOTIONS AND THE PROCESS OF PARENTING

We have described the process and importance of identifying feelings of family members. We have emphasized the beneficial effects of positive feelings and the negative effects of angry feelings. Theodore Dix recently presented a model of parenting that gives a central role to emotions in organizing parents' behavior with their children.[42]

Emotions, both positive and negative, suffuse the parenting process, Dix says. Parental warmth is a major aspect of the caregiving role. Toddlers and children can arouse strong negative feelings in parents because conflicts occur so frequently in the course of daily life—three to fifteen times per hour when children are young. Further, life events can arouse feelings that carry over into parenting—anger stirred up at work can spill out in harsh discipline at home.

Parents' emotional states will determine how parents view children's behavior. When in positive moods, parents are more understanding and empathic with children. Parents' emotional states also determine the type, consistency, and effectiveness of discipline they use. When angry, they may resort to physical punishment and carry it out more forcefully than they would otherwise. Dix concludes: "Thus, perhaps more than any other single variable, parents' emotions reflect the health of parent-child relationships. They are barometers for the quality of parenting, the developmental outcomes that are likely for children, and the impact that environmental stresses and supports are having on the family."[43]

Just as Belsky identified three components to the process of parenting, Dix identifies three sources of parents' emotions—parents' concerns/goals, children's behavior, and life-events/social factors. These factors contribute to the arousal or activation of parents' emotions. The emotions, in turn, influence parents' motivations and beliefs about children and organize and energize parental behavior. Parents regulate and modulate emotional reactions so they are appropriate to the situation.

Figure 3-1 depicts the relationship of these three factors. The following example illustrates Dix's model. A father has goals of raising an independent, curious child. On a particular day, however, he is frustrated and angry because his boss ignores his suggestions and gives impractical orders. When his four-year-old son asks numerous questions and insists on answers, the father, in his frustrated mood, views the child's behavior as defiance of his request to wait until later for the answers. He then punishes the child and feels worse because now he feels inadequate as a parent.

He talks his work situation over with his wife, makes positive plans, and feels better. When his persistent four-year-old returns in a few hours with new questions, the father, in a good mood, interprets the behavior as curiosity about the world and goes to the encyclopedia to look up the answers. The father feels good about taking the time to help his child. In each of the two situations, the father's goals and the child's behavior were the same. The father's mood, negative in one instance and positive in the other, influenced the father's interpretation of the boy's behavior and his own response to it.

The techniques for communicating feelings outlined in this chapter all help parents regulate their emotional responses to children by getting a clear, unbiased

FIGURE 3-1
DIX'S MODEL OF AFFECTIVE PROCESSES IN PARENTING

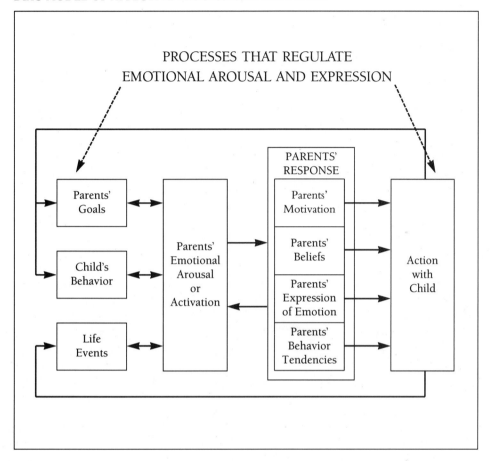

PROCESSES THAT REGULATE
EMOTIONAL AROUSAL AND EXPRESSION

view of the child's actual behavior (active listening) and defusing one's own feelings (I-messages) so they do not result in either over- or under-reactions to parent-child situations.

One might think that communication skills can not modify high levels of negative parental affect caused by real-life events like poverty, chronic marital strife, divorce. Elaine Blechman, however, has found that families with numerous, long-lasting problems benefit significantly from learning effective communication skills that involve (1) clear exchange of information among family members, (2) recognition of family problem, (3) formulation of a plan for solving the problem, and (4) re-appraisal of the situation.[44]

Communication skills not only help solve all kinds of family problems, they are basic tools of negotiating any kind of difference be it a family, business, or

80

CHAPTER 3
Establishing
Close
Emotional
Relationships
with Children

INTERVIEW
with Emmy E. Werner

Emmy E. Werner is professor of human development and research child psychologist at the University of California, Davis. For three decades, she and colleagues Jessie Bierman and Fern French at the University of California, Berkeley, and Ruth Smith, a clinical psychologist on Kauai, have conducted the Kauai Longitudinal Study, resulting in books such as Vulnerable But Invincible, The Children of Kauai, Kauai's Children Come of Age, *and* Overcoming the Odds.

From your experience of watching children at risk grow up on Kauai, what would you say parents can do to support children, to help maximize their child's potential? From your work with children at risk, what helps children survive and flourish even when faced with severe problems?

Let me say that, in our study, we studied the offspring of women whom we began to see at the end of the first trimester of pregnancy. We followed them during the pregnancy and delivery. We saw the children at ages one, two, and ten, late adolescence, and again at thirty to thirty-two. We have test scores, teachers' observations, and interview material at different times on these people. We have a group of children who were at high risk because of three or more factors. They were children who (1) experienced prenatal or perinatal complications, (2) grew up in poverty, and (3) lived in a dysfunctional family with one or more problems.

You ask me to comment on parenting and what parents can do, but first I would like to urge that we redefine and extend the definition of parenting to cast a wider net and include people who provide love in the lives of children. I like to talk about *alloparenting,* the parenting of children by alternate people who are not the biological parents—they can be relatives, neighbors, siblings.

In our study of vulnerable but invincible children, we found that a major protective factor was that at least one person, perhaps a biological parent, or a grandparent, or an older sibling, accepted them unconditionally. That one person made the child feel special, very, very special. These parent figures made the child feel special through acts. They conveyed their love through deeds. They acted as models for the child. They didn't pretend the child had no handicap or problem, but what they conveyed was, "You matter to me, and you are special."

Now, another theme in our findings is that the parent figure, whoever he or she was, encouraged the child to reach out to others beyond the family—to seek out a friendly neigh-

international difference. Negotiators from the Harvard Negotiation Project illustrate the usefulness of communication techniques for the solution of differences that occur between countries.[45] They describe the basic elements of all working relationships as balancing emotion and reason (rationality), understanding how others see things, communicating effectively to minimize mixed messages, being wholly trustworthy, persuading through example and logical and moral argument, and accepting other people as worthy of respect.

bor, a parent of one of their boy or girl friends, and, thus, learn about normal parenting from other families.

The resilient child was temperamentally engaging. He or she encouraged interaction with others outside the home and was given the opportunity to relate to others.

I had no preconceptions about this protective factor, but what came through was that somewhere along the line, in the face of poverty, in the face of a handicap, faith has an abiding power. I'm not referring to faith in a narrow, denominational sense, but having someone in the family or outside of it who was saying, "Hey, you are having ups and downs, this will pass, you will get through this, and things will get better."

Another thing was that these children had an opportunity to care for themselves or others. They became nurturant and concerned, perhaps about a parent or a sibling. They practiced "required helpfulness."

Now, another protective factor is whether the children were able to develop a hobby that waa a refuge and gave them respect among their peers. One of our study members said later, "If I had any doubts about whether I could make it, that hobby turned me around." The hobby was especially important as a buffer between the person and the chaos in the family. But it was not a hobby that isolated you from others; it nourished something you could share with other people.

As many of the children looked back, they describe how a positive relationship with a sibling was enduring and important. As adults they commented with surprise how supportive the relationship was and how these relationships were maintained despite great distances and despite dissimilarity in life and interests.

What do adults say they want to pass on to their own children?

Looking back as an adult, they felt some sort of structure in their life was very important. Even though the family life was chaotic, if a parent imposed some reasonable rules and regulations, it was helpful.

They emphasized faith as something to hang on to and make this clear to their children. As parents now they are quite achievement-motivated. They graduated from high school, and some went back and got additional training. They encourage their children to do well in school.

The main theme that runs through our data is the importance of a parent figure who says "you matter" and the child's ability to create his or her own environment. The children believed they could do it, someone gave them hope, and they succeeded against the odds.

MAJOR POINTS OF CHAPTER 3

Parenting experts reviewed here:

- include Ginott, Gordon, and Briggs who focus on communicating feelings
- include Dreikurs and the behaviorists who focus on changing children's behavior

CHAPTER 3
Establishing
Close
Emotional
Relationships
with Children

- agree on the importance of modeling, communicating positive feelings, respecting children, avoiding ridicule and shaming
- disagree mainly on the importance of external rewards and punishments, the expression of parental anger, and the use of preventive statements to ward off troubles

Close emotional ties rest on the parent's love for the child:

- as a unique person
- expressed in physical affection as well as in sensitive daily care
- and the mutual expression of feelings and thoughts

When parents listen to child's feelings and reflect them:

- child becomes increasingly able to identify feelings and to understand what their causes and consequences are
- child learns his or her own feelings are important
- child's point of view is better understood
- parent and child learn the obvious problem is not always the real problem
- problem is sometimes resolved because feelings are validated

When parents express their feelings, they send I-messages that:

- help parents clarify their own feelings
- state how the parent feels, what behavior aroused the feelings, and why the behavior affects the parent
- convey a message about a problem, about a good act the parent likes, or about a possible problem in the future
- help children understand parents' wishes and point of view

Close relationships grow when parents:

- encourage the child and give the child a sense of self-respect and accomplishment by allowing as much independence as possible
- avoid criticism that discourages the child
- teach children how to do what is wanted so they can contribute positively to family life
- teach children to communicate their needs
- teach children a healthy attitude toward mistakes
- give many opportunities for self-expression in sports, creative activities, hobbies

- discourage the child's seeking the mistaken goals of attention, power, revenge, and inadequacy
- create a democratic family atmosphere of mutual respect and cooperation in accomplishing family tasks and resolving problems that arise

When adults express unresolved anger in the presence of children, the anger:

- disrupts children's physiological functioning
- produces feelings of sadness, anger, and guilt in children
- decreases their level of play with other children
- makes it hard for children to learn to express their own anger—some become overly passive and others become overly aggressive
- makes children feel they are the cause of anger and should fix the situation
- has minimal impact when parents resolve conflict fairly

Happiness comes from:

- feelings of love, affection, and concern others direct to us
- activities that lead to feelings of accomplishment and competence

When people are happy, they:

- show more concern for other people
- feel greater confidence in themselves and their abilities
- perform tasks better
- are more friendly and responsive to others
- respond to unfair treatment generously
- seem inoculated against future difficulties

Close family relationships:

- increase joy and pleasure in life
- promote healthy growth
- buffer members against daily frustrations and disappointments
- expand horizons as members take up new activities together

Dix presents a model of the process of parenting that describes:

- emotion at the center as an organizing, directing force in parenting
- child's characteristics, parents' goals, and life events as the main activators of parents' emotions
- emotion as determiner of parent's view of the child's behavior and the parent's response to it
- regulatory processes that modulate and control parents' emotions

CHAPTER 3
Establishing
Close
Emotional
Relationships
with Children

Communication skills are:

- useful with a variety of family situations
- useful in all forms of interpersonal relationships

Children are resilient under stress when:

- a caregiver feels the children are special
- they have faith that the future will be better
- they reach out to others through sharing a hobby or giving help
- they have an easy temperament
- they have a strong relationship with a sibling

EXERCISES

1. Imagine a time when you were a child and felt very close to one of your parents (if you like, you can do the exercise with each of your parents), and describe your parent's behavior with you. What qualities did your parent show that made for closeness? Share these qualities with class members. Is there a common core? If you do this exercise with each of your parents, note sex differences—do your mother and father show different qualities at times of closeness with you? Do your classmates experience differences in mothers' and fathers' behavior toward sons and daughters?

2. Imagine a time when you were a child and felt very distant from one of your parents (again, you may do this with each of your parents) and describe your parent's behavior with you. What qualities did your parent show that created distance? Again, share these qualities with class members and find the common core. Are these qualities the opposite of qualities that lead to closeness or do they represent very different dimensions? Do the qualities described in Exercises 1 and 2 support what clinicians and researchers say is important?

3. Take turns practicing active listening with a classmate. This can be done in many formats: (a) Describe a time when you were upset as a child as your partner does active listening as a parent might have. (b) Describe negative feelings in a recent exchange and have your partner active listen. (c) Describe scenes you have witnessed between parents and children in stores or restaurants while your partner active listens. (d) Follow directions your instructor hands out for what one child in a problem situation might say while your partner active listens.

4. With a classmate, practice sending I-messages. Again, choose from a variety of formats: (a) Recall a situation when a parent was angry at you when you were growing up and describe I-messages your parent might have sent. (b) Recall a recent disagreement with a friend or instructor, and give appropriate I-messages for that. (c) Describe public parent-child

confrontations you have witnessed and devise appropriate I-messages for parents. (d) Devise I-messages for problem situations presented by your instructor.

5. (a) Recall one of your minor faults or weak points. When did you first become aware of this fault? In many instances, it goes back to what parents said to you when you were a child. Use Martin Seligman's ABCDE method of dealing with negative beliefs to give different interpretations to that quality. (b) Recall a recent example, no matter how minor, in which you confronted adversity and felt negative. Follow Seligman's recommendations for dealing with it.

ADDITIONAL READINGS

Briggs, Dorothy. *Your Child's Self Esteem*. Garden City, N.Y.: Doubleday, 1975.

Faber, Adele, and Mazlish, Elaine. *How to Talk So Kids Will Listen and Listen So Kids Will Talk*. New York: Rawson Wade, 1980.

Ginott, Haim G. *Between Parent and Child*. New York: Avon, 1969.

Gordon, Thomas. *P.E.T. Parent Effectiveness Training*. New York: New American Library, 1975.

Gordon, Thomas. *Teaching Children Self-Discipline*. New York: Times Books, 1989.

Seligman, Martin E. P. *Learned Optimism*. New York: Pocket Books, 1990.

Notes

1. Haim G. Ginott, *Between Parent and Child* (New York: Avon, 1969).
2. Haim G. Ginott, *Between Parent and Teenager* (New York: Avon, 1971).
3. Adele Faber and Elaine Mazlish, *Liberated Parents/Liberated Children* (New York: Avon, 1975).
4. Adele Faber and Elaine Mazlish, *How to Talk So Kids Will Listen and Listen So Kids Will Talk* (New York: Rawson Wade, 1980).
5. Thomas Gordon, *P.E.T. Parent Effectiveness Training* (New York: New American Library, 1975).
6. Thomas Gordon with Judith G. Sands, *P.E.T. in Action* (New York: Bantam, 1978).
7. Thomas Gordon, *Teaching Children Self-Discipline* (New York: Random House, 1989).
8. Dorothy C. Briggs, *Your Child's Self-Esteem* (Garden City, N.Y.: Doubleday, 1970).
9. Rudolf Dreikurs, *The Challenge of Parenthood*, rev. ed. (New York: Hawthorn, 1958).
10. Rudolf Dreikurs with Vicki Soltz, *Children: The Challenge* (New York: Hawthorn, 1964).

11. Gerald R. Patterson, *Families: Applications of Social Learning to Family Life,* rev. ed. (Champaign, Ill.: Research Press, 1975).
12. Gerald R. Patterson, *Living with Children,* rev. ed. (Champaign, Ill.: Research Press, 1976).
13. Wesley C. Becker, *Parents Are Teachers* (Champaign, Ill.: Research Press, 1971).
14. Robert Eimers and Robert Aitchison, *Effective Parents/Responsible Children* (New York: McGraw-Hill, 1977).
15. John D. Krumboltz and Helen B. Krumboltz, *Changing Children's Behavior* (Englewood Cliffs, N.J.: Prentice-Hall, 1972).
16. *American Heritage Dictionary,* 2nd college ed. (Boston: Houghton Mifflin, 1982), p. 744.
17. Ginott, *Between Parent and Child,* pp. 39–40.
18. Gordon with Sands, *P.E.T. in Action,* p. 47.
19. Judy Dunn, Jane Brown, and Lynn Beardsall, "Family Talk About Feeling States and Children's Later Understanding of Others' Emotions," *Developmental Psychology* 27 (1991): 448–455.

CHAPTER 3
Establishing
Close
Emotional
Relationships
with Children

20. Faber and Mazlish, *Liberated Parents/ Liberated Children.*

21. Jane B. Brooks and Doris M. Elliott, "Prediction of Psychological Adjustment at Age Thirty from Leisure Time Activities and Satisfactions in Childhood," *Human Development* 14 (1971): 61–71.

22. Dreikurs with Soltz, *Children: The Challenge.*

23. Ibid., p. 39.

24. Gordon, *Teaching Children Self-Discipline.*

25. Dreikurs with Soltz, *Children: The Challenge,* p. 108.

26. Gail D. Heyman, Carol S. Dweck, and Kathleen M. Cain, "Young Children's Vulnerability to Self-Blame and Helplessness: Relationship to Beliefs about Goodness," *Child Development 63* (1992): 401–415; Martin E. P. Seligman, *Learned Optimism* (New York: Pocket Books, 1990).

27. Seligman, *Learned Optimism.*

28. Ibid., pp. 221–222.

29. Ibid., p. 222.

30. Mona El-Sheikh, E. Mark Cummings, and Virginia Goetsch, "Coping with Adults' Angry Behavior: Behavioral, Physiological, and Verbal Responses in Preschoolers," *Developmental Psychology* 25 (1989): 490–498.

31. John M. Gottman and Lynn F. Katz, "Effects of Marital Discord on Young Children's Peer Interaction and Health," *Developmental Psychology* 25 (1989): 373–381.

32. E. Mark Cummings, "Coping with Background Anger in Early Childhood," *Child Development* 58 (1987): 976–984.

33. Jennifer S. Cummings, Davis S. Pellagrini, Clifford S. Notarius, and E. Mark Cummings, "Children's Responses to Adult Behavior as a Function of Marital Distress and History of Interparent Hostility," *Child Development* 60 (1989): 1035–1043.

34. E. Mark Cummings, Mary Ballard, Mona El-Sheikh, and Margaret Lake, "Resolution and Children's Responses to Interadult Anger," *Developmental Psychology* 27 (1991): 462–470.

35. Katherine Covell and Rona Abramovitch, "Understanding Emotion in the Family: Children's and Parents' Attributions of Happiness, Sadness, and Anger," *Child Development* 57 (1987): 985–991.

36. E. Mark Cummings et al., "Children's Responses to Different Forms of Expression of Anger between Adults," *Child Development* 60 (1989): 1392–1404.

37. Eleanor E. Maccoby and John A. Martin, "Socialization in the Context of the Family: Parent-Child Interaction," in *Handbook of Child Psychology,* eds. Paul H. Mussen and E. Mavis Hetherington, vol. 4: *Socialization, Personality, and Social Development,* 4th ed. (New York: John Wiley, 1983), pp. 1–101.

38. John A. Clausen, Paul H. Mussen, and Joseph Kuypers, "Involvement, Warmth, and Parent-Child Resemblance in Three Generations," in *Present and Past in Middle Life,* eds. Dorothy H. Eichorn et al. (New York: Academic Press, 1981), pp. 299–319.

39. J. Kirk Felsman and George E. Vaillant, "Resilient Children as Adults," in *The Invulnerable Child,* ed. E. James Anthony and Bertram J. Cohler (New York: Guilford, 1987), p. 298.

40. Charles R. Carlson and John C. Masters, "Inoculation by Emotion: Effects of Positive Emotional States on Children's Reactions to Social Comparison," *Developmental Psychology* 22 (1986): 760–765.

41. Brooks and Elliott, "Prediction of Psychological Adjustment at Age Thirty from Leisure Time Activities and Satisfactions in Childhood."

42. Theodore Dix, "The Affective Organization of Parenting: Adaptive and Maladaptive Processes," *Psychological Bulletin 110* (1991): 3–25.

43. Ibid., p. 4.

44. Elaine A. Blechman, "Effective Communication: Enabling Multiproblem Families to Change," in *Family Transitions* ed. Philip A. Cowan and Mavis Hetherington (Hillsdale, N.J.: Lawrence Erlbaum, 1991), pp. 219–244.

45. Roger Fisher and Scott Brown, *Getting Together: Building Relationships As We Negotiate* (New York, Penguin, 1989).

MODIFYING CHILDREN'S BEHAVIOR

C H A P T E R   4

Whether or not the loving is easy, your second primary task—modifying children's be-
havior with fair and firm limits—is a challenge. Deciding what is "fair" is no simple task.
What are realistic expectations for that particular child of that particular age? What
behaviors are appropriate? The next challenge—getting the child to meet the expectations
you have set—can be even more difficult. How do you effectively communicate what you
expect? What your limits are? What if your expectations are clear but your child fails to
meet them? To establish firm boundaries, parents must enforce limits by using appropriate
problem-solving techniques to modify behavior.

Children do not naturally do all the things parents want them to do. This chapter
focuses on ways of shaping children's behavior so they can adapt to family and social
standards. As in many other areas of parenting, parents change their own behavior
to ensure children will follow guidelines. In this chapter we cover ways of (1) establishing realistic expectations, (2) structuring the environment to help children meet
them, (3) teaching new, socially approved behaviors to children, (4) setting limits,
and (5) enforcing limits.

KINDS OF LEARNING

Psychologists identify three kinds of learning—classical conditioning, operant or
instrumental conditioning, and observational learning. **Classical conditioning** occurs when new signals are learned for already existing responses. Classical conditioning is especially important in understanding how new responses are attached to
an individual's emotional and physiological responses. In everyday life, a stimulus
(trigger) is followed by a response. In Pavlov's first experiment with dogs, the sight of
food caused the dog to salivate. Sight of food was called the **unconditioned stimulus**
and salivating the **unconditioned response**. When a neutral stimulus, a buzzer, was
paired many times with the sight of food, soon the buzzer alone triggered the
response of salivating. The buzzer was called the **conditioned stimulus** because only
after many pairings with food was it able to elicit the response.

INTERVIEW
with Paul Mussen

Paul H. Mussen is professor emeritus of psychology at the University of California, Berkeley. He is a former director of the Institute of Human Development on the Berkeley campus. He has coauthored many books, including The Roots of Prosocial Behavior in Children *with Nancy Eisenberg in 1989. He is also an editor of* The Handbook of Child Psychology.

Parents are very interested in moral development. What can they do to promote this in their children?

With my bias, modeling is of primary importance. It is *the* single most important thing parents can do. Parents create a nurturant environment in which the child wants to imitate the parent's behavior and the parents behave in an altruistic way so that there is an identification with the parents. Parents also can try to get the child to participate when they are doing something for someone else.

Then parents use empathy-eliciting disciplinary procedures in which they make the child aware that he or she has hurt someone. In the early years with toddlers, it is a disciplinary technique that involves showing clearly and emphatically that you disapprove but at the same time, making clear that someone else was harmed by what the child has done—"You pulled her hair. Don't ever do that again. You really hurt her."

In general I think the disciplinary practices are very important. Studies show the empathy-eliciting techniques—so-called induction and reasoning as opposed to power-assertion (spanking and threatening)—are important because they focus not on punishing the child but on pointing up the consequences of what is done. So, first eliciting empathy, then later reasoning with the child are important.

Rewarding altruistic behavior when it occurs is important. The research evidence here is not as strong as one might like, but it does suggest this.

Discussing moral issues at home is critical both from the point of view of moral thinking and from the point of view of moral behavior. Older studies showed that the model's behavior was the critical thing, not what the model said. More recent studies show that verbal

We see the process of classical conditioning in everyday life when people who experience a strong emotional feeling attach that feeling to other stimuli present at the time. Later, other stimuli may trigger the emotional response. For example, a child is frightened by a barking dog who nips him playfully. The next time the child sees a barking dog, he feels frightened because he associates the barking alone with the fear that he felt when the barking was accompanied by a nip from the dog.

Operant or **instrumental conditioning** involves forming new associations between stimuli (triggers) and responses on the basis of positive and negative consequences. When a stimulus-response pattern leads to a positive consequence—a cookie, a parent's smile, extra privileges—the behavior is likely to occur again. When the pattern receives no reward or leads to a negative consequence—a parent's frown or loss of a privilege—the behavior pattern decreases. When the behavior disappears, we say it is **extinguished** or has undergone **extinction**.

responses can be helpful also. You are giving the child some codes or rules that the child can then apply later on when various situations arise. So the discussion and what, for lack of a better word, we used to call preaching—in effect, discussing problems, making principled statements—can be helpful.

Giving children assignments of responsibilities fairly early at the child's level, is also useful. For example, in the schools, a young fifth-grader can help a second-grader; and at home older siblings can help younger siblings. Having chores and assigning tasks in such a way that children get satisfaction from accepting responsibility is important.

Those are the important disciplinary techniques—modeling, a nurturant milieu so the child identifies with the modeling, reasoning, discussing rules and principles so the child can use them later, rewarding positive behavior when it occurs, and giving opportunities for satisfaction from accepting responsibility.

What are the things parents should avoid doing?

One thing to avoid is behaving immorally themselves. Another is being inconsistent—occasionally not reacting to misbehavior that harms someone else and at other times punishing it, and at still other times rewarding it. Inconsistent patterns of reaction should be avoided. Also be very alert in terms of inconsistency with respect to what the parent says and what the parent does.

In general, I feel that power-assertive techniques (like spanking) should be avoided because they produce the wrong orientation. They give the impression that authority can do whatever it wants and the rest of us just have to go along. They result in less independent moral judgment, and they make the point that aggression can be a successful means of getting what you want.

Avoid underestimating children's understanding because I think they are a lot more sensitive to these issues than we might think. And I don't think they should be babied or patronized when you are handling something. Let them be involved in making decisions. Assume that they can understand when you are trying to use inductive techniques. Parents sometimes feel they have to play down to children, and I don't think that's true.

Children also learn by observing **models** and imitating them. A four-year-old imitates the mother's care of a two-year-old sister and reaps the reward of a big smile from daddy. Imitation of a model will occur even when the child receives no reward. Observation of another person's behavior is enough to stimulate imitation. Children often do as we do and not as we say, because they have observed us and are imitating our behavior instead of obeying our words. Children are most likely to imitate models who are warm, nurturing, and powerful. In extreme circumstances, when there is no model of warmth and power to copy, children will imitate a hostile, rejecting figure.

Learning principles help parents teach children how to behave in approved ways. Rudolf Dreikurs commented that parents seem to expect children will naturally observe what is correct.[1] It is indeed true that a first rule of parenting is that parents model the behaviors they wish children to have. Parents, however, must go beyond this simple model and take a more active role, teaching children new skills and limiting behavior. First, though, parents must decide on realistic expectations for children.

ESTABLISHING REALISTIC AND APPROPRIATE EXPECTATIONS

Unrealistic expectations of children's behavior are a major source of parents' frustration. Since there is no one correct way to rear children at each stage of development, how do parents make their expectations realistic? What is realistic, given the variety of family settings that parents and children live in?

Realistic expectations are those that take into account the child's age and characteristics, family pattern of living, social standards, parents' individual characteristics, health and safety factors, and daily events. Parents use the child's age as their first guide. For example, they do not expect toddlers to obey quickly, because they know toddlers are beginning to explore the world and assert their individuality. Parents expect more refusals at this age and are ready to be patient as children learn to master activities themselves. Parents learn what to expect at different ages by reading, going to parent groups, talking to other parents, and by experience.

Having considered the child's age, parents then consider the child's own individual characteristics. Some children develop exactly by the book and parents base their expectations on what is typical for children of that age. Other children may have special needs to take into account. For example, parents of highly active children must learn to have different expectations about how long their children can sit at a movie or musical event. Parents of shy children will have different expectations of how much support their children need when meeting new people in a strange setting. Parents of gregarious, outgoing children will have different expectations about how often friends can come to spend the night. So parents will always ask themselves whether a specific expectation is realistic for a specific child at a specific stage.

Having taken the child's special characteristics into account, parents arrive at expectations based on their own and their family's overall needs. For example, in families where both parents work outside the home and children are in day care after school, it may be more important for children to do chores before school because there is little time before dinner. Or, in families with many children, expectations about sharing toys and possessions and helping each other may be much greater than in two-child families.

Then we have parents' personal expectations. Parents may expect that children will follow in their footsteps—parents who were school achievers may expect very good grades from children; athletic parents may expect children to perform well in sports. Other parents expect children to achieve what they did not—the shy parent who wants a popular child or the early-working parent who wants the child to enjoy childhood. These expectations based on parents' lives are reasonable if they can be abandoned when a child cannot or does not want to meet them. Parents have other expectations based on personal characteristics—parents who like lots of sleep may expect children to be similar; parents who do not like noise may expect very low noise levels. It is always wise for parents to reassess their expectations based on personal values to see whether they are realistic.

Parents also base expectations on their own social values and the social standards of the community. Parents of ethnic groups may have expectations about sharing or independence or about participation in extended family activities that are different from those of the predominant culture. Or parents may live in a community where the standard is participation in some kind of group activity such as Boy Scouts or Girl Scouts; parents may then expect their children to take part, too.

Expectations must be tailored to meet health and safety needs. When families live near busy streets, there will be firm expectations that very young children stay out of the streets. Health needs dictate reasonable amounts of sleep per night, a nutritious diet, toothbrushing. Children can be expected to follow these guidelines even though they do not want to.

Finally, daily events influence the nature of realistic expectations—and precisely in this area parenting becomes an art. If a child had a stressful day, expectations may have to be changed. If a child went to the dentist, had a fight with a friend, lost a pet, it may be realistic and understanding to be tolerant of the child's irritability or inability to perform chores. Similarly, a parent who had a very rough and unusual day, feeling sick with flu or meeting some unusual expense, may want a respite from the expectations of other family members.

Finally, when they assess the appropriateness of their expectations, parents must ask themselves if this is something they expect from themselves or a friend. Parents will occasionally demand that children do things they themselves do not do. For example, parents may demand that children not eat between meals, while snacking themselves and having two or three coffee breaks per day. Sloppy parents may expect neat children. When parents themselves do not perform behaviors they expect of children, they should not be surprised when children follow suit.

All these factors—child's age, special characteristics, parents' characteristics, family lifestyle, community standards, health and safety needs, daily events—influence parents' realistic expectations. In general, children do best when expectations are consistent from one day to the next, especially in matters of importance. Though parents may make occasional allowances for special events and stresses, consistent expectations for the child lead to greater compliance.

HELPING CHILDREN MEET EXPECTATIONS

Having established realistic expectations, parents help children meet them in several ways. First, they structure the child's physical environment. They have storage space for children to put away toys, they have hooks in closets at children's level of reach. They have dressers children can open and storage space marked for clothes in drawers. They have toys children can take care of.

As nearly as possible, the family house should be structured to meet children's needs. Play space outdoors is available. Furniture, rugs, decorations are selected with an active family in mind. Thomas Gordon says many parents refuse to take things off tables or put fragile objects out of children's reach because they believe children should learn early not to touch certain objects.[2] When asked, however, most of these same parents said they would quickly modify their homes if an elderly parent were coming to stay! Gordon believes that if an aging parent with mature faculties needs the home adjusted, all the more so do young children, who are not mature.

Putting dangerous substances out of the way, having locks on drawers containing knives, clearly marking sliding glass doors—all these changes minimize the opportunities for children to harm themselves and help children lead safe, healthy lives. Figure 4-1 presents suggestions for making the home a safe environment for children.

A second major way parents help children meet parental expectations is by establishing a regular daily routine. A regular routine makes a habit of certain behaviors that children learn to do automatically. Regularity has physical benefits for the child as well. Our physiological systems—including secretions of hormones, needs for sleep and food—operate on a 25-hour cycle, but we live in a 24-hour day. So, to help bodies stay in rhythm, both children and adults need a schedule for sleeping, eating, exercising at regular intervals. Human beings function at their best in this kind of routine.

Here again, however, children's individual tempos must be taken into account. Some children are slow to wake from sleep; they must have more time in the morning to get started. Other children need more time to wind down at night, so their bedtime routines may have to be started earlier than usual. Children have different patterns of eating—some eat a lot in the morning, tapering off by dinner; others have opposite patterns. A child can be expected to come to the table for some sort of food, but portions can be varied so that the child's individual needs are kept in mind.

A third way parents help children meet expectations is by monitoring the amount of stimulation children receive. For example, they schedule their children's activities in such a way that children do not become overly tired or overly excited. Parents do not take a preschool child shopping all morning and then send the child off to a birthday party in the afternoon because the child may well be irritable and overly stimulated. As holidays or vacations approach, parents try to schedule rest periods or quiet time so children have a chance to unwind from all the excitement.

Parents also prepare children for difficult situations or changes in routine. They may calmly rehearse a visit to the dentist, letting the child practice with a doll or stuffed animal, so the child will be much less likely to feel overwhelmed when the real event occurs. Parents can use rehearsal to prepare children for other changes in routine. For example, if parents are going on a vacation, or if a parent will not be there to pick up a child at day care, they can go over in advance what the child will do and what other caregivers will do.

REWARDS

Once parents have agreed upon realistic expectations and structured their children's environment, they reward children for appropriate behavior when it occurs. **Rewards** or positive reinforcers are actions that increase the likelihood the behavior will occur again. Rewards are always present when a behavior continues, whether we

FIGURE 4-1
Childproofing the House

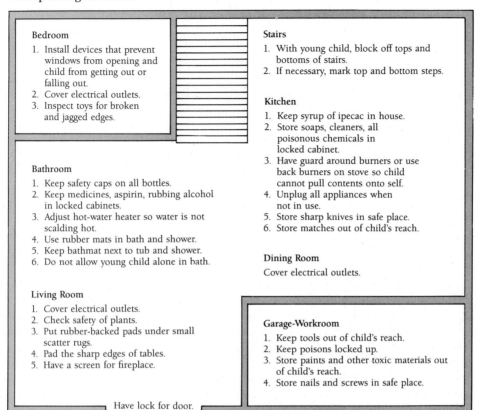

Bedroom
1. Install devices that prevent windows from opening and child from getting out or falling out.
2. Cover electrical outlets.
3. Inspect toys for broken and jagged edges.

Bathroom
1. Keep safety caps on all bottles.
2. Keep medicines, aspirin, rubbing alcohol in locked cabinets.
3. Adjust hot-water heater so water is not scalding hot.
4. Use rubber mats in bath and shower.
5. Keep bathmat next to tub and shower.
6. Do not allow young child alone in bath.

Living Room
1. Cover electrical outlets.
2. Check safety of plants.
3. Put rubber-backed pads under small scatter rugs.
4. Pad the sharp edges of tables.
5. Have a screen for fireplace.

Stairs
1. With young child, block off tops and bottoms of stairs.
2. If necessary, mark top and bottom steps.

Kitchen
1. Keep syrup of ipecac in house.
2. Store soaps, cleaners, all poisonous chemicals in locked cabinet.
3. Have guard around burners or use back burners on stove so child cannot pull contents onto self.
4. Unplug all appliances when not in use.
5. Store sharp knives in safe place.
6. Store matches out of child's reach.

Dining Room
Cover electrical outlets.

Garage-Workroom
1. Keep tools out of child's reach.
2. Keep poisons locked up.
3. Store paints and other toxic materials out of child's reach.
4. Store nails and screws in safe place.

Have lock for door.

General
1. Install smoke alarms in house.
2. Have fire extinguishers.
3. Plan fire escape routes.
4. Keep poison control, fire and police department numbers by the telephone.

Adapted from *Working Mother,* October 1985.

recognize them or not. Sometimes the rewards are pleasurable feelings inside the person and are not observable. For example, children run and jump because they feel good when they do it. They draw and solve puzzles often because such activities are enjoyable in themselves. Sometimes rewards are given by other people. Such external rewards fall into three general categories: **social rewards** of attention, smiles, approval, praise, physical affection; **material rewards** of food, presents, special purchases; and **privileges and activities,** such as trips, special outings to the zoo, or permission to stay up late. Parents are wise to notice the kinds of rewards that appeal to their children and to make a list of activities and privileges that are particularly appealing to each child in the family. Sometimes the reward is allowing the child to continue the pleasurable activity he or she initiated. When parents supply external rewards, behaviorists suggest they rely most heavily on social rewards because those bring the family closer together and create an atmosphere of warmth and trust. Within this category, however, individual preferences exist. Some children enjoy hugs and kisses, while others like verbal compliments.

When behavior patterns are being established, parents give rewards after each successful act. Once the behavior occurs regularly, they can give rewards only occasionally. For example, when Jimmy first started picking up his clothes and putting them in the hamper, his mother commented every day about how helpful he was. As he continued, his mother remarked on it only when he did it rapidly.

How, specifically, should rewards be given? Eimers and Aitchison have outlined seven specific steps.[3] They believe social rewards of praise and approval are more effective than material rewards because they are less costly, less formalized, and have lasting psychological benefits. Specific statements of praise and approval are informative. They may describe positive characteristics that children have not noticed about themselves, thus increasing their self-esteem and self-confidence. Following are the seven recommended steps:

1. Make eye contact with your child. Direct eye contact makes the statement a more personal one.

2. Be physically close to your child. Praise given at close range has more impact.

3. Smile. Sometimes a smile alone is praise, but it should accompany the verbal message so that the child sees your pleasure in your facial expression.

4. Comment on positive behaviors. Send I-messages, telling the child what you like about his or her behavior—"I like it when you help me carry in the groceries." Express appreciation when the child does you a favor—"Thank you for mailing my letter." Children blossom under this attention.

5. Focus on behavior, not on the child. Like all other strategists we have cited, behaviorists recommend comments on specific behaviors, not on the child's characteristics. "Doing the dishes is a big help to me, Linda, and I appreciate it," not "What a good girl you are."

6. Show affection. How we handle our bodies—our gestures, moves, tones of voice—can increase the value of the praise and make the child feel very special. Again tailor the affectionate demonstrations to the child.

7. Deliver the reward immediately. The faster the reward is given, the more effective it is.

Sometimes praise alone is not effective. Children may not want to carry out an activity no matter how approving a parent is. A schoolchild may not like math and may refuse to work hard, even for social rewards. In this situation, tokens or a point system can be useful in motivating the child to take an interest. A token system is

---

BOX 4-1
REWARD MENU

Extra snack	5 tokens	Play cards with parents	5 tokens
Extra story read	5 tokens	Play outside extra hour	10 tokens
Extra game with parents	10 tokens	Trip to park	10 tokens
Trip to library	10 tokens	Movie	15 tokens
Special dinner menu	15 tokens	Special hike	15 tokens

---

one in which children earn tokens or points that they can exchange for privileges or other rewards (see Box 4-1). If a child does not like math and is careless when doing homework, parents may want to establish a program in which the child can earn one token for every correctly completed math problem. At the end of the week, the child presents the homework, corrected by the math teacher, to the parent. The number of math problems correctly done determines the number of tokens earned.

As children improve their behavior, they must do more and more to obtain tokens. For example, as math improves, the child might earn only half a token for each problem correctly done in a week. Eimers and Aitchison recommend giving social rewards of approval along with tokens and eventually switching to social rewards alone.[4] When the child's math skills are firmly established, the entire system can be phased out.

Parents must be careful not to take approved behaviors for granted. They must continue to comment on the chores completed on time, the good report card, the clothes picked up. In the rush of everyday life, it is easy to forget the desirable behaviors performed by all members of the family. The sensitive parent continues to make comments on well-learned but much-appreciated behavior.

Are rewards a form of bribery? This is a charge often made about the use of external rewards. Behaviorists reply that if rewards are increased when the child refuses to carry out an act, then the reward is a bribe. Giving regular rewards for desirable behavior, however, is nothing more than giving a realistic payoff, a common motivation for adults as well as children. For example, a paycheck is a payoff for work; a compliment to a co-worker expresses appreciation of some positive act. Why should we not do this with our children? To the extent that behaviorists rely on social rewards of attention, smiles, and praise, they are conveying positive feelings to the children in the same way that Gordon, Ginott, and Briggs recommend. Reflection of feelings and I-messages are not considered bribes, but they are social rewards that increase communication between child and parent.

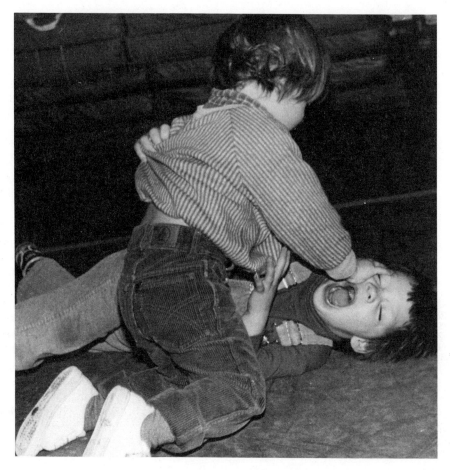

Children may not spontaneously do what parents want them to do, so parents should teach children what they desire them to do. All siblings fight, but families differ in their tolerance of aggression. Children who are allowed to be aggressive in the home will be aggressive in preschool and school.

TEACHING ACCEPTABLE NEW BEHAVIORS

Because children may not spontaneously do what parents want them to do, parents must actively teach children what they desire them to do. When the behavior is already within the child's capacity, parents show the child what they want done. They move very young children through the necessary steps, verbalizing each step as they go—"This is how you put on your shirt." Parents can break the task into separate units and describe what is being done while the child does it. "First you put one arm through the sleeve. Then put the other arm through the other sleeve. Then you put your head through the opening and pull the shirt on." Parents offer encouragement and praise after each step. After the child has thoroughly learned the behavior, only occasional praise is needed.

In some situations the child is not able to carry out the behaviors the parents want to reward, so parents must *shape* the child's existing behavior. For example, suppose a parent wants her five-year-old to begin making his bed, and he does not know how. The first step for the parent is to decide what behaviors come closest to the specific behavior she wants the child to learn. Reward these. Then, as these increase in frequency, demand a higher level of performance before the reward is given. For example, in teaching bed making, a parent might initially reward the young child when the covers and spread are pulled up close to the pillow. As the child masters that skill, then the parent rewards pulling the spread over the pillow. Finally, when that is mastered, the parent rewards the child for having a smooth bed with no wrinkles and the spread over the pillow.

Shaping behavior is a useful approach with schoolchildren who get poor report cards. Parents can reward the highest passing grade on the first report card. They can contract with children for rewards after the next report card if there are specific improvements. Since report periods are usually six weeks long, parents may reward good test performance during that period or contract to give small regular rewards for teacher reports of acceptable work. Report cards are a situation where parents do not want to give a child rewards only for superb performance because they may be a very long time coming; in this situation rewarding improvements in homework and test grades may be more effective.

Theoretically, it is possible to raise children using only rewards and ignoring all misbehavior, which theoretically becomes extinguished for lack of reward. In everyday life, however, parents usually must deal with behavior that violates rules. When the child actively does something not approved, parents have two tasks before them—to state limits effectively, then enforce them.

STATING LIMITS EFFECTIVELY

When rules are clearly and specifically stated, children are more likely to follow them. Say, "I want you to play outside for a while"; not, "Be good this afternoon." Phrase the rule, if possible, in positive form, also stating its purpose. For example, say, "Carry your coat so it stays clean"; not, "Don't drag your coat on the floor." Research shows that when parents say, "Don't" in a loud voice, followed by a few words, the child hears only the few words and continues the action.[5] "Don't jump on the sofa" leads young children to continue the jumping.

Children respond more easily when rules are phrased in an impersonal way. "Bedtime is at 8," or "Dinner at 6" is more likely to result in compliance than "You have to go to bed now," or "You have to be home for dinner at 6."

Parents get best results when they give only one rule at a time. As they give the rule, they gain the child's attention, standing close to the child with good eye contact. Young children can be walked through the desired behavior. For example, as parents say, "It's time to clean up toys," they pick up the young toddler's hand and show her how to put teddy on the shelf, guiding her hand through the movements.

When possible, give the children options. "You can have hot or cold cereal," "You can take the trash out now or right after dinner," "You can wear a raincoat or carry an umbrella." Having choices gives children some control over what is happening. Parents also give options when they prepare for changes in behavior. For example, just before dinner, a parent may prepare a child for coming in by saying, "Dinner is in five minutes," or, "In five more swings, it is time to leave the park." Children have a chance to get ready to follow the rule. Having options and having time to prepare for a change not only make it easier for children to follow rules, but also boost their self-esteem as they see their feelings and wishes respected.

Ginott suggests four steps in stating limits: (1) accept the child's wish without criticism or argument, (2) state what the rule or limit is, (3) when possible, describe how the child can obtain the wish, and (4) accept any irritation or resentment the child feels over being denied a request.[6] For example, with an elementary school child, a parent might say, "I understand that you want to watch an extra hour of TV tonight, but you know the rule is only one hour per day and you have already watched the one hour. If you want to give up tomorrow's hour, you can watch the extra hour tonight." If the child refuses to accept this, the parent can say, "I know you are unhappy you cannot watch TV tonight."

Parents might like to see many changes in their children's behavior, but parents are most effective when they have priorities in the rules. Health and safety rules are most important. Rules about staying out of the street, about always telling parents where they are, and about following curfew rules are the most important and the most carefully monitored. Also in this category are prohibitions against hurting other people and damaging them physically by biting, hitting, kicking. Next are what might be termed rules that ease social living—rules that make being together easier. This category includes rules against destroying other people's property or hurting their feelings deliberately and rules of general consideration (such as being quiet when others are sleeping or being helpful with chores).

Third in priority come conventional rules—how to use a napkin and silverware, what clothes to wear, what social routines to follow. Parents sometimes place great emphasis on this area—chewing with the mouth closed, sitting up in chairs. Even young preschoolers are aware of the difference between rules that concern kindliness and basic consideration of others and rules having to do with social convention.[7] Significantly, they are more impressed with the importance of kindness to others than with social conventions. Parents are wise to accept their preschoolers' reasoning and let them master conventions at a later date.

Last on the list are rules governing behaviors that can be choices for children. What clothes to wear, what games to play are, in most cases, matters of the child's individual preference. These choices usually carry no serious consequences. If parents believe there are consequences—such as very loud music that affects teenagers' hearing or clothing so inappropriate to the weather there is a health risk—then limits must be set. In general, however, children have autonomy in these areas of dress, play, and entertainment. Parents need not expend enormous energies getting children to do things just as they would like them to.

Once they have set priorities on the rules, parents must deal with children's failures to abide by them.

ENFORCING LIMITS

When rules have been stated clearly and children do not follow them, then parents act to enforce them. Before acting, however, parents must do two things. First, they must ask themselves whether children continue to break the rule because, in some disguised fashion, parents are rewarding the rule-breaking behavior. Parents sometimes tell children to stop running or stop teasing, but then undermine themselves with a chuckle and a shake of the head to indicate that the child has a lot of spirit and that they admire that spirit. So, the child continues. Parents must first look to see if they are rewarding behavior they do not approve.

Second, parents must be sure they are in general agreement about enforcing the rules. If there are big differences between them, parents should get off by themselves and negotiate the differences with mutual problem-solving techniques. If parents frequently disagree, they may refuse to set any consequence for a behavior until they have a chance to talk with the other parent because children view any parental conflicts as justification to do what they want to do.

Parents have many options to choose from in enforcing limits.

Mutual Problem Solving

Using Gordon's mutual problem-solving technique is a useful first step.[8] Employing this approach, parents identify the rule-breaking as a problem to them, a problem they want children to help them solve so that children, too, will be satisfied with the outcome. Parents solicit their children's opinions and work together to find a solution agreeable to all concerned. For example, when children are consistently late for dinner or do not come to the table when called, parents present this as a problem they all must solve. The underlying assumption is that the family working together can find an alternative that satisfies everyone. There are six steps to the problem-solving process: (1) defining the problem, (2) generating possible solutions, (3) evaluating possible solutions, (4) deciding on the best solution, (5) implementing the decision, and (6) follow-up evaluation.

Parents begin by explaining to children the exact problem that is troubling them and its effect on them and then say that they are going to try a new method to solve the problem so that everyone's needs are met. Children may be skeptical at first, thinking this may be another way for their parents to get them to behave. But as children realize that their needs are being considered, they become more active participants. Gordon advises parents and children to spend the most time on defining the nature of the problem and exchanging possible solutions.

Parents and children may disagree about a problem. Parents may feel upset by the continual mess in the kitchen on weekend mornings as children trail in one after another and get breakfast at odd times without cleaning up. The mother finds her kitchen in a mess and no one child to hold responsible. The children, in turn, may feel the problem is that Mom won't serve weekend breakfasts at a reasonable time, like 10 or 11 a.m., because she wants to be out doing errands. Active listening by everyone and willingness to hear suggestions can bring agreement.

Parents solicit their children's opinions and work with children to find a solution
agreeable to all.

Gordon advises that, when you start these problem-solving sessions, they should
be frequent. But don't let a discussion last too long. If the list of problems is long,
take the most important ones first. If only two family members are involved, the others need not participate. It is not necessary to resolve a problem the first time it is
discussed. Family members should feel free to think about a problem, discuss it
together, then resolve it at the next session.

As you talk about each proposed solution, try to figure out how it will work. Once
a solution is selected, consider how the results will be evaluated and make sure that
you allow enough time so it has a chance to succeed. During the process of propos-
ing solutions and picking one, each family member needs to listen actively to the
suggestions of all family members. In this situation, as in so many, family members
need to be able to trust each other and to recognize each other's needs.

Sometimes children are reluctant to get involved in mutual problem solving.
Gordon suggests that parents start with a problem that family members are not upset

INTERVIEW
with Parents

What are the joys of parenting for you?

"I have made deals with her. We always call it, 'Let's make a deal. This is what I want. What do you want?' We would come to some agreement, and as long as she was clear about it, she would do it. This was from early, early, early. So now on just about anything, we can negotiate. She wants to watch two programs, and we want to watch something else, and she'll come up with an idea. 'How about you let me watch this, and you tape that? Then I'll go do this.' We have tried a few democratic family meetings which is a little early, and we have done only a few, but she likes them. She'll see a problem and say, 'I think we need a meeting.'" FATHER OF PRESCHOOLER

"We don't have sidewalks, and I have always put a chain at the end of the driveway whenever he is riding his bike so he doesn't go out. The other day he got his bike out to ride and then went and put the chain up. I thought, 'Good for him! He's learning to protect himself; he's learning these adaptive skills of safety for himself.' It made me feel proud of him. It was a good moment." FATHER OF PRESCHOOLER

"Another great joy is like painting a good picture or taking a good jump shot. It's doing something that is just right for your kids. It just hits the target. It might be, after reprimanding him and sending him to his room, going up and talking to him, telling him you love him and to come downstairs now. Just knowing how good a thing that is, how appropriate it is. It may be buying the fishing rod for a child that he desperately wanted. It is the pleasure of pleasing someone you care about and pleasing him on the basis of personal knowledge you have about him." FATHER OF ELEMENTARY SCHOOL CHILDREN

about. For example, in your first problem-solving session you could talk about how the family is going to spend the next vacation. Also, you can help the individual child to understand that the no-lose method is worthy of his participation if you start with a problem that is bothering him. If children can see, concretely, how their life is better when these talks are held, they are more likely to participate.

Once a solution is agreed on, parents may find that children don't follow through. Children break agreements for a variety of reasons—they may not have had enough experience in self-direction, they may forget, they may test the limits to see what will happen, or they may have accepted an unworkable solution just to end the session. When an agreement is broken, parents must send a strong I-message of disappointment and surprise, as soon as possible. Perhaps the child can be helped to keep the agreement. Or perhaps another problem-solving session is needed.

Parents might be tempted to build punishments into the problem-solving agreement—"If you don't carry out the garbage, your allowance is reduced by 25¢." Gordon advises against the use of penalties to enforce agreements. Parents should assume children will cooperate, instead of starting with a negative expectation expressed in the threat of punishment. Children frequently respond to trust.

The **contracting sessions** devised by behaviorists are similar to Gordon's mutual problem-solving sessions. Contracting sessions are an expansion of the token system. When parents use tokens, they may do so to change one specific behavior or to reward the child for doing a particular chore. When parents want to reach agreement on several matters, and children are also asking for some changes, the family holds a contracting session. Contracting sessions are most appropriate with elementary school children and teenagers, but verbal preschoolers can also participate.

In approaching the problem, parents need to be clear about the specific, positive behavior they want to see. You can make a list: (1) vacuuming once a week, (2) dusting once a week, (3) changing the bed once a week. Each task can be worth 30 points, and the total of 90 points can be exchanged for two car rides or staying out an extra hour on a weekend evening. You present the scheme to the teenager, who agrees to clean his or her room once a week for that number of points. Then you monitor the behavior each week and give the number of points earned.

Now let's look at a more complicated example. Suppose you wish to decrease your seven-year-old son's messiness. You decide he should do four things, hang up his coat, clean and put away his lunchbox, put away his toys, and put his dirty clothes in the hamper. The behaviors are clearly stated. Before you propose a contract, observe the boy's behavior—count how many times in a week he does these things. Eimers and Aitchison suggest a chart to record behavior over a seven-day period (Box 4-2).[9]

One mother, after observing and counting for a week, discovered that her son had hung up his coat only once and at no time put his dirty clothes in the hamper or put his toys away. When she told him what rewards he could earn with a point system, the child was excited and eager to try. Mother and child used the same form to record successful completion of each task. After the system went into effect, the mother noticed dramatic differences in the child's behavior. After seven weeks, the child was picking up his toys and putting his dirty clothes in the hamper. The system was gradually phased out after the habits were established.

Some behaviorists disapprove of elaborate programs of special incentives because they are more formalized and less personal than social rewards and can be financially costly. If a child has not responded to other strategies, however, special incentives may produce the desired results.

Natural and Logical Consequences

Suppose that mutual problem solving and contracting sessions do not work. Then a parent might try Dreikurs' natural and logical consequences.[10] A **logical consequence** is the natural outcome of misbehavior in which parents do not interfere. When children experience the logical consequences of misbehavior—for example, eating cold food because they are late for dinner—they learn to anticipate the consequences and to avoid them by not repeating the misbehavior.

Because the consequences are the result of the child's misbehavior, the child and not the parent is responsible for the child's discomfort. The violation, not the parent, brings the penalty. Instead, the parent remains friendly and undisturbed. The following incident illustrates the method of logical and natural consequences. When a

---

BOX 4-2
BEHAVIOR LOG

Behavior	Sun	Mon	Tue	Wed	Thurs	Fri	Sat
1. Hang up coat							
2. Clean and put away lunchbox							
3. Put away toys							
4. Put dirty clothes in hamper							

---

three-year-old crayoned on the walls, the mother told her that they would not be able to go to the beach until she, the mother, washed off the marks. She asked the daughter to help, but after cleaning for a few minutes the girl wandered off. Every few minutes the child came back and asked when they were going to the beach. The mother replied calmly, "As soon as we get this wall cleaned." The child did not complain when she learned that it was too late to go to the beach.

Logical consequences differ from punishment in several ways. Logical consequences are directly related to what the child has done—if children do not put their clothes in the laundry, they have no clean clothes. A punishment may have no logical relationship to what the child has done—a spanking is not the direct result of being late for a meal, but is the result of the parent's authority. The method of logical consequences does not place moral blame or pass moral judgment on the child. The child has made a mistake and pays the price. The parent stands by as an adviser, rather than acting as a judge. Punishment implies that the child has committed a "wrong" act and must atone for the offense.

The method of logical consequences is not always as simple as standing by and letting the natural outcome of the act teach the child not to repeat the act. Parents must sometimes take a more active role. They must be careful not to turn the consequences into punishment by the comments they make. They must not criticize the child or angrily label the child. If a parent, for example, seems gleeful when a child suffers consequences—"You did not finish your homework and now you are paying the price! What did I tell you?"—the value of the method is lost. Children then experience the consequences as punishment, and they resent the parent's reaction.

In some situations parents will have to supply the consequences because not all misbehavior results in unpleasant outcomes. For example, when a child bites or hits another child, the consequence is a howl from the recipient. There is no discouraging consequence unless the other child takes action. Dreikurs indicates that when a child bites, a parent may want to bite back to demonstrate that a bite hurts. Similarly, if a child hits a parent hard, the mother may comment that she, too, can hit. She may then hit the child playfully, but in a way that hurts slightly. Most experts recommend against biting and hitting as being too physically aggressive and suggest restricting children to their room.

Logical consequences cannot be used when they result in danger to the child. We cannot allow children to run into the street and be hit by a car to teach them to stay out of the street. Parents can restrict children to a safe place—either to the house or to the backyard—until they have learned to stay away from the street.

Taking Action

Ginott recommends **taking action**, using some form of behavior to enforce existing limitations.[11]

When reflecting feelings, setting limits, and allowing natural consequences have not worked, parents can take action. Ginott does not believe in punishment, which he defines as a powerful person taking punitive action against a child. Taking action is different because the parent uses some form of behavior to enforce an existing limitation. For example, let's assume that house rules include not bouncing a ball in the house. If a child continues to bounce the ball after being given the choice of going outside to bounce or staying in and not bouncing, then parents act. They either send the child outside with the ball or they take the ball away and permit the child to remain in the house. With teenagers, parents might remove the privilege of using the car if children do not respect the family curfew. Again, removing car privileges would not be punishment; it would be acting to enforce the established rule. The main difference is the parent's attitude. A parent who takes action is not a punishing authority figure but an adult who is acting to enforce the meaning of his or her words.

Punishments

These four methods may not have worked, and parents will have to use punishments. Punishment means giving a behavior a negative consequence to decrease the likelihood of its occurrence. Punishments require varying degrees of effort on the parent's part. Before describing these, let us look at six general principles for using punishments: (1) Intervene early. Do not let the situation get out of control. As soon as the rule is violated, begin to take action. (2) Stay as calm and objective as possible. Sometimes parents' upset and frustration are rewarding to the child. Parents' emotions can also distract the child from thinking about the rule violation. (3) State the rule that was violated. State it simply: do not get into arguments about it. (4) Use a *mild* negative consequence. A mild consequence has the advantage that the child often devalues the activity itself and seems more likely to resist temptation and follow the rule in the future. (5) Use negative consequences consistently. When actions are sometimes punished and sometimes not, they do not decrease. This may seem to contradict what was said earlier about taking into account daily events in establishing expectations. Daily events, however, are rarely sufficiently stressful to change major rules. (6) Reinforce positive social behaviors as they occur afterwards; parents do not want children to receive more punishments than rewards.

Following are punishments, ranging from mild to severe. First, **ignoring** might seem the easiest punishment as the parent must pay no attention to what the child says or does. It requires effort, however, as the parent must keep a neutral facial expression, look away, move away from the child, and give no verbal response or attention to what the child says or does. A parent may be tempted to look or watch the child, and this attention may be enough reward for the child to continue the behavior. To be effective punishment, then, ignoring must be complete. Ignoring is best for behaviors that may be annoying but are not harmful to anyone. For example, children's whining, sulking, or pouting behavior can be ignored. Some experts put temper tantrums in the category of behavior that is best ignored. Although a parent might start out by ignoring a temper tantrum, some children work themselves into such an emotional and physical state that they cannot bring the tantrum to an end. Children can frighten themselves with the intensity of a tantrum. Parents may then want to be more active and use the strategy of time out described later in this section.

A second punishment is **social disapproval**. Parents express in a few words, spoken in a firm voice with a disapproving facial expression, that they do not like the behavior. For example, when a child dawdles, rather than clearing the table after dinner, a parent can say firmly, looking directly at the child with a serious expression, "It's time for the table to be cleared." Parents sometimes make the mistake of requesting behavior in a pleading tone of voice which suggests that the child may or may not comply. Hearing this tone, children know the parent does not mean business and do not comply. Words, physical gestures, and facial expressions must consistently make the point that the behavior is not approved of for change to occur.

When children do not change behavior their parents have disapproved of, parents can institute a **consequence**—removing a privilege, using the time-out strategy, or imposing extra work. When families have contracts, children agree to carry out specified chores or behaviors in exchange for privileges. When certain behaviors do not occur, children lose privileges. For example, TV time is linked to the completion of chores or homework. When homework or chores are not finished by a certain time, there is no TV. If a child does not bring home an acceptable school report about classroom behavior, no friends may stay overnight that weekend.

Time out (Box 4-3) is a method best used for aggressive, destructive, or dangerous behaviors. It serves to stop the disapproved behavior, giving the child a chance to cool off and, sometimes, to think about the rule violation. There are variations on the time-out method: The child can be requested to sit in a chair in the corner, but many children get up. If the child is required to face the corner, parents can keep the young child in the corner for the stated time. With older children, parents may want to add the rule that if the child does not comply with time out for one parent during the day, making the presence of both parents necessary, then the child will spend twice the amount of time in time out. Parents may feel facing the corner or the wall has little negative value because the time involved is only a few minutes. Time out has symbolic value, however. It demonstrates to children that parents are in control; certain behaviors are not permitted, and children will suffer consequences if they do them. Time out excludes the child from the social group for a certain period. Even though the time is short, children dislike being excluded.

It is best to have only two or three behaviors requiring time out at any one time. Otherwise, a child may be in the corner a great deal of time for too many different things. Further, it is important that both parents and all caregivers agree on the two or three things that will lead to time out so the child gets consistent punishment.

Many experts have found that sending a child to his or her room or being grounded there for a period is not effective punishment because the child can find

◆

BOX 4-3
USING TIME OUT FOR MISBEHAVIOR

1. Make a request in a firm but pleasant voice. Do not beg or shout.
2. Count silently to 5. Do not let the child know you are counting.
3. If the child has not started to comply in 5 seconds, look the child in the eye and say firmly, "If you don't _____, then you are going to stand in the corner."
4. Count silently to 5. Do not let the child know you are counting.
5. If the child has not begun to comply, take the child firmly by the hand or arm and say clearly and loudly, "You did not do as you were told, so you will have to stand in the corner."
6. No matter what the child promises, begs, screams, or yells, he or she goes directly to the corner. There is no going to the bathroom or getting a drink. Do not argue with the child.
7. Face the child to the wall and say, "Now you stay here for _____ minutes." If the child leaves the corner, return the child to the corner and stand behind him or her so that leaving the corner is not possible.
8. When the time is up, say, "Now you may _____" (state the positive behavior).
9. If the unacceptable behavior recurs, start the process again.
10. Following the punishment, praise the next positive behavior with positive feedback. Never punish more than you praise.

Where should the corner be? Choose a dull corner—in the hall or dining room where there are no toys or distractions, no TV. You should be able to see the child.

How long in the corner? Young children under four can spend a few minutes. Children between the ages of five and eight can spend 5 to 10 minutes, and children over eight may require between 10 and 30 minutes. A general rule is that the child spends the same number of minutes as his or her age. While he or she is in the corner, the child misses whatever is happening—a meal, TV.

Adapted from Russell A. Barkley, *Hyperactive Children* (New York: Guilford, 1981), pp. 328–330.

many enjoyable things to do there. So, as children get older, extra work and chores may be substituted for grounding. One boy was consistently sent to his room for lying, where he read and listened to his tapes. His lying continued. But he decidedly disliked the negative consequence of raking leaves for 20 minutes for every lie he told, and when this punishment was given, his behavior improved.

The last punishment we will consider is **spanking**. In one study of 150 families, 148 had used spanking at least once.[12] Thus, almost all parents spank their children at some time, but there are problems with using it as a regular form of discipline. First, if parents rely heavily on spanking for discipline, children may behave well only under threat of physical punishment. When away from the spanking parents, children may run wild. Second, children who come from homes where physical punishment is frequently used tend to be more physically aggressive than their peers, and this aggressiveness creates further problems. Most parents use physical punishment only in extreme situations that involve safety—running into the street or trying to get out of a moving car.

When parents use punishments, they are sometimes thrown off track by the child's comment: "I don't care. That doesn't bother me." Parents then give up the punishment, thinking the child does not mind it. The child's comment, however, is often an attempt to save face and be in control when she feels just exactly the opposite. Some children may use the comment to get their parents to stop the punishment. So parents must not be misled by their children's statements of unconcern. Continue to apply the negative consequence.

MANAGING CHILDREN'S BEHAVIOR IN PUBLIC PLACES

Parents feel vulnerable when their children refuse to follow rules in public places. Embarrassed parents imagine that onlookers are highly critical of their attempts to control their children and judge the parents as cruel, incompetent, unloving, and unfair. Many of these imagined criticisms are thoughts they themselves have had observing parents and children before having children of their own. The experienced, effective parent is more likely to feel sympathetic, however, since almost all parents have had to deal with this situation.

Managing behavior in public places pulls together most of the principles of modifying children's behavior. First, parents fit the demands of the situation to the child's individual temperament and condition that day. If a child has a cold and is irritable, that is not the day for a family dinner at an expensive restaurant with a long wait for service; that may be the day for fast food. If a child has been active all morning, that is not the day for a long shopping trip to a department store. Before entering a public place, remind the child of the rules; if the child is young, have him or her repeat them to you. Provide the child with activities in the public place. If it is the grocery store, let the child help get the purchases off the shelf. If it is a restaurant, give the child a drawing pad and pencil to occupy time.

Parents model desired behavior. They show children how to do the approved behaviors—put a napkin in their lap, eat slowly, engage in conversation. Parents give praise and attention, perhaps even a reward, for good behavior—a special dessert, a desired food at the store. When rules are violated, the parent immediately takes action. If a child throws food at a restaurant, gets out of the chair to run around, or leaves the parent in the store, immediate action follows. Parents can express disapproval or immediately take the child to the rest room to do time out in a corner. One family solved the problem by carrying a picture of the time-out chair at home with them. When the child began to violate the rules, parents got out the picture and told the child there would be so many minutes in the chair as soon as they got home if the disapproved behavior did not cease. The behavior stopped.

LEVELS OF INTERVENTION

Martin Hoffman[13] identified three kinds of disciplinary techniques—power-assertion, withdrawal of love, and induction. Power-assertive techniques rely on parental force and include physical punishment, parental commands, threats, and removal of privileges. These methods obtain quick results and are effective in the short term when, for example, a child is about to run into the street or hit another child. They do not, however, help build internal controls in the child so the child complies only when force or the observing parent is present.[14]

Withdrawal of love techniques involve parental disapproval of the child and loss of love when the child violates a rule. They, too, are effective in the short term as the child experiences fear or anxiety and stops the behavior, but they do not help the child learn internal controls and may only increase the child's need for approval from others.[15]

Inductive methods rely on controlling the child's behavior through reasoning and helping the child understand the effects of the behavior on others and their feelings. While they may not stop behavior as quickly as the other two methods, inductive methods enable the child to incorporate parents' standards so approved behavior continues even when parents are not there.[16]

Eleanor Maccoby and John Martin describe the cyclical nature of parents' disciplinary techniques and children's responses to them.[17] Benign cycles occur when parents are warm and involved with children, sensitive to their needs. Children develop secure attachments, are cooperative, and respond to parents' requests with minimal pressure. Parents are pleased and are more likely to grant children's requests, increasing children's cooperation. In a similar fashion, vicious cycles can develop when parents are irritable and/or use power-assertive techniques that get children's immediate compliance but do not build internal controls that prevent continuing misbehavior. So, the parent will then have to use more power-assertion.

How do parents select these different techniques? Most parents use a combination, but parents develop beliefs about the effectiveness of inductive, authoritative methods as opposed to power-assertive, authoritarian methods.[18] Often parents react in terms of these beliefs.[19] As noted in Chapter 3, however, a parent's affect is perhaps a more important determiner of the choice. When parents are under stress, are angry or upset, they are more likely to use power-assertion. This is true with depressed mothers as well. Even though many believed in the importance of low-power techniques, their resentment of the child and the parenting role determined the choice of their parenting behaviors, not their beliefs.[20]

Stresses and affect need not be marked to have an effect. Parenting hassles involving normal children's challenging behavior like whining, demandingness, and resisting routines can distress parents and lead to less satisfied parenting and less functional parenting behavior.[21] Friendship and support from other parents help to minimize the effects of the hassles.

So, choice of technique is related to beliefs about its effectiveness, but more importantly to parents' emotional reactions and the degree of normal daily stress in people's lives.

PROBLEM-SOLVING APPROACH

When children develop difficulties, parents have greatest success when they take action. We recommend a seven-step approach to handling difficulties.

First, parents must identify the child's behavior or concern and describe it specifically. For example, "She does not take out the garbage," not "She is lazy." Then observe when and how often the behavior takes place. Does it happen with one parent and not the other? How often does it happen? When instances are actually counted, the behavior may not occur as often as parents believe. At the end of this step parents have valuable information on the occurrence of the behavior, information that can tell them why it happens and how they can stop it.

Before taking any action, however, parents must go through a step of self-questioning to determine whether the behavior represents a real problem. Parents must ask themselves whether they are taking out frustrations in another area of their lives—marriage, work, extended family—on the child, preferring to see the child's behavior as the problem rather than something in their own lives.

If convinced that the child's behavior is really of concern, parents must ask themselves whether their expectations of a child are realistic for that child at that time. Sometimes, especially with firstborns, parents expect more than a child can do, or they may expect more than that particular child can do. The parent must also ask whether the behavior may be a child's temporary reaction to some special stress, thus not a matter of permanent concern. For example, when a new sibling comes, when the family moves, or when the child changes school, temporary changes in the child's functioning may occur as a result of stress. Although it is important to be aware of the behavior change, the parent may not want to define it as a problem but rather as a temporary indication that the child needs special support during a stressful period.

Once the parent is convinced a problem exists that requires action, the third step involves eliciting the child's point of view on the behavior. If the child is an infant, the parent will have to observe and guess what the child is thinking or feeling, a technique we will discuss further in Chapter 5. But when children are older, a parent should always get their view of what the problem is. They may have the answer to the difficulty themselves. For example, a single mother was about to bring her daughter to a counselor because she could not get her to bed at night. She decided to ask the six-year-old first what would help get her to bed. The child suggested two stories before bed and a chance to look at books in bed before sleep. The mother followed the girl's suggestion and the problem ended.

The fourth step is to pay positive attention to the child while solving the problem. When trouble strikes, parents sometimes become so frustrated that they focus narrowly on the difficulty and overlook all the child's competent, enjoyable behaviors. Thus it is important to spend leisure time with the child, playing games or going on an outing, to gain a more balanced, positive picture of the relationship with the child.

The fifth step is carrying out some intervention to change the child's behavior. Intervention may take the form of setting and enforcing a limit, but it could well be some other action. Providing encouragement when the child is discouraged in mastering new tasks and teaching a new behavior are two examples of interventions to stimulate a change. Sometimes two interventions are carried out at the same time. For example, if a child in third grade lacks friends, the parent might want to increase the child's self-confidence by getting swim lessons and inviting a friend's son over for play to give the child increased social experience.

The sixth step is evaluating the results of the intervention. How successful was it? Try the intervention for two weeks and then count the undesirable behaviors again. Has there been a decrease? If not, go on to the seventh step: starting over again with a new intervention. In the process of trying one intervention, the problem often emerges more clearly and a more effective way of dealing with it comes to mind. For example, in dealing with fights between brothers, a parent may learn that the older boy is frustrated in school and takes out his feelings on his little brother after school during the week. The problem then changes from one of sibling fights to a scholastic problem. The problem-solving approach resumes within this new framework.

To review, the problem-solving approach has seven steps:

1. Identify the problem specifically; observe when and how often it occurs.
2. Question yourself on the reality of the problem.
3. Get the child's point of view.
4. Spend pleasurable time daily with the child.
5. Carry out an intervention.
6. Evaluate the results of the intervention.
7. Start over again, if necessary.

And remember: Changing a child's behavior requires patience and practice from the parent.

A problem-solving approach to difficulties is useful because, as we saw in Chapter 1, parents' circumstances vary and may require different behaviors from the child. For example, when both parents of young children work outside the home, they may have to direct problem-solving skills to morning routines so that everyone leaves home at an early hour in a reasonable mood.

Parents may be members of religious and ethnic groups that value certain behaviors not stressed in the majority culture. A problem-solving approach enables parents to encourage their group's desired qualities. For example, American culture emphasizes developing independence and having many social ties in the community. Yet many ethnic groups value interdependence and close emotional ties with extended family members. Parents who want children to be close and depend primarily on the extended family for social activities can use problem-solving techniques to achieve these goals.

Parents often wish there could be a single solution to each kind of problem situation—one way to handle temper tantrums, one way to deal with refusals to eat, one way to deal with teenagers' rebelliousness. There is no formula that all parents can use to raise all children because each child as well as each parent is a unique individual.

A behavior problem can originate in several ways, and the source of the problem will influence the solution. For example, a four-year-old boy may suddenly refuse to go to bed. Exploration with the child may reveal he is fearful, and reassurance about the absence of monsters may enable him to resume his regular bedtime. Another child may have the same problem, but it may stem from her need for extra attention after the arrival of a new baby brother. Her parents may decide to spend more time with her in the evening after the new baby has gone to bed for the night. Perhaps delaying the older child's bedtime for another 15 minutes spent in play may be all that is required.

A child's age is an important factor when parents are trying to determine the best approach to a particular problem. The same problem will require different approaches at different ages as well as with different children.

Each parent is also a unique individual. One parent may find unacceptable the strategy that another parent finds effective. Some parents are not comfortable with as much confusion, noise, and disorganization as others. They may insist on very clear-cut limits, regularly enforced, while other parents will prefer greater flexibility. Each parent needs to be aware of his or her own reactions to techniques and to decide which techniques are most useful in achieving the desired family atmosphere.

The complexity of using childrearing strategies increases when we realize that children may not be learning by the strategy parents are using. Jane Loevinger, in a perceptive and humorous article, illustrates this problem with the example of a five-year-old who hits his younger brother.[22] The parent who punishes the older child with a spanking may actually be teaching that child that it is permissible to use physical aggression to obtain one's ends. The parent who uses reason and logic in dealing with the older boy may find that the child, seeing that no punishment follows hitting, is likely to do it again.

Why use a strategy—why not just do whatever comes to mind at the time? Because, says Loevinger, those children who have the most difficulties growing up and functioning are raised by parents who are impulsive, self-centered, and unable to follow a set of guidelines. "The chief value of a parental theory," writes Loevinger, "may well be in providing a model for the child of curbing one's own impulses out of regard for the future welfare of another."[23]

THE CHALLENGE OF LEARNING

When parents have growing children, they would be wise to take up a new hobby or athletic activity periodically. Learning a new skill themselves, they can appreciate how slow the process of learning can be and how frustrating it is to want to improve and still make mistakes. Parents will gain a greater appreciation of their children's sturdiness when they realize, that if learning is hard for parents with mature motor and intellectual skills, how difficult must it be for children learning many skills with bodies and minds that are still developing. Further, children are surrounded by others who seem able to do what is required rather easily. That children are as cheerful and patient as they are is a testament to their basic good nature.

DEVELOPMENTAL CHANGES AND PARENTING BEHAVIOR

We have devoted the last two chapters in a general way to two major parental tasks—establishing close emotional relationships and modifying children's behavior.

Eleanor Maccoby summarizes the parental tasks at each age as follows:

In infancy, the parent's function is mainly one of caregiving, and this includes helping the infant to regulate its own bodily functions. During the preschool years, children are learning to regulate their own affective states, and parents are contributing to this, partly through their direct dealings with the child's emotional outbursts, but also by regulating the rate at which the child is exposed to new experiences. In this period, parents do a great deal of monitoring of the child's moment-to-moment activities and provide much direct feedback. During the school-aged years, the amount of direct contact between parent and child diminishes greatly; parental monitoring is more distal. In a sense, much of it involves monitoring the child's self-monitoring. The child must now join the family system as a contributor, a cooperative interactor. In simpler societies, this middle-childhood period is the time during which children begin to participate in family survival enterprises: caring for domestic animals, doing some work in the fields, getting wood and water, caring for younger children. In our own society, children's labor is not needed, and their task is to become educated. Nevertheless, they are able to contribute to the functioning of the family. In adolescence, the child is becoming heavily involved in the larger society outside the family, but the family still has the function in providing both guidance and support for the child's entrance into these larger spheres.[24]

Not only will we look at the parent's task in relation to the child, but we must also examine the stages parents themselves go through as they rear their children. We focus on parents' feelings, frustrations, and pleasures and discuss ways of maximizing the enjoyment of parenting. Parenting is a process that goes beyond meeting daily needs and solving problems. Thus, we need an overview of development so that we may nurture children to realize their full potential.

When we combine the problem-solving approach with the parental qualities and behaviors all strategies advise—modeling of desired traits, respect for the child's and one's own needs, confidence that the child can learn what is necessary, sharing of problems and solutions in family meetings—then parents can effectively foster the growth and development of their children. Each individual has a unique potential to discover and develop. Arnold Gesell and Frances Ilg state it well:

> When asked to give the very shortest definition of life, Claude Bernard, a great physiologist, answered, "Life is creation." A newborn baby is the consummate product of such creation. And he in turn is endowed with capacities for continuing creation. These capacities are expressed not only in the growth of his physique, but in the simultaneous growth of a psychological self. From the sheer standpoint of creation this psychological self must be regarded as his masterpiece. It will take a lifetime to finish, and in the first ten years he will need a great deal of help, but it will be his own product.[25]

Parents have the privilege of serving as guide and resource as their child creates a unique "psychological self."

MAJOR POINTS OF CHAPTER 4

Children learn when:

- new signals are associated with already existing responses
- new associations are made between stimuli and responses on the basis of positive and negative consequences
- they observe models and imitate them

Parents set stage for learning by developing realistic expectations of the child based on:

- goals of the parent
- child's age
- child's particular characteristics and needs
- health and safety issues
- family's needs and values
- events of the day

Parents help children meet expectations when they:

- structure the physical environment with hooks for clothes, storage space for possessions
- establish a regular routine that takes account of children's tempo so they can anticipate what is going to happen and cooperate
- monitor stimulation so children are prepared for difficult situations and are prevented from overexcitement that leads to their falling apart
- take an active role in teaching children by shaping new approved behaviors

Rewards are:

- those actions that increase the likelihood a behavior will occur again
- always present whether recognized or not
- available in many forms from social attention and approval to privileges and material rewards like money and tokens that can be exchanged for privileges
- most useful when given in the form of positive social attention

Parents set limits most effectively when they:

- state rules as clear, objective, positive statements of what they want
- explain the purpose of the rule
- focus on the most important rules of health and safety first, then rules that ease social living
- are consistent with rules and back each other up
- discuss differences of opinion about the rules away from the children and arrive at a joint decision
- offer children options whenever possible
- give a child a chance to prepare for a new activity

When children do not follow rules, parents have many techniques for enforcing the rules. Parents can:

- use a mutual problem-solving session with all family members to arrive at a solution agreeable to all—this may or may not be put in the form of a contract

- remain detached and let the natural consequences of the act teach the child—parents may have to devise logical consequences if no natural ones arise
- take action to enforce limits, accepting the child's disappointment in not having his or her own way and showing how, if possible, the child can get his or her way
- use punishments to decrease the likelihood of the behavior's happening again—for example, ignoring, taking away privileges, requiring time out, and rarely, if at all, spanking

Managing children's behavior in public places involves:

- setting realistic expectations for child
- parents' modeling of appropriate behavior
- rewarding positive behaviors
- giving negative consequences for misbehavior

Disciplinary techniques:

- can be divided into three main kinds—power assertion, withdrawal of love, and induction
- can create benign or vicious cycles in which parents' response tends to perpetuate the child's response, and the child's response perpetuates the parents'
- are often more determined by parents' emotional states than their beliefs about the effectiveness of the technique
- are affected by minor parenting stress
- are modified by having the support and friendship of other parents

The seven steps of the problem-solving approach are:
- identifying the problem
- self-questioning by the parent
- eliciting the child's point of view
- spending enjoyable time with the child
- taking action
- evaluating the action
- starting again if necessary

The advantages of the problem-solving approach are:
- parents can take account of the individual characteristics of the child
- parents can retain their own goals and values for their children's behavior

Parents' behavior changes with the age of the child:

- in infancy, parents are caregivers
- in preschool, parents monitor activities and give immediate feedback
- in school years, parents help children become self-monitors who can guide their own behavior and be cooperative members of the family
- in adolescence, parents help children engage in the larger society

To help children develop caring, prosocial behavior, parents:

- provide a nurturant, warm home atmosphere
- are models of caring and ethical behavior the child can imitate
- use reasoning in talking about rules
- arouse the child's empathy for the distress the child has caused in another person
- involve the child in altruistic behavior
- reward caring behavior with attention
- shun power techniques like spanking
- discuss moral issues and actions so the child learns a code of rules that can be applied in new situations

EXERCISES

1. Write a description of the disciplinary techniques you can recall your parents used with you in elementary school years and high school. How would you characterize your parents' methods and how did you respond to them?

2. Choose some behavior you want to increase—for example, regular exercise—and work out a reward system to increase that behavior. Chart the frequency of the desired behavior before and during the reward system. If time permits, observe the frequency for a week after you stop the reward system. Share your experiences with classmates. What kinds of rewards have been most successful in helping you and other students increase desired behavior?

3. Choose some behavior you want to decrease. Chart the occurrence of the behavior before any intervention. Then choose a negative consequence that will occur after every repetition of the undesired behavior. If you wish, at the same time choose to reward a substitute behavior. Then monitor the occurrence of the undesired behavior. If time permits, observe the frequency of the behaviors after you have stopped the consequences. For example, you may decide you want to decrease procrastination in going to the library. Decide that every time you postpone going to the library for five minutes or longer, you will have to stay at the library an extra thirty minutes. If you go to the library on time, permit yourself to leave ten minutes early.

4. Observe parents and children together at a playground or in the grocery store or other public place. Select pairs of children of approximately the same age and contrast how their parents treat them. Are the parents similar in behavior? What theories of learning do they appear to be using? What parental behaviors seem effective with the children? Observing five minutes with each child, time how often the parent intervenes to maintain or change the child's behavior.

5. Select a friend's behavior that you wish to change. Devise a system of rewards or a system of positive/negative consequences to change the behavior then carry it out for five weeks and note the change. For example, you might decide to change a friend's habit of being late for meetings or of not calling when he or she says.

ADDITIONAL READINGS

Becker, Wesley. *Parents Are Teachers.* Champaign, Ill.: Research Press, 1971.

Dinkmeyer, Don, and McKay, Gary D. *The Parent's Handbook.* Circle Pines, Minn.: American Guidance Service, 1989.

Dreikurs, Rudolf, with Soltz, Vicki. *Children: The Challenge.* New York: Hawthorn, 1964.

Nelson, Jane. *Positive Discipline.* New York: Ballantine, 1987.

Patterson, Gerald R. *Living With Children.* Rev. ed. Champaign, Ill.: Research Press, 1977.

Notes

1. Rudolf Dreikurs with Vicki Soltz, *Children: The Challenge* (New York: Hawthorn, 1964).

2. Thomas Gordon, *P.E.T. Parent Effectiveness Training* (New York: New American Library, 1975).

3. Robert Eimers and Robert Aitchison, *Effective Parents/Responsible Children* (New York: McGraw-Hill, 1977).

4. Ibid.

5. Eli Soltz, Sarah Campbell, and David Scotko, "Verbal Control of Behavior: The Effects of Shouting," *Developmental Psychology* 19 (1983): 461–464.

6. Haim G. Ginott, *Between Parent and Child* (New York: Avon, 1969).

7. Larry P. Nucci and Elliot Turiel, "Social Interactions and the Development of Social Concepts in Preschool Children," *Child Development* 49 (1978): 400–407.

8. Gordon, *P.E.T.*

9. Eimers and Aitchison, *Effective Parents/Responsible Children.*

10. Dreikurs with Soltz, *Children: The Challenge.*

11. Ginott, *Between Parent and Child.*

12. Diana Baumrind, "The Development of Instrumental Competence through Socialization," in *Minnesota Symposia on Child Psychology,* vol. 7, ed. Ann D. Pick (Minneapolis: University of Minnesota Press, 1973), pp. 3–46.

13. Martin L. Hoffman, "Moral Internalization, Parental Power, and the Nature of Parent-Child Interaction," *Developmental Psychology* 5 (1967): 45–57.

14. Eleanor E. Maccoby and John A. Martin, "Socialization in the Context of the Family: Parent-Child Interaction," in *Handbook of Child Psychology,* eds. Paul H. Mussen and E. Mavis Hetherington, vol. 4: *Socialization, Personality and Social Development,* 4th ed. (New York: John Wiley, 1983), pp. 1–101.

15. Ibid.

16. Ibid.

17. Ibid.

18. Rosemary S. L. Mills and Kenneth H. Rubin, "Parental Beliefs about Problematic Social Behaviors in Early Childhood," *Child Development* 61 (1990): 138–151.

19. Ann V. McGillicuddy-De Lisi, "Parental Beliefs within the Family Context: Development of a Research Program," in *Methods of Family Research: Biographies of Research Projects, vol. 1: Normal Families,* eds. Irving E. Sigel and Gene H. Brody (Hillsdale, N. J.: Lawrence Erlbaum Associates, 1990), pp. 53–85.

20. Grazyna Kochanska, "Maternal Beliefs as Long-Term Predictors of Mother-Child Interaction and Report," *Child Development 61* (1990): 1934–1943.

21. Keith A. Crnic and Mark T. Greenberg, "Minor Parenting Stresses with Young Children," *Child Development 61* (1990): 1628–1637.

22. Jane Loevinger, "Patterns of Parenthood as Theories of Learning," *Journal of Abnormal and Social Psychology 59* (1959): 148–150.

23. Ibid., p. 150.

24. Eleanor Maccoby, "Socialization and Developmental Changes," *Child Development 55* (1984): pp. 324–325.

25. Arnold Gesell and Frances L. Ilg, *The Child From Five to Ten* (New York: Harper & Row, 1946), p. 308.

INFANCY AND EARLY CHILDHOOD

C H A P T E R 5

Introducing an infant into a household creates a true full-time job—24-hour-a-day, 365-days a year. How can you prepare for the parenting task? What adjustments must you make in your lifestyle? What can you do to form a positive relationship with a helpless, demanding infant or young child? Since it is largely through healthy interactions with parents that children form positive self-concepts and learn to relate to other people in satisfying ways, how should you interact with your child? By hearing what actual parents wish they had known about infancy, toddlerhood, and preschool years and by anticipating and preparing for children's unregulated emotions, you can enhance your parent/child relationship and focus on the joys of being parent to an infant or young child.

TRANSITION AND ADJUSTMENT TO PARENTHOOD

The arrival of a baby changes every aspect of married life, from finances to sex life, sleeping habits, and social life. The positive changes—having a baby to love, feeling closer to the other parent, sharing the joys of the child's growth—are easy to incorporate. The negative changes require adaptation. Although many first-time parents report that nothing could have adequately prepared them for the experience, knowing what to expect in advance can still help parents cope.

The mother's adjustment to pregnancy, birth, childcare in the first year, and the baby's functioning is predicted from her adaptation to the pregnancy itself.[1] Women who feel positive about the pregnancy, who envision themselves as confident mothers, do indeed adjust more easily to being a mother. Further, their babies seem more competent in social, motor, and cognitive skills. What predicts the mother's positive view of pregnancy? According to current research, in the main it is her own experiences with her parents as she was growing up. These relationships are not absolutely fixed; a woman who had a difficult time as a child will not necessarily be destined to repeat it. Many parents make strong, successful efforts to avoid repeating and passing on parenting behaviors they experienced as children. They feel satisfaction and pleasure at creating the family they would like to have had when they were children. Information on child growth and development and strategies for establishing relationships and positive behavior provide tools for interrupting a negative cycle that began in childhood.

The marital relation affects each parent, the way the parent relates to the baby, and how the baby grows and develops. It is not just that psychologically mature people make happy marriages and parent well. Recent research shows that a happy marriage improves parenting, even when psychological adjustment is controlled.[2]

When mothers and fathers feel support from each other, they are more competent parents and interact with the baby more effectively. Father-infant interactions and fathers' competence, particularly, is related to feeling support from mothers. Even basic activities are influenced by the quality of the marriage. Mothers feed babies more competently when their husbands are supportive and view them positively, whereas marital distress is related to inept feeding by the mother.[3]

Intimate emotional spousal support is related also to parents' satisfaction with themselves in the parental role and with the baby. When parents are happy with each other, they smile at the baby more and play with the baby. Babies profit from this atmosphere of positive regard, are more alert, and have more motor skills.

Ellen Galinsky describes the first year of an infant's life as the **nurturing stage** of parenthood.[4] Parents focus on forming an attachment to the new baby, caring for the child, and accepting their new roles as parents. As they care for the child, they continue to question themselves: "Am I doing okay?" "Am I the kind of parent I want to be?" Though they devote most of their energy to the child during the first few months, gradually parents incorporate the other parts of their lives into caregiving activities. Relationships between mother and father and work activities are expanded to include the baby; relationships with other children and relatives are redefined. A great deal goes on during these early months.

It may be difficult, however, for parents to give each other the support that is so crucial in coping during this period. A significant number of new mothers report specific problems, including: (1) tiredness and exhaustion; (2) loss of sleep, especially in the first two months; (3) concern about ignoring husband's needs; (4) feeling inadequate as a mother; (5) inability to keep up with housework; and (6) feeling tied down.[5] Mothers did not anticipate the many changes that would occur in their lives when their babies arrived, in part because they did not realize how much work is involved in caring for an infant. Fathers had a similar ordering of complaints: (1) loss of sleep for up to six weeks; (2) need to adjust to new responsibilities and routines; (3) disruption of daily routines; (4) ignorance of the amount of work the baby requires; and (5) financial worries (62 percent of the wives were employed prior to the child and only 12 percent afterward). Husbands make such comments as, "My wife has less time for me" and "Getting used to being tied down is hard."

The new father may see the infant as a threat to his relationship with his wife and to their lifestyle. Concern about the amount of time and money and freedom that the baby will surely consume can obscure the joy he expects—and is expected—to feel. No more candlelit dinners, or even impromptu decisions to go to a movie or to make love, not for a while. The father has not had the physical experience of carrying the baby for nine months, nor is he as likely to be as involved as the mother in the care of the newborn. And for a while, at least, the needs of the baby will come before the

WHAT I WISH I HAD KNOWN ABOUT INFANCY

"I remember when we brought him home from the hospital, and we had him on the changing table for a minute, and I realized, 'I don't know how to keep the engine running.' I wondered how could they let him go home with us, this little package weighing seven or eight pounds. I had no idea of what to do. I kind of knew you fed him, and you cleaned him and kept him warm; but I didn't have any hands-on experience, anything practical. In a way I would have liked them to watch me for a day or two in the hospital while I changed him, to make sure I knew how to do it. It's kind of like giving me a car without seeing whether I could drive it around the block." FATHER

"I didn't have enough information about breastfeeding for two months. I almost gave up because it was so painful. I found a good breastfeeding nurse who showed me two things, and it changed the whole experience. It made such a difference, and breastfeeding became a joy." MOTHER

"I wish we had known a little more about establishing her first habits about sleeping. The way you set it up in the beginning is the way it is going to be. Having enough sleep is so important. We went too long before we decided to let her cry for five minutes. Then she got into good sleep habits." FATHER

"I had no idea how tired I would be. I'm not sure anyone can describe the level of tiredness you feel. I am getting eight hours of sleep now but I always sleep lightly and could wake up in an instant. When I wake up in the morning now, I don't feel refreshed. I'm still tired even though he is sleeping through the night." MOTHER

"I wish I had known how it would change things between me and my husband. The baby comes first, and by the time the day is over and he is in bed, we have two hours together, but I just want to curl up and take care of myself." MOTHER

"For me I had knowledge about feeding and what he would be like, and what the days would be like. I wish I had known what only experience can give you. I wish I had known how I would respond and how stressed I would be. I was sleep-deprived, and that was not easy for me. I wish I had had a mother who could be here and give me the benefit of her experience, to say, 'This is all normal, this is part of having a baby.' My mother died in the beginning of the pregnancy, and I had sisters and friends I called." MOTHER

wishes of the husband—and those needs will be frequent and unpredictable, delaying meals and interrupting sleep. But almost all fathers and mothers find that emotional attachment to their babies grows and deepens if they are patient and caring.

In the first few weeks after birth, obstetricians advise restraint from sexual intercourse. During this period the new mother is especially vulnerable to infection, her energy has been drained by pregnancy and birth, and her days and nights are devoted to care of the newborn. She is fulfilling the demand of an inarticulate and

WHAT I WISH I HAD KNOWN ABOUT TODDLERHOOD

"Someone said when you have a child, it's like two appointment books—his appointment book and yours. And first you do everything in the kid's appointment book; and then when you're done, you do everything in the kid's appointment book again. I wish I had known they weren't joking. I knew that it would be a challenge, and in some ways I wish I had known more. But in other ways I think if I had really known exactly how hard it would be sometimes, I might have been more reluctant or waited longer, and that I would really have regretted—not doing it." FATHER

"I wasn't prepared for all the decisions. Is it okay if he does this or not? He's trying to do something; shall I step in so he doesn't hurt himself or shall I let him go? It's making all those choices, making sure what I feel." MOTHER

"There is anxiety, a feeling of vulnerability I have never felt before. If he gets sick, what are we going to do? If he has a little sickness we just hope the doctor is doing the right thing. We went through a great deal in the past few weeks choosing a nursery school for him, and we hope we have done the right thing, but is this the one for him?" FATHER

"I wish we had—because he is our first child—more of a sense of the norms. What is okay versus what is a problem and what is really bad? Is this normal, is this just kids being kids? He pushed someone at school three times; is this par for the course or is this a problem? We don't know when we are reacting and when we are overreacting." FATHER

"I wish I had known how much time they needed between one and two. They are mobile, but they are clueless about judgment. I think it was one of the most difficult times. Even though she did not get into a lot of trouble sticking her finger in light sockets, still she takes a lot of time and watching, so the transition to two was great." MOTHER

very dependent creature that she perform many unfamiliar tasks along with the usual household and personal routines. The fact that lovemaking, a source of pleasure in marriage, is interrupted adds to the stress felt by both parents after childbirth. During this early period of physical and emotional adjustment, the wife—particularly the working wife—needs time to regain her stamina and to establish new routines.

Parents interviewed about easing the transition to parenthood identify six basic ingredients in promoting parental well-being: (1) giving up the illusion of being a perfect parent, (2) looking for information you can apply to your child and your living situation rather than exact prescriptions of what to do, (3) learning the art of making decisions and setting goals (setting priorities on what is most important to

WHAT I WISH I HAD KNOWN
ABOUT THE PRESCHOOL YEARS

"I wish I had known how much frustration comes just because kids are kids and
you have to be tolerant. They don't have the attention span for some things. They
might want to do something with you, but they can only do it for about fifteen
minutes. You have to go places prepared with all his things or with things to keep
him entertained. In the car on a trip, we have a lot of things for him to do. When
you plan ahead, you can still be spontaneous at times. You learn that if you are
prepared, things really don't have to be a hassle." FATHER

"Everything. I wish I'd known more about communication, how to talk to your
children, and the most effective way to help them grow with a strong ego, a good
sense of self. We were raised with a lot of 'Do this and don't do that,' a lot of
demanding and dictatorial things as opposed to trying to solicit participation in
the process of decision making, trying to get in touch with your child's feelings so
you really do understand how they feel about things. That's really hard to learn,
and I don't know how you can learn it without the experience of actually having
the child. But I'm continually learning how to understand her feelings about
things." MOTHER

"I think it is incredible that we don't teach anything about being a parent. I have to
learn it as I go along because I want things to be different for them than they were
for me growing up. I can't use my own experiences as a guide." FATHER

"I wish I had known how to handle them so they could be spontaneous and feel
good about the things they did. How to be spontaneous with them is one of the
hardest things for me." FATHER

do and following through helps restore a sense of effectiveness), (4) considering
parenthood as a series of tradeoffs and realizing that decisions to fill one member's
needs may mean that someone else has to wait, (5) not trying to assume the role of
parent without support from others, and (6) looking after yourself.[6]

Couples who are prepared for the stresses that accompany the arrival of a new
baby experience less anxiety and turmoil. Childbirth courses, parent groups, and
satisfactory marital adjustment before the birth can alleviate stress after birth. The
couple who have a realistic notion of how parenthood will change their lives will
experience less stress from unanticipated problems. And they will be more open to
experiencing joy in their new child and their new roles.

How can couples cope during this transition period? Social scientists emphasize
the importance of communicating feelings and needs in open and nonjudgmental
ways, of negotiating solutions when conflicts arise, and of sharing responsibilities for
care of the infant and for household chores.

Gordon's active listening, I-messages, and mutual problem-solving techniques are
as useful in husband-wife interactions as they are in parent-child relations. Carolyn

Cowan and Philip Cowan identified hidden challenges parents face as they establish effective patterns of communication.[7] Parents have to be able to balance their individual needs with those of the other person and the relationship. Parents can do this when they feel good about themselves and are able to see and discuss both sides of the problem. Successful communication depends on really trying to understand the other person's position—not jumping to conclusions, not reading the other person's mind, and especially not assuming negative motivations on the part of the other person. Parents who are able to accept that differences and strong feelings are bound to arise, and who are committed to finding solutions to those differences, work them out to their own and their children's benefit.

PERSONAL AND SOCIAL DEVELOPMENT

Infants are introduced to the world of human beings by their social experiences in the first year of life. Warm, supportive relationships establish feelings of security and trust in the world.

Parent-Child Relations

Bonding The first meeting between parents and child is an important occasion. In the first hour after birth, babies are more alert and visually attentive than they will be for the next three or four hours. And during that first hour they may be most responsive to contact with parents. The parents' first chance to touch, hold, and explore the baby and to receive some response in the form of the child's eye or body movement is very important.[8]

While early contact is pleasurable and starts the relationship between parents and child on a positive note, Michael Rutter is critical of the concept of bonding that suggests physical contact is essential to strengthen the attachment.[9] He points out that relationships are multifaceted and not dependent on a single sensory modality like skin contact. Relationships develop over time, and strong attachments can be formed with caregivers even if the early bonding is not possible for some reason.

Attachment to Parents

Cultural lore, literature, and psychologists have long emphasized the warmth, comfort, security, and trust the child derives from the mother-child attachment. Chapter 3 discussed forming relationships; here we discuss how a parent develops a relationship with an infant. The baby's attachment to the mother begins in the early weeks of infancy. At about five months, the baby may give joyful kicks and gurgle and laugh to engage the mother in play. If the mother has been away, the baby will lift its arms or clasp its hands in greeting when the parent returns.

At four to five months, babies show signs of apprehension in the presence of strangers—freezing, lying or sitting still, and barely breathing. At seven to eight months, they show pronounced fear of strangers, sometimes crying as an unknown person approaches. This occurs at about the same time that babies develop an aware-ness that the mother exists even when she is not physically present, and this is followed by development of fear of separation from mother and other important persons.

Attachment is a strong psychological bond to a figure who is a source of security and emotional support. By seven or eight months, babies show such attachment to parents. When parents are accepting of the child, emotionally available, sensitive to the baby's needs, and cooperative in meshing activities with the tempo of the child, then a strong, *secure attachment* develops.[10] Infants with these secure attachments explore more and are more persistent in tasks. About 65 percent of babies develop such attachments.[11]

About 35 percent of babies develop insecure attachments that are revealed in one of two ways. When parents are intrusive and overstimulate the child, babies form *anxious avoidant* attachments and avoid the parent after separation. When parents are uninvolved and unavailable, babies form *anxious resistant* attachments and alter-nately cling to the parent and push the parent away.[12]

Attachment to Both Parents Until recently, the mother-child bond was considered the only attachment of importance in infancy. As researchers have observed parent-child interactions and attachments in nuclear families, however, they have found that babies become attached to both parents, although most will seek comfort from the mother if distressed. Mothers and fathers interact differently with babies. First, mothers spend more time with infants even though a high percentage are employed in the work force.

There are differences not only in the quantity of time but also in the way parents spend time with babies.[13] Mothers, even when working, are significantly more en-gaging, responsive, stimulating, and affectionate. They are caregivers and nurturers. Fathers, on the other hand, take the role of playmates who teach children how to get along with others. Through physical play, infants and toddlers learn how to interpret others' emotional signals and how others respond to theirs so that social competence grows.[14] As children grow, mothers spend less time in caregiving, and their interac-tions with children become similar to those of fathers.

Though fathers spend less time with infants than mothers do, they are sensitive caregivers, as perceptive as mothers in adjusting their behavior to children's needs and children securely attach to them. Fathers are most likely to be highly involved in caregiving and playing when the marital relationship is satisfying and wives are relaxed and outgoing. Both fathers and mothers give most care and physical affection in the first three months when babies are settling in. As babies become less fussy and more alert at three months, both parents in turn become more stimulating and reactive.[15]

Although mothers and fathers interact differently with babies, recent observations indicate parents do not treat their sons and daughters differently in routine caregiv-ing activities at home. They give sons and daughters equal amounts of affection, stimulation, care, and responsiveness.[16]

Sex differences in parents' treatment of children aged one to five are not marked. What differences are found occur at about eighteen months of age.[17] Parents of boys give more positive attention to their aggressiveness and negative attention to their attempts to communicate. Fathers give positive responses to boys' playing with "sex-appropriate" toys and negative responses to their playing with "female" toys. Girls' aggressiveness appears to be ignored, but their attempts to communicate receive positive attention from mothers. In most ways, however, boys and girls are treated similarly.

Future Correlates of Attachment The baby uses the interactions with the attachment figure to form an internal model of the way people relate to each other in the world. The child comes to expect certain reactions on the part of adults and plans his or her own behavior accordingly. Further, the child develops a sense of personal value in the world. When attachment figures are accepting and available, then babies feel lovable and competent. Conversely, when figures are insensitive and rejecting, babies develop a sense of unworthiness.[18]

The benefits of attachment are seen not only in the present, but they extend into the future as well. Securely attached one-year-olds are more curious later in childhood; they attack a new problem vigorously and positively.[19] While they persist at a task, they are able to accept help from the mother and are not aggressive. Their mothers are supportive and helpful. Children whose attachment is tenuous are anxious, throw more tantrums when presented with problems, and are more negative in response to the mother, ignoring and opposing her in different ways.

Securely attached toddlers are outgoing well-liked preschoolers. They are sympathetic to others, suggest activities, and are able to be leaders. When involved in their own activities, they are self-directed, goal-oriented, eager to learn new skills and develop their abilities. The bond with the mother, then, increases the self-esteem and self-confidence that give the child a positive view of the world and permit exploration and satisfying interaction with others.

Children who had and continue to have anxious-avoidance attachments in infancy suffer many problems in the preschool years. They are dependent, noncompliant, hostile, impulsive, and withdrawn. Children with early and later anxious-resistant attachments lack confidence and assertiveness in their play, and they relate poorly to peers.

Parents' Contribution to Attachment Box 5-1 summarizes the research findings on parental behaviors that promote positive attachments and positive qualities in children of different ages.

As we noted in Chapter 1, parents bring their own personal histories and expectations to parenting. Mothers who reported having secure attachments with their own parents were warm, helpful, and supportive with their own preschoolers. These children, in turn, were securely attached to them and received all the benefits of that close relationship. Mothers who reported remote, detached relationships with their own parents were cool, remote, and very directive with their own children. These children were insecurely attached to them, anxious, subdued, and suffering from behavior problems. A third group consisted of mothers who were also insecurely attached to their own parents but were preoccupied with these relationships. With their own children, these parents were confusing and controlling. They were

When children have warm, secure attachments to a parent, they are more competent, out-going preschoolers.

sometimes warm and gentle, but then could be angry. Their children were negativistic and noncompliant.[20]

Mothers experiencing secure attachments reported as many negative events in their early lives as insecurely attached mothers, but they seemed to interpret them differently. They were able to focus on what was positive in the relationship and value that.

◆

BOX 5-1
QUALITIES OF PARENTS RELATED TO
POSITIVE PARENT-CHILD RELATIONSHIPS

Parents of Infants

Warm
Accepting
Involved
Emotionally available
Sensitive to baby's needs
Synchronizes behavior to baby's signals/moods
Nonrestrictive

Parents of Toddlers

Warm
Accepting
Involved
Emotionally available
Responsive to what child does
Provides safe base for exploration
Synchronizes behavior to child's state
Balances support and guidance with
 independence to promote new skills

Parents of Preschoolers

Warm
Accepting
Involved
Sensitive
Responsive to child's needs
Authoritative
Appropriately controlling, not overcontrolling

Parents who grew up with alcoholic parents have a particularly difficult time. Carolyn Cowan and Philip Cowan report that, to their surprise, 20 percent of the parents in their study grew up with an alcoholic parent. Though none reported current problems with alcohol, "On *every* index of adjustment to parenthood—symptoms of depression, self-esteem, parenting stress, role dissatisfaction, and decline in satisfaction with marriage—men and women whose parents had abused alcohol had significantly greater difficulty."[21]

Even more distressing was the generational legacy the children (the grandchildren of the alcoholics) in their study received. Parents saw their preschoolers as less successful though objective measures suggested these children functioned as well as others. "This suggests that parents who grow up with troubled and ineffective parenting develop unrealistic expectations of what they can expect of their children, and as a result, have difficulty seeing their children's behavior in a positive light."[22]

A parental expectation that can have long-term negative impact is the parent's preference for a child of a different sex. A recent longitudinal Swedish study documented that when both parents wanted a child of the opposite sex, that child experienced difficulties.[23] Parents played less with the child; mothers reported children had more problems. Children were aware they were not the preferred sex and could report this clearly when they were adults. Father-daughter relations were particularly troubled when the father would have preferred a son.

Parents, as we have pointed out, are not doomed to repeat patterns of behavior they do not like. At any point in the pattern, they can act to break negative cycles with education, psychological interventions, and concerted effort.

Babies' Contribution to Attachment   In addition to parents' behavior, other qualities influence attachment. As we noted in Chapter 1, a baby comes with his or her own temperament that can influence the ease of establishing and maintaining the relationship. Temperament is defined as constitutionally based biases towards certain moods and ways of reacting.[24] Activity level, rhythmicity (regularity, eating, sleeping), fussiness, distractibility, readiness to adapt to new situations, attention span, intensity of response, threshold of sensory stimulation (how quickly aware of outside stimuli), and persistence in responding are commonly identified dimensions.

Parents are curious to know how long and to what degree these early differences persist. Research has focused mostly on stability of activity level, irritability, fearfulness, and shyness. All babies are in an unsettled state for about the first three months. Differences noted very early in this period may disappear as babies' behavior becomes more organized. Nevertheless, research has found that a small cluster of this group seem to maintain early differences. For example, vigor of neonatal movements in the newborn nursery was related to children's daytime activity level when the children were between four and eight years of age. Active neonates were still perceived by parents at ages four to eight as outgoing and quick to approach new experiences.[25]

Early difficult temperament, measured at six months, predicted difficult temperament at thirteen and twenty-four months and behavior problems when the child was three years old.[26] While early crying and fussiness did not endure, irritability at age seven months tended to endure for the next year or two. Shyness appeared to be a temperamental quality that endures and is related both to genetic influences and to social experiences in the family. So shyness and low sociability appearing by the end of the first year seem to be enduring and are related to both genetic and environmental influences.[27]

Thus, differences among babies appear early. As the nervous system settles down in the first three to six months of life, some of these differences disappear. A small number of certain behaviors, however—such as vigorous response—will persist. Whether such differences persist will depend in part on the ways parents interact with their infants. These differences do not dictate the security or insecurity of the attachment, but they do make special demands on a parent's sensitivity.[28]

Crying

All babies cry. This distresses parents and can create stress in the growing relationship. There are great individual differences, however. In newborn nurseries, babies
cried from 1 to 11 minutes per hour. The average daily total per baby was about two
hours of crying. Researchers who classified reasons found hunger was a significant
cause, as well as wet or dirty diapers. The largest single category, however, was
"unknown reason." It may be that crying expressed a social need for cuddling,
warmth, or rhythmic motion.[29]

Babies' crying increases to an average of about 3 hours at six weeks and decreases
to an average of 1 hour per day at about three months. Though hunger seems a predominant reason, unknown causes remain the second highest category. As crying
increases, it comes to be concentrated in the late afternoon or evening hours, with
little during the day.

Sylvia Bell and Mary Ainsworth[30] conducted a thorough study of crying in the
first year of life and found that babies had as many crying episodes at the end of the
year as at the beginning, but they spent much less time in each episode. Mothers
tended to be consistent in how much they ignored the baby's crying, and there were
marked differences among the mothers. One mother ignored only 4 percent of the
cries, and one mother ignored 97 percent. Although each mother's behavior was consistent from quarter to quarter, the crying of each baby was not consistent until the
last two quarters.

How does the baby's crying relate to the mother's behavior? In the first quarter,
there was no relationship. In the second quarter, a trend appeared and was significant in the third and fourth quarters. Those mothers who responded immediately to
the cries of the baby had babies who cried less! Conversely, ignoring a baby's cries
seemed to increase the amount of crying as measured by frequency and duration.
Those mothers who responded most at the beginning of the year had less to respond
to at the end of the year.

What strategy is most effective in terminating crying? Picking up and holding the
baby stopped the crying in 80 percent of the situations in which it occurred. Feeding,
which involves physical contact, was almost as effective. The least effective method
was to stand at a distance and talk to the child. Judy Dunn reviews ways of providing comfort to crying babies and finds that caregivers around the world soothe by
"rocking, patting, cuddling, swaddling, giving suck on breast or pacifier."[31] Effective
techniques provide a background of continuous or rhythmic—as opposed to variable—sensations for the child. For example, constant temperatures, continuous
sounds, and rhythmic rocking at a steady rate reduce the amount of time the infant
cries. Effective soothing techniques also reduce the amount of stimulation the baby
receives from his or her own movements. Thus, holding and swaddling reduce sensations from the child's flailing arms and legs and thus decrease crying.

Physicians Urs Hunziker and Ronald Barr recently speculated that American
babies might be more content and cry less if they were carried more, as babies are
in other cultures.[32] They studied two groups of mothers and babies—one group
consisted of mothers who received infant carriers and carried babies three extra
hours per day, when babies were not crying as well as when babies were crying; the

INTERVIEW
with Jacqueline Lerner and Richard Lerner

Richard Lerner is director of The Institute for Children, Youth, and Families at Michigan State University, and Jacqueline V. Lerner is professor of psychology at Michigan State University.

Parents are interested in temperament and what this means for them as parents. What happens if they have a baby with a difficult temperament that is hard for them to deal with? Is this fixed? Will they have to keep coping with it?

R. Lerner: We don't believe temperament necessarily is fixed. We believe that temperament is a behavioral style and can, and typically does, show variation across a person's life. We're interested in the meaning of temperament for the person and the family in daily life.

J. Lerner: Although we know temperament is present at birth, we don't say that it is exclusively constitutionally derived. Temperament interacts with the environment. We find children who do seem to stay fairly difficult and children who stay fairly easy. Most children change, even from year to year. Given this, we can't possibly believe that temperament ever becomes fixed unless what happens in the family becomes fixed.

R. Lerner: What we are concerned with are individual differences. They are identifiable at birth, but they change, we believe, in relation to the child's living situation. We find that what one parent might call difficult is well below the threshold of another parent's level of tolerance for difficulty. What some people find easy, others find quite annoying.

In fact, you can find in our case studies examples of how difficult children ended up developing in a particular context that reinterpreted their difficulty as artistic creativity. One girl picked up a musical instrument at age thirteen or fourteen and began playing. She had a gift for that. Prior to that, she had a difficult relation with her father who found her temperamental style totally abhorrent to him. As soon as she had this emerging talent, he said, "Oh, my daughter is an artist. This is an artistic temperament." They reinterpreted the first thirteen years of their relationship, believing they had always been close.

We believe the importance of temperament lies in what we call "goodness of fit" between the child's qualities and what the environment demands. The child brings characteristics to the parent-child relationship, but parents have to understand what they bring and how they create the meaning of the child's individuality by their own temperaments, and their demands, attitudes, and evaluations. Moreover, I think parents should understand that both they and the child have many other influences on them—friends, work, or school.

When you think about the fit with the environment, how do you think about the environment, what is it?

R. Lerner: We have divided demands from the environment into three broad categories: physical characteristics of the setting, the behavioral characteristics of the environment, and the behaviorial and psychological characteristics of the other important people in the child's life.

J. Lerner: The setting has physical characteristics, and the people have behavioral characteristics and demands, attitudes, and values.

R. Lerner: Parents need to understand the demands of the context (the living situation) they present to the child by means of their own values and behavioral style. Even the features of the physical environment the parents provide can affect the child's fit with the context. Parents need to understand there are numerous features of the context; and because of the child's individuality, a better or lesser fit will emerge. For example, if your child has a low threshold of reactivity and a high intensity of reactions, you don't want to put that child's bedroom next to a busy street. If you have a choice, you'll put that child's bedroom in the back of the house or won't let the child study in any part of the house where he or she will get distracted.

A poor fit also occurs if you have a child who is very arrhythmic and you demand regularity, not necessarily as a verbal demand but perhaps in the way you schedule your life. You begin to prepare breakfast every morning at 8:00, the bagel comes out at 8:05 and disappears at 8:15, and some days the child makes it and some days not. The parents have to see how they may be doing things that create poorness of fit. It's not just their verbal demands but also their behavioral demands and the physical set-up of the house.

J. Lerner: Some parents don't see what they are reinforcing and what they are teaching their child through their demands. There has to be consistency between the demands and the reinforcements. Sometimes you don't want to be too flexible. I learned this the hard way. My nine-year-old tells me about what I have done in the past. "But when I did this last week, it was okay and now it isn't."

In actively trying to get the child to behave or in trying to change a temperamental quality, parents need to focus themselves on what behaviors they want reinforced and what ones they don't. They need to be perceptive on both ends of the response—the demands they are setting up and what they are actually reinforcing. If you know a child is irregular in eating in the morning and you want to change the pattern because you know he'll get cranky and won't learn well if he doesn't have a full stomach, be consistent. "You don't walk out the door unless you have had at least three bites of cereal and a glass of juice." But if you let it go one morning, you can expect the child to say, "Well, yesterday you didn't make me do that."

From your research, do you see areas that can be supports for children as they are growing up?

R. Lerner: More and more children experience alternative-care settings, and this has to become a major support. The socialization of the child is moving out of the family more and more, and we are charging the schools with more of the socialization duties. Throughout infancy and childhood, the alternative caregiving setting is the day care, the preschool, and, obviously, the school. These settings have to be evaluated in terms of enhancing the child's fit and the ability to meet the demands of the context.

THE JOYS OF PARENTING INFANTS

"I love babies. There is something about that bond between mother and baby. I love the way they look and smell and the way they hunker up to your neck. To me it's a magic time. I didn't like to babysit particularly growing up, and I wasn't wild about other people's babies, but there was something about having my own; I just love it. And every one, we used to wonder, how are we going to love another as much as the one before; and that is ridiculous, because you love every one." MOTHER

"There is joy in just watching her change, seeing her individualize. From the beginning it seemed she had her own personality—we see that this is not just a little blob of protoplasm here, this is a little individual already from the beginning. She has always had a real specialness about her. It was exciting to see her change." FATHER

"I think it's wonderful to have a baby in the house, to hear the baby laugh, sitting in the high chair, banging spoons, all the fun things babies do. They seem to me to light up a household. When there's a baby here, a lot of the aggravations in the household somehow disappear. Everyone looks at the baby, plays with the baby, and even if people are in a bad mood, they just light up when the baby comes in the room. I think there is something magical about having a baby in the house." MOTHER

"What I've discovered about parenting is there is a constant process of loss and gain. With every gain you give up something, so there is sadness and joy. The joy

other was a control group of mothers who carried their babies as usual. They monitored crying of the babies from three to twelve weeks and found that the supplemental carrying eliminated the peak of crying that usually occurs at six weeks, reduced crying overall, and modified the daily pattern of the crying so there was less in the evening hours. For example, at six weeks, those babies who received extra carrying cried 43 percent less overall than the control group. At twelve weeks both groups decreased, but the carried babies still cried slightly less (23 percent less). Equally important, babies who were carried more were more content and more visually and aurally alert.

The supplemental carrying provides all the kinds of stimulation that we know soothes babies—rhythmic, repetitive movement with postural changes. Close physical contact with babies also gives mothers a better understanding of their infants' needs and reactions so that caregiving is more sensitive and responsive.

Another recent suggestion for soothing crying babies takes a different approach. In clinical and research training, pediatrician William Sammons observed many different kinds of babies and gradually developed the belief that babies have the ability to calm themselves, but they must be given the opportunity to develop this skill.[33] Babies suck on fingers, wrist, or arm; get into a certain body position; or focus on certain visual forms like walls or objects or light to soothe themselves. In

133

Strengthening
Reciprocal
Relationships
to Develop
Autonomy and
Self-Regulation

comes when he does something new, different. He crawls and that's great, but the loss is you no longer have to get him something or carry him there. Now I have to do less for him. My role shifts the less I do for him. So, it's a mixed thing. He's growing up too fast. I want to hold on to each phase; I like the new phase, but I want to hang on to each one too." MOTHER

"As he gets older, I relate more, play more. He is more of a joy. Some of the joys are so unexpected. I would stop myself and open up and think, 'Oh, this is my son, he's so joyful. He's smiling for no particular reason.' I am not that joyful, but he's joyful for no reason. He reminds me of joy." FATHER

"It's the first time in my life, I know what the term 'unconditional love' means. The wonder of this little girl and nature! I have never experienced anything like that. It is 'Yes,' without any 'Buts.'" FATHER

"I enjoy seeing her and her father together, hearing them talk, seeing him so happy with her all the time." MOTHER

"Crawling was just so wonderful for me, it just seemed to reveal something about his personality, his persistence. It was strenuous for him physically. I would be across the room, and he would start out across the room; and you could hear him, breathing, kind of panting, working and working and working to get himself across the room. There was something about that, so valiant. And his laughter; he loves to laugh, and he had such joy, such a sense of accomplishment he communicated when he got across the room." MOTHER

his pediatric practice he has encouraged parents to engage in a mutual partnership with babies so that the infants can find their own ways of self-calming.

Parents help babies develop their skills by organizing a comfortable environment at home for the infant, attending to needs babies communicate, and learning the meanings of their babies' cries. When babies do cry and they are not clearly in need of food or some other specific intervention, parents intervene in a minimal way, talking to them, stroking them, giving them a chance to find their own particular way to calm themselves. The great advantage is that developing skills to do this enables babies to deal with a whole variety of unpredictable and unpleasant events like noise, heat, fatigue, and overstimulation. Babies become happier as do all family members.

STRENGTHENING RECIPROCAL RELATIONSHIPS TO DEVELOP AUTONOMY AND SELF-REGULATION

In the first eight or nine months of life, parents have the active role of nourishing and giving physical care to babies, meeting their needs and helping them regulate their functioning. Babies cooperate in the care, but parents are the more active partners, relying on their own sensitivity to understand what babies want.

THE JOYS OF PARENTING TODDLERS

"There is the excitement of baby talk becoming real words." MOTHER

"What I appreciate about this age is that he is so into exploring everything about the world. He'll try everything. He has no preconceived ideas—he's so willing, so open, so excited. He loves his vitamin pill, and he gets so excited about it. When he can do something, he is so proud. The look on his face when he can feed himself pasta is so special." MOTHER

"I like sharing, teaching him. His attention span is limited now, but he does imitate us completely. I enjoy learning about myself as I see him with me and with my parents." FATHER

"It is wonderful now, he comes into a room and sees me, and he runs across the room and yells, 'Daddy,' and leaps on me. I like that. Or we had company, and I came down the stairs and he started to say over and over my whole name— 'Michael_____. Michael_____.' I like that." FATHER

"To see him put ideas together, to see him remember something that happened one time four months ago and tell us about it—I am sure all children do these things, but they continue to be the miracle of this evolving person and who he is; it's such a thrill. The four-month thing came up yesterday because we were talking about his old day-care person. In the summer we went to visit her, and I took her fresh-ground coffee. Yesterday I told him we were going to see her, and he said, 'Oh, I want to take her ground coffee.' It just came out of the blue, and that was

Toward the end of the first year, babies' increasing motor and cognitive skills enable them to plan and carry out actions that do not meet parents' approval so even in the first year, parents begin guiding and modifying children's behavior. Babies also have the capacity to comply with simple requests. The way parents go about shaping children's behavior to meet standards establishes behavioral patterns that children use in interactions with others.

In the second year of life, toddlers gain increasing control of their behavior. Table 5-1 on page 138 presents the phases of control Claire Kopp believes children go through to attain self-regulation. The process takes several years, and the goal is not simple compliance with rules but autonomy or self-regulation, the capacity to monitor and control behavior flexibly and adaptively even when an adult is not present.[34]

Parents take many actions to encourage children's cooperation with parental requests. The term "receptive compliance" refers to a "generalized willingness to cooperate with (or perhaps, to 'exchange compliances with') a partner."[35] When parents have secure attachments to children, are sensitive and responsive to their needs, they create a climate in which children are more likely to comply because parents attend to their needs and wishes as well. Noncompliance is low, but when it occurs,

135

Strengthening
Reciprocal
Relationships
to Develop
Autonomy and
Self-Regulation

four or so months ago. There's a real person who remembers things that are important and significant to him." MOTHER

"I've heard of this, and it's true; it's rediscovering the child in yourself. Sometimes, it's the joy that he and I hop around the couch like two frogs on our hands and knees. Or we're in the bathtub pretending we are submarines and alligators. Sometimes he likes to ride around on my shoulders, and I run and make noises like an airplane or a bird. And I am not just doing it for him, but we are doing it together, playing together." FATHER

"The joy comes from the things we do as a family, the three of us—going to see Santa Claus together or to see miniature trains and take a ride. Early in the morning we have a ritual. When he gets up, early, he has a bottle of milk and gets in bed with us; the lights are out, and we are lying in bed, and he tells us his dreams and we watch the light outside and see the trees and see the sun come up. We do that in the morning, and it is a quiet joy." FATHER

"When he began to learn words, he said the dog's name, but he called her 'Hotcha' for Sasha. And then he learned how to say it correctly, and he would say it all day long, 'Sasha.' I remember the first moment when I knew he understood language in that sense. One time we were in one room, and across the next room, outside on the deck, Sasha scratched at the door to come in; and he heard her. I heard her too, and he looked at me and said, 'Sasha,' as if to say 'Sasha wants to come in.' For the first time it was a definite, clear communication to do with Sasha, and that was wonderful." MOTHER

parents use reasoning, explanations—low-power techniques that result in a sharing of power. Sharing power with children may have strong impact because it communicates essential respect for the child as a person.[36]

In addition to creating an atmosphere for receptive compliance, parents often take preventive actions to head off conflicts before they arise. Parents divert children's attention from tempting forbidden activities, suggesting interesting substitutes. For example, in grocery stores, they suggest children pick out items or they make a game of identifying products or colors or items to prevent whining for candy.[37]

Resistance to parents' requests continues for years, but children adopt varying strategies for expressing their resistance.[38] Initially toddlers rely on direct, often angry, defiance and passive noncompliance. These methods decrease somewhat with age as toddlers develop more skill in bargaining and negotiating. Despite these age changes, there is "modest stability" in children's general choice of behavior. Those children who used the most unskilled forms of resistance as toddlers used the most unskilled as five-year-olds. Those who used simple refusal and negotiating as toddlers were most likely to use bargaining at age five.

THE JOYS OF PARENTING PRESCHOOL CHILDREN

"When she was four, she was the only girl on an all-boy soccer team. Her mother thought she was signing her up for a coed team, but she was the only girl, and she enjoyed it and liked it even though she is not a natural athlete. She watches and learns and gets good at it, and we got a lot of joy out of watching her." FATHER

"Well, every night we have a bedtime ritual of telling a story and singing to her. This is probably beyond the time she needs it, but we need it." MOTHER

"He's very inventive, and it's fun for both of us when he tells stories or figures out ways to communicate something he's learned or heard. When his mother had morning sickness, he heard the baby was in her tummy so he figured out the baby is making the morning sickness, pushing the food out." FATHER

"It's fun to get home in the evening; he comes running out and jumps up which is really fun. It's a wonderful greeting." FATHER

"One of the delights that comes up is reading him stories, telling him the adventure of John Muir, at the four-year-old level. We were talking about places to go, and I said, 'Maybe we could go visit the home of John Muir.' He said, 'Oh, great, then I could go up there and have a cup of tea.' And I remembered I had told him a story about Muir's having tea in a blizzard, and he remembered that. He put that together, and it came out of nowhere. It knocked me over that he remembered that image." FATHER

"I enjoy her because I can talk to her; we have these wonderful conversations, and she can tell me about something that happened to her today at school that was really neat for her, and I just love to hear about it." MOTHER

"It's fun to hear him looking forward to doing things with us. He'll ask how many days until Saturday or Sunday because on those days I wait for him to get up before I have breakfast. Usually I'm up and gone before he gets up. He likes to come out and get up in my lap and share my breakfast, and it's a ritual. He looks forward to that and counts the days." FATHER

Children often adopt similar methods in resisting parents and in influencing them to get their own way. Children who use outright defiance to resist parents use forceful methods like demanding and whining to get what they want. Children who bargain and negotiate to resist use persuasion to influence parents.

Defiance occurs most frequently when parents use high-power strategies like commands, criticisms, threats, physical punishments to control children's behavior. Suggestions and guidance in the form of explaining, persuading, directing, and verbally assisting the child to do what is wanted all increase compliance. Giving verbal feedback about difficulties is also helpful.[39] These primarily verbal methods may

137

Strengthening
Reciprocal
Relationships
to Develop
Autonomy and
Self-Regulation

"She's really affectionate, always has been, but now out of nowhere, she'll tell you she loves you. She likes to do things with you, and when you give her special attention, one on one, she really likes it. We play games—Candy Land or Cinderella—or just one of us goes with her to the supermarket or to the park. We read stories every night and do some talking. Sometimes I put a record on and we dance." FATHER

"I miss this since the baby came, but we used to have special time together. We would go off and do things by ourselves. We would go driving in the car, go shopping, and have a lot of time to communicate, just the two of us. Four and a half is a really wonderful, talkative, growing stage. She would talk about the stuff going on in her life, questions she has: 'Why does it rain?' We would sing songs she learns in school." MOTHER

"The time I like best with her is hanging out together, and she loves doing projects with me. She likes to help me with a project when I am working in the garage, and I'll show her how to use tools, and it's a special time with Dad." FATHER

"He's four, and he's so philosophical. He's always thinking about different things, and sometimes he'll tell me, and I am amazed. One day we were driving and he said, 'Can God see me riding here in the car?' Or one night at dinner, he was watching his little sister who's one, and he said, 'Do you think when she gets to be a big girl she'll remember what she did as a baby?'" MOTHER

"I like going for a walk with her, and we went skipping rocks at the reservoir. I was going to show her how to skip rocks because she had never seen that before. Of course, she wanted to try it, and I didn't think she was old enough to do it. I had found the best skipping rock; it was just perfect. I was going to hold her hand and do it with her. She said, 'No, I want to do it myself.' I thought, 'Oh, no!' The best skipping rock and it was just going to go plunk. No, I thought, it is more important to just let it go. So I said, 'Here let me show you how.' So I showed her, and she said, 'No, I can do it.' She threw it and it skipped three times! The first time she ever threw one! She wanted to stay till she did it again, and we did a little; but it will be a while before she does that again, I think." FATHER

succeed because they make clear to the child what is wanted. Two-year-old negativism may occur primarily because children do not understand the request.[40]

The time and involvement required for promoting self-regulation is enormous. Mothers of two-year-olds intervened every 6 to 8 minutes to make a request or stop a behavior.[41] Parents must realize, however, that children most often comply with the request. In fact they take pleasure in matching their actions to the words of another. The pleasure of accomplishing a goal is a powerful incentive for toddlers' obeying commands. Toddlers who were asked to do easy and interesting tasks happily repeated the tasks when no adult was involved.[42]

TABLE 5-1
PHASES OF CONTROL

Phases	Approximate Ages	Features	Cognitive Requisites
Neuro-physiological modulation	Birth to 2–3 mo.	Modulation of arousal, activation of organized patterns of behavior	
Sensorimotor modulation	3 mo.– 9 mo.+	Change ongoing behavior in response to events and stimuli in environment	
Control	12 mo.– 18 mo.+	Awareness of social demands of a situation and initiate, maintain, cease physical acts, communication, etc. accordingly; compliance, self-initiated monitoring	Intentionality, goal-directed behavior, conscious awareness of action, memory of existential self
Self-control	24 mo.+	As above; delay upon request; behave according to social expectations in the absence of external monitors	Representational thinking and recall memory, symbolic thinking, continuing sense of identity
Self-regulation	36 mo.+	As above; flexibility of control processes that meet changing situational demands	Strategy production, conscious introspection, etc

From C. B. Kopp, "Antecedents of Self-Regulation: A Developmental Perspective," *Developmental Psychology* 18 (1982): p. 202.

HELPING CHILDREN REGULATE EMOTIONS

Parents want children to regulate not only their behavior but also their emotional outbursts. Parents can most effectively help children learn to live comfortably with their feelings when they understand the emotional life of young children. By the end of the first year babies express interest, surprise, joy, anger, fear, and disgust. As self-awareness grows, toddlers express embarrassment, pride, guilt, and empathy.[43]

Mothers begin to guide babies to control their emotional reactions in the first few months of life. They do this with both nonverbal and verbal techniques. They avoid negative facial expressions that the baby can copy; and, as mentioned, they empha-size the positive emotions. Verbally, they encourage positive emotions with such phrases as "Give me a smile," "Laugh for Mommy." At the same time they discourage negative reactions with such phrases as "Don't cry" and "Don't fuss now." In the sec-ond half of the first year, mothers discourage the overt expression of feelings. There is evidence that mothers of boys are more responsive to them and match their son's behavior more.[44]

While babies are clearly responsive to others' feelings, they are not totally depen-dent on caregivers. When confronted with negative stimulation, they can cope and soothe themselves.[45] In fact, a basic task of infancy is to begin learning to regulate feelings.[46] When mothers of three-month-olds adopted depressed expressions for just 3 minutes, babies cried and fussed, then turned away and comforted themselves. Babies soothe themselves by sucking hands or fingers, manipulating themselves, finding a neutral scene to fix upon.[47]

Babies take an active role not only in soothing themselves but in giving them-selves pleasure as well. Babies smile when they can make something happen.[48] Babies just a few months old get pleasure from making a mobile go or a rattle shake. As soon as toddlers can talk, they talk about feelings. By the beginning of the third year toddlers talk about positive feelings such as being happy, having a good time, feeling good, and being proud. They talk about negative emotions as well—being sad, scared, angry. They talk about uncomfortable physical states—being hungry, hot, cold, sleepy, and in pain. Words play an important role in helping toddlers learn how to handle negative feelings by enabling them to communicate these states to parents, get feedback about how appropriate the feelings are, and think about how to manage them.[49]

Toddlers also use objects to handle negative feelings. They frequently have transi-tional objects like stuffed animals, blankets, pieces of cloth, and dolls to provide comfort in times of distress. The use of such objects reaches a peak in the middle of the second year when as many as 30 to 60 percent of children have them.[50]

Toddlers also enlist the help of parents and caregivers to resolve negative feelings and situations beyond them. They call or pull parents to what they want remedied. As they move beyond two, toddlers seem to have a greater understanding of when they need the extra help and call for it more quickly.[51]

Toddlers are aware, too, of others' feelings, and they develop ideas about what actions cause feelings and what actions change feelings. Following are examples of comments from twenty-eight-month olds: "I give a big hug. Baby be happy." "Mommy exercise. Mommy having a good time." "I'm hurting your feelings 'cause I mean to you." "Grandma's mad. I wrote on wall." "You sad, Mommy. What Daddy do?" Toddlers also learn that one person's feelings can stimulate another person's actions. "I cry. Lady pick me up." "I scared of the shark. Close my eyes."[52]

Preschoolers become increasingly accurate in understanding the connections between feelings and the events and social interactions that produce them. While they at first believe that feelings are temporary, by the end of the preschool period, they recognize that feelings can persist and are influenced by what one thinks.[53]

Children are accurate in identifying what triggers emotions, especially when there is a social cause for the feelings. In one study, preschoolers agreed 91 percent of the time with adults in giving reasons for other preschoolers' feelings as they occurred in the course of everyday activity.[54] Preschoolers were most accurate in understanding anger and distress and less accurate in understanding happy and sad reactions.

While there are common areas of agreement between preschoolers and adults in understanding feelings, still there are differences; and parents are forewarned that they may well not understand their preschoolers' reactions. Preschoolers evaluate events by their outcome. If a wrongdoer is successful at getting what he or she wants, the preschooler assumes the child feels good about that. They may know an act is wrong, but not necessarily feel wrong or bad for doing it.[55] When adults were asked to predict how children of different ages would react emotionally in different situations, adults were not so skilled in understanding preschoolers as they were third- and sixth-graders.[56] Adults and all children agreed in predicting emotional outcomes to failure, nurturance, and justified punishment. Adults, however, did not anticipate how happy preschoolers would be to evade punishment while still getting what they want. Adults thought preschoolers would feel sad or mad, but the children reported they would feel happy. Preschoolers were highly sensitive to punishment, feeling angry or sad whether it was deserved or not.

Anger

Parents most want to help children deal with anger. The research of Florence Goodenough on anger and temper outbursts provides valuable information on how and why temper tantrums develop and on effective ways of handling anger.[57] She found that many factors influenced the occurrence of anger. Outbursts peak in the second year and are most likely to occur when children are hungry or tired (just before meals and at bedtime) or when they are ill. Thus, when reserves are down for physical reasons, tempers flare. Outbursts are usually short-lived—most last less than 5 minutes—and with young children under three the aftereffects were minimal. With increasing age, children tended to sulk and to have hard feelings. From one to three years, the immediate causes of anger seem to be conflict with authority, difficulties over the establishment of habits (eating, baths, bedtime), and problems with social relationships (wanting more attention, wanting a possession someone else has). With older children, social and particularly play relationships trigger more outbursts. After the second year, boys seem to have more outbursts than girls.

The parents of the children who had the fewest outbursts used a daily schedule as a means to an end, and had a more tolerant, positive home atmosphere. They were consistent and fair in the rules they established. They had realistic expectations that children would be independent, curious, stubborn; they anticipated problems and found ways to prevent them. These parents tried to help children conform by preparing them for changes in activities. They announced mealtimes or bathtimes in advance so children had 10 minutes or so to get ready. In these homes, parents focused on the individuality of the child. When a real conflict arose, however, they were firm.

Parents of children with many outbursts were inconsistent and unpredictable, basing decisions on their own wants rather than the child's needs. These parents tended to ignore children's needs until a problem forced them to respond. In some of these families, parents imposed a routine regardless of the child's activity of the moment and forced the child to act quickly in terms of the parent's desire. Criticism and disapproval characterized the home atmosphere. In short, when children are tired, hungry or sick, they are likely to respond with anger. Parental behaviors that reinforce attachment—acceptance, sensitivity to children's needs, and cooperativeness—minimize temper outbursts.

Temper Tantrums

With Goodenough's study in mind, let us examine what Ginott, Gordon, Dreikurs, and the behaviorists suggest about parental managing of children's temper tantrums. Ginott recommends accepting all angry feelings, but directing children's behavior into acceptable channels.[58] Parents can do this verbally by saying, "People are not for hitting; pillows are for hitting." Neither parent nor child is permitted to hit. If children's tantrums are not ended by verbal statements, parents take action, even in public, returning home if a child has a tantrum in a store.[59]

Gordon suggests finding substitute activities to head off trouble. If no jumping is permitted on the sofa, parents can allow children to jump on pillows on the floor. Once anger surfaces, Gordon suggests that parents listen actively and provide feedback about the frustration and irritation the child feels—sometimes a child needs nothing more than acceptance of what he is feeling.[60]

Gordon recommends mutual problem solving to find a solution agreeable to both parent and child. But when a compromise is not possible and a child is still upset, active listening may again be useful. He cites the example of a child who was unable to go swimming because he had a cold. When the child's mother commented that it was hard for him to wait until the next day, he calmed down.

Dreikurs recommends many of the techniques that Goodenough found were used by parents whose children had few tantrums.[61] When tantrums occur, parents are urged to ignore them and leave the room. Ignoring a child is appropriate in public as well as at home.

The behaviorists use a similar method of ignoring. Krumboltz and Krumboltz tell of a little boy who learned that if he cried and had a tantrum, his parents would pick him up instead of paying attention to the new baby.[62] When they realized that their actions were creating the tantrums, they agreed to ignore the outbursts. When the boy learned that he gained nothing by banging his head and demanding what he wanted, the tantrums stopped. The behaviorists insist that parents must be firm and consistent. Otherwise tantrums will continue, and each time children will hold out longer because they have learned that they can win by outlasting the parents.

Strategists who emphasize communication of feelings to prevent tantrums suggest parental intervention by reflecting feelings. The parents of the boy who is jealous of a new baby might be advised to comment that if the boy wishes he could be held like a baby; only after attending to feelings would Ginott, for example, take action. The behaviorists and Dreikurs, in contrast, focus on handling tantrums once they have occurred.

Stanley Turecki and Leslie Tonner, who work with difficult children, draw a distinction between the **manipulative tantrum** and the **temperamental tantrum**.[63]

Children who want their way use the tantrum to manipulate the parents into getting them what they want. Turecki recommends firm refusal to give into such tantrums. Distracting children, ignoring their outbursts, and sending them to their rooms are all techniques for handling that kind of tantrum.

In the more intense temperamental tantrum, children seem out of control. Some aspect of their temperament has been violated, and they are reacting to that. For example, the less adaptable child who is compelled to switch activities suddenly may have an outburst, or a child sensitive to fabric may do so when he or she has to wear a wool sweater. In these instances, Turecki advises a calm and sympathetic approach; parents can reflect the child's feelings of irritation or upset: "I know you don't like this, but it will be okay." Parents can then put their arms around the child, if permitted, or just be a physical presence near the child. No long discussion of what is upsetting the child takes place unless the child wants to talk. If the situation can be corrected, it should be. For example, if the wool sweater feels scratchy, let the child remove it and wear a soft sweatshirt. This is not giving in, but just correcting a mistake. All parents can do then is wait out the tantrum.

Throughout a display of the temperamental tantrum, parents convey the attitude that they will help the child deal with this situation. Though parents change their minds when good reasons are presented, they are generally consistent in waiting out the tantrum and insisting on behavior change when necessary.

Empathy

At the same time that anger is on the increase, expressions of affection and empathy increase as well. In the second year babies begin to give signs of affection—love pats and strokings—to parents, particularly the mother. They are also affectionate to animals and younger children.

Empathy develops in stages during the toddler period.[64] At ten to twelve months, babies respond to other children's distress by crying with agitation. In the second year, however, they take action—touching, cuddling, or rubbing the injured party. An eighteen-month-old girl, upset by her baby brother's crying, brought him a diaper to hold because she liked to carry a diaper for comfort. Between eighteen months and two years, children begin to imitate the emotional reactions of the hurt individual, mimicking facial expressions of pain. Many go through a process of referring the pain to themselves. If a mother bumps her arm, the child rubs the mother's elbow, then his own. Compassionate action follows the self-referencing behavior. Investigators suggest that true kindness may depend on the ability to relate the other's distress to oneself.

Preschoolers appear more able than toddlers to adopt the perspective of the other person and respond to him or her. Since they are better able to understand the sources of emotional reactions, their strategies for making things better go more directly to the source of the problem. When another child is angry, they are likely to give some material thing to the child, share with him or her.[65] When another child is sad or distressed, they are more likely to do something positive for the child, playing with the child, comforting the child.

Sharing and giving with friends occurs most frequently in an atmosphere of comfort and optimism. Best friends continue to share when happy, appreciative responses follow. When sharing does not occur, but the friend remains happy and smiling, the conflict does not escalate and sharing is resumed.[66]

What qualities in parents stimulate empathy in a toddler? Children who are kind and helpful in response to the suffering of others have mothers who are warm, caring individuals, concerned with the well-being of others. These mothers expect children to control aggression, and when they do not, mothers show disappointment— "Children are not for hitting," "Stop! You are hurting him." The researchers conclude that mothers of empathetic children model kindness to others, but they go beyond that to teach children how to do what is expected. They maintain high standards and continue a warm, caring relationship with children.[67]

ATTAINING A SENSE OF SELF AND GENDER IDENTITY

As children engage in conflicts with parents, learn to assert themselves and to control their feelings and understand others' feelings, they get a clearer conception of themselves as individuals. By twenty-four months, they begin to use pronouns like "I," "Me," "Mine," and make statements about their activities like "I run," "I play."[68] An important part of a child's sense of self is a sense of gender identity. By two or two and a half, children proudly announce, "I am a boy," or "I am a girl," and by four it is as hard for a child to change a sense of gender identity as it is for an adult.[69]

A 1978 study found that children as young as three years of age agree on what is expected of boys and girls, both in the present and in the future.[70] Boys are active builders who help father and behave aggressively; girls are talkative, help mother, play quietly, never hit, but ask for help. Men are bosses, mow the grass, and can be doctors and pilots; women clean house, rear babies, and are nurses and teachers. Those who hope for less sex stereotyping of behavior in the future will be encouraged by the fact that boys and girls believe that both sexes have a common core of positive and negative traits—both sexes are described as strong, kind, fast runners, unafraid, messy, dirty, smart, and quiet. In addition, boys and girls have positive beliefs about their own sex, valuing traits associated with being a boy or a girl. Neither sex feels slighted; in fact, they tend to view the opposite sex as less favored than they are.

How do children use all the information provided to arrive at a sense of sexual identity? Parents begin sex-typing behavior, perhaps without realizing it, by responding in an emotionally positive way to the child's appropriate sex-typed activities and appropriate object choices.[71] Parents encourage boys to manipulate objects and to learn about the world and discourage them from expressing feelings and asking for help. Parents encourage girls to ask for help and to help with tasks. Parents criticize girls for running, jumping, climbing, and manipulating objects.

Through parents' emotional responses toddlers learn that parents value certain behaviors, and children learn the appropriate gender labels for those behaviors. Sex-role education begins with the parent's positive or negative emotional response.

When the child learns the label, then he or she can organize behavior in terms of whether it is appropriate or not for that label.

Some parents begin sex-typing behavior early, and their toddlers are early (before twenty-seven months) to learn labels and are more sex-typed in their activities and choices of toys than are toddlers of parents who start later and learn labels later (after twenty-seven months). At age four the early labelers and the later labelers are similar in behavior and choice of toys, but the early labelers are more aware of sexual stereotypes.

Parents can help children build a firm, positive sexual identity by giving an emotionally positive response when both boys and girls show qualities of strength, kindness, emotional responsiveness, intelligence, confidence, and competence.

When parents form strong attachments with children, establish reciprocal relationships to encourage autonomy, teach children to regulate negative feelings and express feelings of kindness and consideration to others, parents prepare children to relate positively with others in the family and with peers. Let us look first at sibling relationships in the family.

Sibling Relationships

Growing up with brothers and sisters has long-lasting effects on children.[72] The relationships among siblings are emotional, intense, affectionate, but sometimes aggressive and full of conflict. Older siblings teach young siblings; they model activities for them. Sometimes they care for them and protect them; sometimes they fight.

Older siblings, aged three and four, can act as substitute attachment figures for their toddler siblings in the absence of the mother.[73] Even young toddlers show positive feelings toward their older siblings, miss them when they are gone, and try to comfort them when they are in difficulty. We now know that younger toddler siblings engage in more advanced behavior with their older siblings, playing in more complicated and imaginative ways. Toddlers are also capable of teasing older siblings in clever ways. They learn about family rules and are adept at getting mothers involved when the firstborn has violated a rule, but not when they themselves have. They learn to pay careful attention to the feelings and intentions of others. They learn to stand up for their own rights and argue persuasively with their siblings, and so their social reasoning and ability to protect their own interests increase. They also become skilled in giving sympathy and support to others.[74]

Most firstborn children under five show signs of upset after the baby's birth.[75] The most common change, shown by 93 percent of children in one study, was an increase in misbehavior—refusing to follow rules and regular routines, being demanding when the mother was interacting with the baby. Over 50 percent of the children became more clinging and dependent—wanting bottles and seeking to eat, toilet, and play like a newborn—but these behaviors began to decrease after the first month or so.[76]

Positive changes occur as well. Eighty-two percent of two- to four-year-old firstborns had positive feelings about being a big brother or sister one month before the birth, and 80 percent remained positive in the first year. They most enjoyed

Even young toddlers show positive feelings toward older siblings, miss them when they are gone, and try to comfort them when they are in difficulty. How well siblings get along is partly determined by the parent-child relationship.

cuddling and smiling with the baby. They reported being upset by the baby's crying, which decreased in the first twelve months, and the infant's increasing interference with their toys and play.

Though upset at times, all firstborns reported helping with the baby, and 95 percent of mothers reported that they did. They got diapers, soothed the baby, and occupied the infant while the mother was busy. Most mothers (75 percent) reported that the two shared and played well by the end of the first year. The fact that 63 percent of firstborns wanted another sibling at the end of the first year suggests that overall it was a positive experience for them.

Many factors influence how firstborns will relate to the child. Children who are most likely to be upset at the birth of a sibling are those who are already irritable, sensitive, difficult to manage, and inclined to engage in many confrontations with their mothers. When mothers are unusually tired or depressed following the birth of the sibling, negative reactions are more common among firstborns. When fathers have close relationships with firstborns, the latter tend to have less conflict with their mothers following the birth of the sibling.

INTERVIEW
with Judy Dunn

Judy Dunn is professor of human development and director of the Center for the Study of Child and Adolescent Development at The Pennsylvania State University.

What are the most important ways to help children have satisfying relationships with brothers and sisters?

It is reassuring for parents to learn how common it is for brothers and sisters not to get on. They fight a great deal. The main variable is the children's personality. This child is one way and that child is another, and they don't get along. They don't have any choice about living together, and so it's easy to see why they don't get on. It is such a "No holds barred" relationship. There are no inhibitions, and both boys and girls can be very aggressive.

It is reassuring for parents to know that fights occur not just in their family. No one really knows what goes on in other families, and so you think it is just in your own. But children can fight a lot and still end up with a close relationship.

When there is the birth of a new sibling, keep the level of attention and affection as high as possible for the firstborn. I think it's almost impossible to give too much attention to the first child at this time.

Also, keep the firstborn's life as similar as possible. Routine things matter a lot to little children. They like predictability. The mother structures their whole world, so that after a baby comes, they can be upset just by any changes mother makes in their routine.

In middle childhood, there is a strong association between sibling fights and feelings that the other child is favored by the parent or parents. It is important to be aware how early and how sensitive children are to what goes on between parents and children. It is never too early for parents to think about the effects of what they are doing on the other child. So always be aware of how sensitive children are and avoid favoritism.

Birth of a Sibling

Ginott tells parents that because no one likes to share center stage with another, a child is bound to feel some jealousy and hurt. Preparation does help, however. Parents can say that soon there will be a new baby in the family and that a baby is both fun and a nuisance. They should express, and permit the child to express, negative as well as positive feelings. Before the baby arrives, parents can help the child to anticipate both the love and the left-out feelings that he or she will experience. After the child arrives, parents can be alert for signs of jealousy, acknowledging the older child's jealousy, resentment, and hostility. Ginott suggests special attention and "extra loving" for the older child during these times of stress.[77]

Gordon recommends active listening, listening to behavior as well as to words and realizing that when the child becomes irritable, aggressive, or immature, jealousy lies just under the surface. A parent can simply comment, "You are unhappy," "sad," or "lonely."[78]

Dreikurs has a thorough discussion of sibling rivalry.[79] He shows how children's responses to the new baby depend on both their own feelings at the time and on the characteristics of the new arrival. Dreikurs recommends accepting any verbal statements of hostility, any talk about wanting to get rid of the baby. The main way to help older children cope is by making them your partner in caring for the baby. Point out the older children's advantages, how big they are, how well they bring a diaper for the baby, how smart they are to figure out that the baby wants company. If possible, the father can spend more time with the older child. When the older child makes unreasonable demands for attention, parents should overlook these. Parents can also try to plan special treats for the older child while the baby is asleep. To minimize difficulties as children grow, parents are urged not to compare them.

The behaviorists suggest that when a new baby arrives, the older child can learn to do special tasks that will increase self-esteem. Eimers and Aitchison cite the case of a child who was always asking her parents if they loved her.[80] At first they answered, but as the question became repetitive, behaviorists advised them to ignore the question and instead to build the child's self-esteem by giving positive attention for what she did well. They began playing games with her and spending more time talking and reading to her. The child felt valued and no longer needed to ask whether she was loved.

Briggs suggests opportunities for verbal and creative expression of jealousy. One mother gave her daughter a doll to hit to express the anger the child felt toward a younger sister. Coloring, drawing, and molding clay can also help to express feelings. Briggs also suggests building the older child's self-esteem by teaching new skills that increase the child's competence.[81]

Again the strategists are in general agreement, although they focus on slightly different aspects of the problem. Ginott prepares the child for the birth. Gordon and Briggs elicit feelings through active listening. Briggs suggests ways to drain tension and, along with Dreikurs and the behaviorists, recommends building the child's self-esteem through attention and interest in positive behavior as well as through teaching new skills.

Relationships in the home prepare children to interact with peers. Learning strategies for getting along well with peers reduces the risk of later psychological problems.

Peers

Young toddlers from thirteen to twenty-four months can play with peers, taking turns and sharing. They develop a social competence that persists into preschool years.[82] They can form stable friendships that persist for as long as a year. Between 50 percent and 70 percent of reciprocated friendships lasted at least a year, and 10 percent lasted two years. Further, these friendships are important emotional attachments for the children. When children remained with the same group of friends or moved with their group of friends, their play remained reciprocal and interactive. When a change occurred without a friend or a friend moved, play became less interactive. It is important for parents to realize the depths of these relationships for some children.

In the preschool period, friends have as many fights as casual acquaintances, but they handle them differently.[83] Whereas casual acquaintances stand up for their rights until someone wins, friends tend to disengage and find an equal solution that gives each partner something. Friends are then able to continue to play with each other while casual acquaintances drift away from each other after a fight.

Preschoolers like each other because they share the same activities and play together well. Preschoolers want to enjoy themselves and have fun with a minimum of friction. Those who disrupt play and cause trouble are disliked by other children.[84] Observations of children's nursery school behavior indicate that the majority of interactions between children are friendly.[85] Children spend a high percentage of time in friendly encounters that include asking, suggesting, starting an activity with a smile or comment, saying, "Let's do. . . ." Only a small proportion of interactions (14 percent) are of a demanding, aggressive nature, and just 5 percent involve whining, begging, and crying. Even when others are domineering, many preschoolers are mature enough to either ignore the response or agree with the other child and thus avoid a conflict. Preschoolers enjoy a friendly atmosphere and tend to return the positive overtures of others. Those children who reach out to others are sought out as companions.

The quality in relationships with peers is influenced by relationships in the family. Toddlers and preschoolers who have secure attachments with their mothers are more sociable, more friendly and cooperative with their peers than those lacking strong attachments. Experience within the family creates ways of relating to others in the world outside.[86]

PARENTS' EXPERIENCES

From the child's second to fourth or fifth year parents are in Galinsky's **authority stage**.[87] Parents must deal with their own feelings about having power, setting rules, enforcing them. Parents have to decide what is reasonable when children mobilize all their energy to oppose them and gain their own way. In the nurturing stage parents were primarily concerned with meeting babies' needs and coordinating their own with caregiving activities. Usually the appropriate childcare behavior was clear—the baby had to be fed, changed, bathed, put to bed. Although judgment was required in deciding about letting the child cry or timing sleep patterns, still the desired aim was clear.

In the authority stage parents must develop clear rules and have the confidence not only to enforce them, but also to deal with the tantrums that follow. Parents require self-assurance so they can act calmly and neutrally when they meet with opposition from their children. Many parents, bogged down in battle with their toddler, find themselves doing and saying things they vowed they never would—the very words they hated to hear from their own parents when they were children. Parents are shaken and upset as their ideal images of themselves as parents collide with the reality of rearing children.

Parents' images of themselves undergo revision in light of the way they actually behave. This can be a painful process because it involves change. Parents must change either their ideal image or their behavior to come closer to living up to their own standards. Parents' images of children are revised as well. They discover that children are not always nice, loving, cooperative, and affectionate. Children can be extremely aggressive, breaking things, hitting parents, pulling their hair.

One father described how he coped with these feelings by revising the kind of parent he wanted to be and by finding new ways to relate to children so that he met the images he wanted to keep of himself as parent.

> Stanley and his wife have one son, eighteen months old. Stanley is a doctor. "In my family, growing up, when someone got angry at someone, they'd stop loving them—which made me feel abandoned as a child.
>
> "When my son gets angry, the easiest thing for me to do would be the same—walk out and slam the door.
>
> "But when you've suffered that yourself you don't want to see it repeated. What I do is to stay and let the rage go through my ears and try to think clearly about what's going on.
>
> "I tell him that even though I've said no, I still love him. I hold him while he's having a temper tantrum, and I tell him it's okay for him to be angry with me.
>
> "Being able to do this is recent, new, and learned, and it's hard work. In the past, I couldn't see beyond my own feelings. What I've now learned is that I have to see past them.
>
> "Another thing I've learned is that if I've gotten angry at my son or if I've done something that I feel I shouldn't have, I'm not the Loch Ness monster or the worst person in the world. I learned the reparability of a mistake."[88]

Parents must also deal with each other as authorities. It is wonderful if both parents agree on how and when to enforce rules. But this is frequently not the case. One parent is often stricter or less consistent; one may dislike any physical punishment, and the other may believe it is the only technique to handle serious rule breaking. Communicating with each other, finding ways to handle differences, is important for parents. Parents sometimes agree to back each other up on all occasions. Other times, they agree to discuss in private any serious misgivings they have about the others' discipline; then the original rule setter is free to revise the rule. Still other times, one parent may decide to let the other handle discipline completely. This is a less desirable solution because it means one parent is withdrawn from interaction with the child. Parents need to find ways to resolve differences so they can give each other the support they need in childrearing. Mutual support is the most important source of strength in parenting.

Single parents and employed parents must work with other authorities, such as day caregivers or relatives who provide major care, to develop consistent ways of handling discipline. Again, communicating with other caregivers helps provide consistent solutions to problems. When authorities do not agree, children become confused and are less able to meet expectations.

As parents become aware of their personal feelings about being authorities and learn to deal with them, they can put these misgivings aside and deal as neutrally with rule enforcement as possible. As with handling infancy, a range of preparations such as reading books, gaining information from groups, taking parenting courses, and talking with other parents helps parents handle the demands of conflicting feelings in the authority stage.

MAJOR POINTS OF CHAPTER 5

As they make the transition to parenthood, parents:

- often do not anticipate the stress produced by all the changes
- are exhausted, unable to keep up with routine household chores, meals
- give up the illusion of being a perfect parent
- learn to set priorities and make decisions in terms of them
- seek support from each other and their social network
- seek expert help if mothers' postpartum depression continues without change
- experience many joys
- are able to be more competent when they receive support from their spouse
- use active listening and mutual problem-solving techniques to handle stress

Bonding at birth:

- is pleasurable for parents and baby
- gets the relationship off to a good start but is not essential for attachment to develop

Attachment:

- is a bond the baby forms with a caregiver
- is secure when parents are accepting and sensitive in meeting the baby's needs
- is insecure when parents are either unavailable and uninvolved or intrusive and controlling
- develops between babies and both parents
- is the basis for the baby's sense of being lovable and worthwhile
- in infancy relates to social competence in toddler and preschool years
- provides a model to young children about how people relate to each other
- is influenced by parents' experiences with their own parents

Mothers and fathers:

- interact with babies in different ways with mothers being nurturing caregivers and fathers being stimulating playmates
- treat boys and girls differently around eighteen months—giving positive attention to boys' aggressiveness and ignoring aggressive behavior in girls

Individual differences in babies:

- appear early
- influence parents' behavior in caring for them

Parents soothe babies when they cry by:

- responding to them quickly
- giving them additional carrying time
- giving babies a chance to soothe themselves

Parents whose children function well and have secure attachments:

- are available, attentive, and sensitive to the child's individual needs
- grant the child as much independence as possible within safety limits
- balance independence with support to overcome barriers the child may meet
- provide models of kind, caring, controlled behavior
- share the experiences of exploration and discovery with the child
- provide reasonable limits to give the child structure
- talk with the child to explain reasons for what is done, to understand the child's view of what is happening, and to let the child express himself or herself
- play with the child to increase the child's positive mood and desire to cooperate in routines and activities

Parental techniques that encourage autonomy and self-regulation include:

- creating an environment of receptive compliance
- using low-power parenting strategies of reasoning, suggesting, persuading, guiding to control the child's behavior
- sharing power with the child
- decreasing defiance by clearly explaining what is wanted

Children's emotional control increases when parents:

- listen to children's feelings and accept them as valid
- put children's needs ahead of their own
- use low-power parenting strategies
- use mutual problem-solving techniques to settle differences

As they develop a greater sense of individuality, toddlers develop a sense of sexual identity that:

- is proudly announced at about two to two and a half

- initially is based on parents' positive and negative emotional responses to sexually appropriate activities
- organizes activities so that boys manipulate objects and explore the world more and girls express feelings, ask for help, and give help more
- includes the belief that both boys and girls share common positive and negative traits—both sexes are strong, kind, fast runners, unafraid, messy, dirty, smart, and quiet
- views one's own sex as the more favored

As their independence grows, children also develop closer relationships with others, and they:

- are more physically affectionate with family, friends, and pets
- become more concerned about others, imitating their distress when they are hurt
- are helpful and loving with newborn siblings
- are kinder
- take delight in complying with some adult requests and meeting a standard of behavior

Parents are learning to be fair authorities when they:

- reason with children and explain the rules
- act to deal firmly with temper tantrums so children know their own intense feelings are controlled
- work together to settle their own conflicts about authority so children get a set of consistent limits
- do not abuse their power

Joys include:

- physical pleasures of babies
- playing with babies
- joy and laughter of babies
- child's delight in personal achievements
- child's increasing abilities and skills
- child's helping behaviors
- communication via verbal language
- playing with the child
- children's reasoning
- affection
- joint projects

EXERCISES

1. Discuss the father's statement on page 120 of the book, that he knew so little about babies that he should not been permitted to take one home from the hospital. Should parents have to apply for a parenting license and demonstrate a certain level of knowledge about babies before they can take one home from the hospital? Each group can devise an exam that would be taken by all parents and then the class can compare suggestions.

2. Go to a toy store and spend an imagined $150.00 on toys for an infant or toddler. Justify your choices.

3. In small groups, discuss the role of siblings in your lives. (a) What have been the positive and negative contributions to this point in time? (b) If you were having children now, how many would you want and why? (c) What would you do to discourage sibling rivalry?

4. A parent of an almost-three-year-old toddler comes to you and says that the child is angry, physically aggressive at day care—kicking, hitting, and punching children as well as the teacher. He has alredy been asked to leave two babysitters' homes and is in a center that takes care of many children who have lived in families where parents have been physically abusive with each other, so the teacher is experienced with this kind of problem, but she is having a difficult time. The mother works days and the father works nights and sometimes cares for the child in the day. The parents have recently separated but the anger occurred prior to the separation. What information would you want to get from the mother to understand the problem better, and what general guidelines would you give her in seeking a solution for the anger?

5. In groups, recall early experiences of sex-type learning. (a) Did the teaching deal with activities, appearance, feelings? (b) Who was teaching you about sex-appropriate behavior—parents, siblings, peers, relatives, teachers? (c) Were you more likely to accept the teachings of adults as opposed to peers? (d) Are similar experiences occurring today? Make a group list of the kinds of experiences your members had.

6. Survey other students on their parents' use of physical punishment. This can be done by breaking into small groups and tabulating information on the following topics. (a) Did your parents use physical punishments? (b) If so, which ones—spanking, hitting? (c) Was this punishment frequent (several times a month), occasional (a few times a year), or rare (can only recall one or two occasions in their life)? (d) For what misbehavior did your parents use physical punishment? (e) How do you recall feeling at the time of the punishment? (f) How do you feel now about it? (g) Would some other punishment have been more effective? (h) If so, what and why? (i) Do you now or do you intend to use physical punishment with your child or children? (i) Why or why not? Small groups can report to the class at large and entire class results on the topic can be tabulated.

ADDITIONAL READINGS

Brazelton, T. Berry. *Infants and Mothers*. Rev. ed. New York: Dell, 1983.

Brazelton, T. Berry. *Toddlers and Parents*. Rev. ed. New York: Dell, 1989.

Cowan, Carolyn Pape and Cowan, Philip A. *When Partners Become Parents*. New York: Basic Books, 1992.

Eisenberg, Nancy, and Mussen, Paul H. *Roots of Prosocial Behavior in Children*. New York: Cambridge University Press, 1989.

Fraiberg, Selma. *The Magic Years*. New York: Charles Scribner's Sons, 1959.

Galinsky, Ellen, and David, Judy. *The Preschool Years*. New York: Times Books, 1988.

Turecki, Stanley, and Tonner, Leslie. *The Difficult Child*. New York: Bantam, 1985.

Notes

1. Eleanor E. Maccoby and John A. Martin, "Socialization in the Context of the Family: Parent-Child Interaction," in *Handbook of Child Psychology,* eds. Paul H. Mussen and E. Mavis Hetherington, vol. 4: *Socializaion, Personality, and Social Development.* 4th ed. (New York: John Wiley, 1983), pp. 1–101.

2. Martha J. Cox, Margaret Tresch Owen, Jerry M. Lewis, and V. Kay Henderson, "Marriage, Adult Adjustment, and Early Parenting," *Child Development* 60 (1989): 1015–1024.

3. Ross D. Parke and Barbara J. Tinsley, "Family Interaction in Infancy," in *Handbook of Infant Development,* 2nd ed., ed. Joy Doniger Osofsky (New York: John Wiley, 1987), pp. 579–641.

4. Ellen Galinsky, *Between Generations: The Six Stages of Parenthood* (New York: Times Books, 1981).

5. Myra Leifer, "Psychological Changes Accompanying Motherhood and Pregnancy," *Genetic Psychology Monographs* 95 (1977): pp. 55–96.

6. Roberta Plutzik and Maria Laghi, *The Private Life of Parents* (New York: Everest House, 1983).

7. Carolyn Pape Cowan and Philip A. Cowan, *When Partners Become Parents* (New York: Basic Books, 1992).

8. Marshall H. Klaus and John H. Kennell, *Maternal-Infant Bonding* (St. Louis: C. V. Mosby, 1976).

9. Michael Rutter, "Continuities and Discontinuities from Infancy," in *Handbook of Infant Development,* 2nd ed., ed. Osofsky, pp. 1256–1297.

10. Russell A. Isabella, Jay Belsky, and Alexander von Eye, "Origins of Infant-Mother Attachment: An Examination of Synchrony during the Infant's First Year," *Developmental Psychology* 25 (1989): 12–21.

11. Alicia F. Lieberman, Donna R. Weston, and Jerie H. Paul, "Preventive Intervention and Outcome with Anxiously Attached Dyads," *Child Development* 62 (1991): 199–209.

12. Isabella, Belsky, and von Eye, "Origins of Infant-Mother Attachment."

13. Ross D. Parke, "Perspectives on Father-Infant Interaction," in *Handbook of Infant Development,* ed. Osofsky, pp. 549–590.

14. Lisa J. Bridges, James P. Connell, and Jay Belsky, "Similarities and Differences in Infant-Mother and Infant-Father Interaction in the Strange Situation: A Component Process Analysis," *Developmental Psychology* 24 (1988): 92–100.

15. Jay Belsky, Bonnie Gilstrap, and Michael Rovine, "The Pennsylvania Infant and Family Development Project, I: Stability and Change in Mother-Infant and Father-Infant Interaction in a Family Setting at One, Three and Nine Months," *Child Development* 55 (1984): 692–705.

16. Beverly I. Fagot and Richard Hagan, "Observations of Parent Reactions to Sex-Stereotyped Behaviors: Age and Sex Effects," *Child Development* 62 (1991): 617–628.

17. Parke and Tinsley, "Family Interaction in Infancy."

18. Everett Waters, Judith Wippman, and L. Alan Sroufe, "Attachment, Positive Affect, and Competence in the Peer Group: Two Studies in Construct Validation," *Child Development* 50 (1979): 821–829.

19. Martha F. Erickson, L. Alan Sroufe, and Byron Egeland, "The Relationship Between Quality of Attachment and Behavior Problems in Preschool in a High Risk Sample," in *Growing Points of Attachment Theory and Research,* ed. Inge Bretherton and Everett Waters, Monographs of the Society for Research in Child Development 50 (1985), serial no. 109, pp. 147–166.

20. Judith A. Crowell and S. Shirley Feldman, "Mother's Internal Models of Relationships and Developmental Status: A Study of Mother-Child Interaction," *Child Development* 59 (1988): 1273–1285.

21. Cowan and Cowan, *When Partners Become Parents,* p. 142.

22. Ibid.

23. Hakan Stattin and Ingrid Klackenberg-Larsson, "The Short- and Long-Term Implications for Parent-Child Relations of Parents' Prenatal Preferences for Their Child's Gender," *Developmental Psychology* 27 (1991): 141–147.

24. Alexander Thomas and Stella Chess, *Temperament and Development* (New York: Bunner/Mazel, 1977).

25. Anneliese F. Korner, Charles H. Zeanah, Janine Linden, Robert I. Berkowitz, Helena C. Kraemer, and W. Stewart Agras, "The Relation Between Neonatal and Later Activity and Temperament," *Child Development* 56 (1985): 38–42.

26. John E. Bates, Christine A. Maslin, and Karen H. Frankel, "Attachment Security, Mother-Child Interaction and Temperament as Predicators of Behavior Problem Ratings at Age Three Years," in *Growing Points of Attachment Theory and Research,* eds. Bretherton and Waters, pp. 167–193.

27. Denise Daniels and Robert Plomin, "Origins of Individual Differences in Infant Shyness," *Developmental Psychology* 21 (1985): 118–121.

28. Sarah Mangelsdorf et al., "Infant Proneness-to-Distress Temperament, Maternal Personality, and Mother-Infant Attachment: Associations and Goodness of Fit," *Child Development* 61 (1990): 820–831.

29. Marc Weissbluth, *Crybabies* (New York: Arbor House, 1984).

30. Sylvia M. Bell and Mary D. Salter Ainsworth, "Infant Crying and Maternal Responsiveness," *Child Development* 43 (1972): 1171–1190.

31. Judy Dunn, *Distress and Comfort* (Cambridge, Mass.: Harvard University Press, 1977), p. 23.

32. Urs A. Hunziker and Ronald G. Barr, "Increased Carrying Reduces Crying: A Randomized Controlled Trial," *Pediatrics* 77 (1986): 641–647.

33. William A. H. Sammons, *The Self-Calmed Baby* (Boston: Little, Brown, 1989).

34. Claire B. Kopp, "Antecedents of Self-Regulation: A Developmental Perspective," *Developmental Psychology* 18 (1982): 199–214.

35. Maccoby and Martin, "Socialization in the Context of the Family," p. 65.

36. Susan Crockenberg and Cindy Litman, "Autonomy as Competence in Two-Year-Olds: Maternal Correlates of Child Defiance, Compliance, and Self-Assertion," *Developmental Psychology* 26 (1990): 961–971.

37. George Holden, "Avoiding Conflicts: Mothers as Tacticians in the Supermarket," *Child Development* 54 (1983): 233–240; Thomas G. Power and M. Lynne Chapieski, "Childrearing and Impulsive Control in Toddlers: A Naturalistic Investigation," *Developmental Psychology* 22 (1986): 271–275; George W. Holden and Meredith J. West, "Proximate Regulation by Mothers: A Demonstration of How Differing Styles Affect Young Children's Behavior," *Child Development* 60 (1989): 64–69.

38. Leon Kuczynski and Grazyna Kochanska, "Development of Children's Noncompliance Strategies from Toddlerhood to Age 5," *Developmental Psychology* 26 (1990): 398–408.

39. Maccoby and Martin, "Socialization in the Context of the Family;" Crockenberg and Litman, "Autonomy as Competence in Two-Year-Olds."

40. Sandra R. Kaler and Claire B. Kopp, "Compliance and Comprehension in Very Young Toddlers," *Child Development* 61 (1991): 1997–2003.

41. Cheryl Minton, Jerome Kagan, and Janet A. Levine, "Maternal Control and Obedience in the Two-Year-Old," *Child Development* 42 (1971): 1873–1894.

42. Harriet L. Rheingold, Kay V. Cook, and Vicki Kolowitz, "Commands Cultivate the Behavioral Pleasure of 2-Year-Old Children," *Developmental Psychology* 23 (1987): 146–151.

43. L. Alan Sroufe, "Socioemotional Development," in *Handbook of Infant Development,* ed. Osofsky), pp. 462–506; Michael Lewis,

Margaret W. Sullivan, Catherine Stanger, and Myra Weiss, "Self Development and Self-Conscious Emotions," *Child Development* 60 (1989): 146–156.

44. Carol Zander Malatesta and Jeannette M. Haviland, "Learning Display Rules: The Socialization of Emotion Expression in Infancy," *Child Development* 53 (1982): 991–1003.

45. Kopp, "Regulation of Distress and Negative Emotions; Edward Z. Tronick, "Emotions and Emotional Communications in Infants," *American Psychologist* 44 (1989): 112–119.

46. Carroll E. Izard and Carol Z. Malatesta, "Perspectives on Emotional Development I: Differential Emotions Theory of Early Emotional Development," in *Handbook of Infant Development,* 2nd ed., ed. Osofsky, pp. 494–554.

47. Tronick, "Emotions and Emotional Communication in Infants."

48. John S. Watson, "Smiling, Cooing and 'the Game,'" *Merrill-Palmer Quarterly* 18 (1972): 323–339.

49. Inge Bretherton, Janet Fritz, Carolyn Zahn-Waxler, and Doreen Ridgeway, "Learning to Talk about Emotions: A Functionalist Perspective," *Child Development* 57 (1986): 529–548; Kopp, "Regulation of Distress and Negative Emotions."

50. Kopp, "Regulation of Distress and Negative Emotions."

51. Ibid.

52. Bretherton et al., "Learning to Talk about Emotions."

53. Sally K. Donaldson and Michael A. Westerman, "Development of Children's Understanding of Ambivalent and Causal Theories of Emotions," *Developmental Psychology* 22 (1986): 655–662.

54. Richard A. Fabes, Nancy Eisenberg, Sharon E. McCormick, and Michael S. Wilson, "Preschoolers' Attributions of the Situational Determinants of Others' Naturally Occurring Emotions," *Developmental Psychology* 24 (1988): 376–385.

55. Gertrude Nunner-Winkler and Beate Sodian, "Children's Understanding of Moral Emotions," *Child Development* 59 (1988): 1323–1338.

56. Frank A. Zelko, S. Wayne Duncan, R. Christopher Barden, Judy Garber, and John C. Masters, "Adult Expectations about Children's Emotional Responsiveness: Implications for the Development of

Implicit Theories of Affect," *Developmental Psychology* 22 (1986): 109–114.

57. Florence L. Goodenough, *Anger in Young Children* (Minneapolis: University of Minnesota Press, 1931).

58. Haim G. Ginott, *Between Parent and Child* (New York: Avon, 1969).

59. Adele Faber and Elaine Mazlish, *Liberated Children* (New York: Avon, 1975).

60. Thomas Gordon, *P.E.T.: Parent Effectiveness Training* (New York: New American Library, 1975).

61. Rudolf Dreikurs with Vicki Soltz, *Children: The Challenge* (New York: Hawthorn, 1964).

62. John D. Krumboltz and Helen B. Krumboltz, *Changing Children's Behavior* (Englewood Cliffs, N.J.: Prentice-Hall, 1972).

63. Stanley Turecki and Leslie Tonner, *The Difficult Child* (New York: Bantam Books, 1985).

64. Marion Radke-Yarrow et al., "Learning Concern for Others," *Developmental Psychology* 8 (1973): 240–260; Herbert Wray, *Emotions in the Lives of Young Children,* Department of Health, Education, and Welfare Publication no. 78-644 (Rockville, Md.: 1978).

65. Fabes, Eisenberg, McCormick, and Wilson, "Preschoolers' Attributions of the Situational Determinants of Others' Naturally Occurring Emotions."

66. David Matsumoto, Norma Haan, Gary Yabrove, Paola Theodorou, and Caroline Cooke Carney, "Preschoolers' Moral Actions and Emotions in Prisoner's Dilemma," *Developmental Psychology* 22 (1986): 663–670.

67. Radke-Yarrow et al., "Learning Concern for Others."

68. Michael Lewis and Linda Michalson, *Children's Emotions and Moods* (New York: Plenum, 1983).

69. John Money, "Human Hermaphroditism," in *Human Sexuality in Four Perspectives,* ed. Frank A. Beach (Baltimore: Johns Hopkins University Press, 1976), pp. 62–86.

70. Deanna Kuhn, Sharon Churnin Nash, and Laura Brucken, "Sex Role Concepts of Two- and Three-Year-Olds," *Child Development* 49 (1978): 445–451.

71. Beverly I. Fagot and Mary D. Leinbach, "The Young Child's Gender Schema: Environmental Input, Internal Organization," *Child Development* 60 (1989): 663–672.

72. Judy Dunn, *Sisters and Brothers* (Cambridge, Mass.: Harvard University Press, 1985).

73. Robert B. Stewart, "Sibling Attachment Relationships: Child Infant Interactions in the Strange Situation," *Developmental Psychology* 19 (1983): 192–199.

74. Judy Dunn and Penny Munn, "Becoming a Family Member: Family Conflict and the Development of Social Understanding in the Second Year," *Child Development* 56 (1985): 480–492; Judy Dunn and Penny Munn, "Development of Justification in Disputes with Mother and Siblings," *Developmental Psychology* 23 (1987): 791–798.

75. Dunn, *Sisters and Brothers.*

76. Robert B. Stewart, Linda A. Mobley, Susan S. Van Tuyl, and Myron A. Salvador, "The Firstborn's Adjustment to the Birth of a Sibling: A Longitudinal Assessment," *Child Development* 58 (1987): 341–355.

77. Ginott, *Between Parent and Child.*

78. Gordon, *PET: Parent Effectiveness Training.*

79. Dreikurs with Soltz, *Children: The Challenge.*

80. Robert Eimers and Robert Aitchison, *Effective Parents/Responsible Children* (New York: McGraw-Hill, 1977).

81. Dorothy C. Briggs, *Your Child's Self-Esteem* (Garden City, N.Y.: Doubleday, 1975).

82. Carollee Howes, *Peer Interaction of Young Children,* with Commentary by Kenneth H. Rubin, Hildy S. Ross, and Doran C. French, Monographs of the Society for Research in Child Development 53 (1 Serial No. 217) (1987).

83. Willard W. Hartup, Brett Laursen, Mark I. Stewart, and Amy Eastenson, "Conflict and the Friendship Relations of Young Children," *Child Development* 59 (1988): 1590–1600.

84. Donald S. Hayes, "Cognitive Bases for Liking and Disliking Among Preschool Children," *Child Development* 49 (1978): 906–909.

85. Michael P. Leiter, "A Study of Reciprocity in Preschool Play Groups," *Child Development* 48 (1977): 1288–1295.

86. Donald L. Pastor, "The Quality of Mother-Infant Attachment and Its Relationship to Toddler's Initial Sociability with Peers," *Developmental Psychology* 17 (1981): 326–335.

87. Ellen Galinsky, *Between Generations: The Six Stages of Parenthood* (New York: Times Books, 1981).

88. Ibid., pp. 136–137.

THE ELEMENTARY
SCHOOL YEARS

C H A P T E R   6

The first day of elementary school will launch your child on a sea of opportunity to increase competence. Additional stresses will accompany the greater independence. How will your child manage in his or her expanded world, away from the protection and nurturing of the family environment? Your role as a parent will change dramatically as you encourage independence yet continue to guide the child's behavior. What can you do to foster your child's development when he or she is away in school? To promote reliable habits, self-regulation? How will you encourage your child in school and discourage too much television? Parents remain a powerful influence as the young child copes during the elementary school years.

These years from five to eleven are a time of expansion for children. They have mastered the routines of living—eating, dressing, toileting—and can take care of many of their own needs. They have mastered language and can express themselves easily. Their world expands as they go off to school, meet new friends, and adjust to more demanding tasks. While they are growing in competence, stress increases in their lives as well. Because they are able to compare themselves to others and to external standards, they worry about their competence in many areas and feel vulnerable to embarrassment and feelings of inadequacy. Parents have a powerful role in helping children cope with these new demands.

PARENT-CHILD RELATIONSHIPS

Parents' acceptance, attention, involvement, and sensitivity to children's needs continue to be major forces in helping children become responsible, competent, happy individuals.[1] But changes are occurring in parent-child relationships. Parents spend half as much time with their school-age children as with preschoolers. They are less affectionate and demonstrative.[2] But parents are still the number one figures in their children's lives, and children's greatest fear, as we shall see, is losing their parents.

WHAT I WISH I HAD KNOWN
ABOUT THE ELEMENTARY SCHOOL YEARS

"I wish I'd known how much you need to be an advocate for your child with the school. When we grew up, our parents put us in public school and that was it. Then it was up to the teachers. Unless there was a discipline problem, parents did not get involved. Now, you have a lot more options, and the public schools aren't always great; so you realize how active you need to be in order to insure a good education for your children." MOTHER

"The main thing, I think, is how important temperament is. I knew about temperament, but I did not know how important it is to go with the child's temperament. My daughter was in one school that was very noncompetitive; that's a wonderful philosophy, but it wasn't right for her. She is very competitive, and in that atmosphere she did not do as well. So with the second child, we are going to be more careful to see that there is a good fit between her temperament and what she is doing." FATHER

"I was surprised that even though the children are older, they take as much time as when they were younger; but you spend the time in different ways. I thought when they started school, I would have a little more time. Instead of giving them baths at night and rocking them, I supervise homework and argue about taking baths. Instead of taking them on Saturday to play in the park, I take them on a Brownie event. Knowing that things were going to take as much time would have made me less impatient in the beginning, and I would have planned better." MOTHER

"I learned that especially from five to eight, say, children are not as competent as they look. They really can't do a lot of things that on the surface you think they can. They have language, and they look like they're reasoning, and they look like their motor skills are okay. So you say, 'When you get up in the morning, I want you to make your cereal,' and they can't do it consistently. And so because we didn't know that with the first child, I think we made excessive demands on her, which led to her being a little harsher on herself. Now with the second one, if she can't tie her shoes by herself today, even though she could two weeks ago, we're more likely to say, 'Okay,' instead of, 'Well, you can tie your shoes; go ahead and do it.' If you give them a little help, it doesn't mean you are making babies of them; it means they have room to take it from there." FATHER

"I wish I'd known more about their abilities and work readiness. My daughter had some special needs in school. In preschool, she did well, although I could see there were immaturities in her drawings and writing; but she got lots of happy faces. I was misled by the positive comments they always wanted to make to her, and I thought she was doing better than she was. When she got to school, it came as quite a shock that she was having problems. With my son, I have been more on top and I ask more questions abut how he is really doing, because I want to get any special needs he has addressed. My advice to any parent is that, if at all possible, volunteer in your child's school. I gave up half a day's pay, and in my financial situation that was a real hardship. It is very, very important to keep a handle on not just what is happening educationally, but also who the peers are and what is going on." MOTHER

Changes are occurring because parents no longer have exclusive control of children who now spend several hours a day in school under the control of other adults. So parents begin to permit children to make decisions that parents monitor and supervise; parents have final approval of what children do. This sharing of control with children serves as a bridge to the preadolescent and adolescent years when children will assume more control.[3]

Conflicts between parents and children center on children's interpersonal behavior with others (their fighting, teasing), children's personality characteristics (their irritability, stubbornness), and parents' regulating activities like TV watching, chores, bed time, curfews.[4] Parents are more likely to justify their point of view in terms of conventionality, practicality, and health issues. Children are more likely to listen to parents' rules that prevent harm and psychological damage to others. Children report they have more conflicts with fathers than mothers.

In the elementary school period, mothers and fathers continue to relate to children in different ways.[5] Mothers take major responsibility for managing family tasks—scheduling homework and baths, for example. Mothers are both more directive with children and more positive in their reactions to them.

Fathers, though more generally neutral in affect, continue to engage in more physical play and give more affection to both boys and girls. When fathers have high-status jobs, they have less time to spend with their children, and so low job salience is related to men's playfulness and caregiving.[6] Men are most likely to be involved as fathers when mothers do not take on all the caregiving and managing, closing fathers out. Nevertheless, the more skillful the mothers are with children, the more skillful fathers become. Both parents are similar in being more demanding of boys and more disapproving of their misbehavior.[7]

When parents make demands on the child, social responsibility increases in boys and self-assertiveness increases in girls. Diana Baumrind suggests that parents actively encourage characteristics outside the usual sex role stereotypes. Unless they exert a specific effort to encourage a broader range of characteristics, the natural tendencies for both mothers and fathers is to encourage assertiveness in boys and cooperation and a more dependent role in girls.[8]

Minority parents, in this period, direct more effort at socializing their children with regard to their racial or ethnic identity. Children reason more logically and better understand parents' statements about ethnic issues. Since children spend more time outside parents' direct control, in schools or other activities, they more likely experience prejudice or, at least, confusion at the different values other people hold.

Parents serve as a buffer between children and the larger society. As in so many areas, they interpret social experiences for their children and help them deal with the situations. To socialize children with regard to racial and ethnic issues, parents first teach children (1) their own cultural values, (2) the values of the majority culture, and (3) the realities of being a member of their own group in the majority culture and how people cope with the realities.[9] Successful socialization goes beyond this to teach pride in one's ethnic group and the importance of one's own self-development.

Let us look at how Afro-American parents socialize children; more is known about this group, and other groups may experience a similar process.[10] Afro-American

---

◆
BOX 6-1
SOCIALIZATION MESSAGES
AFRO-AMERICAN PARENTS IMPART TO CHILDREN*

Message	% Parents
Achieving and working hard: *"Work hard and get a good education."*	22
Racial pride: *"Be proud of being black."*	17
Themes of black heritage: *"Taught what happened in the past and how people coped."*	9
Focus on intergroup relations: *Summary category of many responses—accommodate to whites, use collective action to help blacks*	9
Presence of racial restrictions and barriers: *"Blacks don't have the opportunities whites have."*	8
Good citizenship: *"Be honest, fair."*	7
Recognition and acceptance of racial background: *"Realize you are black."*	7
Fundamental equality of blacks and whites: *"Recognize all races as equal."*	6
Maintenance of a positive self-image:	5
Instruct children to stay away from whites.	3**

* Information from the National Survey of Black Americans, a representative national sample of 2,107 men and women. Statements tabulated from the answers to two questions: "In raising children, have you told them things to help them know what it is to be black?" and "What are the most important things you have said?"

** Remaining categories of 1 or 2 percent include a variety of responses having to do with emphasizing religious principles, discussing personal traits, stressing general self-acceptance.

From Michael C. Thornton, Linda M. Chatters, Robert Joseph Taylor, and Walter R. Allen, "Sociodemographic and Environmental Correlates of Racial Socialization by Black Parents," *Child Development* 61 (1990): 401–409.

---

parents think teaching about their racial identity is important, but not *the* most important information to pass on to children. To parents, being Afro-American means children should learn how to deal with prejudice, feel pride and self-respect, learn the value of a good education, and recognize that their fair and moral behavior is not always reciprocated.

Many parents do not discuss ethnic issues with their children. In a national sample, over one-third of parents reported making no statements, and few of the two-thirds who reported making a statement touched on more than one area. Which parents are most likely to talk to their children? Older, married parents who live in racially mixed neighborhoods with a sizeable white population are most likely to talk to children. Mothers are more likely to socialize children than fathers. Parents living in the Northeast are more likely to discuss racial matters, perhaps because, as in mixed neighborhoods, there is more contact between the two races.

What do parents say to children? Box 6-1 summarizes what parents say. Only about 22 percent teach racial pride and a positive self-image. Yet this is the area parents are most uniquely fitted to address. Both majority and minority children evaluate themselves as others close to them do, and so what parents convey strongly affects self-esteem. Since a minority child may get inaccurate and negative messages from other children, the media, and authority figures like coaches or teachers, it is even more important for minority parents to encourage a positive self-image and racial pride.

When parents emphasize awareness of social restrictions and barriers and at the same time encourage self-development and ethnic pride, children are happy and high in self-esteem and are successful in school.[11]

SIBLING RELATIONSHIPS

The variety and intensity of feelings that marked sibling relationships in earlier years continue through the elementary school years.[12] Some children like to play with brothers and sisters and report they hardly ever fight. An equal number report they almost never play but fight all the time. Feelings, however, are often mixed. When questioned, one-third report they would be happier without siblings; yet despite all their criticism, 75 percent of the group would like another sibling.[13]

Positive relationships between siblings are associated with parents' reactions to the children. When parents are responsive and meet children's needs, children share, comfort, and help each other more. Hostility increases when parents play favorites and respond to one child's needs but not the other's.[14]

Parents minimize the intensity of sibling rivalry when they emphasize and treat each child in the family as a unique individual. They do not compare children—not even if the comparisons are accurate and are meant to be informative. There are no statements like, "You are more responsible," "You are lazier than your sister," "She is more popular," "He is shyer." Parents avoid assigning children to particular roles in the family. They avoid describing one child as a student, another as the family joker, still another as a politician. Each child is valued for his or her special qualities.

When children are angry, jealous, frustrated with siblings, parents listen and accept the feelings without trying to change or modify them. To help parents understand the intensity of these feelings, Adele Faber and Elaine Mazlish encourage parents in their workshops to imagine how they would feel if their spouse took a second husband or wife and expected them to accept it.[15] Using that example, they present several vignettes that parallel the many experiences an older child has with a second or third baby. Parents are surprised at the intensity of their own reactions and have greater empathy for their children's feelings.

When conflict occurs, parents have several alternatives for action depending on the intensity of the conflict. When minor bickering or arguing occur, parents can ignore it as a behaviorist might recommend or leave it to the children to settle as Dreikurs would recommend. Thus, one does not give undue attention to undesirable behavior. Dreikurs' unique contribution is his suggestion that when one child disrupts the family, all children receive the same treatment and get the message that all are responsible for getting along together. Such treatment insures that misbehavior does not result in undue attention to the instigating child as that may be the main purpose in the misbehavior.[16]

When conflict escalates, parents can intervene and offer children an opportunity to problem-solve the situation as Gordon would recommend.[17] If children can not settle their differences, parents must intervene to guarantee that no child is hurt. Children can be sent to separate places until they are willing to settle differences. Faber and Mazlish recommend children be encouraged to draw or write down their grievances so siblings can understand their point of view. Parents' responsibility is to stop fighting when a child might get hurt. Many adults have bitter memories of their parents allowing intense physical fighting. Parents protect children and provide opportunities for them to learn how to solve conflicts in constructive ways.

Development of the Self

Children continue to define themselves in terms of their physical features, possessions, activities, and capabilities. Note this self-description by a nine-year-old boy: "My name is Bruce C. I have brown eyes. I have brown hair. I have brown eyebrows. I'm nine years old. I LOVE! Sports. I have seven people in my family. I have great! eyesight. I have lots! of friends. I live on 1923 Pinecrest Dr. I'm going on ten in September. I'm a boy. I have an uncle that is almost seven feet tall. My school is Pinecrest. My teacher is Mrs. V. I play Hockey! I'm almost the smartest boy in class. I LOVE! food. I love fresh air. I LOVE School."[18]

Abilities and actions are still prominent in self-descriptions, but now children begin to make comparisons between themselves and other children. We see this in Bruce's self-description as "almost the smartest boy in class." In older children we begin to see mention of social aspects of the self. Children mention membership in groups: "A Girl Scout," "a member of the soccer team." Psychological traits are also mentioned, as in Bruce's description of his intelligence.

As children develop a greater sense of identity and become more aware of other children's qualities, they evaluate themselves and their own self-worth. Children from four to seven evaluate themselves in terms of two factors: (1) their overall level of competence and (2) their social acceptance. Just as children's conceptions of self become more differentiated with age, so the dimensions on which they evaluate themselves become more complex. Children of eight and older evaluate themselves on four dimensions: (1) their physical competence in sports, (2) their cognitive competence in school work, (3) their social competence with peers, and (4) their general self-worth.[19] As you'll recall, in Chapter 2 we noted the close relationship between feelings of overall self-worth and feelings of social competence and physical attractiveness.

In this period, minority group children are learning about their own ethnic identities and what it means to be part of that culture. By age ten, they know their identity and prefer their own group. Mary Jane Rotheram-Borus and Jean Phinney suggest children show ethnic differences on the four basic dimensions of behavior listed in Box 6-2.[20]

As they progress through elementary school, minority students become more attached to their cultural traditions, and the children with the highest self-esteem are most identified with their cultural behavior pattern. Still, some children identify with the majority culture. How this occurs and what it means for the child's well-being are not known.

As children begin to make comparisons with other children, parents may want them to be accurate. However, evidence suggests that it is better to overrate your abilities and to see yourself more positively than objective tests or ratings might warrant. For example, children who overrate their abilities in school are more likely to respond to failure by getting help, finding out what they did wrong, and remedying the situation because it does not fit with their view of themselves.[21]

Albert Bandura, who has written on the importance of believing in one's own abilities to take effective action (self-efficacy), states that in hazardous situations, accuracy in self-perception of abilities is essential; for example, if you overestimate your ability to swim in heavy surf, you are in trouble and may not have a chance to correct the perception. In many nonhazardous situations, though, people are more effective when they overrate their abilities.[22]

Life is full of problems and, to overcome them, we have to persevere. People are most likely to persist when they believe in themselves. Optimistic views of the self, then, help people make the most of their talents. Young children appear naturally optimistic as they enter school and as they look ahead in life. Parents need to encourage and nurture this beneficial optimism.[23]

DEVELOPMENT OF SELF-REGULATION

Children in these years are learning to control aggression, fearfulness, and worry. **Aggression** decreases in the elementary school years, and when it does occur, it is more likely verbal than physical. Children's **fearfulness** decreases as well, and children are no longer worried about the dark or animals in general though they continue to fear some specific animals like snakes.

What are the events children find stressful? Table 6-1 lists children's ratings of stressful events from 1 (least upsetting) to 7 (most upsetting). Children around the world, regardless of sex or socioeconomic status, agree with each other on what is upsetting even more than the adults and children within the same culture do.[24]

Loss of a parent is the most devastating, and the birth of a sibling, the least upsetting. Parental fights are highly stressful as well. Children reveal their sensitivity in their distress at embarrassing situations—wetting their pants, being caught in a theft, being ridiculed in class. Although many students like school, it is also a source of

---

BOX 6-2
FOUR BASIC DIMENSIONS OF ETHNIC DIFFERENCES IN CHILDREN

1. An orientation toward group ties, interdependence, and sharing versus an orientation toward independence and competition
2. Active, achievement-oriented approach that changes a situation versus a passive, fatalistic approach that insists on self-change to remedy the situation
3. Acceptance of, respect for, and belief in powerful authorities versus an egalitarian view that allows questioning of authority
4. Overtly expressive, spontaneous style versus an inhibited, formal style

Adapted from Mary Jane Rotheram-Borus and Jean S. Phinney, "Patterns of Social Expectations among Black and Mexican-American Children," *Child Development* 61 (1990): 543.

---

anxiety, frustration, and unhappiness with worry about grades, being retained, and making mistakes. Adults may be surprised at children's sensitivity to embarrassing situations and their concern about school. The data emphasize that children may have a different life perspective that may not be immediately apparent to parents.

When children ages six to twelve are asked how to handle stressful situations—like having a friend move away, going to the doctor's office for a shot, having a parent angry at them—their solutions generally attack the source of the problem to change the upsetting circumstances.[25] They are most likely to strike at the roots of the difficulty when the problem focuses on peers or school, where they feel they have more control.

Children are most likely to suggest adjusting to situations—like doctors' visits—that are seen as inevitable.[26] Younger children are the most active in changing the upsetting circumstances. As children grow older, they are more likely to adapt to circumstances, particularly when others are seen as having control.

Parents have a powerful role in helping children cope with fears of tragic events and worries about school events. Parents can not control the occurrence of these events, but they can help children master their reactions to the events. Parents' interpretations of the events shape children's attitudes about difficulties and adversities. Recall Martin Seligman's views described in Chapter 3 on the importance of teaching optimistic attitudes about life.[27] Optimistic attitudes motivate individuals to exert effort to get what they want.

Seligman documented the nature of pessimistic attitudes that lead to discouragement and withdrawal from challenging tasks. Pessimistic individuals consider difficulty a sign of a pervasive, permanent problem that is one's personal fault. They see the problem as unchangeable. Pessimistic children see a poor math grade as the result of their own stupidity and inability to do math. They sometimes avoid studying because they are discouraged and feel they are no good at the subject.

As outlined in Chapter 3, parents can supply new interpretations of the problem. Perhaps the child did not study enough and that can be changed. If the child has a special difficulty with math, a tutor can be obtained. The teacher may have given a

TABLE 6-1
SCALE VALUES* OF CHILDREN'S RATINGS ON STRESSFULNESS OF LIFE EVENTS

Life Event	Egypt	Canada	Australia	Japan	Philippines	USA(a)	USA(b)
Losing parent	6.88	6.88	6.92	6.90	6.76	6.90	6.76
Going blind	6.83	6.75	6.83	6.68	6.70	6.86	6.58
Academic retainment	6.83	6.32	5.94	6.78	6.21	6.82	6.30
Wetting in class	6.73	6.17	6.58	6.73	5.43	6.74	5.78
Parental fights	6.83	5.57	6.16	6.23	6.32	6.71	6.54
Caught in theft	6.62	5.71	6.08	6.73	4.29	6.63	5.20
Suspected of lying	6.62	5.58	6.04	6.73	5.88	6.53	5.86
A poor report card	6.69	5.46	5.69	6.61	5.57	6.23	5.52
Sent to principal	6.63	4.45	5.11	6.63	3.22	5.75	4.68
Having an operation	6.55	4.35	4.58	5.82	4.28	5.51	4.80
Getting lost	6.52	4.22	5.22	5.01	3.90	5.49	4.52
Ridiculed in class	6.63	4.25	4.67	6.11	6.26	5.28	4.65
Move to a new school	6.52	3.41	4.17	5.21	2.55	4.60	4.09
Scary dream	6.59	3.69	4.63	5.07	4.80	4.08	4.06
Not making 100 on test	6.46	2.94	2.94	5.04	3.15	3.75	4.05
Picked last on team	4.73	3.94	2.40	5.92	3.45	3.30	3.30
Losing in game	5.68	2.79	2.23	4.48	3.33	3.16	2.75
Going to dentist	4.87	2.42	1.43	3.05	2.30	2.73	2.54
Giving class report	3.08	2.98	1.53	2.75	1.78	2.58	2.79
New baby sibling	1.20	1.42	1.18	1.43	1.25	1.27	1.46
N**	296	283	191	248	156	367	273
Grade	3–6	7–9	3–8	4–6	5–6	4–6	4–6

*Scale Value: 1–7 (low–high)
**N = Number in sample

From Kaoru Yamamoto, Abdalla Soliman, James Parsons, and O. L. Davies, Jr., "Voices in Unison: Stressful Events in the Lives of Children in Six Countries," *Journal of Child Psychology and Psychiatry* 28 (1987): p. 857.

very hard exam or not allowed enough time. A child has no control over these factors, but can deal with them by being overly prepared for the next test.

Parents help their child to see that the outcome of any school or social event is determined by multiple causes, and the child is never the sole determiner of the events. Children must, however, work on those factors that are within their control. Parents can take the broad view over and over again to help children see that most situations can be improved with effort. Parents encourage children to use their time and energy selectively. When children have reached the maximum benefit of effort, they move on to other activities. For example, when a child feels rejected because she is not invited to a peer's bithday party, parents can suggest ways she might be a more outgoing friend. If new techniques do not work with that friend, the child has to move on and make new friends to be happy. Parents remain optimistic that children will either remedy a situation or find pleasure elsewhere.

Since children adapt their reasoning about difficulties from their parents' ways of reasoning, parents must be careful how they interpret events in their own lives. When they see a problem as unremediable and pervasive, they predispose their children to similar interpretations of events. When parents rely on derogatory criticism, no matter how accurate the criticism may be or how helpful the parent wants to be, the child becomes self-blaming and discouraged. The negative words—"You'll never have any common sense"; "You never learn anything. You just fool around"; "You don't care about anybody but yourself."—last some children a lifetime, and they never escape the impact of such discouraging messages.

Parents play an active role, too, in helping children deal with anger and aggression.

Ginott suggests that parents accept the child's anger with sympathy and understanding, although physical and verbal abuse must be controlled.[28] When nine-year-old Eric came home furious because rain had canceled a class picnic, his mother's impulse was to say, "There will be other days," or to criticize him for complaining. Instead, she commented that he seemed disappointed and frustrated. She was astounded when Eric's anger vanished—often his rages upset the entire household.

Gordon[29] suggests sending I-messages when children act aggressively. This permits the child to resolve the problem. When safety is involved, however, parents must send the message in a forceful tone and, if necessary, must take action so the child will respond.

Dreikurs believes parents should ignore fighting among children. Let siblings settle the differences themselves.[30] If a child fights with neighborhood children, parents stand back and let the other children teach the natural and logical consequences of fighting. Peers will either fight back or refuse to play with the child. Parents can talk about the difficulties later, raising questions about consequences of other ways of relating. But parents do not intervene actively.

For the child who has developed many aggressive behaviors—hitting, yelling, teasing—and uses these negative behaviors in response to the parent's discipline, Gerald Patterson and his co-workers have developed an effective behavioral program.[31] Patterson describes the coercive, or forcing, process the child uses to get family members to do what he or she wants. To change these behaviors in the child, all family members must change. The program, developed at the Oregon Research Institute, requires parents to specify behaviors they wish to change. A trained team observes the family at home for two weeks to record and understand patterns of interaction in the family.

Parents then read either *Families*[32] or *Living with Children*,[33] on behavior modification techniques. After they pass a brief test on these ideas, parents pinpoint exactly the behaviors they wish to change. Parents record the occurrence of negative and positive behaviors before making any changes in order to understand exactly what is happening before interventions are made.

The parents and child draw up a contract. The child gets points or tokens daily for behavior. For example, a child could accumulate 2 points for bedmaking, 2 points for making a school lunch, 3 points for completing homework by a specific time, 2 points for picking up the bedroom, 1 point for brushing teeth without being reminded. The child could use the points for an extra 30 minutes of TV (5 points), extra story (2 points), extra 30 minutes up in the evening (3 points). A child loses points for sibling fighting (2 points), yelling at parents (2 points). Parents deduct points without nagging, criticizing, or scolding. The number of points are added up daily, and rewards are given each evening. Psychologists from the institute contact families at certain times to note progress in changing behavior.

The Oregon Research Institute treatment has the following effects: (1) significant and persistent changes in the child's behavior, (2) modest decrease in coercive behavior of all family members, (3) increased positive perception of the child by parents, (4) no further unconscious parental rewards for negative behavior, (5) more effective punishments, (6) a more active role by fathers in controlling children's behavior, (7) mothers' perception of their whole family as happier.

Lying and Stealing

Ginott makes several basic points about lying. First, lying may represent the child's basic hopes and fears and, in that sense, is an accurate statement of feelings although not an accurate statement of fact. This is particularly true of preschool children. When a parent knows a young child is lying, the parent can reflect the child's feelings: "You wish you owned a horse," or "You wish you were going to the zoo." Second, parents sometimes encourage lying about feelings. They punish a child who says she hates her sister or tells a relative she is ugly. The child learns it is best to lie about how she really feels. Parents are wiser to accept the child's feelings. They can also explain that polite refusal to comment is a way of being both kind and honest. There really are times when "if you can't say something nice, you shouldn't say anything at all."

Third, parents must avoid provoking a lie by asking an embarrassing question to which they already have the answer. For example, if a parent finds an overdue library book that the child has said he returned, the parent should not ask, "Did you return that book to the library?"

Dreikurs takes an understanding attitude toward lying and urges parents not to view it as a terrible act. If parents are not severe when children commit a misdeed, children will not be afraid and will not feel that they must always present themselves in the best possible light. When parents are truthful in their everyday lives, children are more likely to be truthful. When lying does occur, Dreikurs suggests parents remain unimpressed. Children may be lying to get attention or to win a power struggle and make the parents feel helpless. Dreikurs advises a game in which the parent demonstrates how important truthfulness in the family is. In the game, everybody is free to say whatever they like, whether it is true or not. Mother may call a child for a meal that is not there or promise a movie and then say she did not mean it. A child may come to prefer the truth after such a game. When lying stems from a need to boost confidence, parents need to show approval and appreciation for positive behavior, so that lying is not the only route to attention.

Like Dreikurs, the behaviorists urge parents to make telling the truth worthwhile. They illustrate how lying is rewarded in the following episode.[34] A young boy knocked over his mother's highly valued vase and broke it. Although he initially denied any knowledge about what had happened to the vase, a few days later he admitted he had broken it. His mother immediately restricted him to the house for the rest of the month, saying that would certainly teach him a lesson. From this incident, the boy learned he could avoid punishment if he lied and that if he told the truth he could get into trouble. The mother could have said that she was glad the boy had told the truth and asked him to contribute chore money to help pay for a new vase. If she had done that, her son would have learned that honesty is rewarded with respect and that he would have to help replace things he broke.

Like lying, stealing is not that uncommon among children. Ginott urges parents to remain calm and to insist that the child return the object or make restitution. If, as often happens, the child steals from the parent, the parent asks for return of the object or deducts the cost from the child's allowance. Children are expected to discuss their needs for money or possessions with parents. When stealing occurs, however, parents do not get angry. They express disappointment and hurt. As with lying, if parents know that a child has broken a rule, it is unwise to try to trap the child with questions like, "And where did you get this new whistle?" Once a parent has expressed frustration and upset, it is the child's responsibility to change his or her behavior.

Gordon recommends mutual problem solving, as in the following example. A father discovered that his five-year-old son was stealing loose change from the dresser. Father and son held a mutual problem-solving session. The father agreed to give the boy a small allowance, and the boy agreed to save for the special things he wanted.

Dreikurs recommends taking a calm approach in which the child is not criticized or blamed but helped to be honest.

Stealing results from a variety of motives. Often the child hopes "to put something over" on the adult and to get attention, power, or revenge. Often children do not know precisely why they steal. Calm insistence that articles be returned usually teaches the child not to steal again.

SCHOOL

School is a huge step forward in a child's life. The child masters new skills, meets new friends, and adjusts to a new group of adults who evaluate the child in terms of external standards of excellence. Recall Richard Lerner's diagram in Chapter 2, depicting an interactional model of child and parent development. The school is a major force in both children's and parents' lives, as important a force as parents' work, marriage network, and family social network.

As parents are in the family, teachers are the most important persons at school. What teacher characteristics relate to learning? When teachers are flexible, when they maintain a calm, friendly atmosphere in the classroom and use gentle disciplinary techniques, then students learn.[35] When teachers give opportunities for active learning, when they have high, positive expectations for students and are personally involved in supervision and monitoring of students, then students learn. So, active learning in a calm, controlled environment with high expectations for students predicts children's achievement.

THE JOYS OF PARENTING ELEMENTARY SCHOOL CHILDREN

"You enjoy seeing them learning to read. You take pride in their accomplishments, and you know they are accomplishing a lot on their own because you do not have a lot of time to spend with each one." FATHER

"It's the beginning of having friends over and seeing them go over to friends' houses, watching some of that." MOTHER

"I have a real memory of doing some of the same things my children are doing now. I remember kindergarten and first grade, and they are playing some of the same games I did. Jenny is jumping rope to the same rhymes and songs. That is a real joy." MOTHER

"I love watching them become little people who can take responsibility for chores, and also every now and then want to cook me dinner. Now they use the microwave; they can heat something up. They'll make tuna fish and raw vegetables." MOTHER

"Well, I take her to a dance lesson on Saturday morning, and this is one of our times together. We turn on the radio and we listen for certain songs." FATHER

"There is a lot of companionship. In the car now when we are driving any distance, Jenny stays awake, and we can have full conversations. Driving into San Francisco she's become a real companion in many ways. She is fun to go shopping with. She likes to talk about friends, what we've been doing, what we are going to be doing." MOTHER

"She's very interested in my childhood, what it was like when I was a little girl, what about my parents, what was it like where I grew up in New York. That is fairly new and fairly consistent. And that's a joy." MOTHER

Who most easily makes the transition to kindergarten from preschool? The child who gets along well with other children and can play and interact cooperatively adjusts most easily to kindergarten. Children who enter school with friends or who have a stable group of friends outside of school adjust more easily. The aggressive child who has negative peer contacts in preschool is seen as hostile and aggressive by teachers and is rejected by peers.[36]

Most children start school with positive self-evaluations of their abilities and high levels of confidence about their abilities to learn.[37] Children in first grade believe all children can learn whatever is required, and it is just a matter of putting out effort—those who do well have worked harder. As children progress through school, they experience failure and develop more differentiated views of intelligence and ability.[38] They then come to view their own abilities less positively. Girls are consistently more critical of their work and more complimentary of others' work.

"It's really fun learning more about girls. She is a lot like her mother in her interests and her understanding of people. I wasn't a reader; I was out on my bike, and I really like it that she is such a big reader and enjoys many of the books her mother had as a girl." FATHER

"This is the time when I can start instilling my values, why I do what I do, how people become homeless. When they were younger, you just had the rule, 'No play guns in the house,' and now you can talk about why you have the rule, and you are interacting on a whole new level." MOTHER

"Now they really are able to help. When it comes time to take snacks to school, they really can take a big part of the responsibility of doing much of the work. In terms of making cookies, they are really able to do a lot of the work." MOTHER

"I like to watch him draw and do projects. Once I came home with a paper eight feet square, and the three youngest ones got pencils, markers, and pens and crayons, and made up all these sketches and then colored them in and covered the whole paper. They started at about 7:30 one evening on the weekend and just kept going till I had to force them to bed. Then they hung it on one of their walls. Or they took all these cardboard boxes that I brought large amounts of food home in, and they cut them up, and pasted them, sometimes with wood, to make these fancy guitars. They painted them all up with magic markers, and they had a stack of twenty cardboard instruments at one time." FATHER

"Even taking them places like the zoo or the aquarium is different now. Their interest or attention span level used to be minimal, but now their interest level is higher." MOTHER

"I love to teach French, and I do it at the school, so I have had both my children as students. It is really fun to do what I like doing and do it with them." MOTHER

continued

In forging an academic self-image, first graders ignore social categories and do not base their academic self-images on race, parent background, or family constellation. However, there are sex differences in academic self-image.[39] From first grade on, girls are eager to do what they believe parents and peers expect. They are very slow to form their own self-expectations about school performance. Boys, in contrast, are more oriented to their own self-evaluations and negatively value what parents want. They compete and want to learn quickly. Learning math is important to them, whereas it is unimportant to girls even though girls score as high on math tests and on math work as boys.

Academic self-image is initially independent of achievement. By the end of the first year a positive image is related to doing well in school. There is strong evidence that children base their self-image on their parents' beliefs about their abilities.[40] Debra Phillips found that about 20 percent of students in third and fifth grades,

THE JOYS OF PARENTING
ELEMENTARY SCHOOL CHILDREN *continued*

"He's nine, and for the last several months, maybe because I'm the Dad, he's come and said, 'Now there's this girl who's written me a note, what do I do?' Or, 'I have an interest here, how do I act?' I never heard any of this from my daughters. Then he says, 'What were you doing in the third grade? How would you deal with this when you were in the third grade?'" FATHER

"One of the joys is you are learning or relearning through your children, whether it's actual subject matter or reexperiencing things and seeing the way they handle something versus the way you did. It gives me insight into their independence that they think of different solutions for things. There's always another way besides 'Mom's way.'" MOTHER

"Every night we have a talking time just before he goes to bed, either he and his Dad or he and I. He's a real deep thinker and he likes to get advice or get a response, and he just needs that verbal connection. So a few years ago when he was five, he was talking about being afraid of death and that he might not be married and he might not have children and that would be the worst. I can hear parts of what he might hear at church or other places like school, and he takes it all very seriously; when it collides, he wants to know what the answer is. They are always things we don't know the answer to either." MOTHER

"I enjoy the rituals we have developed. I don't know how it started but every night we eat by candlelight. One lights the candles, and one turns down the dimmer, and it's a very nice touch after a day at work." MOTHER

"I can say as a father of two girls between five and ten that to be a father to girls is delightful. It's nice being looked on as a combination of God and Robert Redford. They have a little glow in their eyes when they look at Dad, and it's great. The younger one said, 'When I'm ticklish, you know why? Because I love you so much.'" FATHER

"It's wonderful to have a conversation with them that isn't about some nursery rhyme. You can sit down and have an extended conversation." MOTHER

"He does well in school because he's willing to put in time on things. It is fun to work with him on projects. He wanted a Nintendo, and we said no because it is addictive and you spend too much time on it. He had a science fair project at school, and he decided to make up a questionnaire on how kids used their Nintendo, which he handed out to everyone. I helped him analyze the answers; and he proved the longer kids had it, the less they used it, and so it wasn't addictive. When his birthday came, we got it for him. He proved he was right." FATHER

"I enjoy having them jump into bed with us. I like the way they look and feel, knowing they are my children and I can claim some of the credit." MOTHER

"One of the things that's most fun is to see my daughter sit down and read a book that I read as a child, to see her eyes light up over certain parts, and to have a conversation with her about what part was special for her." MOTHER

The most important event of these years is the child's entrance into school. Apart from the child's family, school is the most influential socializing force. School serves as a meeting place for peers and a setting for interpersonal interactions.

equal proportions of boys and girls, underestimate their abilities as measured by tests. They think they are incompetent. Because these students view their abilities poorly and expect less success, they are less persistent and less likely to succeed than more confident students. Their lack of success only reinforces their underestimations of their abilities.

Parents interpret children's performance in school and give them feedback that the children incorporate in their own self-image. How parents develop their own misperceptions of their children's abilities is not clear; but their views are passed along, and no degree of success seems to alter the children's feelings of incompetence.

Children's academic expectations of themselves gradually become related to their teachers' expectations.[41] Even first graders are aware of teachers' perceptions of their abilities, and they come to view their abilities as the teacher does. Fifth graders too perceive teachers' opinions and perform the way teachers expect.

What do students consider is a fair way to handle the ability differences in a class? Students from first grade to college all felt that the fairest way was to let fast students complete their work and then help slower students to complete theirs.[42] This option was selected far more frequently than the traditional method of letting fast students go to other activities like reading or computers after work was completed. They selected this even though most had never experienced peer helping.

Schools are structured so that girls' abilities are most valued.[43] Girls tend to be less physical, more verbal, more responsive to auditory stimuli, and more able to concentrate on a task as early as the preschool years. Not all girls have these characteristics, but many do. Boys, on average, are active and curious. They learn from doing, manipulating, and seeing. They have greater difficulty concentrating for extended periods of time. Given these sex differences, it is not surprising that boys are described as hyperactive nine times as often as girls and that they are much more likely to experience reading problems. Until schools change to take greater account of the growth patterns of boys, parents can expect their sons may have more problems in school than their daughters.

School is often the place where minority group children get their first taste of discrimination. In the years before school, children are in environments that their parents select for them. If they experience and report an unhappy event, parents can change nursery schools or day care. But for many minority parents, there are no choices outside the public school because of lack of finances.

Just as school settings do not value boys' characteristics, they do not value the cultural traditions of many minority groups. The schools most often reward the majority culture's values of competition and independent achievement. Some minority groups, like the Chinese and Japanese, stress compatible values of hard work, individual effort, a strong drive for achievement, and respect for authority. Students from these groups do well and, in fact, often exceed the performance of majority group students.

Children from different cultural backgrounds, however, with different values, may feel at a loss to achieve in a foreign environment. Parents who are aware of the mismatch that can occur between the values of the child's culture and the values of the school or teacher will be able to help both teacher and child to modify behavior so that learning takes place. Here we can list only a few of the possible kinds of mismatches to help make parents aware of what to look for if their minority children experience difficulty.

Janice Hale-Benson describes several characteristics that influence Afro-American children's learning in schools.[44] Afro-American children enter school accustomed to a high level of noise, much activity, many people, and an abundance of stimulation. They are then expected to sit still, listen to one adult speak, and work by themselves when they would really rather be expressing themselves in activity with other children. The school stifles the enthusiasm of these children and labels many of them hyperactive, just as it does many boys.

Afro-Americans are feeling-oriented people who frequently express themselves in body language rather than words. Their use of words and their style of speech differ from that of the majority culture, so there may be a mismatch between children and teacher.

A careful study carried out by S. Brice-Heath (cited in Diana Slaughter-Defoe et al.) illustrates how subtle this mismatch can be.[45] Brice-Heath observed that both parents of Afro-American students and their teachers complained of poor communication between teachers and pupils. Teachers said the children did not answer their verbal questions. The children complained the teachers asked stupid questions, didn't listen, and had their own set of rules.

Brice-Heath studied the use of questions by teachers and the Afro-American community. Teachers ask questions with obvious answers for several reasons—to start conversations with children, to draw their attention to an area they want them to think about, to direct their attention to behavior the teacher wants changed ("Are you finished talking to your friends now?" is a question we can all remember). In the Afro-American community, questions are asked to get new information, to make accusations ("Did you eat all the ice cream?"), and to get children to think.

Brice-Heath approached teachers, parents, and children to make them aware of the different uses of questions. Teachers took responsibility for making themselves clear to children.

Although minority students' achievement in school has improved in the last fifteen years, still there is a gap between their achievement and that of the majority students. Recent work suggests, however, that in certain areas (for example, math computation) skills are comparable at school entry, but achievement differences emerge as children move through the grades.[46]

For some years, experts thought achievement differences were related to minority students' low self-esteem and low level of aspiration or to lack of family interest and encouragement. New studies indicate these are not the source of achievement differences.[47] Now we find that Afro-American and Hispanic-American mothers of elementary school children place greater emphasis on their children's achievement than do Anglo-American mothers. Minority mothers want more homework, longer school days, and more competency testing of their children. Mothers have both high evaluations of their children's abilities and high expectations for their achievement in school and in later work. Minority mothers take an active part in seeing that homework gets done, though Hispanic mothers feel less capable of helping with the work of a foreign school system.

Minority children share their mothers' enthusiasm for education. They enjoy school, feel good about themselves and their achievements, and expect to do well in the future. They work hard and are self-disciplined.

While there are differences in minority students' level of achievement in the elementary years, these are minimal when social status is taken into account. Investigators do not understand why the high rates of failure and school dropout occur in the later years, when indicators at the fifth-grade level seem to predict future achievement for minority students. One speculation is that families may be so positive that they do not help children isolate those areas where they need improvement. Inappropriate curriculum content seems a factor in lowering minority children's reading level and also may play a role in their later decrease in achievement.

The important point here is that minority parents are currently as motivated, involved, and positive about their children's education as are majority parents of similar social class. Minority elementary school students are as motivated and excited about learning as their peers in the majority culture. So, we have to look at the curriculum and teaching strategies that maximize students' abilities because the present ones may interfere with learning.

Getting to School on Time, Howework, and Grades

In dealing with issues of lateness, homework, and grades, parents combine common strategies that give children both support and independence. Parents establish structure and routine that encourages the desired behavior. For getting to school on time,

INTERVIEW
with Barbara Keogh

Barbara K. Keogh is professor of educational psychology at the University of California at Los Angeles. Her research interests include the role of children's temperament in children's adjustment to school.

For many parents with children in the elementary school years, issues concerning school have a very great importance—how to get children ready for school on time, how to help them behave in school, how to get them to do school work. You have done a great deal of research on children's temperament and school, and I think temperament plays a role in many children's adjustment.

It intrigued me when I started work in this area, a long time ago, that most of the work with temperament had been done with interactions in families, and yet when you think of the number of interactions that teachers have with children per hour, per day, in a classroom and add that up over the school year, temperament is an enormous potential influence.

When we began our research, we found that teachers have a very clear picture of what teachable children are like. One of the very important contributors to teachability is the stylistic variables or temperament variables that characterize children. Some children are easy to teach. They settle down better, they are not as active, they are not as intense, their mood is good, they adapt well, they like novelty, they are curious. All those things make teachers think, "Gee, I am a great teacher," when they have a whole classroom full of children with those characteristics.

So we are really operating on the assumption that children's experiences in school are influenced by individual variations in temperament. We have tried to document and understand the kind of impact these variations have on the teachers. We have used the concept of "goodness of fit" in a loose way.

I am convinced, and this is not a new idea, that teachers do not operate at random. They make decisions based on how they attribute the reasons for the behavior. They may think that active, distractible children are mischievous and need to be restricted and punished, and that children who are very slow to warm up or are withdrawn are lazy and uninterested. When we work with teachers and make them aware of temperamental characteristics, we get a very consistent response: "Oh, I never thought of that." Making teachers sensitive to temperament variations helps them reframe the child's behavior, and it makes the behavior much less upsetting to teachers.

It also carries planning implications. If you know a youngster is very distractible, very

parents suggest children pick out their clothes the night before, and parents get them up in plenty of time to get ready for school, not permitting TV or stereos until the child is ready for school. If lateness continues, parents use Gordon's active listening, I-messages, and mutual problem-solving to deal with the problem.

For getting homework completed, parents establish a regular time for homework. Some families decide that after school is the best time. Other families believe children need play time to exercise after school and homework can come after dinner.

active, and very intense, then you can predict that every time you have a long wait in line, there's going to be a problem with him. It's predictable.

When teachers begin to think of the individual variations on a temperamental rather than motivational basis, they begin to manipulate the environment more effectively. Temperament helps teachers reframe the problem behavior so it is not viewed as purposeful. This is true for both temperamentally "difficult" and "slow to warm up" children.

Another example I like is that most of the youngsters in an elementary class are delighted by novelty. The teachers says, "Oh, we are going to have a wonderful surprise today. At ten o'clock the fire department is coming." Most of the kids are excited. There will be a few little "slow to warm up" youngsters who will say, "But at ten o'clock we are supposed to do our reading." They are upset because the usual routine is not followed. The teacher thinks, "What's the matter with that child? Why isn't he interested?" The child has a need for routine and a tendency to withdraw from newness or change. These children can profit from advance preparation. If they know a day in advance, they get a little forewarning.

Do you have any advice for parents as to how to help their children adjust to school?

Certainly parents have to be advocates for their child. That is absolutely necessary even if it means being confrontational, which is often not too productive. But certainly parents need to be aware when their child is unhappy at school, when their child is having problems, and address the problem with school people.

It has to be recognized that when we are working on a ratio of twenty-five youngsters to one teacher, there are going to be good matches and very poor matches in any class. In no sense does that demean the quality of the teacher or the nature of the child. But there are differences in style, and some styles match better than others.

One thing parents can do is to provide teachers with some recognition that their child might not be a good match for this classroom. It helps the teacher to know that the parents are aware of that. So they can direct their mutual efforts to modify the class so the demands are more reasonable, or they can give the child extra help in modifying his or her behavior so it is more compatible with what is going on in that class.

Do you feel most teachers are willing to change?

Yes, I do. We have worked with a lot of teachers in our research, and I think it helps them to think of ways that they can structure the situation so it is more compatible with the student without loss of educational goals. Yes, we have found teachers to be very open, and they were able to relate what we were saying to different children they have known: "Oh, yes, that's like Joey."

dren need play time to exercise after school and homework can come after dinner. Parents encourage children to keep books and papers in the same place so they are easily located for school. Parents take an interest in homework, making sure the child understands what has to be done, answering questions about it, checking it over; but they do not do the homework or stay there while the child does it.

With regard to grades, parents need to know their children well in order to establish reasonable expectations. Earlier in the chapter we discussed how parents encouraged children to have optimistic, confident views of their own abilities. Parents pay attention and encourage children to identify and remedy those stumbling blocks within their power to control, and to enjoy and take credit for the successes they attain.

Peers

Children want to have friends and to have good times with them. In the school-age period, they spend about 40 percent of their time with peers, a significant increase over the 20 percent at age four.[48] Children like other children who are outgoing and supportive of others. As we noted earlier, physical attractiveness also plays a role. Children who are physically unattractive, immature, disruptive, and aggressive are rejected. **Popular** children tend to socialize with their own network of friends; **rejected children** find a small group of either younger children or unpopular children to associate with. A third group of children who often go unnoticed have been termed **neglected children**. Not enough is known about these children to describe them in any consistent way. They are neither well liked nor rejected. They do not engage in negative behaviors as rejected children do, but they do not have friends because they are so retiring.[49]

School-age children, on average, have about five friends, somewhat more than in preschool and adolescent years. About 90 percent of children report friendships and are selected by others as friends. Friends stress equality of treatment, mutuality, reciprocity in their relationships. The ability to sustain friendships is an important one and is related to later good adjustment. Conversely, when children are rejected in elementary school, especially as they get to be about ten years old, continuing rejection, along with difficulties in overall adjustment, are more likely.[50]

When parents are affectionate, warm, and accepting of children, when there is harmony at home, then children are more outgoing and sociable. Differences appear early and are persistent for long periods of time; further, there are resemblances among family members in ways that suggest a biological component. Life experiences contribute to these behaviors as well, however. Parental correlates of peer sociability and effectiveness include parents' affection, warmth, and acceptance of boys and girls, general parental satisfaction with children, and an absence of family tension. When fathers are both warm and dominant, boys seem more competent; when mothers are warm and dominant, girls are more competent. Thus, competence with peers is related to general family adjustment and warmth. When the family is under stress, as during a divorce, peer relationships change.[51]

Zimbardo and Radl list experiences that appear related to shy behavior: (1) specific failures in social settings like school, (2) loss of social supports, as may occur when a family makes many moves or becomes disorganized with separation or divorce, (3) poor parental role models, (4) lack of experience in social settings, and (5) feelings of shame.[52] These authors consider shyness the result of feelings of low self-worth and shame and of being so labeled by others.

Some argue that as peers become more important to children, their ties to parents and family lessen. This does not appear accurate. Children use both parents and peers as anchors for positive behavior, but they do detach from parents as anchors and misbehave in the preadolescent period. Peer standards of misconduct are increasingly important from third grade to eighth grade but do not increase beyond that point.[53]

The Isolated Child

If a child shows little interest in other people but has many activities that absorb attention and seems happy, parents may not want to intervene because the child has interests and seems content. Activities, however, are sometimes used as substitutes for friends, and many children who do not have friends wish they did. There are two major reasons for not having friends, and they require somewhat different actions on the part of parents.

First, shy children who hesitate to reach out are uncertain what to say to other children, uncertain how to join in games, worried about rejection. They are the *neglected* children mentioned above. Other children do not dislike them, but rather overlook them. These children have to learn to be more friendly, outgoing, and confident with others. A second group of children are actively *rejected*. They often demand attention, are aggressive, disruptive with other children, wanting to direct the games, accusing others of being unfair to them. Underneath their outgoing, aggressive behavior they may have the same feelings and worries as shy children, but they handle them differently. They must learn to curb their aggressiveness, however, and also learn friendly behaviors.

Helping shy children requires several actions, as seen in the example of a mother who used Ginott's method. She discussed the problem with his teacher, who said she would involve him in more group activities.[54] The teacher also gave the mother a list of boys' names, so the mother could organize a group activity. After talking it over with her son, the mother started a bowling club. The club lasted only a week— at the first meeting her son had the lowest score, and he refused to try again. A few days later, however, one of the boys invited him over to play, and a friendship began to grow.

As the mother observed her own and her son's behavior, she realized she had encouraged the boy to depend on her for companionship and had protected him from the rougher and more critical companionship of his older brother and father. She decided to give up her role as protector and to encourage a closer relationship between father and son. Thus, the mother modified her own behavior and at the same time increased the child's skills, just as a behaviorist would.

Gordon considers the child owns the problem with friends. Parents can encourage children to talk about this problem and can listen actively. As children talk about what is bothering them, they may find ways of solving their problems. But until then, or until the child asks for help, parents must accept isolation as the child's problem.

Dreikurs also stresses the child's need to learn how to get along and to accommodate his or her interests and activities to those of peers. He believes that bashfulness and timidity may stem from overindulgence by parents. The child seeks attention and regard from others by doing nothing rather than by taking an active role. Parents can encourage positive interaction and ignore demands for attention. Although it sounds like Dreikurs recommends doing very little, nevertheless he does advise paying appropriate attention to children, playing games and working on projects with them, and encouraging them to participate in activities with other children.

More than other strategists, behaviorists have focused on strategies for helping children to make friends. Sherri Oden and Steven Asher have devised a system of coaching children in interpersonal skills.[55] They give children verbal instructions about effective ways of interacting and provide opportunities to apply the rules in play sessions. Instructions cover four topics: (1) participating in group activities (getting started, paying attention to the game), (2) cooperating in play (sharing, taking turns), (3) communicating with partner (talking or listening), and (4) validating and supporting the peer (giving attention and help). Benefits persisted and were measurable a year later.

Parents can try to do this coaching as they observe their children's interactions with others. When parents comment later, in a calm way, on troubles that interfered with the child's having optimal fun and ask how such problems might have been avoided, they help to increase the child's social competence. The parents should not sound critical and interfering when making these remarks.

Zimbardo and Radl offer many suggestions for the parent of the school-aged shy child (Box 6-3).[56] All these actions are designed to increase self-esteem, confidence, and socially outgoing behavior. Despite Gordon's and Dreikur's beliefs that shyness is a child's problem, parents are advised to help their shy children develop social skills. Research suggests that shy behavior in the early grades persists into middle childhood. Because social competence is so important to children, being shy is related to feeling especially incompetent and lonely and to lacking the feeling of self-worth, thus these feelings persist as well as the shyness.[57]

Parents of rejected children can adopt all these methods, too, in addition to helping their children curb aggressiveness. First, parents must have a detached attitude about tales of being picked on or discriminated against by peers. Parents must talk to teachers and principals to determine what really does happen at school. If children fail to see their part in provoking others' rejection, parents can go over events with them, after the children have cooled down, and present the other child's point of view. If children get in many fights at school or are very disruptive of others' play, a reward system can be set up with the teacher so that children earn privileges each day a positive report comes home. The teacher is involved and sends home a card with checks for all acceptable behavior in class, at recess, and at lunch. If children do not bring home the report at all, there are no TV or other privileges for that day. This procedure is followed every day.

Again, aggressive behavior in early childhood persists and is related to being aggressive and rejected in middle childhood. In contrast to the shy child, the aggressive child may not internalize the problem and feel incompetent, but it is still very important for the parent to act to reverse a cycle of behavior that is related to continuing rejection.[58]

TELEVISION

Television is a powerful teaching tool not only because children spend more time watching it than engaging in any other activity (except sleeping), but also because the visual medium has a powerful impact on children. Children begin to watch TV in infancy, and by the preschool years are watching about twenty-eight hours per week. Average viewing times are similar for school-aged children and adolescents, and do not include time spent with video games and videotapes.[59]

BOX 6-3
THINGS TO DO WITH YOUR SHY CHILD

1. Actively listen to your child and try to see the social situation from the child's point of view.
2. Talk about what you have done or thought during the day while the child was at school and encourage the child to share his or her day.
3. When you ask a question, wait and listen for the answer. Do not jump in to answer it yourself. Shy persons take a while to answer, but the answer will come.
4. Enroll the child in drama or dance lessons if he or she might like that.
5. Encourage physical skills that can be used in a team sport.
6. Help the shy child step out of that role in fantasy play at home—with puppets, dolls—and in activities like shouting for a brief period or dressing up in crazy costumes.
7. Share some of your own difficult childhood experiences with your child; describe how you overcame them.
8. Pretend you are the child's grandparent for the weekend and see how your view of the child changes.
9. Help the child make eye contact while speaking.
10. Notice how often your child smiles and do all you can to increase the smiles.
11. Encourage laughter and a sense of humor.
12. Teach and display listening skills—paying attention to what others say, reflecting back at times what the person says to be sure you are clear on it.
13. Encourage children to speak for themselves—order their own meals in restaurants, get information by telephone.
14. Teach them to identify themselves and take accurate phone messages.
15. Teach friends and relatives to talk to children on matters of interest to both.
16. Give compliments to all family members and make it clear you enjoy receiving them in return.
17. Teach the child to interrupt politely to make a parent give more information if needed—"Excuse me, I have a question," "Excuse me, I didn't understand what you wanted me to do."
18. Watch your child play with other children and note any inappropriate behavior that needs changing. Discuss it later.
19. Have slightly younger playmates over occasionally so the child has a chance to practice skills with children who may be a little less dominant.
20. Involve other children in car rides to school or invite them along to the movies.

Adapted from Philip Zimbardo and Shirley Radl, *The Shy Child* (Garden City, N.Y.: Doubleday, 1982), pp. 152–155.

Like school, TV is an external influence that may or may not reflect family values. Yet it can have tremendous impact on both parents and children. After a five-year study of its impact on children, psychologists at the American Psychological Association conclude TV is not inherently harmful; used wisely it can promote learning and social skills.[60]

Television becomes an enriching family experience when parents and children watch a program together and discuss it.

With wise use—watching educational programs like Sesame Street when young or special programs on selected topics when older—children can absorb information. Television can also change social attitudes, breaking down social stereotypes and providing models of positive social actions. The day after Fonzie got a library card on "Happy Days," the number of children applying for library cards increased five-fold.

Television can also change feelings. Children who saw a presurgery film describing how people might feel about surgery were less fearful before and after the operation and had fewer postoperative problems. So, there are many benefits to be had from TV.

But there can also be problems. Television can perpetuate social stereotypes about groups or activities. By depicting violence and aggression, it can harden individuals. One eleven-year-old boy commented, "You see so much violence that it's meaningless. If I saw someone really get killed, it wouldn't be a big deal. I guess I'm turning into a hard rock."[61] Also seeing too much of adult problems can upset and worry young children about difficulties they may face as adults.

Even if TV has no direct negative impact on children, it deprives them of time for growth-enhancing activities like sports, reading, studying, interacting with others. In that sense, it can be harmful to children.

There is almost no research on how parents can counteract what their children see on TV. However, when adults discuss with children what they are watching, when adults ask questions and stimulate thinking, children become more questioning of what they see. Parents can then spend time watching programs with children, talking about their reactions, what parents liked and disliked. This provides children with guidelines for thinking about what they have seen.

Television is here to stay. It will not go away just because we see its negative aspects. Parents can help children make the wisest use of this powerful medium by limiting the amount of time children watch, encouraging selective viewing so they learn material that is compatible with family values, and discussing programs. Television then becomes a social and enriching experience for children and parents.

PARENTS' EXPERIENCES

Children's entrance into school marks a new stage in parenthood. Children spend more time away from parents, in school and with peers. They are absorbing new information and are exposed to new values. Ellen Galinsky describes this parental stage as the **interpretive stage**.[62] Parents share facts and information about the world, teach values, and guide children's behavior in certain directions. They decide how they will handle the child's greater independence and involvement with people who may not share similar values.

At this point, parents have a more realistic view of themselves as parents and a greater understanding of their children as individuals. Parents have been through sleepless nights, the crying of infancy, the temper tantrums of the toddler, and the instruction of their children in basic routines and habits. They have a sense of how they and their child will react in any given situation. Though some parents have a very negative view of themselves as parents, most have developed a sense of their strengths and difficulties and a confidence that, by and large, they and their children are okay. Children, however, leave their control and enter a structured environment with rules and regulations. Children are evaluated in terms of their ability to control their behavior and learn skills that have reference to the adult world. For the first time there are external standards, grades, which compare children to each other. Parents must deal with, and help their children deal with, these external evaluations, which may be different from those parents have formed at home.

For parents, bridging the gap between the way they treat their children and the way their children are treated by teachers, group leaders, and peers may be a constant struggle. Parents will develop strategies for dealing with teachers who may not see the child as they do, with doctors, and with principals. An attitude that stresses cooperation among adults seems most effective. When parents seek information about the child and offer observations from home, if the focus is on eliminating the problem or settling the difference, adults can work together to make the child's experience in that environment an optimal one.

In the process of explaining the world and people's behavior, parents refine beliefs and values. They may discard some beliefs and add others. Children often prompt changes when they discover inconsistencies and hypocrisies in what parents say. If lying is bad, why do parents tell relatives they are busy when they are not? If parents care about the world and want to make it a safer place, why are they not doing something to make it safe? In the process of answering these questions, parents grow as well as children.

MAJOR POINTS OF CHAPTER 6

Parenting tasks in this period include:

- monitoring and guiding children from a distance as children move into new activities on their own
- interacting in a warm, accepting, yet firm manner when children are present
- strengthening children's abilities to monitor their own behavior
- providing opportunities for children to develop new skills and positive identities
- structuring the home environment so the child is able to meet school responsibilities
- serving as an advocate for the child in activities outside the home—for example, with schools, with sports teams, in organized activities
- interpreting difficult events so children feel optimistic and exert effort to achieve their goals
- encourage constructive sibling relationships

Children value themselves on four dimensions:

- physical competence
- intellectual competence
- social competence with peers
- general self-worth

Children's self-control increases, and by the end of this period, they have:

- gained greater control of their aggressiveness
- become less fearful
- learned to remedy situations they control and adjust to situations others control

Children interact with peers:

- in an egalitarian, give-and-take fashion
- and prefer those who are outgoing and supportive of other children
- and become friends when they enjoy the same activities
- more effectively when parents have been affectionate, warm, and accepting with them
- less effectively when there is stress in the family

Schools:

- are the major socializing force outside the family
- are structured so that verbal and listening skills are valued in students and physical skills are devalued

- create stress in children's lives because children worry about making mistakes, being ridiculed, and failing
- promote learning when they provide a calm, controlled environment and teachers are gentle disciplinarians with high expectations for students
- often do not reward the values of ethnic groups that emphasize cooperation and sharing among its members
- often make learning more difficult for children who use different styles of speech and communication patterns
- are highly valued by many ethnic group members who wish their children to spend more time there, do more homework, and have more proficiency tests

Socializing forces outside the family include:

- schools
- TV
- organized groups like athletic teams, Scouts

Television:

- has beneficial effects in giving new information, changing attitudes, and creating positive feelings
- can reinforce negative social stereotypes
- can harden individuals to violence
- takes time from growth-enhancing activities

Parents are in Galinsky's interpretive stage, in which they:

- have achieved greater understanding of both themselves as parents and their children
- help children meet external evaluations that may be different from those at home
- develop strategies for helping children cope with new authorities like teachers, coaches

Problems discussed center on:

- helping children meet school responsibilities
- dealing with social problems such as social isolation
- changing rule-breaking behavior such as lying

Joys include:

- observing increasing motor, cognitive, and social skills
- reexperiencing one's own childhood pleasures through child's experience

- sharing mutually enjoyable experiences and companionship
- sharing or experiencing emotional closeness

EXERCISES

1. Break into small groups of four or five persons per group. Take turns recalling (a) how your parents prepared you for school, (b) how you felt the first
   days you can remember, (c) what your early experiences were, (d) how confident or not confident you felt about your abilities. Then identify ways parents and teachers could have helped more. Share your group's experiences
   with the class and come up with recommendations for parents and
   teachers.

2. In small groups, take turns recalling the pleasurable events you experienced
   during the years from five to ten. Then come up with a class list of twenty
   common pleasurable events for that period.

3. Take the list of twenty pleasurable events developed in the group discussion
   (see above exercise) and rate each event on a scale of 1 to 7 with 1 being
   least pleasurable and 7 being most pleasurable as you would have when you
   were a child of nine or ten. As Kaoru Yamamoto did with stressful life
   events, get average pleasurable ratings for each pleasurable experience. (See
   articles, "Children's Ratings of the Stressfulness of Experience," *Developmental Psychology 15* (1979): 581–582, and Kaoru Yamamoto et al., "Voices in
   Unison: Stressful Events in the Lives of Children in Six Countries," *Journal
   of Child Psychology and Psychiatry 28* (1987): 855–864). What are the most
   pleasurable events? How do parents contribute to them? (Recall from Chapter 3 that children six to fifteen saw friends as major sources of pleasure
   and parents as major sources of frustration.)

4. Rate the list of twenty stressful events from 1 (least stressful) to 7 (most
   stressful) as you would have when you were nine or ten. Are the rankings
   similar to what Yamamoto found for groups around the world? If not, why
   not?

5. Divide into small groups and discuss major activities that built sources of
   self-esteem in this period. Were these athletic activities? group activities like
   Scouts or Brownies? school activities? Come up with recommendations for
   parents as to the kinds of activities children find most confidence-building.

ADDITIONAL READINGS

Armstrong, Thomas. *Awakening Your Child's Natural Genius*. Los Angeles: Jeremy P. Tarcher,
1991.

Blechman, Elaine A. *Solving Child Behavior Problems at Home and at School*. Champaign,
Illinois: Research Press, 1985.

Damon, William. *The Moral Child.* New York: The Free Press, 1988.

Dunn, Judy. *Sisters and Brothers.* Cambridge, Mass.: Harvard University Press, 1985.

Healy, Jane M. *Endangered Minds.* New York: Simon & Schuster, 1990.

Notes

1. Eleanor E. Maccoby, "Middle Childhood in the Context of the Family," in *Development During Middle Childhood,* ed. W. Andrew Collins (Washington, D.C.: National Academy Press, 1984), pp. 184–239.
2. Ibid.
3. Ibid.
4. Judith G. Smetana, "Adolescents' and Parents' Reasoning about Actual Family Conflict," *Child Development* 60 (1989): 1052–1067.
5. Graeme Russell and Alan Russell, "Mother-Child and Father-Child in Middle Childhood," *Child Development* 58 (1987): 1573–1585.
6. Frances K. Grossman, William S. Pollack, and Ellen Golding, "Fathers and Children: Predicting the Quality and Quantity of Fathering," *Developmental Psychology* 24 (1988): 822–891.
7. Russell and Russell, "Mother-Child and Father-Child in Middle Childhood."
8. Maccoby, "Middle Childhood in the Context of the Family."
9. Michael C. Thornton, Linda M. Chatters, Robert Joseph Taylor, and Walter R. Allen, "Sociodemographic and Environmental Correlates of Racial Socialization by Black Parents," *Child Development* 61 (1990): 401–409.
10. Ibid.
11. Algea O. Harrison, Melvin N. Wilson, Charles J. Pine, Samuel Q. Chan, and Raymond Buriel, "Family Ecologies of Ethnic Minority Children," *Child Development* 61 (1990): 347–362; Margaret Beale Spencer and Carol Markstrom-Adams, "Identity Processes among Racial and Ethnic Minority Children in America," *Child Development* 61 (1990): 290–310.
12. Judy Dunn, *Sisters and Brothers* (Cambridge, Mass.: Harvard University Press, 1985).
13. Rona Abramovitch, Carl Corter, Debra J. Pepler, and Linda Stanhope, "Sibling and Peer Interaction: A Final Follow-up and a Comparison," *Child Development* 57 (1986): 217–229.
14. Brenda K. Bryant and Susan Crockenberg, "Correlates and Dimensions of Prosocial Behavior: A Study of Female Siblings with Their Mothers," *Child Development* 51 (1980): 529–544.
15. Adele Faber and Elaine Mazlish, *Siblings Without Rivalry* (New York: Avon, 1987).
16. Rudolf Dreikurs with Vicki Soltz, *Children: The Challenge* (New York: Hawthorn, 1964).
17. Thomas Gordon, *P.E.T.: Parent Effectiveness Training* (New York: New American Library, 1975).
18. Raymond Montemayor and Marvin Eisen, "The Development of Self-Conceptions from Childhood to Adolescence," *Developmental Psychology* 13 (1977): 317.
19. Susan Harter, "Developmental Perspectives on the Self-System," in *Handbook of Child Psychology,* eds. Paul H. Mussen and E. Mavis Hetherington, vol. 4, *Socialization, Personality and Social Development* (New York: John Wiley, 1983), pp. 275–385.
20. Mary Jane Rotheram-Borus and Jean S. Phinney, "Patterns of Social Expectations among Black and Mexican-American Children," *Child Development* 61 (1990): 542–556.
21. James P. Connell and Barbara C. Ilardi, "Self System Concomitants of Discrepancies between Children's and Teacher's Evaluations of Academic Competence," *Child Development* 58 (1987): 1297–1307.
22. Albert Bandura, "Regulation of Cognitive Processes through Perceived Self-Efficacy," *Developmental Psychology* 25 (1989): pp. 729–735.
23. Mariellen Fischer and Harold Leitenberg, "Optimism and Pessimism in Elementary School-Aged Children," *Child Development* 57 (1986): 241–248.
24. Kaoru Yamamoto, Abdalla Soliman, James Parsons, and O. L. Davies, Jr., "Voices in Unison: Stressful Events in the Lives of Children in Six Countries," *Journal of Child Psychology and Psychiatry* 28 (1987): 855–864.
25. Eve Brotman-Band and John R. Weisz, "How to Feel Better When It Feels Bad," *Developmental Psychology* 24 (1988): 247–253.

188

26. Jennifer L. Altshuler and Diane N. Ruble, "Developmental Changes in Children's Awareness of Strategies for Coping with Uncontrollable Stress," *Child Development* 60 (1989): 1337–1349.

27. Martin E. P. Seligman, *Learned Optimism* (New York: Pocket Books, 1990).

28. Haim G. Ginott, *Between Parent and Child* (New York: Avon, 1969).

29. Thomas Gordon, *P.E.T.: Parent Effectiveness Training* (New York: New American Library, 1975); Thomas Gordon with Judith Gordon Sands, *P.E.T. in Action* (New York: Bantam Books, 1978).

30. Rudolf Dreikurs with Vicki Soltz, *Children: The Challenge* (New York: Hawthorn, 1964), p. 285.

31. Gerald R. Patterson, John B. Reid, Richard R. Jones, and Robert E. Conger, *A Social Learning Approach to Family Intervention,* vol. 1, *Families with Aggressive Children* (Eugene, Ore.: Castalia, 1975).

32. Gerald R. Patterson, *Families: Applications of Social Learning to Family Life,* rev. ed. (Champaign, Ill.: Research Press, 1975).

33. Gerald R. Patterson, *Living with Children,* rev. ed. (Champaign, Ill.: Research Press, 1976).

34. John D. Krumboltz and Helen B. Krumboltz, *Changing Children's Behavior.* (Englewood Cliffs, N.J.: Prentice-Hall, 1972).

35. Jean Ann Linney and Edward Seidman, "The Future of Schooling," *American Psychologist* 44 (1989): 336–340.

36. Gary W. Ladd and Joseph M. Price, "Predicting Children's Social and School Adjustment Following the Transition from Preschool to Kindergarten," *Child Development* 58 (1987): 1168–1189.

37. Karin S. Frey and Diane N. Ruble, "What Children Say about Classroom Performance: Sex and Grade Differences in Perceived Competence," *Child Development* 58 (1987): 1066–1078.

38. John G. Nicholls, Michael Patashnick, and Gwendolyn Mettetal, "Conceptions of Ability and Intelligence," *Child Development* 57 (1986): 636–645.

39. Doris R. Entwisle, Karl L. Alexander, Aaron M. Pallas, and Doris Cadigan, "The Emergent Academic Self-Image of First Graders: Its Response to Social Structure," *Child Development* 58 (1987): 1190–1206.

40. Deborah Phillips, "The Illusion of Incompetence among Academically Competent Children," *Child Development* 55 (1984): 2000–2016; Deborah A. Phillips, "Socialization of Perceived Academic Competence among Highly Competent Children," *Child Development* 58 (1987): 1308–1320.

41. Rhona S. Weinstein, Hermine H. Marshall, Lee Sharp, and Meryl Botken, "Pygmalion and the Student: Age and Classroom Differences in Children's Awareness of Teacher Expectations," *Child Development* 58 (1987): 1079–1093.

42. Theresa A. Thorkildsen, "Justice in the Classroom: The Student's View," *Child Development* 60 (1989): 323–334.

43. Diane McGuiness, "How Schools Discriminate against Boys," *Human Nature,* February 1979.

44. Janice E. Hale-Benson, *Black Children: Their Roots, Culture, and Learning Styles,* rev. ed. (Baltimore: Johns Hopkins University Press, 1986).

45. Diana T. Slaughter-Defoe et al., "Toward Cultural/Ecological Perspectives on Schooling and Achievement in African- and Asian-American Children," *Child Development* 61 (1990): 363–383.

46. Doris R. Entwisle and Karl L. Alexander, "Beginning Math Competence: Minority and Majority Comparisons," *Child Development* 61 (1990): 454–471.

47. Harold W. Stevenson, Chuansheng Chen, and David H. Uttal, "Beliefs and Achievement: A Study of Black, White, and Hispanic Children," *Child Development* 61 (1990): 508–523.

48. Willard W. Hartup, "The Peer Context in Middle Childhood," in *Development During Middle Childhood,* ed. Collins, pp. 240–282.

49. John D. Coie, Kenneth A. Dodge, and Heidi Coppotelli, "Dimensions and Types of Social Status: A Cross-Age Perspective," *Developmental Psychology* 18 (1982): 557–570.

50. Hartup, "Peer Context in Middle Childhood."

51. Ibid.

52. Philip G. Zimbardo and Shirley Radl, *The Shy Child* (Garden City, N.Y.: Doubleday, 1982).

53. Hartup, "Peer Context in Middle Childhood."

54. Adele Faber and Elaine Mazlish, *Liberated Parents/Liberated Children* (New York: Avon, 1974).

55. Sherri Oden and Steven R. Asher, "Coaching Children in Social Skills for Friendship Making," *Child Development* 48 (1977): 495–506.

56. Zimbardo and Radl, *The Shy Child*.

57. Shelley Hymel et al., "Children's Peer Relationships: Longitudinal Prediction of Internalizing and Externalizing Problems from Middle to Late Childhood," *Child Development* 61 (1990): 2004–2021.

58. Ibid.

59. Jane M. Healy, *Endangered Minds* (New York: Simon & Schuster, 1990).

60. "A.P.A. Says Television Has Potential To Be Beneficial," *The Brown University Child and Adolescent Behavior Letter,* March 1992.

61. Patricia Marks Greenfield, *Mind and Media: The Effects of Television, Video Games, and Computers* (Cambridge, Mass.: Harvard University Press, 1984), p. 51.

62. Ellen Galinsky, *Between Generations: The Six Stages of Parenthood* (New York: Time Books, 1981).

ADOLESCENCE

C H A P T E R   7

As your child experiences the physical and psychological changes that launch him or her into adulthood, you will both encounter even greater challenges. The adolescent will face temptations of sex, alcohol, drugs and deal with problems such as choice of friends, peer approval, dating. What can you do to maintain a close relationship while your teenager is pulling away from you to establish his or her unique identity? What specific problems do ethnic minorities face while establishing identity? What parenting strategies are effective when teens become relative strangers—sometimes uncontrollable, often noncommunicative, occasionally isolated? Balancing the freedom teenagers demand with the guidance they need, parents shift their role as nurturer/monitor toward resource/ consultant.

The adolescent years are a turning point for children, who leave the childhood years of stable and steady growth and experience all the stresses of rapid physical growth, a changing hormonal system, and physical development that results in sexual and reproductive maturity. As their bodies and hormones change, children's emotions often become more intense and harder to control. Their thinking changes; they become more aware of possibilities; they think more abstractly. At the same time that children undergo these physical and cognitive changes, they are reaching out socially to peers, becoming independent of their parents. They are beginning to search for their own identity—who they are, what they like, and what goals they will set for themselves.

As adolescents seek a sense of who they are, they question parents' authority, rebel against restrictions, and argue their own point of view for long hours. Parents must encourage the growth of their children's independence and self-esteem, helping them become more competent. Yet parents must not permit so much freedom that children get into trouble they cannot handle. Though it is taxing for parents, this is an exciting time to watch children blossoming as they take their first steps out of childhood into a new life.

PARENT-CHILD RELATIONSHIPS

A majority of adolescents say their greatest fear is losing a parent (see Table 7-3 on page 202). Having heard much about the generation gap and how distant teens want to be from their families, parents may be surprised to learn how important they are to their children. An extensive review of psychological research arrives at the same conclusion concerning the importance of parents.

> The single most important external influence in aiding or hindering the average adolescent (particularly the younger one) in the accomplishment of the developmental tasks of adolescence—at least in today's relatively isolated nuclear family—is his or her parents. The real question is not whether parental models are any longer important; rather, it is what kinds of parental models are necessary or appropriate in preparing contemporary adolescents to cope with the largely unpredictable world of tomorrow.[1]

Although family relationships are changing, the dimensions of parenting which predict competence in the preschool years continue to predict adolescent competence reflected in self-reliant, independent behavior and in the capacity for meaningful relationships with others. Diana Baumrind followed her sample from the preschool years through adolescence and identified three major components of parenting in the adolescent years—parental *commitment* along with the balance between *demandingness* (establishing rules, monitoring compliance, and enforcing rules) and *responsiveness* (being supportive of the child and paying attention to the child's needs and interests).[2] How parents relate to children during adolescence years is more important in determining adolescent competence than earlier parenting techniques.

Baumrind describes six different parenting patterns and relates them to the child's drug use. *Authoritative* parents have strong commitments to children and balance demands with responsiveness to children's needs: "Unlike any other pattern, Authoritative upbringing *consistently* generated competence and deterred problem behavior in both boys and girls, at *all* stages."[3] *Democratic* parents who have strong commitment to children and are highly responsive to their needs are only average in demandingness. Their children are highly competent as well, but are freer to explore drugs.

Nonauthoritarian Directive parents who are high on conventional control and value conformity have children with the least drug use, but this is accomplished by strict obedience to rules so that children are conforming and dependent upon adult approval. *Authoritarian-Directive* parents are even more restrictive and less supportive and have less competent children. Parents of both types are moderately committed to their children.

Unengaged parents are neither demanding nor responsive nor committed to children. They either actively reject or neglect parenting responsibilities. Children from these families are free of adult authority, but they have little direction and so are described as immature. These adolescents have had problems dating back to the preschool years, and they lack competence in many areas of adolescent functioning. The *Good Enough* parent is about average on the different dimensions, and their children are about average in competence.

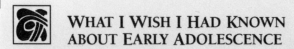

WHAT I WISH I HAD KNOWN ABOUT EARLY ADOLESCENCE

"They seem to get caught up in fads in junior high. They do certain things to the max to be part of the crowd. I wish I'd known how to handle that. At what point are these fads okay, because it's important to identify with your peer group, and at what point do you say no? If they are really dangerous, then it's easy; but with a lot of them, it's a gray area, and I wish I'd known what to do better." FATHER

"I wish I had realized that she needed more structure and control. Because she had always been a good student and done her work, I thought I could trust her to manage the school tasks without my checking. But she lost interest in school, and I learned only very gradually that I had to be more of a monitor with her work than I had been in the past." MOTHER

"I wish I had known more about the mood swings. When the girls became thirteen, they each got moody for a while, and I stopped taking it personally. I just relaxed. The youngest one said, 'Do I have to go through that? Can't I just skip that?' Sure enough, when she became thirteen, she was moody too." MOTHER

"I wish I'd known how to help the boys get along a little better. They have real fights at times, and while they have a lot of fun together and help each other out, I wish I knew how to cut down on the fighting." FATHER

"I wish I knew what to expect. They are all so different, and they don't necessarily do what the books say. Sometimes, I'm waiting for a stage; now I'm waiting for adolescent rebellion, and there is none." MOTHER

"I wish I had known about their indecisiveness. He wants to do this; no, he doesn't. He gets pressure from peers and from what we think is right, and sometimes he goes back and forth. I am more patient about that now." MOTHER

"I wish I had known that if we had dealt with some behaviors when they were younger, we would not have had a problem from eleven to fourteen. He was always a little stubborn and hardheaded, wanting to do what he wanted. But right now, I wish we had done something about the stubbornness because it is a problem. He does not take responsibility, and it gets him into trouble at school. Looking back it has always been a problem, but we did not deal with it." MOTHER

While Baumrind's sample was a smaller, primarily white, middle class sample, her family classifications were equally applicable to a large, ethnically diverse sample of 4,100 adolescents between 14 and 18.[4] Regardless of the adolescent's sex, socioeconomic or ethnic background, authoritative parenting was associated with adolescent competence, confidence, and achievement. Neglectful parenting ("unengaged" in Baumrind's scheme) was associated with low competence, psychological distress,

WHAT I WISH I HAD KNOWN ABOUT LATE ADOLESCENCE

"I wish that I had got my children involved in more family activities. When they were mostly through adolescence I heard a talk by a child psychiatrist who said that often when teenagers say they don't want to do something with the family, at times you have to insist because they do go along and enjoy the event. I wish I had known that sooner, because I accepted their first 'No,' when I perhaps should have pushed more." MOTHER

"This may begin earlier, but it goes through adolescence. I had always heard they look for their own independence, their own things to participate in; but until you really experience it with your own, it's hard to deal with it. When you read about independence, it sounds like it's carefully planned out. When it actually happens, all of a sudden they want to do something that they have never done before and which you firmly believe they have no idea how to do. It can be driving for the first time or suddenly announcing they want to go somewhere with friends. I knew it was going to happen; but exactly how to handle it myself and handle it with them so they got a chance to do something new without its being dangerous has been a challenge to me." FATHER

"I wish that I had known that I had to listen more to them in order to understand what they were experiencing. I sort of assumed that I knew what adolescence was about from my own experience, but things had a different meaning to them. What was important to me was not that important to them, and I wish I had realized that in the beginning." MOTHER

"I wish I knew how to raise children in adolescence when you have traditional values and many of the people around you do not. It's very hard to do here in California compared to the South, where we came from. There, everyone reinforces the same values, and it is a lot easier for parents." MOTHER

"I wish I had known to be more attentive, to really listen, because kids have a lot of worthwhile things to say and you come to find out they hold a lot of your viewpoints." FATHER

"I wish I had known it was important to spend time with the children individually. We did things as a family, but the children are so different, and I think I would have understood them better if I had spent time with them alone." MOTHER

and acting out. Adolescents from indulged and authoritarian homes scored between the neglectful and authoritative groups on most measures.

An intense study of 133 adolescents as they balanced independence with bonds of family closeness and intimacy also found parental commitment to children a crucial element in parenting adolescents.[5] The ability to "hang in" when times are tough is essential. Parents' nonjudgmental acceptance of teenagers' feelings and

Late teens may spend more time in their bedrooms than in any other setting in the home. Parents are expected to respect the teen's privacy, including phone conversations, mail, and personal effects, but they are also expected to include them in leisure time activities and family events.

ideas, and parents' valuing of novelty and ambiguity as teens find new ways to look at things, help create intimacy among family members. When parents share their own personal experiences growing up, they present themselves as a *reliable resource* for children.

As adolescents become more independent, they want to take control of many areas and make their own decisions. Both parents and teens agree it is the mundane, routine behaviors that cause conflicts, with teens reporting more conflicts than parents. School work and grades become a more frequent topic as early adolescents move into junior high school. As they move into high school, chores become a focus and remain a major topic during later adolescence.[6]

As was noted with preadolescents, early adolescents understand parents' insistence on following conventions. Teens simply do not agree with them. Early adolescents insist that many of these issues should be matters under their personal control. Parents are aware of their children's point of view but will not accept it as valid. Early adolescents recognize that certain behaviors have important effects on other people; and they, like parents, consider these moral issues that they will not challenge—for example, hitting others, not sharing.

Parents and children agree that most of the time conflicts end because children follow parents' wishes. In only 18 percent of conflicts do parents follow children's requests, and joint discussion and decision settle just 13 percent of the disagreements. So although there are conflicts, children acquiesce.[7] The basic relationship between parents and children remains solid.

Mothers, however, bear the burden of the increasing disagreements.[8] It may be that since mothers are more involved in routine household management and scheduling, children argue with them about everyday events. It also may be that mothers are more emotionally reactive with adolescents, so both boys and girls argue with them more. When fathers are present as a third party in disagreements, boys are more respectful and mother-son relations improve. Father-adolescent relations are more open and interactive when mothers are not present as a third party.[9] Mothers seem to dominate the relationship, and fathers withdraw.

Later adolescents understand that some activities are done because they benefit the whole family. While conflicts about everyday issues continue, late teens accept and respect their parents' conventional views on situations, and so parents are pleased. Teens do not necessarily give in, but parents are more likely to grant their requests now perhaps because teens seem to understand their reasoning.[10]

When adolescents struggle less over power with their parents, they are able to become more self-governing and independent without giving up warm family relationships. So late teenagers report a greater sense of well-being in the process of separation from parents. When separation occurs in the context of family misunderstandings and emotional distance from the parents, then teens report greater loneliness and feelings of dejection.[11]

When issues of power are settled, then about half the respondents in a large survey report positive relationships with parents, and they want these close relationships to continue as they move through later adolescence.[12]

What makes for positive relationships?[13] Adolescents want parents to trust and accept them, to be warm, to help but not overprotect, to have fun with them. They do not want orders without explanations, parents' just adding, "Because I said so." They do not want nagging, and a "Do it now!" approach. They do not enjoy the "When I was young . . ." lecture. They also do not like parents who are too busy for them. Further, they do not approve of parents' bad habits—heavy drinking, lying, hypocrisy.

Serving as Resource and Consultant

We have talked about ways parents relate to and interact with their adolescents so children grow into mature adults. The term "reliable resource" summarizes parental activity in readying their adolescents to meet the challenges of this period. Parents provide children with information they need on a variety of topics—sexuality, alcohol, drugs, and ways of maintaining a healthy lifestyle. All too often parents fail to provide their children with information about sex. One survey of college students showed that the students received only 15.5 percent of their information about sex from their parents.[14]

In addition to supplying factual information about the physiology of sex, parents help children form values. Parents need to discuss their own values with their children and how their values have helped them lead richer lives. Parents may want to describe the experiences that led them to their value system, offer the reasoning behind the values. Parents need not dictate attitude but present points of view that their children may not have considered. Parents need not worry about presenting a conservative view—many teenagers want to hear just that. If you are concerned about seeming old-fashioned, remember that about 25 percent of boys and 40 percent of girls wish, in retrospect, that they had waited longer before being sexually active.

If you find sexual matters too difficult to discuss with teenage children, it is best to say that to them honestly and then suggest that they talk to a counselor or a doctor. For example, you might say, "I'd like to answer your questions about sex without getting all flustered, but frankly I can't. As I grew up, this subject wasn't discussed and I feel uncomfortable with it. I'll answer the questions I can, even if I flounder, and I'll get books for fuller details. I only hope you'll be more relaxed talking about this subject when you're a parent."[15]

What can parents do to help adolescents make informed choices? First, parents make sure that adolescents have accurate information about reproduction, fertility control, and the use of contraceptives for protected sex. Many parents may not want to discuss the possibility of having sexual relations, fearing that such discussion may appear to give permission for such activity. Nevertheless, having accurate information is a major safeguard against early sexual activity.

Another major safeguard against the risks of sexual activity is postponing the activity until teens are better able to handle the responsibilities.[16] Parental communication with adolescents is associated with postponement. Equally important, parents encourage teens to have interests and sources of gratification that absorb time and attention so that sexual activity can be postponed more easily.

Adolescents must see the relevance of factual information to their personal lives. Many teens believe that pregnancy could not happen to them, and parents need to help them see that pregnancy can happen. Adolescents also must have the social skills to use the information. Are they able to withstand the pressure for sexual activity? Are they able to seek out information that they need? Are they able to use contraceptives and/or insist that their partner use contraceptives? Parents can discuss in general terms how hard it is to be assertive, yet how important for personal well-being.

In addition to providing information, establishing open communication, encouraging interests and the development of assertive social skills, parents also provide supervision. As far as possible, they do not permit teens to be in situations that can lead to spontaneous sexual activity. For example, since first intercourse most often happens at home, parents do not go away for the weekend and leave teenagers alone at home. Teenagers need to stay with friends. Parental supervision is related to delay in sexual activity.[17]

Just as most parents avoid talking about sex, they also avoid talking about the use of mind-altering substances and tobacco. In one survey, 55 percent of the teens said their parents did not discuss drugs with them.[18] Yet a significant number (42 percent) of younger teens thirteen to fifteen were experimenting with marijuana.[19] So parents are well-advised to become knowledgable about the physical effects of alcohol, tobacco, and drugs like marijuana and cocaine and discuss the information with their adolescent children. This information should be reliable and well documented. Parents do more harm than good when they present exaggerated reports of drug effects because teens then dismiss everything that is said to them.

In addition to providing information, parents provide models of responsible substance use. They do not smoke, drink heavily or excessively, or use illegal drugs. When parents do indulge in these habits, children may imitate them even though the children do not like or approve of their parents' behavior.

Parents also serve as consultants when teenagers want to enter the world of work. Ellen Greenberger and Laurence Steinberg suggest parents play an active role in discussing the pros and cons of work in the light of the child's needs and other demands on the child's time.[20] If work is an option, then parents can help teens decide the kind of job that would meet their needs—how many hours, how far from home, the exact time of day for working, ways to handle the money. Parents then monitor the child's work experience after the job has started to be sure it is not too stressful and does not have negative effects on school work, friendships, and social behavior like drinking. If it does, then parents can discuss changing the job or the hours.

The ways that parents can help teenagers make long-term vocational plans are similar to the ways they help them make choices about sexual activity. Parents can provide factual information about expanding fields and possible careers, about the personal qualities and interests needed to do various kinds of work, and about how teenagers can get more information and test their interests. Parents can also provide information about possible occupations based on their observation of children's skills and interests. Ginott has an excellent section on the importance of parental appreciation of those very special acts and traits that can only be seen at home and about the need to tell children about their special talents.[21]

Parents also can help children develop the interpersonal skills and the self-confidence that will enable them to pursue vocational goals. They can talk about how to prepare for interviews, how to present abilities and special qualifications for a job, how to remain at ease in an interview. At times of failure and frustration, parents can offer encouragement and suggest alternative actions. As children make choices, however, parents must stand back and keep silent.

In the past, parents have encouraged a commitment to work for boys but not for girls. Because work is now a more important part of a woman's life across the life span, parents encourage their daughters as well as their sons to search for meaningful work that they can enjoy.

Parents also serve as models and sources of information for minority adolescents who are exploring their ethnic culture and achieving a sense of identity. Psychiatrist James P. Comer states that the entire Afro-American community has to act together "to help each child establish a personal and group identity . . . that allows each young person to feel, 'I am an individual, an Afro-American with a tradition of sacrifice, struggle, and excellence; and it is my job to restore and carry on the tradition for my own sake, for the good of the Afro-American community, and for the good of America.'"[22] These are appropriate feelings for all children to have about their ethnic tradition. Margaret Spencer and Carol Markstrom-Adams make nine recommendations, listed in Box 7-1, to promote positive identity formation of minority youth.[23]

Development of the Self

Adolescents think of themselves in terms of psychological qualities. They describe how they relate to other people, their social style, and begin to see patterns in their behavior. They reflect on their own characteristics, see themselves as fitting certain categories, and have a greater sense of their abilities to do things. Note this self-description of a seventeen-year-old girl.

BOX 7-1

**METHODS TO ENHANCE IDENTITY FORMATION
OF ETHNIC MINORITY YOUTH**

1. Methods should be proposed to keep minority youth in school and academically oriented since lack of education increases the risk of poverty and disadvantage.
2. Efforts are required to heighten health consciousness, because poor health interferes with identity processes. The physical health of many minority youth lags behind that of majority youth.
3. Importance of social networks should be affirmed. Churches and extended families are important resources for minority families as they socialize children.
4. Methods should be proposed to support parents as cultural transmitters. Many ethnic group parents do not discuss their distinctive values and experiences, and parents must receive support as they begin to do this.
5. Proposals are needed to offer a media-focused, cultural emphasis that affirms positive group identity for all youth to combat the negative stereotyping that occurs.
6. Methods are needed to promote teaching of native languages and cultures, particularly for American Indians who are at risk for losing their cultural heritage. Creativity is required to encourage biculturalism at the same time one preserves cultural traditions.
7. Programs are required for the special training of teachers so that they will be sensitive to cultural traditions, communicative patterns, and sometimes the language of minority students.
8. Childrearing support by way of teaching parenting skills is required to promote parents' sense of ethnic pride and enhance the home-school partnership.
9. Improved training is required for mental health workers serving ethnic minority populations.

Adapted from Margaret Beale Spencer and Carol Markstrom-Adams, "Identity Processes among Racial and Ethnic Minority Children in America," *Child Development* 61 (1990): 305–306.

I am a human being. I am a girl. I am an individual. I don't know who I am. I am a Pisces. I am a moody person. I am an indecisive person. I am an ambitious person. I am a very curious person. I am not an individual. I am a loner. I am an American (God help me). I am a Democrat. I am a liberal person. I am a radical. I am a conservative. I am a pseudo-liberal. I am an atheist. I am not a classifiable person (i.e., I don't want to be).[24]

Sex differences in self-descriptions at age eighteen reveal that boys see themselves as more daring, rebellious, and playful in life than girls and, at the same time, more logical, curious, and calm. Girls see themselves as more attuned to people than boys are—more sympathetic, social, considerate, and affectionate—and more emotionally reactive—more worrisome, more easily upset, more needing of approval.[25]

James Marcia believes that following a period of exploration, adolescents make a commitment to values, goals, and behavior and, in doing so, achieve a **sense of identity.**[26]

The process of achieving this identity is gradual, taking several years; and it is the usual path for most adolescents. It is not, however, the only path to identity. Some adolescents make a commitment to traditional values without even considering for themselves what they want to do with their lives. There is no crisis or conflict because these adolescents do not want to deal with issues. Marcia terms commitment without exploration **identity foreclosure** to indicate that possibilities have been closed off prematurely.

A different path is taken by adolescents who experience a **moratorium**. These young people experience a crisis about what they want to do. They have ideas they explore but have not yet made a commitment. So a moratorium is exploration without commitment. Finally, some adolescents experience **identity diffusion** in which they can make no choices at all. They drift without direction.

Achieving a sense of identity is a more complicated task for minority youth. They have two cultures to explore, understand, and integrate in their quest for identity. They begin with a diffused view of their ethnic background. They talk to parents, family friends, and other adults about ethnic issues. They read books and share experiences with friends. They are aware of prejudice and think about its effects on work and life goals. In the eighth grade, about a third of Afro-American students are actively involved in the exploration. By age fifteen, about half of minority students are actively exploring their cultural roots and traditions and an additional one-fourth have already achieved a sense of identity.[27]

Two difficulties arise.[28] First, many minority parents do not talk with their children about their cultural background, and they do not share their own experiences with the majority culture. Perhaps because they do not want to burden their children with experiences that no longer occur or perhaps because they are uncomfortable with issues of culture and race, many parents remain silent and offer no models for children. Children have to seek information elsewhere and cannot consciously pattern themselves after their parents.

Second, minority adolescents have to explore and integrate two cultures. Integrating one set of cultural traditions with the realities of everyday life is difficult enough. When there are two cultures that sometimes conflict, the task becomes very complicated.

Which values does one select? Children and adolescents ideally should be permitted a bicultural identification that includes both cultures. Minority youth who combine, for example, emphasis on both cooperation and sharing found in many ethnic cultures with the assertive independence of the majority culture are effective in a wider range of situations than are those attached to just one set of values. A bicultural orientation is not easy to achieve because peers or family may pressure the adolescent to adopt only the traditional cultural values.

The process of achieving identity is even more difficult when the minority culture is devalued and adolescents experience negative stereotyping. Youth may then refuse to explore their ethnic roots and instead seek a foreclosed identity. There is some evidence that this happens more frequently among minority adolescents.[29] Other adolescents internalize the negative images, feel deficient and worthless, and develop what Erikson calls a **negative identity**. Currently, more minority youth develop a positive cultural identity and feel high self-esteem. A positive ethnic

TABLE 7-1

WHAT ADOLESCENTS WANT MOST IN LIFE

To be loved	41%
To be healthy	38%
To do the kind of work you really like	29%
To be successful in your work	25%
To be rich	22%
To be married	13%
To do something worthwhile for the world	9%

Reprinted with the permission of Rawson Associates, an imprint of Macmillan Publishing Company from *The Private Life of the American Teenager* by Jane Norman and Myron Harris, Ph.D. Copyright © 1981 Jane Norman and Myron Harris.

identity enables youth to replace tension and defensiveness with self-confidence about the future.

In the process of self-reflection, adolescents of all groups come to have an increased respect for what they can accomplish and do, a greater sense of the "I" who wills and acts. It may be this basic self-respect that accounts for the general positive view of the self-concept in these times of change. When self-esteem is measured yearly from the ages of twelve to eighteen, we find that most adolescents are stable in their overall view of themselves.[30] Seven out of ten report they like themselves and there is much to like.[31] Through the period from early to late adolescence, they mature, become more independent, more perceptive of others, and more communicative. By fifteen or sixteen, they are psychologically strong individuals. A small group of adolescents, about 20 percent, appear to experience the tumult and turbulence clinicians often associate with this period. They suffer intense anxiety and extreme mood swings. Still a third group is generally stable and has difficulty only when some unexpected stress occurs.[32] So, though there are occasional times of uncertainty and self-doubt, of loneliness and concern about the future, most adolescents also experience self-confidence, a zest for life, an excitement about the future, a sense of challenge and competence in meeting new situations.

What are the "down" times for early adolescents? Teens are most upset when alone in their room, studying, because they are deprived of company and made to do work they do not enjoy. What concerns most adolescents? Table 7-2 illustrates major worries expressed in a large-scale study and compares thirteen to fifteen-year-olds to older adolescents.[33] For early adolescents, school is the greatest concern. Parents are not as bothersome to them as brothers and sisters and friends. Interestingly, parents' greatest concerns for their children—usually drugs, alcohol, and sexual experiences—are not what bothers teens.

What do teens fear? Table 7-3 is not broken down by age because children between the ages of thirteen and eighteen show few differences. Far and away the biggest fear of teens is that something may happen to their parents. They also fear many things that parents would agree are sources of concern: dying, not getting a good job. As in earlier years, they worry about school. As one would expect in times of expanding social contacts, social fears are important as well.

TABLE 7-2
ADOLESCENT WORRIES

What Bothers You the Most? 13–15-Year-Olds		What Bothers You the Most? 16–18-Year-Olds	
School	30%	School	29%
Brothers and sisters	30%	Parents	28%
Friends	26%	Money	24%
Parents	23%	Friends	22%
Money	13%	Brothers and sisters	21%
Drinking and drugs	10%	Drinking and drugs	9%
Sex	9%	Sex	7%

Reprinted with the permission of Rawson Associates, an imprint of Macmillan Publishing Company from *The Private Life of the American Teenager* by Jane Norman and Myron Harris, Ph.D. Copyright © 1981 Jane Norman and Myron Harris.

Teenagers' depressed moods and nervousness are primarily related to social stressors or life events.[34] Adolescents who reported many negative events not only felt depressed but experienced poor physical health as well following the event. Hormonal changes too may play a role in depressed mood or aggressiveness.[35] The experience of positive events, however, can serve as protection against the effects of negative events when they do occur.

When depressed mood deepens, adolescents may think about suicide. Susan Harter and her co-workers have isolated the significant factors they believe account for the depressed mood and suicidal ideation seen in some adolescents.[36] They believe when adolescents feel incompetent in areas important to them and to others, and also feel lack of support from important others like parents and friends, then they will feel hopeless. Hopelessness leads to a "depression" composite consisting of low self-esteem, general hopelessness, and depressed mood. Depression then leads to suicidal ideation.

Harter concludes,

. . . There are powerful implications for *prevention* as well as *intervention*. For example, our findings suggest that intervening at the front end of the model, by influencing self-concept and social support, will have the biggest impact, since it is here that the chain of causal influences appears to begin. Thus, we can intervene to improve self-esteem, by helping the individual to become more competent in areas in which he/she has aspirations, or by aiding the individual to discount the importance of domains in which high levels of success are unlikely. Self-esteem can also be improved by intervening to provide more opportunities for support and approval from significant others. Such interventions should not only enhance the individual's self-esteem, but prevent the more insidious cycles that involve hopelessness, depression, and associated suicidal thoughts and gestures that may serve as the ultimate path of escape.[37]

TABLE 7-3
ADOLESCENT FEARS

What Are Your Greatest Fears?*	
Losing your parents	58%
Dying	28%
Not getting a good job or being successful	21%
Not doing well in school	18%
Nuclear war	14%
People not liking you	12%
Getting cancer	10%
Not getting married	6%
Getting attacked or mugged	6%

* The participants chose more than one response in some cases.

Reprinted with the permission of Rawson Associates, an imprint of Macmillan Publishing Company from *The Private Life of the American Teenager* by Jane Norman and Myron Harris, Ph.D. Copyright © 1981 Jane Norman and Myron Harris.

Peers

Parents worry about the influence of peer groups in these years. They sometimes fear they have lost their children to their age mates. This is not so. Friends tend to share the same values and backgrounds; they are not that different from each other. Second, peers defer to each other on matters of music and entertainment, clothing and language. But they rely much more on parents in regard to moral and social values, vocational suggestions—just the areas where parents want to have the most influence. Teenagers want input from their parents on the important issues.

The healthiest teenagers strike a balance between acceptance of peer values and parental values. Adolescents who are peer-oriented rather than adult-oriented may be turning to age mates because they lack closeness with adults.[38] Their parents seem to be uninterested in them, neither giving them guidance nor establishing limits. These teenagers are likely to have low self-esteem, a dimmer view of the future, less interest in making and doing things, and less competence in academic work than adolescents who are also adult-oriented. They do not appear to find in their peer attachments the emotional warmth and closeness they require to be productive and effective.

Adolescents who are well liked by other adolescents share many characteristics. They like other people and are sympathetic and understanding of their problems. They are cheerful, lively, and fun to be around. They like to plan events, and their enthusiasm arouses others. Thus, they make others feel comfortable and accepted by promoting positive social interactions or by planning enjoyable events. Other adolescents are less well liked for a variety of reasons. Some are ignored or neglected because they are social isolates who retreat in nervous shyness. Others arouse antagonisms because they are aggressive, demand attention, are critical and complaining.[39]

Time with friends is spent primarily in leisure—joking, talking, fooling around. From friends, adolescents get a clearer view of themselves. They also get positive feedback and encouragement. If they are depressed, peers help them feel better:

> Close friends can be relaxed with each other and don't need to be aware of their actions. Each can talk freely about emotions and show them. With each other, the two friends have a chance to see themselves wide open; they are not afraid of talking too much about themselves. One can say he likes or dislikes someone, and he knows the other won't tell. One can be in a sour mood one day and know that the other will understand. Best friends can complain to each other, and most important, they can act stupid or silly, loud or crazy with one another and understand that there is no need to feel that the silliness endangers the friendship.[40]

Dating

Dating serves many important functions in adolescence. It is a way to learn how to relate to people of the opposite sex; it provides a structure for meeting people, exploring compatibility, and terminating a relationship with a minimum of embarrassment. Finally, dating gives practice in developing feelings of trust and enjoyment with the opposite sex.

Most girls begin dating at about fourteen and boys between fourteen and fifteen. By their senior year in high school, about half of adolescents date more than once a week, and one-third between two and three times a week.[41] Going steady occurs most frequently among older adolescents sixteen to eighteen; 30 percent of boys and 40 percent of girls of this age say they are going steady. Over half the adolescents say they have been in love, with girls reporting this more frequently than boys.[42]

Adolescents who have definite educational and vocational plans and who wish for marriages like those of their parents go steady less often and report being in love less often during adolescence. When girls have high self-esteem, they date more often but go steady less often. Those who are most likely to be going steady do not want marriages like their parents. Involvement in dating that is too early and too intense may block opportunities for same-sex relationships or more casual opposite-sex relationships that develop the capacity for intimacy and closeness at later ages.[43]

A 1990 national survey of 11,000 high school students reveals that over half of high school students have had sexual intercourse. Rates differ with the sex of the student—60 percent of boys have had intercourse, and 48 percent of girls.[44] Teens are less likely to be sexually active if they believe parents do not approve of such activity, if they think peers are not engaged in such activity, and if they are not in a serious relationship.[45]

Adolescents believe that the quality of the relationship between people, the way they treat each other, is the most important factor in making the decision about sexual activity.[46] Although both boys and girls are more liberal than before, girls still tie sexual relations to feelings of love, and 75 percent say they would have sexual relations only if they loved the person. An almost equal number of boys insist that they must like the person, but only 47 percent tie having sexual intercourse to feelings of love for the other person.[47]

Increases in premarital intercourse for girls may cause observers to overlook the

INTERVIEW
with Susan Harter

Susan Harter is professor of psychology at the University of Denver and has carried out extensive studies on self-esteem. This interview is continued from Chapter 2.

Self-esteem seems very important because it gives the person a kind of confidence to try many new activities.

One of the things that I began to fret about was that we had spent a lot of government money examining what feeds into self-esteem. I bolted upright one day and said to myself, "What if self-esteem doesn't do anything? What if it doesn't have any ramifications for everyday lives and happiness? We know what creates it, but if it does not really impact our lives, who cares?"

So, this is how we got interested in depression. We looked at the dimensions of depression, and mood is the most cardinal aspect of depression. To make a long story short, self-esteem has powerful implications for mood. The correlation between how much you like yourself as a person and your self-reported mood on a scale from cheerful to depressed is typically about .80.

Low self-esteem is invariably accompanied by depressive affect. We have extended these findings in developing a model that helps us understand suicidal thinking in teenagers. We included Beck's concept of hopelessness and have measured specific hopelessnesses corresponding to the support and self-concept domains. We ask, "How hopeless are you about getting peer support, parent support, about ever looking the way you want in terms of appearance?" "How hopeless are you about your scholastic ability?" There are various separate domains.

The worst consequences occur if you feel inadequate in an area in which support is important and feel hopeless about ever turning that area around. Moreover, if you don't have support and feel there is nothing you can ever do to get that support, this feeds into a depression composite of low self-esteem, low mood plus general hopelessness. Thus, the worst case scenario is the feeling that I am not getting support from people whose approval is important, I am not feeling confident in areas in which success is valued, I am hopeless about ever turning things around, I don't like myself as a person, I feel depressed, and my future looks bleak. That, in turn, causes kids to think of suicide as a solution to their problems, as an escape from painful self-perceptions leading to depression.

conservative views many adolescent girls hold. Girls are usually going steady with their first sexual partner, and a large number plan on marrying the partner. Girls are more likely to feel anxious and fearful after their first intercourse, and about 40 percent wish they had waited. In contrast, boys usually feel positive and optimistic about their first intercourse, even though in nearly half the instances the girl was not someone they knew well.[48]

Even though adolescents are more active sexually today than previously, they are not using contraceptives on a widespread basis. Only about one-third of sexually

There is another scenario that may also lead to suicidal thinking, namely, the teen who has done extremely well in all these areas. Then they experience their first failure, for example, scholastically (they get their first B), athletically (they feel they are responsible for a key loss), or socially (they don't get invited to a major party). As a result, they consider suicide as a solution to their humiliation. These teens seem so puzzling, but we think that conditional support plays a role here. We saw kids whose support scores were reasonable, but when we interviewed them, they would say, "Well, my parent only cares about me if I make the varsity team or if I get all As" or whatever the formula is for that family. So conditionality of support is important.

Another aspect about suicide is the co-occurrence of symptoms. People have talked about internalizers and externalizers as though you are one or the other. Most people have both qualities. When you look at measures of internalizing and externalizing symptoms, a correlation is about .65. Typically, you don't have a separate group of internalizing people who only engage in behaviors directed against the self. In clinical samples, it is often difficult to predict whether problem adolescents will act out against themselves or take it out on someone else. It may depend on the specific circumstances. Is the other person actually there when the adolescent is distressed or is the adolescent alone? Is there a weapon available? These factors partially determine whether one acts against the self or against the others.

That leads to another point. We asked teenagers who reported depressed affect which specific emotions comprise depression for you? We all suspect it is sadness of some kind, but are there other feelings that are part of the depressive experience? Eighty percent of adolescents tell us it is sadness plus *anger*. Who is the target of that anger—are they angry at themselves (the classic view of depression), or are they angry at someone else? We found that the majority of teens are angry at someone else. They have not yet internalized the anger against themselves. They will tell you, "Yeah, I am really, really sad, and I am angry at my mom. She got divorced and isn't paying attention to me or she is on my case."

Typically, adolescents view the causes of depression to be actions of others against the self. Other people have rejected them or are in conflict with them or aren't treating them the way they want to be treated. A few of them will admit they are angry at themselves, but most anger is directed at others.

I think it is important to point out that the reason people are spending so much energy and and money on studying self-esteem is that low self-esteem has so many consequences such as depressed mood, lack of energy to get up and do age-appropriate tasks, be productive, and, for some, thoughts of suicide. Most parents want their children to be happy, and self-esteem is an important pathway to happiness and the ability to function in today's world.

active women aged fifteen to nineteen always use contraceptives. About 27 percent never use contraceptives, and still another third do only sometimes.[49] Girls with high self-esteem who are confident and happy with their lives and on good terms with their parents are most likely to use contraceptives. Boys who are older, more responsible, and have parents who approve of sexual activity are most likely to use contraceptives. When used, the most popular methods are condoms, withdrawal, and the pill.[50]

ROUTINES, PROBLEMS, AND STRATEGIES

The problems encountered during adolescence relate to physical and intellectual functioning, social behavior, and family interactions. Among the most prevalent and difficult are those associated with family, school, friends, and social behavior—shyness, dress, sexual activity, and limit-setting that involves curfew and the use of alcohol and drugs.

The Noncommunicative Adolescent

Parents complain that children come home, go to their rooms, and shut the door. When they emerge for meals or snacks, they say little, answer any question with only a word or two. They don't talk about what they are doing, thinking, or feeling. Children don't seem unhappy, but parents feel they don't know them anymore. Parents may feel hurt when children say little to them but talk for hours on the phone to their friends.

Parents can, however, interact with children to promote conversation. Don Dinkmeyer and Gary McKay advise three strategies: (1) comment on nonverbal behavior, (2) ask for comments, (3) be a model of conversing.[51] For example, parents can try commenting on facial expressions or body language: "Looks like you had a good day today," or "You look happy." Teens may not follow up with any comments, but parents have made an effort.

Parents can ask for comments, saying, "How's school going?" or "What are you and Jenny doing tonight?" If the child answers with one word or two, parents drop the conversation and wait for another time. Parents can remain good models of communication, however, talking about their day, their friends, their plans.

Once teens begin to talk, parents listen and communicate feelings. If parents jump in with criticism, judgments of the child or others, blame, or sarcasm, all children clam up. Reflecting feelings helps teens to continue to talk. If teens talk about problems they are trying to work out and want to discuss them, parents can encourage them to list options, explore the advantages of each, and then act.

There are many *don'ts* to the process of encouraging conversation. Don't force the child to reveal feelings. Don't give advice once the teen has begun to talk. Don't rush to find the solution. Don't hurry to answer questions; delaying an answer can stimulate thinking. Adele Faber and Elaine Mazlish give the example of a girl who asked her mother, "Why don't we ever go to any place good on vacation like Bermuda or Florida?" The mother answered, "Why don't we?"

The girl replied, "I know, I know. Because it's too expensive. . . . Well, at least can we go to the zoo?"[52]

Faber and Mazlish describe useful techniques when teens begin to talk about discouragement or frustration. They suggest showing respect for the child's struggle with comments like "That can be hard," "It's not easy," or "Sometimes it helps when . . ." and then parents give a piece of information: "It helps when you're rushed to concentrate on the most important item." Teens are free to use the information or not. Parents have to watch their tone of voice or the information can sound like advice.

A nurturing, supportive parent-child relationship is the best insurance against some of
the problems that may face adolescents.

Faber and Mazlish also present interesting alternative responses to saying "no."
Since teens are very sensitive to control and may not like to ask if they hear a lot of
"nos" in response, having other ways to respond is useful and will encourage greater
talkativeness. Suppose a teen wants you to take him to the store at 5:30 while you
are cooking dinner. Instead of giving a flat "no," a parent can say, "I'll take you after
dinner." If you are completely unable to do it, you can say, "I'd like to be able to help
you out, but I have to get dinner on the table and get to that meeting at 7:00." A parent
can leave out the "no" and just give information. For example, if a teen asks for an

extra, expensive piece of clothing, the parent can say, "The budget just won't take it this month." If there are ways the teen can get the item, the parent can pass that information on. "If you want that as a birthday present at the end of the month, that would be fine."

All strategies recommend fostering self-esteem and autonomy by focusing on the positive things teens do. When children feel good about themselves, they talk more. Dinkmeyer and McKay describe how parents use encouragement to foster self-esteem at times of frustration. Encouragement focuses on effort, improvement, and interest and is reflected in phrases like, "You really worked hard on that," or "I can see a lot of progress," or "You were really a big help to your brother in cleaning his room."

Using all these different strategies does not guarantee a talkative teenager in the home, but it increases the likelihood of conversation.

School Problems

Experts are divided on the handling of school problems. Some give all the responsibility to the early adolescent to handle the problem; others encourage the parent to take an active role.

Ginott cites the example of a thirteen-year-old boy who brought home a note from the teacher about his poor behavior.[53] His mother said, "You must have felt terrible to have to bring home a note like that." He agreed he did. His mother wrote the school that she was sure he would handle the problem. (In the past she would have yelled and screamed.) The next day she met the principal, but her son had already begun to improve his behavior.

Gordon, as well as Dinkmeyer and McKay, consider that the child has the problem. This is an issue he or she must deal with. A parent can be a model of effective work habits, can be interested in the child's feelings about school, but essentially schoolwork is up to the child.

Not so with the behaviorists. Eimers and Aitchison describe recommendations to help an eleven-year-old boy who was failing school.[54] Testing revealed he was bright and had no special learning problem. He just misbehaved in class and did not do homework. Eimers and Aitchison described the problem as the boy's not getting sufficient rewards for doing work. Parents found a suitable work place in the dining room, and the boy was given a choice of rewards for spending so much time on his homework. Initially, the amount of time he put in was brief, but gradually it was increased so that he could obtain the reward.

But as the boy's homework improved, his classroom behavior still required changing. He was given points for working predetermined amounts of time at his desk. When he clowned in class, he was put in time out for a brief period. The teacher also praised the boy for on-task behavior. We can see here that parents and teachers can do many things to change school behavior—organize the environment, give praise and rewards for appropriate behavior, and give punishment for inappropriate behavior.

Exactly which method—giving the child the problem to handle or setting up a behavioral regime—will work in individual cases depends on the parents' values and the seriousness of the problem. Given the age of early adolescents, mutual problem-solving sessions and sending strong I-statements of concern might be appropriate tactics. If this does not lead to an effective plan for change, then parents can try the behavioral system. If children fall behind in school because they aren't doing the work, they can find it very hard to catch up when they finally decide to take action. For that reason the more active approach of the behaviorists has merit.

The Isolated Child

Although the socially outgoing child presents some problems to parents, these can usually be worked out with contracting sessions or mutual problem solving. The aggressive child often has the same problems as the isolated child with an extra layer of aggressiveness that can be controlled with rewards and negative consequences. The isolated child, however, requires action on a variety of fronts as described in Chapter 6. We raise the issue again here, however, because adolescence gives a special poignancy to such a problem. Because the emphasis in these years is on getting along with others, isolation is especially frustrating.

Philip Zimbardo, a psychologist who has studied shyness in all age groups and has established a Shyness Clinic at Stanford, and Shirley Radl recommend several actions.[55] Theirs are the only suggestions specifically geared for the adolescent years of twelve to seventeen. Because appearance is so important in the early and late adolescent years, Zimbardo and Radl suggest working from the outside in, concentrating first on appearance so that a teenager looks as well as possible from their point of view. Skin problems should be attended to immediately. Acne, which can create real misery, comes from many causes. Medicines likes creams, lotions, and antibiotics prescribed by a dermatologist can be used on severe cases. Weight, too, can be a problem. A pediatrician can discuss weight and put the child on a diet. Parents then have suitable foods available and serve as models of good eating patterns.

Teeth sometimes need attention. Since most children and many adults wear braces, they are not the source of embarrassment they once were. Parents may be concerned about expense, but many dentists have a no-interest payment plan. Grooming and clothes also aid appearance. Parents can provide the current fashion so far as the budget allows. When clothes are more expensive than parents can afford, possible solutions include buying, for example, one or two pairs of expensive pants rather than four or five cheaper ones. Or teens can earn money to make up the difference between what the parents can afford and what the clothes cost.

At home, parents do all the things that increase children's sense of security and importance. Respecting privacy, treating the child with respect, keeping lines of communication open, giving responsibility, giving appropriate praise, not prying into the child's thoughts and feelings, having rules and structure all contribute to a sense of security that enables the child to reach out to others in these sensitive years.

Choice of Friends

By the time children reach their teens, they are aware of the qualities that their parents value in people. They sometimes seem to pick friends we find less than desirable.

THE JOYS OF PARENTING EARLY ADOLESCENTS

"Seeing him care for younger children and babies is a great pleasure. He's a great nurturer with small children. He has endless patience." MOTHER

"He is a talented athlete, and his soccer team got to a championship game. He scored the winning goal, and when he took off with the ball down the field, I was very proud of him. It was a unique feeling of being proud that someone I had helped to create was doing that. He had felt a lot of pressure in the game, so to see how incredibly pleased he was gave me great joy." FATHER

"Now that they are older, they bring new skills into our lives. I did not learn algebra in school, but to help him with problems now and then, I learned algebra from the book. I am very pleased to be able to help." MOTHER

"It is gratifying to me to see him learn the rules. He makes sure his homework is done, and he does it on his own steam." MOTHER

"I like that he does things I did, like play the trumpet. He started at the same age I did and since he took it up, it has rekindled my interest and I started practicing again. This last weekend, we played together. He also brings new interests too. Because he likes sailing I have started that and really like it." FATHER

"She is in that dreamy preteen state where she writes things. She wrote a poem about the difference between being alone and loneliness. She has a real appreciation of time on her own and how nice being alone can be. I like that because I had that at her age." MOTHER

"It's nice just being able to help them, feeling good because they are being helped out and benefited." FATHER

"It's nice to see her being able to analyze situations with friends or with her teachers and come to conclusions. She said about one of her teachers, "Well, she gets

All the strategies discussed in this book agree that parents should not intervene directly to forbid or end a relationship. Instead, they should do what behaviorists call "letting the behavior run its course." The child's choice is respected, and the child respects the parents' feelings. The strategies differ on how parents should express their reservations. The possibilities include waiting to comment, refusing to encourage or facilitate the relationship, and arranging situations in which the child can see the problem as the parents do.

When teens pick same-sex friends with different values, parents may worry that their children will be led into situations they cannot handle—heavy drinking, speeding in cars, cutting school. Parents should first examine their own reactions. Is the friend really likely to create trouble for your child? Or are you objecting to less important characteristics, such as appearance and manners? If the friend really is a problem, does your child have some underlying conflict or need that attracts him or her to such a friend? Does your child feel insecure and seek out a daredevil to mask excited and she never follows through with what she says, so you know you don't have to take her seriously." MOTHER

"I really enjoy being in the scouts with the boys. Once a month we go on a camping weekend, and I really look forward to that." FATHER

"I was so impressed and pleased that after the earthquake, he and a friend decided to go door to door and offer to sell drawings they made of Teenage Mutant Ninja Turtles. He raised $150 that he gave for earthquake relief. I was very proud that he thought this up all by himself." FATHER

"I was very happy one day when I found this note she left on my desk. It said, 'Hello!!! Have a happy day! Don't worry about home, everyone's fine! Do your work the very best you can. But most important, have a fruitful life!!!' I saved that note because it made me feel so good." MOTHER

"He enjoys life. He has a sense of humor. He's like a butterfly enjoying everything; eventually he'll settle in." MOTHER

"He's very sensitive, and his cousins two years older than he ask his advice about boys. They may not take it, but they ask him even though he's younger." FATHER

"It's very rewarding to see them in their school activities. My daughter sings in the school chorus, and I enjoy that, and my son is in school plays." FATHER

"I am very pleased that she is less moody now than she used to be. We used to refer to her lows as 'Puddles of Frustration,' but she has got past that now." MOTHER

"Well, they have their friends over, and we have Ping Pong, pool, cards, and we stressed having these things available. I enjoy playing all these games with them." FATHER

the insecurity? If so, it is best for parents to deal with the underlying problem and try to find ways of bolstering confidence.

If you object because the friend has a terrible driving record, cuts school frequently, or is failing courses, sit down and share your concerns with your teenager. Respect the child's right to have this friend, but point out the possible consequences to your child. If not pressured, the child will be able to understand what you are saying and may begin to spend less time with the friend. If the two continue to spend time together, it is possible that the friend may change. It is also possible that, as you get to know the friend, you may begin to understand why your child values this friendship. If the friendship continues and trouble does result for your child or seems about to occur, you may want to take action to end the relationship by forbidding it. This is difficult to enforce if the teen is determined to see the friend. In some situations, however, this firm action may be what your child wants.

Ginott tells of a situation in which parents gave their teenager freedom of choice yet exerted influence by raising questions for her to consider. Their eighteen-year-

THE JOYS OF PARENTING LATE ADOLESCENTS

"I think it's really fun to watch them grow up and mature. It's fun to see them discover things about themselves and their lives. The older ones have boyfriends, and I'm seeing them interact with the boyfriends." MOTHER

"Sometimes the kids have friends over, and they all start to talk about things. It's nice to see them get along with their siblings as well as their friends. It gives you a good feeling to see them enjoying themselves." FATHER

"I felt very pleased when my son at sixteen could get a summer job in the city and commute and be responsible for getting there and doing a good job." MOTHER

"I like it when they sit around and reminisce about the things they or the family have done in the past. They sit around the table and talk about an outing or a trip we took, saying 'Remember this?' It's always interesting what they remember. This last summer we took a long sightseeing trip, and what stands out in their minds about it is funny. They remember Filene's basement in Boston or a chicken ranch where we stopped to see friends. One father took the scouts on a ski trip. They got stuck in the snow on the highway for hours, and the car almost slid off the road. He said, 'Never again.' I said, 'Don't you realize that because of those things, the boys will probably remember that trip forever. You have given them wonderful memories.'" MOTHER

"I really enjoy her happiness. She always sees the positive side to a situation. Things might bother her from time to time, but she has a good perspective on things." FATHER

"I really like to see them taking responsibility. Yesterday they had a school holiday, and I was donating some time at an open house fundraiser. They got all dressed up and came along and helped too. The older one coaches a soccer team of four-year-olds, and the younger is a patrol leader in the Scouts, so they both have responsibility for children. They complain sometimes that it's hard to get the little kids' attention to show them things, but I think they like it." MOTHER

old daughter felt she had met the boy of her dreams. Her mother worried she was being swept away in a world of fantasy and physical attraction, and was not asking practical questions about how compatible they might be in a permanent relationship. The mother, however, did not raise these issues while her daughter was up in the clouds. Empathizing with her daughter's feelings, she waited for the best time to suggest realistic considerations.[56]

Gould cites the example of a boy in his late teens who became interested in a girl his parents disapproved of. Gould advises being pleasant to the girl, but says the parents do not need to lend the car for dates nor entertain her in their home.[57]

In another example, described by Krumboltz and Krumboltz, a couple found that their sixteen-year-old daughter was serious about an older boy they disliked, and

"I enjoy that she is following in the family tradition of rowing. I rowed in college, and my brothers did, my father and grandfather did, and she saw a city team and signed up. She does it all on her own and has made a nice group of friends through it." FATHER

"I can't believe that she has had her first boyfriend and it worked out so well. They met at a competition; and he lives some distance away, so they talk on the phone. He has a friend who lives here, and he comes for a visit sometime and does lots of things with the family. We all like him, and it is nice for her to have a boyfriend like that." MOTHER

"The joys are seeing them go from a totally disorganized state to a partially motivated, organized state. You can see their adult characteristics emerging." FATHER

"I enjoy seeing my daughter develop musical ability, seeing her progression from beginning flute to an accomplished player who performs, and seeing how much pleasure she takes in her accomplishment." MOTHER

"It really gives me a lot of pleasure to see the two of them help each other. They seem to have respect for each other. She is the brain and helps him with school, and he helps her too at times." FATHER

"I enjoy his maturity. He's so responsible. He tests us, but when we're firm, he accepts that. I'm real proud of him because he looks at the consequences of what he does." FATHER

"I enjoy his honesty and the relationship he has with his friends. He is real open with his feelings, and his friends look up to him. He's a leader." MOTHER

"He's not prejudiced. His best friends are of different ethnic groups. People trust him and like him because he's real concerned about people." FATHER

"I feel really pleased about the way the boys get along together. There is rivalry, but there is a lot of love. The older one takes the younger one under his wing, and the younger one looks up to him." FATHER

they feared an early marriage would occur.[58] They were worried because their daughter wanted to go steady. Instead of forbidding the relationship, they invited the boy to eat all weekday dinners with them and to spend time on weekends going on family excursions. The parents came to like certain qualities in the boy, but after three months their daughter ended the relationship and started dating other boys.

Sexual Behavior

Parents can provide as much information as they feel comfortable with and refer teenagers to physicians or other professionals who can answer questions. Parents discuss their values because these influence teens' behavior. Experts disagree on whether the parent should go with the adolescent to get contraceptive devices. Dodson recommends this active approach, but Ginott does not. In light of the deadly risk of AIDS, parents might want to take an active role.

One million teenage girls get pregnant each year. Katherine Oettinger discusses teenage pregnancy and how to handle it in *Not My Daughter.*[59] Parents and daughter must consider the circumstances, the maturity of the partners, and the emotional and financial supports available. Professionals emphasize that once a teenage girl is pregnant, there are no simple, easy alternatives. It is important that everyone communicate feelings openly, consider all the alternatives, and keep a clear focus on handling the problem without making accusations or placing blame. In making plans for the future, it is very important to keep in mind the adolescent's continuing education. When adolescents continue in school, their future, with or without children, can be very like that of women who get pregnant when more mature.

Sexually transmitted diseases are another problem being experienced by an increasing number of teenagers. Ginott describes the case of a mother who was horrified when confronted with the possibility that her daughter might have gonorrhea. The mother did not blame or criticize the child, however. She remained calm and talked about what they would do—see the doctor, get the diagnosis, and obtain treatment if necessary. Of primary importance from any perspective is dealing with the infection. Then the girl must decide whether and how she will protect herself in the future. If this is a divisive issue for family members, then family counseling is in order.

Curfews

Once children have friends, they want to stay out. When adolescents come home after the agreed-upon time, parents worry. Ginott and Gordon both recommend expressing the fear and worry that underlie the anger parents often express when children are late. One parent who had been following Ginott varied the curfew with the occasion and encouraged her daughter to call if she were to be late. The mother told the girl that she would like a worry-free evening; the girl accepted her parent's concern and called.

Krumboltz and Krumboltz describe an active way to handle lateness.[60] Parents can set an alarm clock for 15 minutes after the curfew. If the child is home, then he or she turns off the alarm before it goes off. If the child is still out, the alarm alerts the parents. Dodson, using behavioral principles, suggests overlooking lateness of 15 or 20 minutes.[61] He says if children come home 45 minutes or an hour late, parents are entitled to make a ruckus.

A more unusual curfew problem was cited by Briggs.[62] A teenager asked her mother to come downstairs five minutes after she came home from a dance with her boyfriend and insist that she come to bed. When the mother asked why, the daughter said the boy liked to "make out," and she was not interested. The mother came down as instructed and delivered her message. As she went upstairs, she heard her daughter whisper, "She's a drag, isn't she?" Briggs explains that the daughter needed a scapegoat, so that her denial seemed not to be what she wanted but what she was forced to do. Briggs advises parents to help children be assertive, clear about what they want, and able to communicate their own wishes in a gentle but firm way.

Express your concern about the child's welfare. Adjust curfews if they are unreasonable. If lateness is habitual, this should be discussed in a family session.

Alcohol and Drugs

Two longitudinal studies provide information on the antecedents and implications of substance use and abuse in the high school years.[63] Both samples were followed from the preschool years with careful assessments of both parents and children. Children's substance use was determined in interviews in the 1980s.

Though investigators categorized substance use slightly differently, both found that the most serious use of alcohol and drugs in their samples was related to serious psychological problems both in adolescence and in early and middle childhood. In both studies, adolescents with the most serious alcohol and drug use lack general competence, have poor impulse control, and experience emotional distress. In Diana Baumrind's study, these problems date back to preschool years; and in Jonathan Shedler and Jack Block's study, frequent users have different personality characteristics from experimenters and abstainers as early as age seven, when they relate poorly to other children and feel generally insecure.

Both studies find that adolescents who experiment casually with drugs do not have serious psychological problems and, in fact, are competent, outgoing adolescents. These studies find, too, that many abstainers are anxious, conforming individuals who are fearful of taking risks. Baumrind divided abstainers into two groups—risk-avoidant nonusers and rational nonusers who justify their choice for realistic reasons—"I don't like my mood changed chemically." Risk-avoidant nonusers are less explorative, less resilient, and less competent than rational nonusers who are more socially and intellectually confident.

Several family variables are identified as antecedents to substance use or nonuse. Baumrind found that adolescent substance use parallels parent use. Abstainers come from families where parents do not use substances, and abusers come from families where parents abuse substances. Adolescents with the lowest substance use come from nonauthoritarian-directive and authoritative homes (see the Parent-Child section for descriptions of these parenting patterns), and the abusers from unengaged families where they lack direction and encouragement. Findings from the Shedler and Block study reinforce the view that abusers come from disorganized, unprotective families and abstainers come from homes where parents exert control over children. But the families in the Shedler-Block study are not as supportive and encouraging as are the families of nonusers in the Baumrind sample.

The agreement in the findings of the two studies is noteworthy. Both indicate casual or experimental use occurs in the context of competent, outgoing social behavior in adolescents. The most serious use of substances is associated with lack of competence and psychological problems dating back to early and middle childhood. Shedler and Block point out the importance of recognizing the long-standing nature of the substance abuser's problems and the need for extensive help if the problem is to be dealt with.

Many parents overlook indicators of possible drug use because the idea is painful to them. They ignore their children's grade changes, lack of energy, lack of interest in usual activities, changes in friends, and changes in aggressive behavior. They engage in what writer Beth Polson and psychologist Miller Newton term **parent denial**, refusing to look at the problem and pretending it is not there.[64] Parents find many excuses for their teen's altered behavior, and most teens who are using drugs are happy to accept the excuses put forth by parents.

Newton's experience with his son provides an illuminating example. Newton served as the executive director of the state association of alcohol treatment in Florida, and his wife was a supervising counselor at a treatment agency. Both parents were knowledgable about the use of at least one drug. Their two older children, nineteen and twenty, were both happy and competent people. The first time their fifteen-year-old son Mark came home drunk, the family rallied around him, gave him information about alcoholism in the family, and began to monitor his behavior more closely. He was a bright, curious boy with many interests and a passion for healthy living, so the family was unprepared for the next drunk episode two months later. Mark was violent and threatening with his father and brother. At that time he admitted he was using some pot as well.

Close family supervision followed, and Mark was allowed to go only certain places and had to be home at certain times. His parents said that if there were recurrences, Mark would go into a treatment program. When a fight erupted a few months later, the parents found evidence of much drug use. Mark entered a residential treatment program and has been free of drugs for four years.

In their book *Not My Kid: A Parent's Guide to Kids and Drugs,* Polson and Newton outline actions parents can take to promote a healthy, drug-free adolescence.[65] They insist that how families live day by day is the most important factor. Parents need to be involved family members who know what their children are doing and who their children's friends are. Then they make it clear to adolescents that theirs is a drug-free family in which there is (1) no use of illegal drugs or misuse of legal drugs or prescriptions; (2) no routine use of alcohol by parents; (3) no intoxication by adults; (4) no alcohol use by underage children; (5) no use of drugs to lose weight, sleep, relax, or wake up. Every family member agrees to this contract. If a child is found to be using some drugs, parents call the parents of all the child's friends to discuss ways of promoting organized student activities.

If a child tries drugs, the family contract is repeated. If the behavior continues, the child is taken to some additional form of counseling that deals with the child and the family. Since family members can help drug-oriented children, family counseling is important in addition to any individual therapy prescribed. As in many other areas, the family joins together with other families to provide support and activity to promote a healthier, safer adolescence.

PARENTS' EXPERIENCES

Parents report they do not feel ready to have teenage children. The childhood years have gone so fast, it seems too soon to have a daughter with a mature figure and sons with bulging muscles and low voices. Parents find their children's sexual maturity disconcerting. They are surprised to see sons with *Playboy* magazines and hear girls talking about the sexual attractiveness of boys.

Their adolescents' mood swings and desires for greater freedom throw parents back to some of the same conflicts of the early toddler and preschool years. The elementary school years were stable because parents could talk and reason with children, but now they are back to dealing with screaming, crying, moody creatures who sometimes act younger but at the same time want more freedom. Parents may have felt they themselves have grown and matured as parents, able to handle crises, only to find themselves back at square one, yelling and feeling uncontrolled by their children.

It is difficult to give up images, but that is what parents must do. Children are no longer children; they are physically and sexually mature. They are not psychologically mature, however, and they still need the guidance parents can give. Parents often have to give up images of themselves as the perfect parent of an adolescent. We all recall our own adolescence, the ways our parents handled us, and in many cases we want to improve on that. Sometimes we find we are not doing as well as we want and have to step back and see where we are going off the track.

Adolescents are maturing and gain the physical glow and psychological vitality that comes from feeling the world is a magical place while parents are marching to or through middle age. Parents often do not feel vibrant and alert, and it is hard to live with offspring who may present such a physical contrast to how parents themselves feel. Further, the world is opening up to adolescents just as parents may feel it is weighing them down. Parents have heavy work responsibilities, often duties of taking care of aging parents as well as growing children. Parents feel they have little time and money at their own disposal, yet they live with young people who seem to have a great deal of both.

Thus, parents have to be careful not to let resentment of the freedom and excitement of their teenagers get in the way of being effective parents. As parents develop reasonable expectations of the amount of freedom and responsibilities their children are to have, they must be careful not to overrestrict or overcriticize out of envy.

Ellen Galinsky calls this the **interdependent stage** of parenting to highlight the greater freedom and control children have.[66] Parents have several years to work through these issues before their children are launched. When parents can become more separate from their children, be available to help them grow yet not stifle them in the process, then parents' and children's relationships take on a new dimension and richness.

MAJOR POINTS OF CHAPTER 7

In this period parents:

- continue to be the single most important influence in aiding or hindering the adolescents' development
- provide role models of ethical, principled behavior
- must be available and listen to children
- are likely to get their way in conflicts with children most of the time
- serve as consultants and provide factual information on topics of importance to teens

- share more power in decision making with teens so they can be more self-governing in the context of warm family relationships
- encourage children to separate with a sense of well-being when they share power

When adolescents consider themselves, they:

- describe themselves in psychological terms and through introspection begin to see patterns to their behavior
- reveal sex differences in their self-descriptions, with boys seeing themselves as both more daring, logical, and calm than girls, and girls seeing themselves as more attuned to people and more emotionally reactive than boys

Sense of identity:

- develops gradually over a period of time
- depends on exploring a variety of alternatives and making a commitment to values, goals, and behavior
- can be foreclosed if youth make a commitment without exploring their options
- is diffused if adolescents drift and take no action at all
- is not achieved when early adolescents experience a moratorium and explore without making a commitment
- is achieved in a more complicated way by youth of different ethnic groups

Early adolescents of different ethnic groups:

- must integrate two cultures
- must consider prejudice and its effects on their lives
- must engage adults in their culture in talking about their roots and their experiences in integrating two cultures

Peers:

- are major sources of support and pleasure in life
- seek friends who are sympathetic, understanding, lively, and interested in mutually enjoyable activities
- begin dating at about age fourteen and go steady more frequently in the sixteen- to eighteen-year-old period
- usually seek a sexual partner with whom there is an ongoing relationship

Parents' reactions to their children's growth:

- sometimes include resentment and envy at teens' greater physical vitality and freedom
- sometimes sparks a reliving of their own adolescence

Adolescents' problems discussed center on:

- peer relationships
- dating issues
- school problems
- substance use/abuse
- low self-esteem

Joys of parenting adolescents include:

- observing growing social maturity and closeness with friends
- observing children's growing capacity for responsibility for self
- feeling good to have helped children in some specific way
- seeing children concerned and helpful to others
- growing emotional closeness

EXERCISES

1. See videos of the movies "To Sleep with Anger," "Avalon," and "Parenthood." Compare parenthood in the majority culture with parenthood in different ethnic groups. What are the roles of grandparents and parents in each culture? How does each culture socialize the young to be part of that culture?

2. Break into small groups and describe the kinds of experiences that increased your self-esteem when you were teens. Then with the whole class, write suggestions for parents who want to increase the self-esteem of their teenagers.

3. Divide into pairs. In the first exercise, have one partner take the role of a parent who wants to talk about appropriate sexual behavior for the teenager while the other partner plays the role of the teen who wants more freedom. Then reverse roles, and have the second "parent" try to convey values about appropriate uses of substances in adolescent years to the second "teen." Practice active listening and sending I-messages.

4. Break into small groups and discuss ways parents can talk to teenagers about responsible sexual behavior including the use of condoms. How can parents increase the use of condoms to decrease STDs?

5. Break into small groups and take turns describing the kinds of enjoyable experiences you had with your parents as teens. Then as a whole class, devise a list of highly enjoyable experiences you could have with your own future teens. Are there common elements in what makes for a good time?

ADDITIONAL READINGS

Csikszentmihalyi, Mihaly. *Being Adolescent*. New York: Basic Books, 1984.

Dinkmeyer, Don, and McKay, Gary D. *STEP/TEEN Systematic Training for Effective Parenting of Teens*. Circle Pines, Minn.: American Guidance Service, 1983.

Elkind, David. *The Hurried Child*. Reading, Mass.: Addison-Wesley, 1981.

Gordon, Sol, and Gordon, Judith. *Raising a Child Conservatively in a Sexually Permissive World*. Rev. ed. New York: Simon & Schuster, 1983.

Norman, Jane, and Harris, Myron. *The Private Life of the American Teenager*. New York: Rawson Wade, 1981.

Polson, Beth, and Newton, Miller. *Not My Kid: A Parent's Guide to Kids and Drugs*. New York: Avon, 1985.

Rinzler, Jane. *Teens Speak Out*. New York: Donald I. Fine, 1985.

Notes

1. John Janeway Conger and Anne C. Petersen, *Adolescence and Youth,* 3rd ed. (New York: Harper & Row, 1984), p. 231.
2. Diana Baumrind, "The Influence of Parenting Style on Adolescent Competence and Problem Behavior." Paper presented at the American Psychological Association Meetings, August 1989, New Orleans.
3. Ibid., p. 16.
4. Susie D. Lamborn et al., "Patterns of Competence and Adjustment among Adolescents from Authoritative, Authoritarian, Indulgent, and Neglectful Families," *Child Development* 62 (1991): 1049–1065.
5. Stuart T. Hauser with Sally I. Powers and Gils G. Noam, *Adolescents and Their Families: Paths of Ego Development* (New York: Free Press, 1991).
6. Judith G. Smetana, "Concepts of Self and Social Convention: Adolescents' and Parents' Reasoning about Hypothetical and Actual Family Conflicts," in *Development during the Transition to Adolescence: Minnesota Symposia on Child Psychology,* vol. 21, ed. Megan R. Gunnar and W. Andrew Collins (Hillsdale, N.J.: Erlbaum, 1988), pp. 79–122; Judith G. Smetana, "Adolescents' and Parents' Reasoning about Actual Family Conflict," *Child Development* 60 (1989): 1052–1067.
7. Smetana, "Concepts of Self and Social Convention."
8. Laurence Steinberg, "Impact of Puberty on Family Relations: Effects of Pubertal Status and Pubertal Timing," *Developmental Psychology* 23 (1987): 451–460.
9. Per F. Gjerde, "The Interpersonal Structure of Family Interaction Settings: Parent-Adolescent Relations in Dyads and Triads," *Developmental Psychology* 22 (1986): 297–304.
10. Smetana, "Concepts of Self and Social Convention."
11. DeWayne Moore, "Parent-Adolescent Separation: The Construction of Adulthood by Late Adolescents," *Developmental Psychology* 23 (1987): 298–307.
12. S. Shirley Feldman and Thomas M. Gehring, "Changing Perceptions of Family Cohesion and Power across Adolescence," *Child Development* 59 (1988): 1034–1045.
13. Jane Norman and Myron Harris, *The Private Life of the American Teenager* (New York: Rawson Wade, 1981).
14. H. D. Thornberg, *Development in Adolescence* (Monterey, Calif.: Brooks/Cole, 1975).
15. Dorothy C. Briggs, *Your Child's Self-Esteem* (Garden City, N.Y.: Doubleday, 1970), p. 302.
16. Jeanne Brooks-Gunn and Frank J. Fursten-berg, Jr., "Adolescent Sexual Behavior," *American Psychologist* 44 (1989): 249–257.
17. Ibid.
18. Melvin Zelnick and John F. Kantner, "Sexual Activity, Contraceptive Use, and Pregnancy Among Metropolitan-Area Teenagers: 1971–1979," *Family Planning Perspectives* 12 (1980): 230–237.
19. Conger and Petersen, *Adolescence and Youth.*
20. Ellen Greenberger and Laurence Steinberg, *When Teenagers Work* (New York: Basic Books, 1986).

21. Haim G. Ginott, *Between Parent and Teenager* (New York: Avon, 1969).

22. James P. Comer, "What Makes the New Generation Tick?" *Ebony,* August 1990, p. 38.

23. Margaret Beale Spencer and Carol Markstrom-Adams, "Identity Processes among Racial and Ethnic Minority Children in America," *Child Development* 61 (1990): 290–310.

24. Raymond Montemayor and Marvin Eisen, "The Development of Self-Conceptions from Childhood to Adolescence," *Developmental Psychology* 13 (1977): 318.

25. Jack Block, "Some Relationships Regarding the Self from the Block and Block Longitudinal Study." Paper presented at the Social Science Research Council Conference on Selfhood, October 1985, Stanford, Calif.

26. James E. Marcia, "Identity in Adolescence," in *The Handbook of Adolescent Psychology,* ed. Joseph Adelson (New York: John Wiley, 1980), pp. 159–187.

27. Jean S. Phinney, "Stages of Ethnic Identity Development in Minority Group Adolescents," *Journal of Early Adolescence* 9 (1989): 34–49.

28. Margaret Beale Spencer and Carol Markstrom-Adams, "Identity Processes among Racial and Ethnic Minority Children in America"; Michael C. Thornton, Linda M. Chatters, Robert Joseph Taylor, and Walter R. Allen, "Sociodemographic and Environmental Correlates of Racial Socialization by Black Parents," *Child Development* 61 (1990): 401–409.

29. Phinney, "Stages of Ethnic Identity Development in Minority Group Adolescents."

30. Conger and Petersen, *Adolescence and Youth.*

31. Norman and Harris, *Private Life of the American Teenager.*

32. Daniel Offer and Judith Offer, *From Teenage to Young Manhood: A Psychological Study* (New York: Basic Books, 1975).

33. Norman and Harris, *Private Life of the American Teenager.*

34. Judith M. Siegel and Jonathan D. Brown, "A Prospective Study of Stressful Circumstances, Illness Symptoms, and Depressed Mood among Adolescents," *Developmental Psychology* 24 (1988): 715–721.

35. J. Brooks-Gunn and Michelle P. Warren, "Biological and Social Contributions to Negative Affect in Young Adolescent Girls," *Child Development* 60 (1989): 40–55.

36. Susan Harter, "Visions of Self: Beyond the Me in the Mirror," University Lecture, University of Denver, 1990.

37. Ibid., p. 16.

38. John Condry and Michael L. Siman, "Characteristics of Peer- and Adult-Oriented Children," *Journal of Marriage and the Family* 36 (1974): 543–554.

39. Conger and Petersen, *Adolescence and Youth.*

40. Tina deVaron, "Growing Up," in *Twelve to Sixteen: Early Adolescence,* ed. Jerome Kagan and Robert Coles (New York: W. W. Norton, 1972), pp. 340–341.

41. Norman and Harris, *Private Life of the American Teenager.*

42. Conger and Petersen, *Adolescence and Youth.*

43. Ibid.

44. "Sexual Behavior among High School Students—United States, 1990," *Morbidity and Mortality Weekly Report* 40: 885–888, 1992.

45. Melody A. Graham, "The Effects of Parent-Adolescent Communication on Adolescent Sexual Behavior." Paper presented at the American Psychological Association Meetings in August 1992, Washington, D.C.

46. Robert C. Sorenson, *Adolescent Sexuality in Contemporary America: Personal Values and Sexual Behavior Ages 13–19* (New York: Harry N. Abrams, 1973).

47. Vance Packard, *The Sexual Wilderness: The Contemporary Upheaval in Male-Female Relationships* (New York: Pocket Books, 1970).

48. Judith Stevens-Long and Nancy J. Cobb, *Adolescence and Early Adulthood* (Palo Alto, Calif.: Mayfield, 1983).

49. Zelnick and Kantner, "Sexual Activity, Contraceptive Use, and Pregnancy among Metropolitan-Area Teenagers."

50. Conger and Petersen, *Adolescence and Youth.*

51. Don Dinkmeyer and Gary D. McKay, *STEP/TEEN Systematic Training for Effective Parenting of Teens* (Circle Pines, Minn.: American Guidance Service, 1983).

52. Adele Faber and Elaine Mazlish, *How to Talk So Kids Will Listen and Listen So Kids Will Talk* (New York: Rawson Wade, 1980), p. 165.

53. Ginott, *Between Parent and Teenager.*

54. Robert Eimers and Robert Aitchison, *Effective Parents/Responsible Children* (New York: McGraw-Hill, 1977).

55. Philip Zimbardo and Shirley Radl, *The Shy Child* (Garden City, N.Y.: Doubleday, 1982).

56. Ginott, *Between Parent and Teenager.*

57. Shirley Gould, *Teenagers: The Continuing Challenge* (New York: Hawthorn, 1977).

58. John D. Krumboltz and Helen B. Krumboltz, *Changing Children's Behavior* (Englewood Cliffs, N.J.: Prentice-Hall, 1972).

59. Katherine B. Oettinger, *Not My Daughter* (Englewood Cliffs, N.J.: Prentice-Hall, 1979).

60. Krumboltz and Krumboltz, *Changing Children's Behavior.*

61. Fitzhugh Dodson, *How to Discipline with Love* (New York: Rawson Associates, 1977).

62. Briggs, *Your Child's Self-Esteem.*

63. Baumrind, "The Influence of Parenting Style on Adolescent Competence and Problem Behavior," Jonathan Shedler and Jack Block, "Adolescent Drug Use and Psychological Health: A Longitudinal Inquiry," *American Psychologist* 45 (1990): 612–630.

64. Beth Polson and Miller Newton, *Not My Kid: A Parent's Guide to Kids and Drugs* (New York: Avon, 1985).

65. Ibid.

66. Ellen Galinsky, *Between Generations: The Six Stages of Parenthood* (New York: Time Books, 1981).

PARENTING/WORKING

C   H   A   P   T   E   R   8

Combining work and parenting challenges men and women of the 90s. As more mothers are committed to paid work outside the home and more fathers are involved in childcare, men and women face the demands of an 80-hour work week. And they feel pressure. How might you prepare for the double duty of working and parenting? How can you compensate for the time work prevents you from spending with your child? How might you adjust your attitudes and routines to enhance the quality of time you spend parenting? Such are the concerns of the working parent.

A 1990 survey of a thousand men and women reveals that 40 percent of men and 80 percent of women would stay at home and care for their children if they could. Further, 57 percent of men and 55 percent of women report feeling guilty if they spend less time with their children than they should and neglect important rituals like having dinner together as a family.[1]

Although both men and women feel pressure, women have primary responsibility for the home and family. It is the women who feel the effects of these responsibilities on their work. Only 2 percent of men in the survey report family responsibilities have hurt their careers while 41 percent of women feel family demands have negatively affected their careers.[2] While many see working and parenting as "a women's issue," it is not. It is a family and societal concern and requires widespread changes so that both men and women can enjoy the pleasures and challenges of working and parenting.[3]

In this chapter we examine how parents' work influences parenting behaviors and, in turn, children. We look first at men and work, then at women and work. We look at how parents provide childcare in their absence and present guidelines for selecting the care most appropriate for children of different ages. Finally, we examine common problems in integrating work and family lives as well as parents' solutions to them.

MEN AND WORK

The impact of men's work on family life is primarily studied in terms of the effects of unemployment on the family, and the effects of the nature of father's work on family values and childrearing.

Fathers' unemployment has enormous impact on families. This effect was most carefully studied in families before mothers worked outside the home in larger numbers. When fathers did not have jobs, their families had no money at all. Today the impact of a father's unemployment may be different because so many families have two incomes. The most exhaustive and detailed study on this topic is Glen Elder's series of longitudinal studies of children who grew up in the 1930s during the Depression.[4] Elder compared children whose families maintained an income during the Depression with children whose families had lost more than a third of their income. When children were adolescents at the time of their fathers' unemployment, there was a stimulating effect. Families pulled together; everyone did his or her share. Boys got jobs and worked outside the home, as did mothers; girls stayed home and did housework. Boys developed initiative, did better in school, and as adults were more competent and satisfied than boys whose fathers continued to work. Women from families that suffered economic loss tended to marry highly successful men and to remain family-oriented, happy with their roles as wives and mothers, whether they were adolescents or preschoolers during the Depression. These women continued, and enjoyed very much, their traditional interest in the home and family. The effects on boys who were preschoolers at the time of their fathers' unemployment appeared more depressing. These boys did less well in school and were less stable and mature as adults.

The link between economic hardship and children's functioning is parental behavior toward children. Fathers who lost income became more hostile, more rejecting of children, less supportive. Mothers' behavior did not change. Fathers had less impact on adolescent boys, who were out of the home much of the time, than on their preschool sons. They did affect adolescent girls who stayed in the home, and consequently many of these girls had less self-esteem than their age-mates, whose employed fathers were more accepting. For reasons not known, preschool girls seemed to escape this negative influence.[5]

When men work, the nature of their job influences—indirectly and directly—many aspects of family life. The indirect effects of fathers' work are seen, for example, in a recent study comparing family activities and childrearing attitudes in father-absent and father-present homes.[6] Father-absent homes were those in which fathers were gone for periods of time because of work in remote areas or because of unusual shifts; as a result, fathers were not home during the child's waking hours. When fathers are absent, mothers engage in fewer community and social activities—they see fewer friends and participate in fewer organized activities. Mothers then lose support from the social network that nurtures them, and they, in turn, are less playful and stimulating with their children. So, when fathers do not participate in family life, it is less social and stimulating.

Fathers' work directly influences the social status or social class of their family, which in turn affects childrearing and children. Fathers' job classification—professional, business, skilled or unskilled labor—is the major determinant of the family's social status. The family's social status in turn influences social attitudes and child-rearing practices. Middle-class parents value self-reliance and independence in children. To encourage these qualities, parents are more likely to give explanations for what they want, to motivate the child to do what is necessary on his or her own. Working-class parents value obedience and conformity in children and are more likely to use power-assertive techniques to force compliance. They use physical punishment more than middle-class parents; they refuse to give explanations, simply stating, "Because I said so." They are less interested in explanations, saying, "Do it now."[7] As noted in Chapter 1, families with less money use more force in childrearing, omit explanations, and demand obedience because they do not have the time or energy to give detailed reasons or to motivate children to do what is required. High stress makes these parents less understanding when brothers and sisters fight or when problems arise at school because they have fewer material and psychological resources to draw on.[8]

Levels of satisfaction and stress at work affect men's family lives, but the exact effects are not clear-cut. When their occupations are highly stressful, men may return home emotionally drained and highly frustrated, with little to give family members—policemen, for example, are known to have high rates of family problems. Conversely, when men have satisfying work, they may be more giving fathers. But it happens also that satisfying work can so absorb a father that he is not present at home. This is especially true of men in higher-status occupations. In a recent national sample, over half of college-educated men said work interfered with life at home, whereas only 21 percent of grade-school–educated men reported their work as interfering with family life.[9] Men who have less important jobs and few satisfactions at work may invest their energy and time in family members.

So, the nature and extent of fathers' work has a wide-ranging influence on family life and children. When fathers find their work highly absorbing and satisfying, they feel conflict between work and family commitments. When their work is highly stressful, they find it difficult to have the energy to establish stable, happy homes.

WOMEN AND WORK

When Western society was industrialized in the early nineteenth century, the work place became separated from the home—men went off to work and women stayed at home to be caregivers of children. When women first returned to paid employment in increasing numbers, the focus of interest was on the effects of maternal absence on children, the effects of early day care, the effects of stress on mothers. Women's increasing participation in the labor force is now a fact of life. Questions about women and work now center on how father's caregiving and mother's interactions with children change when both parents have paid employment outside the home.

Mothers' Satisfaction and Morale

Numerous studies indicate that the important factor is not whether the mother works or not, but whether she is satisfied with what she is doing. A mother who is satisfied with her decision is a more effective caregiver and her children flourish. For example, in a recent study of kindergartners' academic and social performance, those children who scored least well came from homes in which mothers stayed home even though they thought having a job would benefit the child.[10] Next lowest were children from homes in which mothers worked but felt children would be better off if they stayed home. Higher scores were earned by children from homes where mothers worked and thought they were better mothers because of it. Highest scores were obtained by those from homes where mothers stayed home and thought that was best. So, their mothers' satisfaction with what they are doing is the critical factor in understanding the impact of mothers' employment on children. From existing research it is impossible to say whether children do well because their mothers are satisfied with their own activities or whether their mothers' overall satisfaction comes from the fact their children are doing well; longitudinal research is required to determine cause and effect.

There are indications that being unemployed when they want to work produces strain in mothers. According to several studies, women who wish to get out of the house are the most frustrated and depressed. This is especially true of women who are well educated and have skills. They feel less competent, less attractive, more lonely and uncertain about who they are when they do not work.[11]

Amount of Work

Though more women are working now, there is great variation in how much time they work. Of a random Boston sample of women with children ages five to fourteen, 56 percent were employed but only 15 percent were working more than 30 hours a week; 21 percent worked 20 to 29 hours during the time their children were in school. Many did not work during school vacations. Taking full-time work as 35 hours per week or more, when mothers' employment was categorized as full-time, part-time, and none, studies from 1974

> found part-time employment an unusually successful adaptation to the conflict between the difficulties of being a full-time housewife and the strain of combining this role with full-time employment. These mothers seemed to be physically and psychologically healthy, positive toward their maternal roles, and active in recreational and community activities. Their children compare favorably to the other groups with respect to self-esteem, social adjustment, and attitudes toward their parents; scattered findings suggest that the marital satisfaction is the highest of the three groups.[12]

Part-time employment, however, has the disadvantages of being lower paid, more difficult to find, and less useful in advancing a career than full-time employment. It may be most beneficial for mothers of very young children. Urie Bronfenbrenner and his colleagues recently found that mothers of three-year-olds are most satisfied with themselves, their work, and most especially their children when they are employed part-time. They have positive views of both sons and daughters. Because mothers' positive attitudes influence fathers' views in turn, the whole family system is affected.[13]

We have little systematic information about the effects of their mothers' long-term employment on children. Does it matter if mothers start work early and continue through the child's growing years? We do not know because no longitudinal studies have followed the same sample of children for a long period of time.

Changes in Mothers' Home Activities

How does a mother's behavior at home change when she returns to work? This is not entirely clear. Much depends on the time when the mother returns to work, the ages of her children, and how many hours she works. Large-scale studies of mothers' time use summarized by Sandra Scarr indicate minimal differences between activities with children of employed and nonemployed mothers.[14] One study found that non-working mothers spend more time watching TV (21 minutes per day) than playing or reading to children (10 minutes). Nonworking mothers tend to do household chores and their children spend only 5 percent of their waking time in direct interaction with them (4 percent is spent in direct interaction with fathers). These time studies show that employed mothers spend as much time in direct interaction with children as nonemployed mothers do.

Lois Hoffman, however, concludes after reviewing several studies that employed mothers generally spend less time with each child, regardless of the child's age, than nonemployed mothers.[15] There is minimal difference between educated employed mothers and educated nonemployed mothers because they give up their personal time to spend with their children. The differences may be greatest when children are youngest. Recent work indicates that when mothers of infants work an average of 12 hours a week, they are less involved in the direct care of their babies than nonworking mothers. Even when they are home, working mothers spend less time alone with their babies than nonworking mothers because the father is usually there at the same time.[16]

Effects of Mothers' Working on Children

All research thus far indicates that

> taken by itself, the fact that the mother works outside the home has no universally predictable effects on the child. Maternal employment does appear to exert influence, however, under certain conditions defined by the age and sex of the child, the family's position in society, and the nature of the mother's work.[17]

Let us look at what is known about the effects of working mothers on children of different ages. With infants, a major area of research has centered on the attachment relationship between mother and child when the mother is employed. Jay Belsky and Michael Rovine, reviewing five studies of non-risk working- and middle-class families, state there are suggestions that, in this country, at this time, extensive nonmaternal care in the first year of life may be "associated with patterns of attachment that are commonly regarded as evidence of insecurity."[18] When there are more than 20 hours a week of nonmaternal care, then infants may be more likely to avoid the mother. These same studies find, however, that though there is risk, 50 percent of

INTERVIEW
with Susan McHale

Susan McHale is associate professor of human development at The Pennsylvania State University and co-director of the Pennsylvania State University Family Relations Project.

From your experience in studying dual-earner families, what kinds of things make it easiest for parents when both work?

We look at how the whole family system changes when mothers work, and we found very interesting changes in how fathers relate to children between nine and twelve years old when their wives are employed. We collect a measure of "exclusive" or dyadic time—how much time the father spends alone with the child doing some fun activity like attending a concert or school activity. In single-earner families, fathers spend about 90 minutes a week with boys in "exclusive" (dyadic) and about 30 minutes with girls, so there is quite a sex distinction in these families. In dual-earner families, fathers spend equal amounts of "exclusive" time with boys and girls—about 60 minutes per week so mother's working may enhance the relationship between *father* and daughter and decrease involvement between father and son.

We do not get any straightforward sex differences in the effects of mother's working—that is, boys do not necessarily do less well—unless these are mediated by some other process. For example, we have just finished a paper on parental monitoring of children's activities. To collect data on monitoring, we telephone both the parent and the child and ask specific questions about what has happened that day: Did the child do his homework? Did he have a special success at school that day? Our measure of monitoring is the discrepancy between the children's report and the parent's report. (We presume the children are right.) We thought that monitoring might be related to children's adjustment. We do find that in families where the child is

infants have secure attachments with their mothers, and 50 percent of sons have secure attachments with fathers, so about two-thirds of boys experiencing extensive nonmaternal care have secure attachments with at least one parent.

Though other researchers question the interpretation, Belsky and Rovine point to six factors that seem, in thirty-six comparisons, to identify those infants (of mothers working more than 20 hours per week) who are more likely to develop insecure attachments. The six factors are (1) being boys, (2) having a difficult, fussy temperament, (3) having mothers with limited interpersonal sensitivity, (4) having mothers who are less satisfied with their marriages, (5) having mothers who are highly career-oriented, and (6) not having the father as alternative caregiver. In their study, all infants who were cared for by fathers during the mother's absence had secure attachments to the mother.

These risk factors seem important only when mothers work more than 20 hours per week. Even then, as noted, a significant proportion of infants develop secure attachments because, one suspects, they are in the care of sensitive, involved, child-oriented individuals who find satisfaction in caregiving.

less well monitored, boys are a little bit more at risk for problems in conduct and school achievement. This is independent of who does the monitoring; as long as you have at least one parent who is a good monitor, you do not get these effects.

When we look at what helps families function well when parents work, we find one factor is the agreement between *values and attitudes* on the one hand and the *actual roles* family members assume in daily life. This finding applies to adults and children. I am talking about sex-role attitudes. When parents have young children, we found that incongruencies between sex-role attitudes and behavior are related to problems in the marital relation. Specifically, when husbands and wives have traditional sex-role attitudes but the organization of daily life is egalitarian, couples were much more likely to fight, to have lower scores on a measure of love, and to find the relationship less satisfying.

When we looked at children's involvement in household chores, we found additional evidence of the importance of congruence between attitudes and family roles. For example, the more chores boys in dual-earner families perform, the better their adjustment; the reverse was true for boys in single-earner families, however. The mediating factor seems to be the father's sex-role attitudes. In single-earner families, fathers are more traditional and less involved in tasks themselves. Therefore, when sons do a lot of housework, their behavior is out of concordance with their fathers' values. In both kinds of families, dual and single earners, boys whose roles are incongruent with their fathers' values feel less competent and more stressed, and they report less positive relationships with their parents.

The congruence between values and beliefs and the kinds of family roles children and adults assume is what predicts better adjustment. Whether you can change people's attitudes and beliefs or whether it is easier to change family roles is hard to say. Part of the problem is that the work demands in dual-earner families require that family roles change before people feel really comfortable with that.

Beyond the infancy period, a growing number of studies indicate high-quality day care—reflected in experienced directors, well-trained staff, and a good staff-child ratio—is related to a variety of positive outcomes: language development,[19] toddlers' ability to self-regulate in a laboratory situation,[20] social development[21] and participation,[22] and later performance in school.[23]

Highly motivated parents seek out high-quality care for their children, and so development is promoted at home and at school by sensitive caregivers. Of concern, however, is that a vicious cycle may develop for those children in low-quality day care. Their families are often highly stressed, so children receive little attention at home and then go to day care where there are fewer adults per child with whom to interact.[24] So these children have less contact with adults and get less stimulation. This is not a necessary consequence of mothers' employment; it is possible to establish more high-quality day care programs.

Preschool children in day care are both more outgoing and empathic and more pushy and aggressive than children reared at home. They appear more skilled in the social world, better able to get what they want from other children and adults outside the home.[25] Full-time working mothers regard their preschool children differently than part-time and nonworking mothers. Bronfenbrenner and his co-workers found that educated full-time working mothers tend to regard their daughters positively and their sons negatively.[26] Less-educated full-time working mothers regard both their sons and daughters negatively. Mothers who work only part-time, regardless of their level of education, regard both their sons and daughters positively. Because boys may be so active, requiring more supervision and monitoring than girls, full-time working mothers are frustrated by them. Less-educated mothers may have so many demands on them that both sons and daughters are a strain.

In the elementary school years, daughters of working mothers appear more self-confident and more independent than daughters of nonworking mothers. They make better grades at school and are more likely to think about careers for themselves. Here it seems likely that their mothers become role models of competence and independence. Both boys and girls see men and women as contributing equally to the family and so they become less stereotyped in their views of men's and women's roles. They also become more independent themselves as they do chores around the house and take responsibility for household activities.[27]

Elementary school–age boys may suffer more than girls from their mothers' employment. Middle-class sons of working mothers do not appear to do as well in school as middle-class sons of nonworking mothers. Whether this is a temporary finding (it is not found among adolescent boys) or whether it reflects a real deficit in experience is not known. Bronfenbrenner and colleagues speculate that sons need more parental supervision and contact than girls for optimal behavior.[28] Working-class mothers usually give their children the same amount of supervision regardless of whether or not they are employed. Middle-class mothers traditionally provide more supervision, and when they are employed and absent, their boys' functioning tends to decrease. Hoffman offers a similar possible explanation.[29] Boys are generally allowed more independence than girls. When they are allowed more independence than they can handle, as in the middle-class homes of working mothers, boys' intellectual performance decreases. As Susan McHale noted, it may be that boys do less well because they do not have as much individual attention from fathers.

Working-class sons admire their fathers less and see them as less competent if their mothers feel burdened by work or the social context is disapproving. When their mothers feel comfortable and their fathers support their mothers' activities, sons' perceptions of their fathers' competence do not change.[30]

Studies of children in the adolescent years have found mainly positive effects from working mothers. The benefits appear pronounced for daughters of employed mothers, who are more active, independent, and competent in both social and intellectual activities than daughters of mothers who are not employed. Boys, too, show social and personal effectiveness when their mothers are employed.

Knowing what research says about possible negative effects of mothers' employment allows parents to compensate for these problems. As all researchers note, working mothers are here to stay. The evidence suggests that close contact with a caregiver is important in infancy, and, as we shall see, appropriate monitoring of the child is important as that child grows.

Timing of Working

Boys' intellectual performance appears to be inhibited when their mothers began work before they were three.[31] Effects were confined to intellectual functioning for boys; girls showed no negative effects.

One study of divorcing families suggests that when mothers were working before the divorce, the work had no negative effect on the children.[32] When mothers started to work immediately following the divorce, then children seemed to develop behavior problems. They experienced the loss of two parents, and the disruption resulted in problems. Again, not the fact of employment but the number of stresses contributes to problems of this nature.

In this section we have looked at amount of time worked, mothers' attitudes about work, how mothers' behavior at home changes, the effects of employment on children's behavior, and the timing of working. There is no information available, as there is for men, on the effects of different kinds of women's work on family values or childrearing behaviors. Let us now look at what happens in the family as men and women adapt to two wage earners in the family.

MEN AND WOMEN AT WORK

We have limited information on the impact of two working parents on children. We do know that men become more involved in childcare and housework when women work. This is especially true of young fathers who participate actively in childbirth classes and learn caregiving skills. The more hours mothers work, the more caregiving fathers do. Interestingly, when fathers are involved in physical caregiving, the whole family spends more leisure time together.

When fathers become primary caregivers (while mothers go off to work) or equal caregivers, they manage the routine and care for children much as mothers do. The tasks of running a household and caring for children demand the same behaviors whether one is a man or woman. Children fare well under this system. Homes are more enriched, and parents, less punitive with children, when fathers are equal or primary caregivers.[33]

In most families, however, fathers do not help out on an equal basis. When wives are employed, fathers of preschoolers work around the house about 12.8 hours per week—20 minutes more than fathers with nonworking wives. Because both parents are home with their children in the evenings, fathers with employed wives spend somewhat less time with their children in the evenings than fathers with nonworking wives. Nonworking mothers, who have been with their children much of the day, reserve evening time for fathers. Mothers who have only evenings and weekends as their main time to spend with children get some of the time that children usually spend with their fathers.

Sociologist Arlie Hochschild has interviewed men and women, day-care workers and sitters, observed them in their homes, and followed them in their activities with their families to understand how men and women combine work and families in what she terms the "stalled revolution."[34] Although women have paid employment

INTERVIEW
with Arlie Hochschild

Arlie Hochschild is a professor of sociology at the University of California at Berkeley. She is the author of The Second Shift: Working Parents and the Revolution at Home. *It describes how couples combine work, children, and marriage.*

How can couples negotiate so they work out issues around family and work? How can people know how they will react and what they want before they marry and have children?

I think this is something young people can become more self-conscious about. I think it is especially important to talk with one another about the division of labor before a child arrives. This kind of problem has both private and public solutions. I think we have to look at both equally, simultaneously.

I was sitting next to a young woman who is a metallurgist at a manufacturing company, where I was giving a talk on issues of corporate reform—getting part-time work and parental phases of work. This woman was 8 months pregnant; she was a manager at this company, and she said to me, "My husband and I work all the time. Just yesterday I got up at 5:15 with him; he was out the door at 5:45, and I was out the door at 6:00 A.M. and returned at 6:00 P.M." She described this tremendously loaded day. She said to herself, "If I can't get all the things I have to do done now, what am I going to do when the baby comes?"

This is what we ought to be avoiding. She hadn't sat down and talked this over with her husband. He was not planning to make any modifications in his schedule when the baby arrived, and she was only going to take the 6-week maternity leave and then hop right back on the horse. She was involved in a highly workaholic culture, and her entire community was based at work; I could already foresee that in that 6 weeks she would feel guilty that she was not at work.

What is the solution for such a woman's problems? I think it is not simply negotiating things with her husband, but also getting working couples together in neighborhoods to discuss making time for childhood and parenthood. It requires corporations making revolutionary changes in the very social structure of work.

I don't even use the word *part-time* because it sounds like it is part of something whole. I talk about having parental phases in every regular job so that when you have a child, you would automatically go on 60 percent time or 80 percent time with a cut in pay. Perhaps the company can pay you for full-time and you can pay them back later. There are arrangements that could be made financially as well. This would last through the child's preschool years, after which a parent could go back to full-time work.

I would like to see every parent get job relief for the period of parenthood. This could be done, and it wouldn't be a loss of productivity for the company. It takes some creative thinking and coordinating of work schedules, but I think we need something that profound to really address the problems of modern parents.

Modern parents are workers. Today you have women joining men in a basically male culture of work that was initially premised on a provider husband who had a full-time wife at home. It just won't do to put two parents in that structure of work. I don't think that focusing on day care (I hear talk of weekend day care) is the answer. We have to do other things to restructure work, creating an alternative to the "Mommy track," because I don't envision a change that creates a track or that is confined to women. This is the crucial issue, really, giving children a piece of their parents back.

So the solution to the problems of a young parent like the one I sat next to is both a public and a private one. I would like to see her get together with other young parents, male and female, to pressure their employers to make these accommodations.

Do you feel it is usually the woman who takes the initiative in establishing a more equal division of family responsibilities?

Usually it is, because by tradition the second shift falls to her.

Will women have to be socialized differently to insist on this negotiation?

Women have to feel empowered, have to feel that what they want will matter.

In your book, when men were interested in being equal partners, it was not clear exactly how they arrived at this point.

Most of the men in *The Second Shift* had a father whom they were critical of. Men in their teens and 20s now may not be similar.

Were there characteristics of women who wanted equal relationships?

Yes, they tended to have high educations and to be invested in their careers, and that's about where my work stopped. In *The Third Sex*, Patricia McBrum finds that women who feel empowered generally identify with their mother, regardless of whether she was a housewife or career woman. It didn't matter. The girl experienced the mother as efficacious, and that had a positive effect on her.

We have a whole new generation of young people coming up who want to avoid the pitfalls of their parents. Yet at the moment they are not thinking of the big picture. They are living with a Reaganesque presumption that they can live the private lives they want to live without structural changes. I don't believe they can.

To live the happy, stable lives they aspire to, we need changes in the work place, new governmental supports for families, and a new cultural emphasis on the needs of children. Sometimes you have to look out before you look in. The larger structural changes make it easier to make the private ones you want.

If we don't make these larger structural arrangements children will suffer. All the trends in the family point away from investing in our children; I don't yet see the reforms at work, and I don't see the government doing anything. The struggle is asked of us to organize locally and nationally for progressive programs to ease the strain on two-job families. It is a matter of urgency.

in increasing numbers, society has made few changes to accommodate the fact that family needs must be met in new ways. There is little subsidized day care, only a few family leave policies just being put into effect, little job sharing, and only sporadic plans for flexible hours.

Until society as a whole provides more assistance, men and women will struggle to meet the goals of meaningful family relationships in the context of satisfying work. Because women have been traditional child caregivers and home maintainers, in most instances they continue this role while they work. Although many men's attitudes have changed, and many men care for children in addition to working, it is rare that the husband and father feels equal responsibility for seeing that the family's needs are met. In one study, 113 of 160 fathers reported they were responsible for no childcare tasks, and 150 of the 160 fathers said they did no traditionally feminine household chores.[35] As a result, women put in what Hochschild calls a "second shift" of work before and after paid employment and, in the course of a year, have an extra month of 24-hour-a-day work beyond what men do.

Hochschild believes that both men and women develop a gender strategy for meshing personal desires for work and family with societal options. Women make decisions about where to concentrate their energy (work or home), what kinds of help they want and need, what kinds of help they will insist upon, and what priority they will give to their work and what to their husband's work. Men, too, decide how much responsibility they want to shoulder for providing economic resources for the family and what family needs they will meet.

In traditional strategies, men and women agree that the wife/mother takes responsibility for home and children, even when working, and the husband's/father's work comes first. Men may share family responsibilities when and if they want. In egalitarian strategies, there is equal sharing of work and family tasks. There are also transitional strategies that are blends of these two. Each couple will work out daily activities based on their gender strategies, and harmony will depend on their working out compromises where differences exist. Where differences in values exist, even positive behavior may meet with a negative response because it does not fit the gender strategy. For example, traditional women sometimes resent the help husbands give because they are not meeting their own standards of doing it all themselves.

Longitudinal research illustrates that the couple's satisfaction with the solution is a crucial ingredient in determining how successful a solution will be for that family.[36] For example, dual-earner fathers who share in childcare and feel this is what they want to do increase in love for their wives, whereas dual-earner fathers who resent the same amount of time in childcare feel more negatively towards their wives and marriage, perhaps blaming them for the extra work.[37]

Hochschild believes society must establish a stronger family policy (outlined in Box 8-1) that will make it easier for men to enjoy the enriching experience of caring for children and will relieve women of the extra work that creates resentment between men and women. She concludes:

> But as the government and society shape a new gender strategy, as the young learn from example, many more women and men will be able to enjoy the leisurely bodily rhythms and freer laughter that arise when family life is family life and not a second shift.[38]

◆

```
┌─────────────────────────────────────────────────────────────────┐
│                                                                   │
│                          BOX 8-1                                  │
│                    A PROFAMILY POLICY                             │
```

An honestly profamily policy in the United States would give tax breaks to compa-
nies that encourage "family leave" for new fathers, job sharing, part-time work, and
flex time. Through comparable worth, it would pull up wages in "women's" jobs. It
would go beyond half-time work (which makes it sound like a person is only doing
"half" of something else that is "whole") by instituting lower-hour, more flexible
"family phases" for all regular jobs filled by parents of young children.

 The government would give tax credits to developers who build affordable housing near places of work and shopping centers, with nearby meal-preparation facilities, as Delores Hayden describes in her book *Redesigning the American Dream*. It
would create warm and creative daycare centers. If the best daycare comes from
elderly neighbors, students, grandparents, they could be paid to care for children.
Traveling vans for daycare enrichment could roam the neighborhoods as the ice-
cream man did in my childhood.

 In these ways, the American government could create a "safer environment" for
the two-job family. It could draw men into children's lives, reduce the number of
children in "self-care," and make marriages happier.

From Arlie Hochschild, *The Second Shift* (New York: Viking, 1989), p. 268.

CHILDCARE

Several kinds of childcare are available when both parents work outside the home.
Parents can select the kind that best suits their own and their children's needs.
Recent data concerning childcare for children under five reveal that 28 percent are
cared for by a nonrelative at home or in another home, 24 percent are in day care
or nursery school, 15 percent are cared for by father, 9 percent by mother at her
work, 21 percent by another relative, and 1 percent in some other form of care.[39]

 Parents and relatives have the advantage that children know them and special
ties already exist. If, however, this is not possible, then parents may seek other substitute care.

 Substitute care at home or in a family day care situation can provide warmth, consistency, and the caring attention young children need. As Belsky noted, the quality
of the caregiver-child relationship, its stability, and the relationship between
caregiver and parent are three basic criteria in selecting a caregiver. If financial considerations are not foremost, parents may wish to hire someone to care for the child
in the home. Employment agencies can provide names, but parents are wise always
to check references thoroughly. Parents can check on the quality of the care by coming home unannounced or having a friend or relative drop by—a sitter in your home
is totally unsupervised, and even though many are fine, distressing incidents can
occur. Back-up arrangements are always needed, however, because caregivers can get
sick or have emergencies.

INTERVIEW
with Jay Belsky

Jay Belsky is Professor of Human Development at The Pennsylvania State University in College Park. He is the initiator and director of the Pennsylvania Infant and Family Development Project, an ongoing study of 250 firstborn children whose parents were enrolled for study when the mothers were pregnant in 1981. He has done systematic research on the effects of day care.

What advice would you give to parents in the first two years about day care?

The most important thing, as Urie Bronfenbrenner used to say, is that parents have some biological advantages in caring for young kids. They are theirs; they have an investment in them that other people simply don't have. So I tell parents that if they can and want to (and when I say can, I mean are we talking about food on the table or are we talking about two-week vacations or wardrobes?), certainly stay home part of the time. I find it hard to believe that most American women who want to have a baby also want to be back at work in six weeks. I think most women—economics and personal aspirations being what they are—would say, "I'd like to be home with my baby for the first year, or part of that year, and return to work gradually." From a company policy perspective that would mean parental leaves without pay at first, and then part-time work with pay that reverts to full-time work after one year. For people who can't take leaves, quality care arrangements would be a part of the policy.

Family day care—that is, care in the home of another family with other children—is cheaper than home care and has some advantages. Sally Provence, Audrey Naylor, and June Patterson believe that the family day care setting provides a more varied environment for children in the toddler years than a day care center.[40] There are kitchens, laundry areas, bedrooms, and a wealth of activities that cannot be duplicated in a center. In family day care, children can engage in many of the same activities they would if they were at home with their mothers.

Family day care is also more flexible in meeting children's individual needs, because there are fewer children. Some single parents choose family day care because it provides a family atmosphere that may be missing after a death or divorce. Family day care homes are licensed; some are part of a larger umbrella organization that supplies toys and training to home caregivers. Day caregivers who are part of such a network can give higher quality care than untrained caregivers. Box 8-2 contains guidelines for making a choice. It is wise to make one visit with the child and one visit alone.

Day care centers provide care for children from infancy, and many provide after-school care for children in the elementary grades. In most states such centers must meet specific standards intended to assure the health and safety of the children. The parent whose child goes to a day care center is sure of having childcare available every day, at some centers from seven in the morning until seven in the evening. Many centers have credentialed personnel who have been trained to work with

For working parents I say again and again that nothing matters as much as the person who cares for your baby. All too often parents don't look "under the hood" of the childcare situation. They walk in, the walls are painted nicely, the toys are bright, the lunches are nutritious. Especially with a baby, once the minimal safety standards are met, what matters more than anything else psychologically is to find out about this person who'll care for the baby. So, who is this person, and what is his or her capacity to give individualized care? Because babies need individualized care, this issue matters above all else.

The second thing to consider is whether the caregiver and parent can talk together easily. Each person spends less than full time with the baby. The time factor is not necessarily handicapping them, but it can if information is not being communicated back and forth. So the trick then is, "If the caregiver gets to know my baby during the day, what can she tell me in the afternoon, and if I have the baby in the evening and the morning, what can I tell her when I drop the baby off?" There has to be an effective two-way flow of information.

The third thing to consider in selecting care is that the arrangement has to last a decent interval of time. That doesn't mean that you must take the child to the same center for a year's time, it means that the same *person,* or *persons,* takes care of him or her for a year or so. If you find a great person who treats the child as an individual and communicates well with the parent, but stays for only a few months, you are not buying yourself a lot. In a baby's life, changing caregivers more than once a year will be stressful. If a baby goes through three or four changes in a year, it may not matter what kind of caregiver he or she gets. Even though the caregivers may get to know the child, the child won't know them. Each has to know the other.

children, and many centers have play equipment and supplies not found in most home care situations. All centers provide opportunities for contact with children of the same age.

However, day care is more expensive than family care, the child receives less individualized attention because each caregiver is responsible for more children, and changes in the staff may be frequent. Other mothers are likely to have firsthand knowledge of various day care centers. And some social service departments have lists of licensed centers. Plan at least two visits to each center you are considering, and observe the responsiveness and competence of the caregivers. Perhaps most important, pay attention to your gut reactions—to the director, to the staff, to the physical environment, and to the children being cared for.

Some years ago, a group of child development advisors drew up the Federal Interagency Day Care Requirements. Congressional approval was sought but not obtained. These represent minimal requirements for what is considered adequate day care:

1. A daily planned program of age-appropriate activities to stimulate physical, intellectual, social, and emotional development.

2. Trained care providers who have had courses in childcare, health, safety, and programming for the center.

3. Healthy meals.

BOX 8-2
CHOOSING A FAMILY DAY CARE HOME

1. Physical characteristics: Are the physical surroundings safe (fenced outdoor area, protected stairs), clean, spacious enough for the number of children enrolled? Are lunches and snacks nutritious? Is the home licensed? If not, why not? Remember that licensing regulations are intended to protect the children but may not be rigidly enforced.

2. Do toys and equipment provide a variety of activities for children? Are they appropriate for the ages of the children? What happens on rainy or snowy days?

3. Do children have special areas apart from family living quarters? Children need some small area to hang coats, keep belongings. Where do they rest?

4. Does the day care mother plan small excursions to the store, post office, library?

5. Does the day care mother seem to be a competent person? Can she cope, physically and psychologically, with the demands of the children? How does she respond when a child cries or several demands are made of her at the same time?

6. Are any other family members available—husband, children, grandparents? If so, do they enjoy and interact with the children?

Adapted from Gloria Norris and JoAnn Miller, *The Working Mother's Complete Handbook* (New York: E. P. Dutton, 1979), pp. 66–68.

---

4. Information to give to parents about health services in the community and records of immunizations.

5. Opportunities for parents to become familiar with the day care center and how it is run, and to have access to any evaluations of the center.

6. Recommend group sizes and staff-to-child ratios as given in Table 8-1.[41]

When children start elementary school, they receive care there for 3 to 6 hours per day and require special provisions only before or after school and on vacations. Approximately two to ten million children six to eleven year olds are unsupervised after school.[42] Financial pressures and lack of available care encourage parents to permit children to come home and care for themselves. Edward Zigler and Mary Lang cite four possible dangers to this system—(1) children alone may feel bad and rejected, (2) accidents or mistreatment may befall these children when alone, (3) children may not develop appropriate skills when unsupervised; for example, they may not become responsible for school work and other chores, and (4) children may engage in disapproved activities like delinquent acting out or premature sexual behavior.[43] It is not surprising that many parents of school-aged children are working to establish more before- and after-school programs.

Availability and Affordability of Care

We have described the kinds of care possible, but how available and affordable are they? The average cost of quality full-time care for a child prior to school age is

TABLE 8-1
RECOMMENDED DAY CARE GROUP SIZES AND STAFF : CHILD RATIOS

	Age of Child	Staff : Child Ratio	Maximum Size
Day care center	birth–2 years	1 : 3	6
	2–3	1 : 4	12
	3–6	1 : 8	16
Family day care home	birth–2 years	1 : 5	10
	2–6	1 : 6	12

Sandra Scarr, *Mother Care/Other Care* (New York: Warner, 1985), p. 186.

approximately $3,000 per year. Infants and toddler care can cost close to $5,000 per year. In certain geographical areas the costs are higher.[44] Childcare, then, becomes a large expense for two-parent families and can be the major portion of the after-tax income of a single parent.

Families receive little government support in arranging childcare. A tax credit of $2400 does not cover the full cost of the care and helps primarily middle and upper-middle class families. Single parents and lower-income parents do not pay sufficient taxes to get a large benefit from the credit. Though federal subsidies provide some block support for childcare expenses of poorer families, only about 10 to 15 percent of those eligible receive such benefits.

There are disagreements about the availability of care. Most agree, however, that shortages in service exist for infants and school-age children. As noted, between two and ten million children between the ages of six and eleven are unsupervised at home before and after school. Further, services are limited for children at certain times of the day—early mornings, early and late evenings, and at times of a child's illness.

Even when care is available, quality of care is uneven. Approximately 70 percent of day care homes are unlicensed. Many day care centers have rapid turnovers of staff and too few staff for the ages and number of children attending.[45] Chapter 10 takes up the question of how to provide affordable and adequate childcare.

RETURNING TO WORK

Following the birth of a baby, many parents wonder about the best time for mothers to return to work. Some professionals have been quoted as saying the best time is before seven or eight months, "when stranger anxiety" hits, or before twelve to fourteen months, when children begin saying "no" frequently. Sidney Greenspan, director of the Clinical Infant Program at the National Institute of Mental Health, says there is no best time, but there is a best process, for returning to work.[46] Ideally, the mother should have a prolonged time to get to know her baby and form an intimate relationship. But parents, other children, and businesses have needs, too, so mothers must sometimes return to work sooner than they would like. This means finding a suitable caregiver.

When a caregiver is selected—either at home, at family day care, or at a day care center—the child is eased gradually into the relationship with the person, first going for short visits, then for longer ones. When mothers actually return to work, it is best if mother and caregivers can overlap by 30 minutes so each can catch up on what has happened during the day or the preceding night. When mothers are optimistic about caregivers, babies often are, too.

Greenspan says it is especially important for infants to have special play or quiet time with their mother when she gets home so that their relationship can be reestablished after the day's absence. Mothers are not to be concerned if their babies are sometimes negative after an absence and turn away from them. Accepting the baby's annoyance and going on to share a more rewarding time are helpful ways to respond.

MAINTAINING TIES TO CHILDREN

When both parents are at work all day and the children are home, with a caregiver when young or unattended when older, parents and children want to keep in touch during these hours of separation. When the child is old enough to use the phone, a regular call at a time convenient for both—during the parent's midmorning or midafternoon break, just after the child's nap, or when the child gets home from school—provides contact and gives them a chance to share news, to talk about an incident on the playground or what is planned for supper. Some parents leave messages where the child will find them. Others send postcards, to the delight of the child who doesn't receive much mail.

Families find a tape cassette useful. The imaginative parent can use time during lunch hour or after the children are in bed to tape a "letter" or a story, perhaps chapters from a child's favorite book. These are for the child to listen to during the parent's absence. Older children can use the tape recorder to tell parents about important events at school, make suggestions for meals or family activities, and leave messages if they are going to be away when the parents get home. Tapes should be used to enhance communication, not as a substitute for communication between parent and child. Tapes should not be prepared during time that parent and child could be spending together.

Working parents find it helpful to meet with children's teachers at the beginning of each school year to describe their work schedules and clarify how each parent would like to be involved in school projects. Communicating the interest and willingness of both parents to help is sufficient to prompt the teacher to include both.

Parents can strengthen ties with children by including them in their work lives whenever possible, just as parents participate in school events and observe classes. The child who visits the parent's office, shop, or factory and even helps there on a vacation day learns a little about what the parent does all day and something about a particular vocation. When parents discuss their jobs with each other, children begin to get some sense of what is involved in working with other people, of what it means to have a job with responsibilities and opportunities and frustrations and satisfactions.

The working parent may find it difficult to take the time to go even to evening PTA meetings. Events during the day—school plays, games, class days when parents can observe teachers and children—are at least as important. But rare is the working parent who has not had to miss these opportunities. When your child comes home with an announcement of an event you cannot possibly attend, be clear in expressing your disappointment, and explain why you cannot be present. The child will be at least somewhat comforted by the knowledge that you would like to attend. And you can set aside some special time to spend only with that child.

Conflict between home and work demands makes working outside the home difficult for many women. Each parent must decide how often and when children take precedence over work and when work comes first. Effective parents take care of themselves as well as of their families. They learn when to say no as well as when to say yes. How do you balance the desire to share your child's world with the demands of your job and your need for time for yourself? There are no easy answers, but certainly it helps to be clear about what you want and flexible in how you respond to each day.

Separation Anxieties

Separation anxiety is not experienced solely by children. Working parents—both mothers and fathers—often feel guilt about leaving children with a caregiver, and their separation anxiety is as traumatic for them as it is for young children.

Looking at mothers' anxiety in the first year of the baby's life reveals that mothers' anxiety about separation from the infant, particularly separation related to employment, changes with time.[47] Educated, older career women have strong feelings of anxiety about separation from their infant for the baby's first two months, seeing the child as vulnerable and in need of nurturance. In the course of the first year, such anxiety decreases; and it decreases most rapidly in those women who want to return to work. Among women who do not want to return but do, anxiety about their ability to balance work and family needs increases, but this anxiety too decreases with time. Women who continue to stay home as their infant grows continue to have strong concerns about their ability to be both mothers and workers, and no doubt these concerns keep them at home.

Anxiety about balancing home and work commitments is a distinguishing feature for those mothers who have secure attachments with their infants, regardless of whether they work or not.[48] This anxiety again may be what keeps mothers at home, but even employed mothers who had strong concerns in this area had infants with secure attachments to them. It is possible that the anxiety motivates employed mothers to find the best nonmaternal care.

A parent who believes that it is reasonable for him or her to work and that doing so does not deprive the child of anything essential can handle crying or pouting at separation calmly. The child's feelings are recognized and accepted—he or she is entitled to feel disappointed that the parent will not be available for several hours. But the parent's behavior is not changed to suit the child's wishes. Children learn to find satisfaction in other activities as they come to understand and accept the parent's absence. Box 8-3 gives some strategies for coping with separation anxiety.

♦

BOX 8-3
MINIMIZING SEPARATION ANXIETY AT DAY CARE CENTERS

1. Ease entry into the day care center by remaining with the child for a significant amount of time each day for the first few weeks and by having extra time to stay a few minutes when the child first arrives.
2. Give the director and staff information about the child's home life—brothers and sisters, pets, daily routines—so that caregivers can talk about home during the day.
3. Give the child something from home—a favorite toy, a pillow, or blanket—to keep at the school to remind the child of home during the day.
4. Give the child pictures of family members to keep at school; a child sometimes finds it reassuring to go to her locker and look at the pictures.
5. Telephone children over two years old to maintain contact during the day.
6. Exchange information with caregivers at the end of the day so that you can talk about what has happened in school and be aware of any special experiences the child may have had.
7. Caregivers can ease separations by helping children wave hello or goodbye and by encouraging the child to talk about home.
8. Caregivers can help children build skills and competencies, increasing a sense of self-esteem and mastery that can help children deal with separation. When children feel more in control and less helpless, they are better able to cope with stress.
9. Caregivers can help children cope with feelings of separation by encouraging games of coming and going, hiding and rediscovering, losing and finding. Even though these games have nothing to do with the parents, the theme of separation and reunion helps handle feelings.

Adapted from Sally Provence, Audrey Naylor, and June Patterson, *The Challenge of Day Care* (New Haven: Yale University Press, 1977), pp. 65–67.

Gloria Norris and Jo Ann Miller[49] use the term **reentry frenzies** to describe the bedlam that breaks loose when a mother opens the front door at the end of her working day or picks the children up at the sitter's or a center. The children may have been playing happily, absorbed in an activity. When their mother appears, they leap at her with pieces of news or demands, a detailed description of an event or a game, expressing feelings and thoughts they have saved all day. One couple complained that their four-year-old son refused to let anybody else talk in the car on the way home from the day care center. When the parents realized that this was the child's way of saying that he has missed his parents, they were able to be more patient and accepting of this nonstop chatter.

Dinner time may be the most difficult hour of the day for both parents and children. Feelings run close to the surface. Young children especially are hungry and easily frustrated, and tantrums are not unusual at this hour. Some parents spend the first half hour at home listening to children's conversations, settling arguments, and talking over the day. This is a good strategy with young children, who may not be able to wait for an hour until after dinner. A second strategy is for parents to devote the first half hour to relaxing from the day. This time can be spent resting, taking a shower, reading the mail. Then the parent seeks out the children and listens to their news while preparing dinner.

Quality Time

The parent who works spends less time with children than the parent who is home and available to the children all day. And the working parent must, during nonworking hours, manage to do chores and errands and eat and sleep and play. Time is precious. And the *quality* of the time shared by parent and child is important.

Dorothy Briggs's definition of a genuine encounter provides a good definition of **quality time**: "focused attention [on the child]. . . . attention with a special intensity born of direct, personal involvement. . . . being intimately open to the particular, unique qualities of your child."[50] Having a genuine encounter means being "all there" with the child. The quality of the relationship, not the nature of the specific activity, is the crucial factor.

Genuine encounters differ according to the age of the child. In infancy, quality time may be active play with the baby, expanding his or her world by introducing new objects or toys or by taking time with routine care, smiling and talking. In the toddler years, quality time may be watching as your child explores an area, waiting for the child to bring you the latest discovery. It is resisting the urge to help the child who tries to climb the stairs or sweep the kitchen floor. In the preschool years, quality time may be arranging a special experience—a trip to a dairy farm or fruit orchard or a special occasion at home with his friends. It may be getting a puppy or kitten and taking the time to show the preschooler how to play with and care for the animal. In the elementary school years, it is helping the child create a work area and a routine for school work. It is going on excursions with a group, like the Cub Scouts or Brownies, or listening as the child practices a musical instrument. In the adolescent years, it is listening to long discussions on the merits of different kinds of jeans or the advantages of a particular kind of sports equipment.

We think less often of shared experiences doing household work as quality time. Yet in the course of working together, parents and children learn about each other's special strengths and weaknesses as they can in no other situation. The teenager who keeps her room a mess may reveal unexpected competence as she devises shortcuts while working in the yard with her mother. Working together also provides time for conversations that might never occur otherwise. With the activity as a common focus, children may talk about their friends and their opinions in ways they would not if they sat down with parents to "have a talk." One full-time mother described several years ago how her relationships with both her teenage daughters improved when she started doing dishes with each of them separately. In the course of that routine activity, the girls discussed their friends, their hopes and worries without her asking a single question.

Quality time is also attention focused on the needs of the child even when that child is not present. Quality time is planning some special event for him, thinking about the wisdom of getting her into a sport, encouraging him to take on a volunteer

For dual-career couples, quality time with their children is especially important. Dorothy Briggs defines a genuine encounter as "focused attention (on the child) . . . attention with a special intensity born of direct, personal involvement . . . being intimately open to the particular, unique qualities of your child."

activity, searching the stores on a lunch hour for special jeans or shorts. Although no direct interaction with the child occurs, this time is devoted to actions that convey to the child that he or she is special and worthy of attention. The parent who spends a Saturday afternoon helping to paint playground equipment, or a Tuesday evening baking cookies for a school bake sale, demonstrates that the child's activities are important and worthy of support. It may be precisely this kind of quality time that is most likely to be lost when both parents work outside the home.

How is quality time related to quantity of time? Quality time is time spent with children when parents have the energy and interest to focus on the children. Other concerns and worries must be put aside, which may be difficult when so much must be done. Spending large amounts of time in the general vicinity of the child does not guarantee quality time. The parent who can arrange quality time will have a different kind of communication with the child. The working parent who is able to set aside a few hours for himself or herself will have a chance to mull over the child's needs in a more relaxed way and will be rested and calmer with the child. It is harder for a mother to give quality time when she works, but not impossible. Many women believe that their work makes them more alert and interested companions for children, able to give a kind of attention that they could not before.

SETTING APPROPRIATE LIMITS

As in all families, reasonable limits are required. Ellen Greenberger and Wendy Goldberg find that having high investment in work does not mean parents must drastically change their standards for behavior or their disciplinary methods.[51] In fact, parents can have high investments in both areas; and when this is the case for mothers, they are most likely to rely on authoritative disciplinary techniques that have been found successful with children of all ages. Parents using these techniques are more likely to view their children's behavior positively and see them as having fewer behavior problems.

It is of course important to set and enforce appropriate limits as described in Chapter 4. Parents may be inclined to indulge children to compensate for being gone all day, but the working parent needs to remember that chores are not an imposition but a shared responsibility in the home.

Parents who permit immature and emotional behavior are also being indulgent. Working parents sometimes feel children are justified in being angry at their absence. When a four-year-old has a temper tantrum because both parents are leaving the house and he cannot go, the parents are sometimes apologetic and comforting, giving the child the impression that a tantrum is a realistic response. Susan, the mother of a three-year-old, explained to Billy that she was leaving three mornings a week for work. After exploring his feelings that he wanted her to be home, she said she understood his wish to have her home, but she was going to work. If Billy wanted to continue the tantrums, she was going to ignore them. Billy looked at her for a few minutes and went off to play with the housekeeper. The tantrums did not stop instantly, but they gradually disappeared.

Parents may find that when both work outside the home, they demand too much from children. They may ask them to do chores that are too difficult. They may ask them to care for younger children when they are just able to care for themselves. They may ask energetic children to be quiet while a parent sleeps in the daytime so he or she can work at night. As parents set limits and establish structure, they must check their expectations of children: Is the child able to do the task? If the child is able to, is the amount of work or responsibility so great that the child is robbed of childhood pleasures? There is no easy way to decide just how much to ask of a child. Don't allow yourself to become so overwhelmed by the demands on you that you, in turn, make demands on your children they are not ready for. Often children can do far more than we expect. However, if children begin to develop behavior problems, then parents can decide to change the responsibilities.

THE COOPERATING FAMILY

Although power is shared and the division of labor in the family changes somewhat when women work, women usually retain primary responsibility for household management. Though infrequent, men's participation in feminine household chores serves as a positive example for boys and girls. Boys and girls do less stereotyping when fathers do such chores.[52]

Though women may have traditionally borne the major responsibility for meeting the household needs, they can shift the burden to the family as a whole and establish a cooperating family. When children are young, a cooperating couple will share *all* the tasks. As children grow into the toddler years, they begin to help. Very young children take pride and pleasure in doing things for and like adults. Parents should capitalize on this natural desire to help and should encourage young children to do chores. The child's room can be arranged so there are shelves and boxes for toys, clothes pegs and rods low enough for the child to reach, a place for shoes, and a stool so the child can get to dresser drawers. At eighteen months a child can, with help, put away toys and clothes.

As children get older, they can be given household chores—for example, emptying wastebaskets and putting away plastic dishes. Children of four and five can dust and polish furniture, clean counters, and scrub pots and pans. Children of eight to ten can learn to prepare simple meals, put away groceries, and do the laundry.

Household chores can be organized at weekly family meetings. In the beginning, a list is made of all household jobs. Each family member picks the chores he or she is willing to do for a one- or two-week period. The chores that no one wants can be rotated. Family members may want to work in pairs, particularly when children are young and when chores are time-consuming. When all chores have been distributed, a chart can be made, with the list of chores, the name of the family member responsible for each chore, and spaces for check marks to be made as the chores are completed. Family members have the satisfaction of helping. And parents will be able to tell from a glance at the chart whether chores are being done on time.

Several steps need to be taken to ensure the success of this method. First, the parents must show the children how to do chores they are not already familiar with. Second, and very important, parents must not apply their standards to the child's work. Appreciation of the effort and praise for what is done correctly will improve performance. Third, children may not always complete their chores on schedule. Parents should be patient and understanding, and they should not take over the job. If children select their own chores, they are more likely to get to them. Even if children choose difficult chores, let them try. They may learn about their own limits—and they may surprise you with their skills.

Family meetings should be held weekly—or more often if necessary in the beginning—to talk about how this arrangement is working. A family may need several meetings to design a workable schedule that all members can meet. Don't expect this system to be an instant success. Do be generous with encouragement, appreciation, and praise. One family rewards itself as a group by going out to dinner when everyone completes chores on time. This encourages children to help each other, so everyone can have fun.

The family needs to discuss how to handle neglected chores, and everyone should agree on the method. Some families impose restrictions—no dinner out with the rest of the family, loss of a week's allowance, loss of a privilege. One mother demonstrated what would happen if she didn't do her work—for one week she didn't shop,

Young children learn that laundry is a family job not a mommy job.

cook, or do laundry. After just a few days the children had learned the importance of everyone's doing their share.

The family will be most successful when they set priorities and recognize there are only 24 hours in a day. Organization will be a key factor in accomplishing all the tasks. Values may change as well. It may be more important for the family to go on a picnic at the beach than to rake leaves or scrub the kitchen floor. Priorities shift to focus on relationships and satisfying family time.

THE MARRIAGE

In the excitement and busyness of working, parents forget that the family started with the primacy of the couple. Further, the satisfaction that the couple have with each other and their ways of doing things make solutions effective. The continuance of a strong, loving bond between parents is a primary factor in the success of combining working and parenting. So parents must plan time for each other as they plan time for children. Husband and wife need time together, regularly and as frequently as possible, to talk about things other than household or childcare matters. Some couples reserve one evening a week for dinner out, even if it's just hamburgers and a cup of coffee. Others get away for a weekend. Marjorie Shaevitz and Morton Shaevitz, who counsel two-career couples, suggest the following methods of strengthening the tie:[53]

1. Include your partner in professional relationships when possible.
2. Devote time to individual interests that express your uniqueness, so you have information and enthusiasm to share.
3. Accept your partner as he or she really is and enjoy the positive traits; realize that the positive traits will also have negative features—the conscientious, responsible parent may want children to be superresponsible and may nag to improve behavior.
4. Applaud and appreciate your partner's accomplishments.
5. Please the partner by buying an occasional extravagance or doing a special favor.
6. Develop closeness by touching and sexual expression; because there is less time for sexual encounters, you need to plan to ensure that both partners have time and are in the mood.
7. Take time to plan the future together.

TAKING CARE OF YOURSELF

Working parents who take care of themselves can take better care of their children and of each other. To reduce tension and fatigue associated with the dual roles of worker and parent, you should each set aside some time in the day for rest and relaxation. Such activities may initially seem self-indulgent, but they will increase your ability to manage both roles.

Working parents who take care of their own needs—exercise regularly, eat a balanced diet, and make sure they have private time for thinking and pursuing interests—are less likely to be tense and tired and more likely to enjoy their job and family. Norris and Miller suggest the following ways for parents to be good to themselves:[54]

1. Keep up your own friendships—exercising with a friend several times a week is ideal.

2. Develop ways of easing the transition from office to home—walk the last block or two, take a quick shower before dinner, rest for ten minutes after arriving home.

3. Learn your own personal signs of stress and do not ignore them; get rest and spend time relaxing.

4. Discover the most stressful times of the day and find ways of relieving tension. You may need a different morning or evening routine. Get up an hour earlier to reduce stress—the loss of sleep is worth feeling more relaxed.

5. Develop a quick tension reliever, like yoga exercises, deep breathing, or meditation.

The life of the working parent is challenging and demanding. As mothers, especially, learn to value what they accomplish, they relax and are more efficient and happier. Most working parents find the challenges worth the efforts required, as life becomes richer and more exciting for the whole family.

MAJOR POINTS OF CHAPTER 8

Men's work:

- influences social status of the family
- affects not only family's financial well-being but also its psychological well-being
- influences values in childrearing
- can absorb fathers so they have little time for families

Women's work:

- may be most satisfying on a part-time basis for mothers of young children
- results in fathers' having more exclusive time with daughters
- changes home activities as they spend less individualized time with children
- by itself has no universally predictable effects on children

Working mothers of infant children are more at risk for insecure attachments with children if:

- they work more than 20 hours a week
- their infants are boys
- their infants have difficult, fussy temperaments
- they have unhappy marriages
- the father does not provide alternative care

Beyond infancy, high quality day care is related to such positive outcomes as increased:

- language development
- self-regulation, self-control
- social development
- participation in school

When mothers of preschoolers work:

- full-time and are well-educated, they regard daughters positively and sons negatively
- full-time and are less well-educated, they regard both daughters and sons negatively
- part-time, they, regardless of educational level, view sons and daughters positively

When children are in elementary school, mothers' working may influence:

- girls positively and boys negatively
- amount of child monitoring a parent does
- children differently depending on the social class of the family
- sons' attitudes toward father

When fathers are active caregivers:

- the family spends more leisure time together
- they manage routine care as mothers do
- homes are more enriched and less punitive

Societal supports required to help parents combine work and parenting are:

- job sharing
- part-time work
- flex time
- family phases for jobs filled by parents of young children
- family leave for fathers
- warm, creative, high-quality, easily accessible day care centers

Each form of day care has some advantages:

- at-home care provides a specific caregiver in familiar surroundings
- family day care involves smaller numbers of children in a homelike atmosphere that can provide more individualized attention at a lower cost

- day care centers have trained personnel, greater variety of educational and play equipment, reliable care providing contact with children of the same age
- self-care for older children can result in children (1) having accidents, (2) feeling lonely, (3) doing disapproved activities, and (4) failing to develop skills

Working parents maintain quality relationships with children by:

- including children in their work when possible
- spending time alone with the child
- staying involved in child's school activities
- leaving notes, taped messages for child
- telephoning to touch base

Quality time is time:

- spent focused on child
- working together as well as playing together

Effectively combining working and parenting requires parents to:

- find time for marriage
- find time to attend to their own individualized needs

EXERCISES

1. Break into small groups and discuss the fact that the effect of mother's working seems to depend on the sex of the child. (See the comments of Susan McHale on page 228.) Discuss the fact that boys may experience more negative effects because they need more monitoring. How can parents take action to optimize effects for both boys and girls.

2. Imagine you had a child under the age of five—infant, toddler, or preschooler. Investigate day care available in the community for a child of that age. You might form groups to investigate care for a child of a particular age with each student visiting at least one center to get information and summarize impressions. One group might investigate family day care in the area and compare the care and the cost of care with that available in a center.

3. Design an ideal day care program for infants or toddlers, specifying the number of caregivers, their qualities, the physical facilities, the daily routine.

4. Imagine what your family and work life will be like in ten years. Write diary entries for a day during the week and for a day on the weekend about your life at home and at work.

5. Write a short paper of advice you could give to a parent of the same sex who feels frustrated and pressured trying to incorporate an infant and the care of the infant into their work life.

ADDITIONAL READINGS

Brazelton, T. Berry. *Working and Caring*. Reading, Mass.: Addison-Wesley, 1985.

Hochschild, Arlie. *The Second Shift*. New York: Viking, 1989.

Miller, Angela Browne. *The Day Care Dilemma: Critical Concerns for American Families*. New York: Plenum, 1990.

Olds, Sally Wendkos. *The Working Parents' Survival Guide*. Rocklin, Calif.: Prima, 1989.

Scarr, Sandra. *Mother Care/Other Care*. New York: Warner, 1985.

Notes

1. Lynn Smith and Bob Sipchen, "Workers Crave Time With Kids," *San Francisco Chronicle,* August 13, 1990.

2. Ibid.

3. Arlie Hochschild, *The Second Shift* (New York: Viking Press, 1989).

4. Glen H. Elder, *Children of the Great Depression* (Chicago: University of Chicago Press, 1974); Glen H. Elder, "Families, Kin and the Life Course: A Sociological Perspective," in *A Review of Child Development Research,* vol. 7, ed. Ross D. Parke (Chicago: University of Chicago Press, 1984), pp. 80–136; Glen H. Elder, Tri Van Nguyen, and Avshalom Caspi, "Linking Family Hardship to Children's Lives," *Child Development* 56 (1985): 361–375.

5. Elder, Nguyen, and Caspi, "Linking Family Hardship to Children's Lives."

6. John L. Cotterell, "Work and Community Influences on the Quality of Child Rearing," *Child Development* 57 (1986): 362–374.

7. Melvin L. Kohn, *Class and Conformity: A Study in Values* (Homewood, Ill.: Dorsey, 1969).

8. Lois Wladis Hoffman, "Work, Family, and the Socialization of the Child," in *A Review of Child Development Research,* vol. 7, ed. Parke, pp. 223–282.

9. Joseph Veroff, Elizabeth Douvan, and Richard Kulka, *The Inner American: A Self-Portrait from 1957 to 1976* (New York: Basic Books, 1981).

10. Anita M. Farel, "Effects of Preferred Maternal Roles, Maternal Employment and Socio-demographic Status on School Adjustment and Competence," *Child Development* 50 (1980): 1179–1186.

11. Hoffman, "Work, Family, and the Socialization of the Child."

12. Louis Wladis Hoffman and F. Ivan Nye, *Working Mothers* (San Francisco: Jossey-Bass, 1974), p. 228.

13. Urie Bronfenbrenner, William F. Alvarez, and Charles R. Henderson, "Working and Watching: Maternal Employment Status and Parents' Perceptions of Their Three-Year-Old Children," *Child Development* 55 (1984): 1362–1378.

14. Sandra Scarr, *Mother Care/Other Care* (New York: Warner, 1985).

15. Hoffman, "Work, Family, and the Socialization of the Child."

16. Susan M. McHale and Ted L. Huston, "Men and Women as Parents: Sex Role Orientations, Employment, and Parental Roles with Infants," *Child Development* 55 (1984): 1349–1361.

17. Urie Bronfenbrenner and Ann C. Crouter, "Work and Family Through Time and Space," in *Families That Work: Children in a Changing World,* eds. Sheila B. Kamerman and Cheryl D. Hayes (Washington, D.C.: National Academy Press, 1982), p. 51.

18. Jay Belsky and Michael J. Rovine, "Non-maternal Care in the First Year of Life and the Security of Infant-Parent Attachment," *Child Development* 59 (1988): 164.

19. Kathleen McCartney, "Effect of Quality of Day Care Environment on Children's Language Development," *Developmental Psychology* 20 (1984): 244–260.

20. Carollee Howes and Michael Olenick, "Family and Child Care Influences on

Toddler's Compliance," *Child Development* 57 (1986): 202–216.

21. Deborah Phillips, Kathleen McCartney, and Sandra Scarr, "Child-Care Quality and Children's Social Development," *Developmental Psychology* 23 (1987): 537–543; Deborah Lowe Vandell, V. Kay Henderson, and Kathy Shores Wilson, "A Longitudinal Study of Children with Day-Care Experiences of Varying Quality," *Child Development* 59 (1988): 1286–1292.

22. Patricia J. Schindler, Barbara E. Moely, and Alyssa L. Frank, "Time in Day Care and Social Participation of Young Children," *Developmental Psychology* 23 (1987): 255–261.

23. Carollee Howes, "Early Child Care and Schooling," *Developmental Psychology* 24 (1988): 53–57.

24. Carollee Howes and Phyllis Stewart, "Child's Play with Adults, Toys, and Peers: An Examination of Family and Child-Care Influences," *Developmental Psychology* 23 (1987): 423–430.

25. Jay Belsky, "Daycare Policy and Research: Infant Day Care and Child Development," *Newsletter of Division of Developmental Psychology* (Fall 1984): 46–47.

26. Bronfenbrenner, Alvarez, and Henderson, "Working and Watching."

27. Lois Wladis Hoffman, "Effects on Children," in *Working Mothers,* eds. Hoffman and Nye, pp. 126–166; Lois Wladis Hoffman, "Maternal Employment: 1979," *American Psychologist* 34 (1979): 859–865.

28. Bronfenbrenner and Crouter, "Work and Family Through Time and Space."

29. Hoffman, "Work, Family, and the Socialization of the Child."

30. Hoffman, "Effects on Children."

31. Bronfenbrenner and Crouter, "Work and Family Through Time and Space."

32. E. Mavis Hetherington, "Divorce: A Child's Perspective," *American Psychologist* 34 (1979): 851–858.

33. Scarr, *Mother Care/Other Care.*

34. Arlie Hochschild, *The Second Shift* (New York: Viking, 1989).

35. Grace K. Baruch and Rosalind C. Barnett, "Fathers' Participation in Family Work and Children's Sex-Role Attitudes," *Child Development* 57 (1986): 1210–1223.

36. Ann C. Crouter, Maureen Perry-Jenkins, Ted L. Huston, and Susan M. McHale, "Processes Underlying Father-Involvement

in Dual-Earner and Single-Earner Families," *Developmental Psychology* 23 (1987): 431–440; Susan M. McHale, W. Todd Bartko, Ann C. Crouter, and Maureen Perry-Jenkins, "Children's Housework and Psychosocial Functioning: The Mediating Effect of Parents' Sex Role Behaviors and Attitudes," *Child Development* 61 (1990): 1413–1426.

37. Crouter et al., "Processes Underlying Father Involvement in Dual-Earner and Single-Earner Families."

38. Hochschild, *The Second Shift,* p. 270.

39. Ramon G. McLeod, "U.S. Study Finds Big Shift in Child Care," *San Francisco Chronicle,* August 15, 1990.

40. Sally Provence, Audrey Naylor, and June Patterson, *The Challenge of Daycare* (New Haven: Yale University Press, 1977).

41. Scarr, *Mother Care/Other Care.*

42. Edward F. Zigler and Mary E. Lang, *Child Care Choices* (New York: The Free Press, 1991).

43. Ibid.

44. Ibid.

45. Ibid.

46. Sidney Greenspan, "After the Baby: The Best Time to Go to Work," *Working Mother,* November 1982.

47. Debra K. DeMeis, Ellen Hock, and Susan L. McBride, "The Balance of Employment and Motherhood: Longitudinal Study of Mothers' Feelings About Separation From Their First-Born Infants," *Developmental Psychology* 22 (1986): 627–632.

48. Susan McBride and Jay Belsky, "Characteristics, Determinants, and Consequences of Maternal Separation Anxiety," *Developmental Psychology* 24 (1988): 407–414.

49. Gloria Norris and JoAnn Miller, *The Working Mother's Complete Handbook* (New York: E. P. Dutton, 1979).

50. Dorothy C. Briggs, *Your Child's Self-Esteem* (Garden City, N.Y.: Doubleday, 1975), p. 64.

51. Ellen Greenberger and Wendy Goldberg, "Work, Parenting, and the Socialization of Children," *Developmental Psychology* 25 (1989): 22–35.

52. Baruch and Barnett, "Fathers' Participation in Family Work and Children's Sex Role Attitudes."

53. Marjorie H. Shaevitz and Morton H. Shaevitz, *Making It Together* (Boston: Houghton Mifflin, 1980).

54. Norris and Miller, *Working Mother's Complete Handbook.*

PARENTING AT TIMES OF CHANGE AND TRAUMA

C H A P T E R   9

Biologically speaking, it takes two to parent, and traditionally family meant mother and father and their biological offspring. So, how does life change for children whose parents divorce? Are they doomed to suffer in "broken" homes or are their lives sometimes enriched by these changes? How can parents help children successfully cope with the trauma of divorce and stress of remarriage and blended families? When death, abuse, and violence affect children, how can parents help them not only survive the trauma but thrive? Parenting during such difficult times brings enormous challenges.

When two people marry and have children, they hope to live together in harmony for the rest of their lives, but today such long-term marriages occur less frequently. When parents live together unhappily, that situation has consequences for children's development. In many cases, parents live together, don't get along, and decide to divorce. The divorce rate rose dramatically from 1965 to 1979 and has leveled off. In 1990, 26 percent of children lived in a single-parent household—21 percent headed by a mother and 5 percent headed by a father—while 74 percent of children lived in two-parent families.[1] The vast majority of single households result from separation and divorce.

An estimated 40–50 percent of children born in the 1990s will experience divorce. Many will live in stepfamilies and may experience another divorce, for about 50 percent of these marriages fail.[2] Before discussing divorce, we look at the effects of marital disharmony on children's development; parental conflict is the forerunner of divorce and may well continue to exert strong effects after the divorce.

MARITAL DISHARMONY AND DIVORCE

We are now more aware of the devastating effects that anger has on people. Children become immobilized when they hear unknown adults arguing. When the arguing adults are their parents, children have high levels of stress hormones, are less able to deal with feelings, and play with their friends in unenthusiastic and halfhearted ways.[3]

How does marital disharmony have such widespread effects? When parents are unhappily married, they are often less effective parents. Parents are less sensitive caregivers of infants when they are unhappy with their mates. When parents of toddlers are unhappily married, parents experience more negative emotions in their everyday lives—more anger, guilt, sadness—and they express these emotions in the family, so there is less positive feeling between mother and father and between parent and child.[4] Fathers who are unhappily married are more negative with children and consider them a bother. Both parents tend to see children as difficult in temperament and as interfering with their lifestyle. Unhappily married fathers of school-age children are also more negative and intrusive with children, and mothers seem to try to compensate for this by being more positive and less intrusive.[5]

Children in a negative atmosphere begin to develop behavior problems. Boys, in particular, become more restless, more impulsive, and more resistant; they also manipulate the rules more.[6] These problems persist; and in adolescence, both boys and girls who experienced parental disagreements in the preschool years are poorly controlled and interpersonally less skilled.[7] Boys also show some difficulties with intellectual functioning. So boys whose parents later divorce are already impulsive and poorly controlled ten years before the divorce.[8]

Mavis Hetherington and Kathleen Camara emphasize that divorce is a parental solution to parental problems.[9] Children often view divorce as the cause of all their problems. For both parent and child, however, divorce is a stress. It forces people to change their relationships to those who have been most important to them. And divorce is a stress that brings many other stresses with it. Financial problems arise; there is no way two families can live as cheaply as one. Often mothers must go to work or increase their hours at work, so children may see much less of their father, who is no longer living with them, and less of their mother, who must work more. Reduced income means many families must move, so the child has a new neighborhood, new school, and new friends to deal with. As resources grow more limited, parents may become more irritable, discouraged, impatient with children.

As the divorce rate has risen, society has begun to make accommodations to the needs of divorcing families. The legal system has changed, making it easier for both parents to continue to be involved in the care of children. With joint legal custody, mothers and fathers, though divorced, continue to make decisions about children, with each parent taking an equal part. In some cases there is joint physical custody, in which children spend significant amounts of time with both parents. When parents have difficulty coming to agreement about custody issues, many states now provide court mediation services. Professional counselors help parents explore children's and parents' needs and reach agreement on reasonable living arrangements.

Further, laws have been passed to make it easier for single mothers to obtain child support payments decreed by the court. This is imperative because mothers who are single heads of household have an income far below that of other family units. Two-parent families with children under 18 have a median family income of $38,664 in 1989 dollars—significantly higher because the wife often works. Single-parent families headed by a man have an average income of $30,336—lower because there is a single wage earner. The average income of a household headed by a woman,

256

CHAPTER 9
Parenting at
Times of
Change and
Trauma

however, is $17,383,[10] dramatically below the income of other family units. Indeed, the feminization of poverty—the poverty of single mothers and their children—is a major social concern.

Children's Reactions to Divorce

Emotional reactions common to children of all ages include sadness, fear, depression, anger, confusion, and sometimes relief—the predominant emotions vary with age and require somewhat different reactions from parents.[11] In the preschool years, children often feel abandoned and overwhelmed by the events. They worry that they may have caused the divorce. Although usually they try hard to handle their feelings with denial, they need parents who will talk to them and explain what is happening, not once but many times. Children may regress, begin wetting the bed, have temper tantrums, and develop fears. Parents can help most by providing emotional support. Outside interventions are not as useful as interventions by parents. Parents are urged to (1) communicate with the child about the divorce and the new adjustments, explaining in simple language the reasons for each change that occurs, and (2) reduce the child's suffering, where possible, by giving reassurance that the child's needs will be met and by doing concrete things such as arranging visits with the absent parent.

Preschool children are often protected initially by their ability to deny what is happening. Five- to seven-year-olds are vulnerable because they understand more but do not have the maturity to cope with what they see and hear. The most outstanding reaction of a child this age is sadness and grief. Children may deny that the parents are really divorcing, rationalize that the divorce is between the parents and will not affect them, or pretend that parents will reunite someday. But these often-used defenses do not make the pain go away, and the child is not yet old enough or independent enough to arrange activities that will bring pleasure and some relief from the worry. The divorce dominates the thoughts of a child this age. One little girl, whose parents had just divorced, was asked what she would like if she could have just three wishes. Her reply: "First, that my daddy would come home. Second, that my parents would get back together. And third, that they would never, ever divorce again."[12]

Fear is another frequent response. Children worry that no one will love them or care for them. The world has fallen apart and there is no safe place. Many children feel that only a father can maintain discipline in the family.

Preschoolers and children in the early elementary years have difficulty with counseling because talking about the situation is so painful. A monologue from a therapist who talks about the divorce and describes the fears, the sadness, the worries the child is experiencing can be helpful.[13] For example, one therapist worked with an eight-year-old boy who wouldn't talk because he was afraid he would cry. She told him that she talked to many other children whose parents were divorced and they often felt very sad about the family breakup and sometimes mad at the parents because they would not stay together. She sympathized and said that it was hard for the boy to know how to act because he did not want to hurt his parents. The boy eagerly nodded his head, indicating that was how he felt. Most parents cannot start by saying they have talked to many children about divorce, but they can start by saying they have read an article or seen a television show on divorce that says children sometimes have whatever feelings the child seems to be showing. Then the child has an opportunity to express reactions.

Children nine or ten and older may find outside intervention useful, and three to four weeks of counseling may help them sort out their feelings and begin to decide how they feel about issues of custody and visitation. Counseling provides a neutral third party to validate the child's feelings. When children are depressed, angry, and worried, it is reassuring for them to hear a professional person say, "Yes, this is a very difficult time, and it is understandable that you feel upset and sad." Children can then accept their feelings more easily.

In helping older children handle divorce, parents need to keep in mind that children may feel responsible—they may believe they have done something that has brought about the divorce. Parents need to say clearly and often, when opportunities occur, that the divorce was *not* caused by the children, but it *was* caused by difficulties between the parents. In addition, parents need to remember that children worry about them and how they are doing. It is not always possible to confine grief and distress to times when the children are not there, but you can help the children by trying to wait until you are alone to express your sadness or anger.

The children of a divorcing or divorced couple need, perhaps more than anything else, to be able to talk with their parents about what is happening. Parents can encourage children to ask questions and to express their feelings. And they should respond to questions with clear statements. Children need to know what the practical arrangements for their lives are—where they will be living and with whom. And they need to know that their parents continue to care about their welfare and about their feelings.

Thus far we have described the reactions of children who regret their parents' divorce. Some children, about 10 percent, feel relieved at their parents' divorce.[14] Often they are older children who have witnessed violence or severe psychological suffering on the part of a parent or other family member. These children feel that dissolution of the marriage is the best solution, and progressing from a conflict-ridden home to a more stable environment with one parent helps these children's overall level of adjustment and functioning.

From a follow-up of children fifteen years after the divorce, Judith Wallerstein concludes that it is very difficult to determine the long-term adjustment of the child from the child's reactions at the time of the divorce.[15] Some children who seemed to have very stong, disorganizing reactions were, nevertheless, doing well many years later while others who seemed to make a good initial adjustment had longstanding problems.

Parent's Reactions to Divorce

Parents' reactions are many and varied, but almost all are intense. Parents often suffer many symptoms—headaches, rapid heartbeats, fatigue, dizziness.[16] Their moods and behavior change at the time of the divorce and these mood changes may be one of the most upsetting aspects of the divorce process for their children. Each parent may respond differently at different times, and both may show similar behavior only

258

CHAPTER 9
Parenting at
Times of
Change and
Trauma

when they are angry with each other. Children are helpless in the face of their parents' extreme moods. One parent may be sad, depressed, lacking in energy; the other may be busy, agitated, preoccupied with his or her concerns. Both often lack self-esteem and seek out people or experiences to make them feel good again.

Divorced men and women both start dating again, though men date in larger numbers and older women tend to remain isolated and alone. Heterosexual relationships now become a source of anxiety and tension. Women wonder how to respond to sexual advances, and men worry about sexual performance. Nevertheless, new intimate relationships after divorce tend to boost parents' self-esteem.

Parents must deal with the intense feelings that arise during the divorce process, even if they were not there in the beginning: They feel sad at the ending of their marriage, even if it was necessary. They feel pain as the divorce becomes real—material possessions are divided, money is dispersed, and custody and visiting rights are arranged. Anger keeps the relationship alive for a time, but gradually detachment and distance mean the marital relationship is truly ended. The loss is real.

Factors Affecting Adjustment to Divorce

Several factors influence how well a family adapts to divorce:[17] (1) the amount of conflict among family members, (2) the availability of both parents to their children, (3) the nature of the relationship changes in the family, (4) the responsibilities family members take, and (5) the defensibility of the divorce from the child's point of view.[18]

Most divorces involve conflict at certain points. When parents have hostile battles in front of children, boys are more likely to react with undercontrolled behavior and girls with overcontrolled behaviors.[19] There are indications that moving from a household with two parents always in conflict to a stable household with one parent can lead to better adjustment for children.[20] Parents often continue the fighting when they live separately, however, and this is harmful to children. It is likely that the increased conflict children witness during divorce, not the divorce itself, leads to their poorer adjustment. Increased conflicts can also occur between parents and children in a one-parent household where the second parent is not available as a buffering agent. In addition, a parent may find the child a convenient target for feelings aroused by the other parent. In the midst of this raging conflict, the child feels very alone. Minimizing the fighting in all arenas aids everyone's adjustment.

When children have continuing relationships with both parents, they can adjust well following the divorce process.[21] It is impossible to predict how fathers, who are usually the ones to move out of the home, will respond after the divorce. Some previously devoted fathers find not living with their children so painful that they withdraw and see less of the children. Other fathers, previously uninvolved, discover that caring for children alone on visits deepens their attachment, and thus they increase their contact with their children. Fathers are more likely to maintain relationships with their sons than with their daughters. In fact, many mothers relinquish custody of older sons to fathers because they feel sons need a role model.

Not only do children need relationships with both parents, but they also need to be able to relate to each parent separately as a parent.[22] Parents often find it difficult

---

BOX 9-1
OUT OF HARM'S WAY:
PROTECTING CHILDREN FROM PARENTAL CONFLICT

Children can continue to grow and thrive even through a divorce if their parents insulate them from intense or prolonged hostilities. Parents who accomplish this share some important qualities:

1. They make it clear that they value their child's relationship and time both with them *and* with the other parent.
2. They work out a fair and practical timesharing schedule, either temporary or long-term, as soon as possible.
3. Once that agreement is reached, they make every effort to live up to its terms.
4. They tell each other in advance about necessary changes in plans.
5. They are reasonably flexible in "trading off" to accommodate the other parent's needs.
6. They prepare the child, in a positive way, for each upcoming stay with the other parent.
7. They *do not* conduct adult business when they meet to transfer the child.
8. They refrain from using the child as a confidant, messenger, bill collector, or spy.
9. They listen caringly but encourage their child to work out problems with the other parent directly.
10. They work on their problems with each other in private.

From Robert Adler, *Sharing the Children* (New York: Adler and Adler, 1988).

---

to direct their energy to parenting. At this time of great need in the first year following divorce, when they actually need *more* attention, children receive less attention from their parents. Frequently children's behavior goes unmonitored, and rules are not enforced. The parent outside the home often becomes highly indulgent and permissive with children; seeing so little of them, he or she hates to spend precious time in discipline. But children function most effectively when both parents take time to monitor their behavior and enforce the usual rules, as in the past.

In the family with two households and both parents working, the need is greater for children to take on more responsibilities.[23] When demands are not excessive and are tailored to the abilities of children, then children may feel pleased with their contribution to the family and the new competence they are developing. When the demands are too great, however—when they are given too much responsibility for caring for younger children or doing chores—then children become resentful, feeling they have been robbed of their childhood. Realistic demands for responsibility can help children grow in this situation.

Children seem better able to cope with divorce and its aftermath when the divorce is a carefully thought out, reasonable response to a specific problem.[24] When

260

CHAPTER 9
Parenting at
Times of
Change and
Trauma

the problem improves after the divorce, children are better able to accept it. They are less able to deal with divorce that is an impulsive act, that may have had little to do with the marriage but was related to other problems in the parent's life. For example, one woman divorced her husband following the death of her mother. She later regretted the decision, but could not undo what had hurt four people.

Protective Factors

Protective factors for children as they adjust to the divorce include qualities in the child, supportive aspects of the family system, and external social supports.[25]

The child's age, sex, and intelligence serve as protection. Intelligence can be a resource in coping with all the stress. Children who are younger appear less affected than those who are school-aged or early adolescent at the time of the divorce or remarriage. Later adolescents seem less affected than younger children because they are becoming increasingly independent of the family. Boys appear to suffer more difficulties at the time of the divorce, and girls appear to have more problems at the time of the mother's remarriage.

The child's temperamental qualities also influence the process of divorce. An easy, adaptable temperament helps. Children with a difficult temperament are more sensitive to change and less adaptable to it, and so they can become a center for parental anger. In part, they elicit the anger with their reactive behavior; and, in part, they provide a convenient target for parental anger that may belong elsewhere.

When mothers are not overwhelmed with stress or experiencing personal problems themselves, they are able to treat easy and difficult children in similar ways. However, if stress increases or mothers' coping techniques decrease, then the tendency is to focus on the difficult child. Social supports in the situation minimize this tendency when stress is at a moderate level. Social supports cannot counteract this tendency when stress is at a high level or when mothers' personality problems increase.

When stress is high and support little, both easy and difficult children have problems adapting. For difficult children, the more stress, the more problems. For easy children, the relationship is different. With moderate amounts of stress, easy children actually develop increased coping skills and become more competent than when stress is either low or high.

We have already touched on some forms of family interaction that are protective—reduced conflict between the parents, structure and organization in daily life, reasonable assignment of responsibilities within the family. Mothers must be especially firm and fair in establishing limits with boys as their tendency is to develop a vicious repetitive cycle of complaining and fighting.

Researchers point to siblings and grandparents as potential family supports.[26] When family life is harmonious after divorce, then sibling relationships are similar to what they are in intact families.[27] When there is conflict between parents, siblings fight, with the greatest difficulty occurring between older brothers and younger sisters.

Grandparents can support grandchildren directly with time, attention, and special outings and privileges that help to ease the pain of the divorce. One girl told

Judy Wallerstein, "If it weren't for my grandparents, I don't think I could have made it past sixteen."[28]

Grandparents provide support indirectly by helping one of the parents. In fact, returning to live in the home of one's parents is a solution many young parents choose when they do not have the resources to be on their own. Grandparents can be loving, stable babysitters who enrich children's lives in ways that no one else can. The mother can work and carry on a social life, knowing that her child is well cared for in her absence. And this arrangement usually reduces living expenses. When mother and grandparents agree on childrearing techniques and the mother is respected in the household as a mature adult, this solution may be attractive.

Such an arrangement, however, can reflect neurotic needs of both the mother and the grandparents—and when this is true, it is likely to create additional problems for the child. If the grandmother was a protective mother who refused to allow the daughter to become independent, that relationship may continue. The daughter may have tried to escape into a marriage that did not last. If the daughter returns to her parents' home, she may have to start again to develop her independence. She will have to establish new supports that will enable her to become more independent and to continue her growth as an individual.

School is a major source of support for children. Authoritative, kindly teachers and peer friendship give pleasure and a sense of esteem to children. School and athletic accomplishments contribute to feelings of competence that stimulate resilience in children.

Some of the protective factors are beyond a parent's control—age, sex, temperament of the child—but many are within a parent's control—setting aside anger, establishing structure, monitoring behavior, and seeking out external supports for children.

PARENTING TASKS DURING DIVORCE

The main tasks of parents are (1) to establish effective channels of communication so that emotions are expressed and important information is clearly exchanged, (2) to establish a stable family structure in the home of each parent, (3) to establish reasonable visiting arrangements for the child, (4) to help children cope with the process of divorce, and (5) to establish meaningful lives so all participants in the divorce process have an opportunity for what Wallerstein calls "second chances."

Effective Channels of Communication

Open communication begins with telling children about the divorce.[29] If possible, both parents together should tell all the children at the same time before one parent leaves. Wallerstein suggests wording like this, "We married fully hoping and expecting to love each other forever, but we have discovered that one (or both) of us is unhappy. One (or both) does not love the other anymore. We fight with each other. The divorce is going to stop the fighting and restore peace."[30]

262

CHAPTER 9
Parenting at
Times of
Change and
Trauma

Parents present the decision as a rational, sad one: "The goal is to present the child with models of parents who admit they made a serious mistake, tried to rectify the mistake, and are now embarking on a moral, socially acceptable remedy. The parents are responsible people who remain committed to the family and to the children even though they have decided to go their separate ways."[31] When parents express their sadness at the solution, then children have permission to mourn without hiding their feelings from adults.

It is also important to express reluctance at the solution because children need to hear that parents know how upsetting this will be for them: "Put simply, parents should tell the children they are sorry for all the hurt they are causing."[32]

There are many things divorcing parents should *not* say. Do not burden your children with your own negative views of the other parent. Do not blame the other parent for all the problems. And do not ask children to take sides—they usually need and want to be loyal to both parents. Parents may be surprised at the loyalty that children feel to both parents, to the marriage, and to the family. Even when one parent has abused the other or the children, children often want the abusive parent present in the family. Even when children are willing to accept a parent's absence, they often do not want anything negative said about him or her.

Wallerstein comments on how little support most children get as they go through the initial turmoil of divorce. Often no one talks to them, no one listens to them talk about their feelings or answers their questions, and few relatives give added help and support. Children are often left on their own to maneuver as best they can.

To keep communication going, each parent permits the child to express his or her feelings and guides the child into acceptable forms of behavior that remedy what can be changed. Parents need to hear that children may be angry at them or the other parent. Active listening and sending I-messages are appropriate ways to keep channels of communication open.

Children will complain about the other parent. A parent can acknowledge the feelings and encourage the child to communicate directly with the other parent, who can take action. One parent is unwise to take responsibility for remedying what the other parent does unless there is some form of extreme abuse or neglect.

Stable Family Structure

As we have noted, children adjust best when each parent establishes and enforces stable family routines. The parent who feels, even unrealistically, responsible for having deprived the children of the other parent may try to compensate for the absence of the other by giving gifts and privileges and being flexible about rules and limits. The parent who is inclined to feel guilty may find support in the words of Frances Ilg and Louise Ames:

> Nearly all children have to learn to face some adverse circumstances, to accept them, and to go on from there.
>
> If, as a divorced mother (or father), you allow yourself to feel too sorry for your poor son or daughter who is having to grow up without a father's close companionship, your oversolicitude may well do him more harm than the absence of his father.[33]

When two single parents share the care of their children, the children may, at times, try to play one parent off against the other with such statements as, "I don't have to do that when I am at Daddy's" or "Mommy lets me stay up much later than you do." Thomas Gordon recognizes that parents are different people and that such differences, if openly discussed and handled with children, can be respected by the children.

Parents must help children to develop increased competencies. A single parent who works and cares for children must rely on the children to help keep the family unit functioning. Children may have more chores and greater independence than their peers. Increased responsibility can lead to increased self-esteem, if neither parent nor child perceives it as an unfair burden.

Having established stable routines within the family, single parents must begin to find people outside the family to serve as substitutes for the missing parent. The brothers and cousins of single mothers can serve as male models for their sons, as can athletic coaches or Scout leaders. Time spent with men who can help guide their development is also important for girls, and mothers will have to make special efforts to find male coaches, male music teachers, or male school teachers who will interact with girls as fathers, brothers, or uncles would. It is unwise to have the mother's male friends fill this role. The child needs to feel that the man is interested in him or her and that the relationship is not dependent on the man's attachment to the mother.

Establishing Reasonable Visiting Arrangements

Parents are strongly encouraged to arrange visiting that meets children's needs for contact with both parents and is not stressful to the child. In the past, most children of divorce lived with the mother, who had full custody, and most of what we know about divorce is divorce under these circumstances. Mavis Hetherington reports some evidence that a child does best in the custody of the same-sex parent.[34] Joint physical custody in which children spend about equal amounts of time with both parents has become more popular.

A recent study following families for two years after divorce finds that children's adjustment is no better under voluntary joint custody than under single-parent custody.[35] There are indications that when joint custody is imposed by the courts, children's adjustment is worse.[36]

Custody arrangements may change as the child grows up. Sometimes when boys are adolescents they go to live with fathers. Teenagers, for example, are more likely to want to spend most of their time at one residence so that all their social life is centered there.

At all ages, it is most important that contact be ongoing, even if it is at irregular intervals as children mature, and that arrangements focus primarily on the children's needs while they are still in the process of developing.

Helping Children Cope with Divorce

Children mourn the loss of the family as they have known it. To do this, they need to understand, at whatever level they can, the reasons for the divorce and its permanence. While most children fantasize thta parents will be back together again, they

264

CHAPTER 9
Parenting at
Times of
Change and
Trauma

When children have continuing relationships with both parents, they can adjust well following the divorce process. Not only do children need relationships with both parents, but they also need to be able to relate to each parent separately as a parent.

must come to recognize that they are maintaining a fantasy that in all likelihood will not come true.[37]

They need to deal with their anger at the loss and give up any guilt they may feel. Children may overhear parents arguing about their behavior and feel they are the cause. As we have seen, noncompliance is more likely a result of marital distress than the cause. Even if it is the cause, parents committed to each other find ways to change the child's behavior rather than end the marriage.

As children deal with their feelings, they are able to turn their energy to their own lives and get on with them. Of concern is the possibility that children will become so bogged down in the divorce that it will prevent their making meaningful commitments to work or to loving relationships of their own. Wallerstein noted in her ten- and fifteen-year follow-ups what she termed a "sleeper" effect. Girls seemed to be doing well until it was time for them to become involved in satisfying love relationships. Then fears of intimacy and commitment, uncertainties about the kind of man they wished to be with, all surfaced. This long-term problem that girls experience may balance the behavior problems that boys manifest at the time of divorce and change our view that boys suffer more.

Parents help when they listen to children's feelings and when they foster children's activities at school and with peers. Parents can seek out situations where children can exercise their abilities and feel good about their accomplishments.

Parents also help children when they do not rely on them as confidants, allies, or major sources of support in their own handling of divorce. Children are then much freer to live their own lives.

What are the enduring effects of divorce on children? After two decades of research comparing the behavior of children in intact, single, and remarried families, Hetherington concludes:

> Depending on the characteristics of the child, particularly age and gender of the child, available resources, subsequent life experiences, and especially interpersonal relationships, children in the long run may be survivors, losers, or winners of their parents' divorce or remarriage.[38]

Establishing New Lives

Divorce is a time of upheaval. For some, divorce brings an end to unhappy family experiences; for everyone, it is the beginning of a period of difficulty, challenge, and a second chance to build a new life. Accompanying the second chance are the added responsibilities of children and the necessity to work, but it is an opportunity to create a more meaningful life with new relationships.

Between 70 and 80 percent of single parents remarry—slightly more men than women remarry and more parents under forty than over forty at the time of divorce remarry.[39] In our current society it is estimated that as many as 35 percent of children, 54 percent of women, and 60 percent of men live in second marriages.[40]

EFFECTS OF REMARRIAGE ON PARENTS

Remarriage provides many benefits to parents. First, it provides emotional closeness, intimacy, and sexual satisfaction for parents. In caring relationships, parents feel greater self-esteem, greater contentment and happiness. Second, parents have someone with whom they can share both the financial and the caregiving responsibilities. Judith Wallerstein[41] finds that many parents do not repeat mistakes of the first marriage again, and she and Joan Kelly[42] find that even though extra work and responsibility may follow remarriage, parents are energetic and happy because of the positive emotional experiences.

Remarriages also bring problems because there are more people to consider and few guidelines for how to integrate everyone: "Newly remarried parents report experiencing levels of both positive and negative stress twice that of nondivorced parents."[43] The divorce rate here is thought to be only slightly higher than in first marriages; but in second marriages, parents are quicker to decide that divorce is necessary.

EFFECTS OF REMARRIAGE ON CHILDREN

When two divorced parents postpone remarriage, they are more likely to continue sharing parenting equally. Noncustodial fathers are more likely to remain active and involved parents if they do not remarry. When parents do remarry, this means

266

CHAPTER 9
Parenting at
Times of
Change and
Trauma

children must share them with a widening circle of people—stepparents and step-siblings.

Custodial mothers' behavior changes after remarriage. Mothers report that they are less emotionally responsive to children and that communication between them is poorer. They are less consistent in the rules, supervise and monitor children less, and are more authoritarian in matters of discipline. So, it is not surprising that both boys and girls are more resistant and rebellious in the first two years of the remarriage. This is particularly true if the children are adolescents at the time.[44]

Boys seem to have less difficulty making the transition to the new family. Perhaps because many boys have had a poor relationship with a single mother, they respond to a stepfather who is warm and involved and spends time with them. So after the first two years, they tend to be accepting of such a stepfather.[45]

Girls, however, are not so accepting. Perhaps because they have had a very good relationship with the mother during the period of single parenting, they seem to resent the new husband as a rival for the mother's time and attention, which are now more limited. No matter how supportively the stepfather behaves, girls tend to remain aloof even after two years.[46]

When children live with custodial fathers and stepmothers, it is again girls who have greater difficulty. Frequent contact with their biological mothers seems to increase the difficulty, but this unusual finding may be the result of the mothers' having special problems that argued against their having custody. However, the longer girls live in such families, the more positive the relationship grows between the daughter and stepmother.[47]

Wallerstein and Kelly found that about one-quarter of children in stepfamilies, mostly those children ten and older, had needs that differed from those of their parents.[48] These children often felt ignored and isolated in the new family. Parents seemed to have less time for them, and they felt lonely. This was particularly true when the noncustodial father faded from the picture. Just as during the divorce process, the continuing involvement with both biological parents is an important factor in adapting well to the new stepfamily.

THE SPECIAL PROBLEMS OF STEPFAMILIES

What makes stepparenting even more difficult than parenting? After all, the biological parents of a newborn are not likely to have much more training for their new roles than does a stepparent—and they may have even less, if the stepparent has children of his own. Fitzhugh Dodson presents six reasons.[49] First, in families of biological parents and children, the parents' mistakes are overcome by longstanding emotional bonds. When a stepfamily is formed, such ties do not exist but are created over time. Second, these blended families are more complex than biological families and often include more people. When the wife and husband both have children, the family includes two sets of stepchildren. If each of the former spouses has remarried, the two sets of children will have two stepparents plus various stepbrothers and stepsisters, and perhaps half-brothers and half-sisters. The number of grandparents also increases. Each of these people from all of these families has needs and interests that must be considered.

Third, members of blended families may have deep feelings of jealousy and ambivalence. Because so many more people are involved and have to be consulted about decisions and the newly married parents want to devote time to their relationship, stepparents may have less time to give to individual children. Children may feel that the new marriage is depriving them of the parent. Parents must accept those feelings as realistic—there is less time for each child. Conversely, the parents may feel that the children are intruding on the marriage. Because living intimately with new people causes some stress, both parents and children may develop mixed feelings toward family members. A child's hostility may be directed at the new stepparent or stepsiblings, or at her or his own parent and brothers and sisters.

Fourth, both parents and children are haunted by the earlier marriage. Stepparents may feel insecure as they live with children who are constant proof that the spouse loved another person. Furthermore, the biological parent continues to have contact with the former spouse because of the children. When the stepparent enters the family, children must recognize that the other biological parent is no longer part of the family. If the absent biological parent has died, children may have created an idealized image of this parent that no flesh-and-blood person can measure up to. It is not surprising, then, that research suggests that it is harder for a stepparent to enter a family in which the absent parent has died.

Fifth, former spouses may use the children and their needs to attack the biological parent and the stepparent. One father and stepmother reported that the mother never bought the children clothes, and when the father did this in addition to the monthly payment, the mother did not wash or care for them. She let the children come for visits looking like beggars and told them the father did not care to provide enough money so she could buy clothes. Conversely, one mother reported that the father and stepmother, rather than providing money for clothes for the children, instead bought the children fancy clothes that were appropriate for the father and stepmother's lifestyle, but not for the children's needs at school and play.

Sixth, there are no clear guidelines for being a stepparent. There are few enough for biological parents, but the role of stepparent remains even more vague. The stepparent must create this role depending on his or her individual personality, the ages and sexes of the children, and their living arrangements. When a biological parent is dead or absent and children live with the stepparent, that stepparent has a larger role. When children live with the biological parent and come only for short visits, the stepparent has a more limited role. Whatever the circumstances, stepparents can create meaningful, caring relationships with children with time, patience, and interest.

Stepparents who are forewarned about the problems of stepparenting and who think and talk, in advance, about how to cope with these problems, can find their new roles rewarding and exciting.

NEW RELATIONSHIPS

Everything written about stepparenting attests to its complexity, its intensity, and its challenge. We do not often enough emphasize the rewards. Brenda Maddox sums up the strengths of the stepfamily and the joys of participation in it:

268

CHAPTER 9
Parenting at
Times of
Change and
Trauma

◆
BOX 9-2
EIGHT-STEP PROGRAM FOR STEPPING AHEAD

Step 1: Nurturing Couple Relationship

    a. Plan something you like away from home once a week

    b. Arrange 20 minutes of relaxed time alone each day

    c. Talk together about the running of the household at least 30 minutes each week

Step 2: Finding Personal Space and Time

    a. Take time to make a special "private" place for each adult and child in the house

    b. Each person takes at least 2 hours a week to do something special for that person—reading, TV, hobby, sport

Step 3: Nourishing Family Relationships

    a. Share with one another something you appreciate each day—perhaps at dinner, where each person shares, or in less formal settings

    b. Do not link discussion of problems with what is liked

Step 4: Maintaining Close Parent/Child Relationships

    a. Do something fun together for at least 20 minutes once or twice a week

    b. These times are given no matter what and do not depend on good behavior

Step 5: Developing Stepparent/Stepchild Relationship

    a. Do something fun together 15 or 20 minutes a week—if child only comes occasionally, make this a longer time, less often

    b. If child refuses, accept that and offer to do something at a later time

Step 6: Building Family Trust

    a. Schedule a family event once a month and give each person a chance to choose what to do

    b. Begin special traditions in your remarried family

    c. Do not always schedule events when nonresident children are there because resident children may believe they are less important

Step 7: Strengthen Stepfamily Ties with Regular Family Meeting

Step 8: Work with Child's Other Household

    a. Give adults in the other household positive feedback once a month

    b. Give positive message without expectation of return

Adapted from: Emily Visher, "The Stepping Ahead Program," in *Stepfamilies Stepping Ahead,*
ed. Mala Burt (Baltimore: Stepfamilies Press, 1989), pp. 57–89.

There are a few plain truths about stepparenthood that I learned writing this book [*The Half Parent*]. I was blind not to have recognized them when I got married. Stepfamilies can be happy, even happier than families in which there has never been more than one mother or father but it takes more work. The tensions of the stepfamily are special and real. A stepparent cannot be the same as a real parent. There are no new Mommies and new Daddies. Yet there are compensations for the strains. My own particular reward has been to help two young people who are nothing like me to be more like themselves and to watch the bond grow between the two sets of children. Stepfamilies in general do have positive advantages. When a stranger has to be taken into the family circle, when children have a parent who lives somewhere else, the family has an extra dimension. There is not that claustrophobia that led the anthropologist Dr. Edmund Leach to describe the ordinary family "with its narrow privacy and tawdry secrets" as "the source of all our discontents." The stepfamily is open and tough. It is not a bad place to live for those who can accept the uncomfortable fact that many of the tensions between stepparents and stepchildren will be inevitable as long as spouses are replaceable and parents are not.[50]

Though life in stepfamilies is tough, special pleasures come with seeing children biologically unrelated to you flourish and grow and in taking part in that growth. Such close and warm and sometimes conflictful relationships can serve as examples that people do not need to be either biologically related or romantically connected to produce profound and positive effects on each other's lives. The essential ingredients for both biological parents and stepparents are to feel comfortable with themselves and free of inflexible views of the other parents, so all can help children become "more like themselves." When adults relate to their own or other people's children in this way, there is no distinction between a biological parent and a stepparent.

WHEN A PARENT DIES

Much of what has been written about changes in the family at the time of divorce applies to the family that experiences the death of a parent: One parent assumes all the responsibility; there may be financial changes; and certainly there will be role changes as the surviving parent takes on both roles without relief.

Coping with the Death of a Parent

Earl Grollman writes, "One of the greatest crises in the life of a child is the death of a parent. Never again will the world be as secure a place as it was before. The familiar design of family life is completely disrupted. The child suffers not only the loss of the parent, but is deprived of the attention he needs at a time when he craves that extra reassurance that he is cared for."[51]

Telling Children How can one tell a child a parent has died? Just exactly what is said depends on the age of the child and the family's view of death. Very young children below the age of five have a limited conception of death and may consider it a reversible condition; one dies but comes back to life again at a later time. Between six and eight or nine, children recognize that death happens and is irreversible, but

270

CHAPTER 9
Parenting at
Times of
Change and
Trauma

they believe it happens mainly to other people. Because logical thinking is not yet established, children may associate unrelated events with death. One boy had heard that Abraham Lincoln was shot to death. When told of his grandfather's death, the boy asked, "Who shot him?" Sometimes a child associates death with the place that it occurred and refuses to go there. For example, a child who thinks that hospitals cause death may be afraid to go to a hospital. Children from three to nine can be both very cautious and emotional about death. As children move into the preadolescent years, they begin to understand death about as well as adults do.

In giving explanations about death, parents should be truthful and should phrase the information in a way that makes sense to the child. The child's questions will indicate the need for more information, which the parent can then give. It is not always possible to be both truthful and helpful. In telling her daughter about the death of the child's brother, one mother found herself telling a lie to help the child understand the reason for the death.[52] Robby had died of a chronic heart condition after years of illness and treatment. When the mother told her daughter that he had died because he was sick, her daughter answered that he had been sick many times, but he always got well. In desperation, the mother finally said Robby had died because he had been in pain, although, in fact, he had not been. The child could understand this. Years later she said that that statement, although false, was the only one that made sense to her. She was grateful that her mother, who was usually very honest, had told a lie. Remember, though, that in most situations it is possible to be both honest and helpful.

Because each situation is unique and needs to be handled with sensitivity, it is impossible to determine exactly what a parent should say. Grollman does list explanations to avoid. Do not describe heaven and tell the child that the dead parent is happy for eternity if you do not believe this yourself. A child will sense the discrepancy between what a parent says and how the parent feels and will become more confused. It is unwise to say that a parent has gone on a long journey, because the child may focus on the return or feel angry at being abandoned. One child, told that his mother had gone on a journey, cursed every time he heard her name, until he was told she had died and was shown her grave. When he understood his mother's absence, the boy was sad but no longer felt abandoned or rejected by her. It is also unwise to say that the parent died "because God loves good people and wants them in heaven." If goodness is rewarded with death, the child may shun good behavior or assume that those who live long lives are, in some undetectable way, bad. When death is equated with sleep, some children begin to fear sleep and are unwilling to go to bed.

Children's Reactions   Once the information is given, how can we expect the child will experience the grief? John Bowlby of the Tavistock Clinic in London describes three phases similar to those experienced by adults: (1) protest when the child cannot accept the death and tries to regain the parent, (2) pain and despair as the child gradually accepts the death, and (3) acceptance and hope that life goes on.[53]

After the child has been told of the parent's death, experts agree it is wise to include the child in as much of the funeral and formal mourning process as seems comfortable to parent and child. Experts agree that, unless children protest, they should view the body to understand that the parent is truly gone. This is not a rigid rule, however, and if either parent or child feels too upset, or if the body of the dead parent has been devastated by disease or injury, then this is not wise. During the mourning period surrounding the funeral and burial, family members may be surprised when young children, although devastated with grief, may scamper away to play, only to cry bitter tears an hour later. Parents should not hold back their own tears and they should not discourage children from crying. Tears are a healthy release of emotion, and many books on grief and mourning recognize the healing quality of tears. Also, do not encourage children to "Be brave!" or "Be a little man!" Rather, say realistically, "Yes, this is a hard time for you. Life is very sad now." Such statements acknowledge grief without minimizing it. Parents, however, should not insist on a display of grief.

Grollman lists a variety of children's reactions to death; many adults have similar responses.[54]

1. Denial: "I dreamt it! Mommy is coming home tomorrow." The child cannot accept the death because it is too painful.

2. Anxiety expressed in bodily symptoms: The child develops symptoms the dead parent had or symptoms expressing tension and sadness. "I can't eat," "I have stomach pains."

3. Hostile reactions: "Why did Mommy leave me like this?" These reactions may be very upsetting to the surviving parent.

4. Guilt reactions: "Daddy died because I didn't wash the dishes right. I killed him."

5. Hostile reactions: Anger at doctors, nurses, or the surviving parent, who did not do what they should have to save the parent.

6. Panic: "Who will love me now?" The child anticipates being abandoned by the remaining parent through death or remarriage.

7. Replacement: The child looks for a family member or friend who will move in and take the parent's place.

8. Taking on mannerisms or habits of deceased parent: The child tries to be like the dead person in interests, activities, and personal traits, as a way of replacing the person who had died.

9. Idealization: "No one can say anything against Mommy. She was wonderful."

Healthy mourning may include some or all of these reactions. Mourning becomes unhealthy when such reactions persist without stopping many months after the death and interfere with a return to satisfying activities. It is important to note that the reactions of some children and adults may be so marked during the grieving period that they hallucinate about the dead person. This is one of the few situations in life in which hallucinations can occur in the course of a healthy adaptation to a crisis.

A frequent reaction in a serious crisis, and one that has to be handled carefully, is guilt. Young children, particularly, often assume they are personally responsible for what happens even though they are in no way involved. The surviving parent

272

CHAPTER 9
Parenting at
Times of
Change and
Trauma

must be very alert to pick up on statements suggesting guilt and should introduce the possibility that the child feels guilt, even if the child has not mentioned it. For example: "Sometimes when a person dies, those close to her wonder if something they did was related to the death. I sometimes think, 'Would things have been different if I had called the doctor sooner?' But I know everything was done that could be done. Do you ever wonder or have thoughts like that?"

Gordon gives the example of a mother who actively listened as her three-year-old asked such painful questions as, "When is Daddy coming home?" and "Where did they put him?"[55] One night, two months after the father's death, the boy awoke and began crying and saying that his daddy was dead. As the mother reflected his upset, the boy was able to talk about how much he missed his father and wanted him back. The mother thought that after this expression of feeling her son seemed less anxious about the death. This three-and-a-half-year-old child asked many questions that were hard for the mother to answer. But she responded as well as she could, without criticism or complaint.

When you understand and accept your child's feelings and respond with empathy and love, you help the child move through the grief process. As memories of the parent are recalled and relived, the death gradually becomes real. At times the child may want to express unbearable pain or anger by striking at pillows or engaging in some physical activity. This can be encouraged. The child's individual reaction to death always should be respected. Grollman sums up the most helpful parental responses:

> Demonstrate in word and touch how much he [the child] is truly loved. A stable and emotionally mature adult who accepts the fact of death with courage and wisdom will bring the truth to the youngster that the business of life is life. Emotional energy formerly directed toward the absent person must now be directed toward the living. This does not mean wiping out the memories of the deceased. Even in death, the absent member can and should remain a constructive force in family life and be remembered in love without constant bitterness or morbidity.[56]

DEALING WITH ABUSE AND VIOLENCE

As we noted in Chapter 1, children in our society are at increased risk for a variety of traumatic experiences. Among them are sexual abuse, physical abuse, and community violence. Since all have the potential to cause lasting physical and/or psychological harm, parents must handle such situations with care.

Sexual Abuse

The National Center on Child Abuse and Neglect defines child sexual abuse as, "Contacts or interactions between a child and an adult when the child is being used for the sexual stimulation of the perpetrator or another person. Sexual abuse may also be committed by a person under the age of 18 when the person is either significantly older than the abuse victim or when the perpetrator is in a position of power or control over another child."[57]

Abusive experiences can range from intercourse to touching, to viewing an exhibitionist. Abuse can occur within the family (incest or intrafamilial) or outside the family (extrafamilial). Abuse need not involve an adult, but can occur when one child is significantly older (usually defined as five or more years) or has power over the child. While much of the research on abuse has focused on girls, we are increasingly aware of abuse perpetrated on boys.

Determining the incidence and prevalence of sexual abuse in childhood is extremely difficult, as the acts are disapproved and most are not reported. In a sample of 1,800 college students, one-third of both men and women reported experiencing sexual abuse in childhood. Only half the women and a tenth of the men reported the incident to an adult. Estimates are that one in four girls and one in six boys has experienced some form of sexual abuse by age eighteen.[58]

Diana Russell interviewed a random sample of San Francisco women concerning childhood sexual abuse.[59] Her definition of abuse was narrower than that of the National Commission, including only sexual contact and not exhibitionism. She found that, by the age of eighteen, 16 percent of women had been abused by a family member and 31 percent by a person outside the family. When both categories of abuse are combined, 38 percent of 930 women reported at least one experience of abuse by the age of 18, and 28 percent reported an experience by the age of 14. Only 2 percent of intrafamilial abuse and 6 percent of extrafamilial abuse were ever reported to police.

In intrafamilial abuse, 38 percent were members of the nuclear family (parents or siblings). The most frequent other relatives were uncles, male first cousins, and grandfathers. Of extrafamilial abusers, only 15 percent were strangers; 42 percent were acquaintances, and 43 percent were friends of the victim or family.

Karen Meiselman describes the family at high risk for incest as having one or more of the following components: (1) an alcoholic and violent father; (2) a mother who is away from home, physically ill, depressed, or passive; (3) an older daughter who has had the responsibility of a mother; (4) parents who have failed to establish a satisfying sexual relationship; (5) fathers and daughters who spend too much time alone with each other; (6) any condition, such as psychosis or below-average intelligence, that reduces an individual's capacity for self-control; (7) previous incest in a parent's family; and (8) a romantic attachment with unusual amounts of physical affection between adult and child.[60]

Diana Everstine and Louis Everstine report a variety of symptoms that sexually abused children may show: fear (the most common reaction), difficulty trusting others, anger and hostility, inappropriate sexual behavior, depression, guilt/shame, problems in school, physical complaints, sleeping and eating disturbances, regressive behavior, avoidant behavior, self-destructive behavior, runaway behavior in older children.[61]

The impact of the sexual abuse on the child depends very much on the child and the specific conditions of the abuse. David Finkelhor and Angela Browne conclude that substantial work is still needed for the effects of different types of child abuse to be understood.[62] They consider, however, the following types usually are more traumatic for children: (1) abuse by fathers and stepfathers, (2) force and/or intercourse, (3) male adult perpetrators (as opposed to adolescent perpetrators).

Finkelhor and Browne suggest that the most useful dimensions for understanding the impact and trauma of abuse are: (1) traumatic sexualization, (2) betrayal, (3) powerlessness, and (4) stigmatization.

"Traumatic sexualization is the process by which a child's sexuality is shaped in developmentally inappropriate and interpersonally dysfunctional ways."[63] A child is taught sexually inappropriate responses through rewards of attention and affection, or a child's anatomy is fetishized, or pain/fear are associated with sexual activity. A child who is too young to understand the sexual implications of the activity may be less traumatized.

Children may experience the pain of betrayal, the feeling that someone they trusted or depended on has harmed them. Feelings of betrayal may come from the abuse itself or from the way the family responds to the abuse. When the adult is a trusted family member, or when a family member knows and does not act to protect the child, the child feels betrayed. The family's response to disclosure can also trigger a sense of betrayal. If the focus of concern is on the perpetrator or on the consequences to other family members, or when the child is blamed or rejected, then the abused child may feel betrayed.

Children also feel powerless and helpless when someone has completely disregarded their feelings and forced them to do or experience unwanted activities. If the child is threatened or feels trapped, or is not believed or supported at the time of disclosure, then the child experiences powerlessness. If the child can act to end the abuse and is supported, these feelings are lessened.

When a child is stigmatized for the sexual activity, the experience of abuse then may become part of the child's self-image. Sometimes the abuser blames the child or makes the child feel shameful for the activity. Others in the family or community may blame the child or feel the child is now "damaged" goods because he or she has had such experiences. Keeping the abuse a secret may heighten the child's sense of shame. When a child learns that abuse happens to other children and children are not at fault, he or she may feel less stigmatized.

When a child is sexually traumatized, feels betrayed, powerless, and stigmatized, then the abuse is most traumatic for the child. All supports that lessen such feelings lessen the impact of the abuse.

Angela Browne and David Finkelhor review 26 studies to determine the impact of abuse on children and women.[64] Since few studies in the past included boys, less is known about the impact on boys. The impact of the experience can be looked at in terms of its initial impact and its long-term impact. The best study on the initial impact of abuse on children was carried out at Tufts Medical School where researchers used standardized measures of psychological functioning administered within six months of the event. They found 17 percent of four- to six-year-olds were considered to have clinically significant pathology—more than that found in the general population of children that age, but less than that found in children under psychiatric care. The amount of disturbance was greater in abused children between seven and thirteen—40 percent scored in a seriously disturbed range; few of the abused adolescents did. The most common reactions of children seven to thirteen are fear (40 percent in one study, 83 percent in another) and anger/hostility (45 to 50 percent in the Tufts' study showed such feelings). Shame/guilt, physical complaints, and behavior changes were the most common other reactions.

INTERVIEW
with Jill Waterman

Dr. Jill Waterman is adjunct professor of psychology at the University of California in Los Angeles. She is co-author of Sexual Abuse of Young Children: Evaluation and Treatment *and* Behind the Playground Wall: Sexual Abuse in Preschools.

Parents worry that their children may be sexually abused. Do you think there is a greater risk for children or is the increase in reports of child abuse a function of greater sensitivity to the problem?

I think the increase in the number of reports is due to the awareness of the problem and breaking the taboos about telling. There is more support for children who do tell. About ten years ago Diana Russell did a survey of adult women. Only six percent of those women who had been abused by someone outside the home and two percent of those abused by someone inside the home ever reported it. So in the past, the vast majority of sexual abuse in childhood went unreported.

Some parents fear sending their children to preschool because of the possibility of abuse there.

For preschoolers the likelihood of being abused in day care, including preschool, is less than the risk of being abused at home. Currently, 5.5 children per 10,000 are abused at day care whereas 8.9 per 10,000 are abused at home. To reduce the risk at preschool, parents need to be sure that (1) they are welcome at the school at any time (there should be no time when they are barred from the school); (2) the school is an open environment where all personnel are easily observed (avoid schools with isolated areas or classrooms); (3) they can observe and feel confident about the way the adults in the school interact with children.

In the past girls were more at risk for abuse than boys. Now, however, at the preschool level, the risk is about equal for boys and girls. Boys' experiences were underreported, perhaps because boys worried about being victims or being seen as wimpy, but now there is an increase in reporting of boys being abused. Still, in the latency and adolescent years, more girls than boys are abused.

There is more awareness now that women may also be molesters. When women are molesters, they are more likely to be part of a team with a man rather than be a solo molester—an aunt and an uncle, for example. Still the great majority of molesters are males.

There is a real increase in those identified as juvenile offenders or older children who molest other children. In almost all cases they are repeating abuse done to them by adults.

How can a parent minimize the likelihood that the child will be abused?

First, teach children that their bodies are their own and no one has the right to touch them. Children have a right to stop whoever does touch or tries to touch their bodies. Second, teach children the concept of private parts of the body—that area that is covered by a bathing suit—and teach the concept of good touch and bad touch. When parents are comfortable with affection and have children who feel comfortable with giving and receiving affection, then children have a sense of what feels good and is good touch. Those children are more likely

continued

276

CHAPTER 9
Parenting at
Times of
Change and
Trauma

INTERVIEW with Jill Waterman *continued*

to identify bad touches quickly. Third, help children identify an adult they can go to if bad touching occurs. Teach them which adults can help—teachers, principals, group leaders. Role-play with them how they would tell someone.

Who are children most likely to tell about abuse?

Whether the abuse is inside or outside the home, the child is most likely to tell the mother. An adolescent may tell a friend who then tells her mother who then reports. Most molesters never admit what they have done. Often there is no way to prove it because much abuse does not involve penile intercourse. Touching and oral sex may leave no evidence at all.

In the event a child does not tell a parent, what are signs by which a parent might tell whether a child has been sexually abused?

In most cases, there are no blatant behavioral indicators of sexual abuse. Rarely, the child may have genital bruising or bleeding. If the child begins sexual play with other children repeatedly, I would be concerned. If a child becomes preoccupied by masturbation to the extent of preferring to masturbate rather than interact with family or other children, I would also be concerned. More commonly, a sexually abused child may show signs of distress that could be due to a variety of causes, not just abuse. Some of these distress signs are: nightmares, sudden fears, withdrawal, or depression. However, these signs would alert a parent only to distress in a child, not necessarily sexual abuse.

If a child has been abused, how can parents act to minimize the impact of the event on the child?

The most important factor is how the parents respond. When parents believe the child and act to protect the child from the molester and get therapy and help for the child, then the child is best able to handle what has happened. When parents do not believe the child or support the perpetrator, the child does least well. This may seem counter to what you would expect, but mothers are more likely to believe a daughter if she is reporting the biological father than if she reports a stepfather. The explanation may be that the mothers have a greater stake in a relationship with a boyfriend or stepfather—it is a newer relationship than with the biological father, and are therefore more likely to support the newer man in their life.

A mother may not support her daughter because she has been abused herself and has not yet resolved that issue in her mind. To support her daughter she would have to face what has happened to herself as well. Or the mother may have blocked from her mind the experience of her own abuse with only occasional flashbacks. Since these trigger a lot of internal conflict, she needs to deny her child's abuse.

The worst outcomes for abused children occur when a close family member has abused the child so the child has difficulty developing trust in other relationships. There is mixed evidence concerning how much the severity (frequency, length of time, types of acts) of the abuse affects the outcome for the child. Sometimes, the severity seems to have great impact, sometimes not. Still, the response of the parents is the most important determiner.

Research shows that sexual abuse of a child is a family trauma and has a major impact on parents. In a study of children abused outside the home, many couples found it difficult to have sex in the first nine months. The parents got images of the child in a sexual situation and could not continue. A small but significant number of couples developed alcohol and drug problems, and a significant number of parents reported they were depressed. They had a decreased trust in all societal institutions—the law, religions, schools, police, media. They lost their belief in a fair, just world.

In another follow-up study we did of children, 46 percent of abused children had scores in the clinical range on behavior problem checklists at the time of the disclosure. Five years later, only 17 percent had scores in that range. Remember, though, that only 2½ percent of a representative sample score in that range. All the abused children received treatment, but many still experienced internal distress several years later. These children are more likely to have symptoms of anxiety and somatic concerns than acting out, aggressive problems.

What kinds of therapy are most helpful for children who have been abused?

Well, everyone in the family needs some form of individual therapy. Each member needs someone to talk to, to explain what the experience is like for them and to express their feelings. Groups are helpful for children of all ages, even for little children. Linda Damon of the San Fernando Valley Child Guidance Clinic developed parallel groups for mothers and children in therapy. Some therapists work with the mothers on a series of topics, and other therapists work with the children on the same topics. The therapists talk to the mothers about what to expect from the children on that week's topic. For example, on the topic that it is okay to say "No," the therapists tell mothers that this week they might expect the children to say a lot of "Nos." Moms, instead of getting angry at them, should help children see the situations in which it is appropriate to say, "No," and those in which, like going to bed, you have to do it anyhow.

Groups for all ages of children over four have the advantage of reducing children's feelings of being weird. They don't feel like "damaged goods" because they see other children who have gone through the same thing and are doing well. So the group helps to take the stigma away from being abused.

Family therapy has a place down the road, I think, only when the perpetrator admits what he has done and the family has made a decision to stay together. Then you really need family therapy.

How long does it take for the child to come to terms with the abuse?

It depends on what happened as well as the age of the child. Some people argue that if the child is really young, he or she does not really understand the meaning of the events and is less likely to experience negative outcomes. The research data is mixed about the age at which children are most or least affected. As children get older—in mid-latency—they may feel they are responsible for what happened, that it is their fault. Adolescents may feel guilty as well. Treatment helps them to deal with these feelings.

Depression is the most common long-term feeling reported by adults abused as children. Even where the abuse was defined very broadly, those who experience it report more depression. The likelihood for victimization in adulthood is also greater. Rape and serious physical abuse were more common in women who reported childhood sexual abuse. These women are also less likely to trust others and more likely to develop substance abuse problems.

In understanding the impact of abuse, it is difficult to disentangle the effects of emotional neglect and conflict in the family prior to the abuse, the effects of the abuse itself, and the effects of family's and society's reactions to disclosure. Browne and Finkelhor comment that people tend to see the impact of abuse in childhood as less serious if symptoms appear only at the time of the abuse and disappear in adulthood, but adult rape is seen as painful and traumatic even if the effects do not persist to old age. The fact is that pain and suffering, even if limited to the time of the experience, are still traumatic and of serious import.

We have looked at the prevalence of sexual abuse and its effects on children. What can be done?

What should be done when abuse has occurred and has been reported? First, the security of the child should immediately be arranged. Second, the child should have the opportunity to vent feelings of anger, fear, guilt, and shame about the act with a therapist. Although some children may be initially hesitant to talk, the experienced therapist can encourage the child to talk and can offer reassurances that help the child deal with the feelings created by abuse. Play therapy can also help the child deal with feelings of betrayal and powerlessness. In play, the child regains feelings of personal power and confidence. Support of these feelings helps the child rebuild trust. The child learns to control his or her world again, and healing and growth proceed.[65]

Groups for children help them to deal with the experience of abuse, and participation in such a group may do even more than a therapist to help the child talk and handle what has occurred and what she is feeling. When a young girl hears that others have had a similar experience, when she realizes that she has not been singled out for some inexplicable reason and hears that others also were victims, it may be easier for her to accept this interpretation of herself.

Family therapy helps all members cope with their reactions to the abuse. Parents and siblings may have strong feelings of sadness, anger, sometimes guilt. They, too, need help in coming to terms with what has happened.

Physical Child Abuse

There is no commonly agreed upon definition of physical child abuse. In defining an act as abusive, consideration is given to the nature of the act, its intensity and frequency, its impact on the victim, the intent of the perpetrator, community standards. Some acts are so clearly abusive that everyone would label them as such—e.g., physical discipline that resulted in a broken bone or severe injury—and some acts are clearly not abusive—e.g., talking to a child calmly and respectfully about a misdeed. Between the two extremes, people cross a line and label an act abusive. Some define violence as any physical act that the recipient does not want; others consider extreme yelling and pushing abusive; others, any spanking; still others, any spanking that results in a bruise or injury. Robert Emery suggests that the same standards of violence that apply to acts between strangers in public be used to define violence in the home with family members.[66]

David Hamburg states that each year approximately 1,200 to 5,000 children die of physical child abuse, and up to a million children are severely abused by parents.[67]

Child abuse rose 10 percent from 1990 to 1991. Seventy-nine percent of the children are under five, and 54 percent are one or under.[68]

Despite the difficulty in defining abuse, research has focused on perpetrators of physical abuse, its effects on children, and treatment when it happens.

Abusive parents are often under a high level of stress, with little support from others. Financial pressure is often present and parents are frequently young. Comparing poverty areas with high and low abuse rates, however, reveals that abuse is more likely to occur in those poor areas in which parents are experiencing much change with little help from family or neighbors.[69] There is much moving in and out of the home and the neighborhood; childcare is not easily available; families have little recreation time together.

Abused children are likely to have some qualities that make caregiving difficult. Such children may be highly active, have some physical problems, or be especially demanding. These children are unable to satisfy the high expectations parents have of them. Instead of being able to give to the parents, they demand more than the average child.[70]

Jay Belsky has put forward an ecological model of maltreatment that includes attention to (1) current family relationships, (2) characteristics of the child, (3) social influences like poverty and unemployment, (4) characteristics of the social community itself, and (5) general cultural values accepting of physical violence.[71] While some abusing parents have themselves experienced abuse as children, still the vast majority of people who have been abused are not abusers themselves.

Initially, social scientists thought a parent had to have a serious psychological problem to abuse a child. Researchers, however, have found no "abusive personality." Rather, *situational factors* like poverty, alcoholism or drug use, and *cognitive factors* like lack of childrearing knowledge, inappropriate demands of children, and lack of tolerance for children's behavior like crying lead to abuse.[72]

The accepted view now is that family aggression is learned and reinforced.[73] At times the reinforcement is clear—a spouse or child stops what is disapproved when physically punished. At other times, the reinforcement is not clear—when a crying child is hit, the crying usually continues. Psychologists speculate that some adults become so upset and angry as a result of any negative, aversive experience that they lose control, overreact in a physical way, and abuse the child. The task with such individuals is to teach them ways to inhibit their angry response or to direct the anger in other ways. The behavior of such hyperactive, poorly controlled individuals is extremely difficult to predict because a wide variety of events—in fact, any negative event—can trigger such an emotional response.

As a group, physically abused children show difficulties in many areas—increased aggressiveness, depression, greater difficulties in peer relationships, decreased cognitive performance, poor social judgment, lack of empathy. When physical abuse occurs early in life, the child's whole model of interpersonal relationships is disrupted, and this may account for the variety of symptoms observed.[74]

Robert Emry states that it is not clear whether the many symptoms come from the abuse itself or from family interactions leading up to the abuse.[75] He points to the fact (described in Chapter 3) that angry episodes, even those not involving the child, distress the child. Children's distress motivates them to get involved in parental

280

CHAPTER 9
Parenting at
Times of
Change and
Trauma

conflicts in order to end them. Child misbehavior distracts parents from their quarrels, and so children are likely to repeat misbehavior to stop conflicts even if they become victims themselves.

Just as with sexual child abuse, there are two forms of intervention—(1) providing security and safety for the child, and (2) getting psychological services. There is some indication that at least with spousal abuse, having the perpetrator arrested prevents recurrence more effectively than mediating the dispute informally or having the perpetrator leave the property for 48 hours. In child abuse cases, children deserve at least as much physical protection as they would get if a stranger attacked them. Richard Gelles commented recently that he believes some parents are so abusive on a single occasion that family reunification should never be considered.[76]

Therapeutic interventions are directed at both the victim and the perpetrator. Physically abused children need the same kind of therapy directed at letting them vent and understand their feelings as sexually abused children. Physically abused children need ways to express their own anger appropriately. They must learn that one can feel strong and powerful without being aggressive, hurtful, or cruel to others. Play therapy provides such help.

Interventions are also directed toward the abusing parent. When appropriate, perpetrators are referred to abuse treatment programs. Parenting skills are taught and parents learn other ways to manage anger. Sometimes home visitors are sent to teach and monitor parenting skills.

Community Violence

We have emphasized that in any form, exposure to unresolved anger and aggression is hurtful to children, whether they witness it or experience it. Children meet aggression not only in their personal lives. Our society has become an increasingly violent place with traumatic events occurring in the lives of many children. While a large proportion of violence occurs in lower socioeconomic areas, violence also occurs in restaurants, schools, and community activities. No children are immune from the effects of community violence. Even if violence does not touch a child personally, a child may be acquainted with someone who has had a family member die or experience harm.

Children exposed to community violence develop many of the symptoms of children who have been physically or sexually abused. They have difficulty sleeping, remembering, and concentrating, and they exhibit anxious attachment to parents (not wanting them to leave), aggressive play, severe limitation of activities and exploration, and regressive behavior.[77] Lenore Terr describes the denial and numbing children use to block out frightening reality.[78] There are also feelings of grief and loss when a significant loved one dies as a result of violence.

All these reactions make it hard for children to develop intellectually and socially in appropriate ways. They view the violence as expectable and develop a sense of futurelessness or fatalism about their lives. Plans are not important because one may be crippled, or die.

What does it take to survive such experiences? James Garbarino and his coworkers summarize the parents' role, and its dangers

If parents, or other significant caregivers, can sustain a strong attachment to their children, can maintain a positive sense of self, and can have access to basic resources, children will manage, although it may be at great cost to the psychic and physical welfare of those parents, who may be "used up" caring for their children.[79]

Several factors influence how children cope with the experience of violence.[80] Characteristics of the child—intelligence, self-confidence, self-esteem, sociability, easy-goingness, affectionateness, good nature—all increase coping. Such children demand little, yet relate positively and happily to others, and are likely to receive support. Environmental factors include the presence of at least one stable emotional relationship with a caregiver who serves as a model of coping, social relationships outside the family with relatives and family friends. The community can give support in many ways—friends, neighbors, teachers, and church people can provide support and encourage the competence of parents and children.

The school is a major refuge for children who confront difficult experiences. After the family, the school is the most important social institution in children's lives. Many resilient children find school activities a source of self-esteem and competence. They make friends with and get support from schoolmates and from teachers who take an interest in them.

In *Children in Danger*, James Garbarino and his co-workers describe the schools as a major unit of intervention to counteract the community violence in children's lives. He outlines a school-based intervention program in which teachers form close emotional attachments with students to promote their development. The researchers believe that these relationships serve as the basis for learning in all areas. Children take in the values, behavior, attitudes of a significant other person. Teachers and programs provide structure and control for students.

Day care centers can be included in programs to reach children below school age. An attachment teacher is assigned to every six or seven students, and a consistent substitute attachment and subgroup are assigned to each child. Children have an unvarying placement in small groups. Formal teaching programs stimulate the child's curiosity and level of development.

The organized school environment with familiar teachers and programs provides security and predictability in a changing world. Teachers are specially trained to work with these children, taking courses in child development and in understanding children's reactions to stress, violence, and loss. Teachers remain available to students who exhibit modulating emotions and deal with them.

Therapy can help children cope with their emotional reactions to trauma.[81] All major personality shifts resulting from trauma require treatment. Such personality changes occur in almost all physically and sexually abused children as well as those who experience some form of trauma.

Parents should arrange psychiatric treatment for a child as soon after a trauma as possible. If several children are involved, participants can be seen in a mini-marathon group session with a highly trained professional. When each member shares his or her experiences, the possibility of anyone's denying the situation (thus prolonging traumatization) are lessened. Schools serve as the familiar places appropriate for such group sessions. If a family has been traumatized, then the family can be treated as a unit. However, family therapy is not recommended when a parent has physically or sexually abused a child as the child is not really free to express the anger felt in the presence of the abuser.

Behavioral therapy is useful for children who have developed fears as a result of the trauma. Deconditioning is useful as an addition to individual treatment designed to deal with the emotional reactions, but behavioral therapy by itself is limited.

The sooner after the trauma a person gets treatment, the better. However, treatment is useful any time a person recognizes that he or she is suffering the effects of a trauma, even if it can not reverse all the effects of the experience.

Parents want to know what to do to prevent violence and trauma in their children's lives. Nothing can completely prevent violence, but children who are street smart are more likely to be able to protect themselves.

THE CHALLENGE MODEL

Therapy can help children deal with the effects of traumatic events and troubled family situations. Concern has arisen, however, that some forms of intervention so emphasize the pain and damaging effects of these difficulties that children and adults believe they are doomed to impoverished lives as a result of the trauma.

Psychiatrist Steven Wolin and psychologist Sybil Wolin term this the "Damage Model" of human development as it focuses on the harmful effects and damage produced by traumas; therapy in this model can only help individuals to understand the damage and how it occurred. Drawing on clinical insights and on the research of such people as Emmy Werner and Ruth Smith (see the interview with Emmy Werner in Chapter 3), the Wolins have developed a Challenge Model of development.[82] While adversity brings stress, harm, and vulnerability to the individual, the Wolins believe it also stimulates the person to branch out, to take measures to protect themselves and find other sources of strength that promote development. So, the individual experiences pain, but develops resiliencies that can limit the pain and promote accomplishment and satisfaction.

In their book, *The Resilient Self,* the Wolins identify seven resiliencies that help individuals rebound in the face of difficult circumstances:

Insight: The habit of asking tough questions and giving honest answers
Independence: Drawing boundaries between yourself and troubled parents; keeping emotional distance while satisfying the demands of conscience
Relationships: Intimate and fulfilling ties to other people that balance a mature regard for your own needs with empathy and the capacity to give to someone else
Initiative: Taking charge of problems; exerting control; a taste for stretching and testing yourself in demanding tasks
Creativity: Imposing order, beauty, and purpose on the chaos of your troubling experiences and painful feelings
Humor: Finding the comic in the tragic
Morality: An informed conscience that extends your wish for a good personal life to all of humankind.[83]

Their book describes the many ways resiliencies grow in childhood, adolescence and adulthood and offers an optimistic approach which encourages survivors of

This family's home was distroyed by the 1989 Loma Prieta earthquake in Northern California. Family or community traumas can affect all members of a family as well as their relationships with people outside the family.

traumas and difficult childhood experiences to review their lives in terms of the strengths they have developed. As a result, people experience pride in their ability to overcome hardships and confidence in their capacity to make further changes as needed. In focusing on pain and the sources of pain in the past, the Damage Model tends to discourage individuals because the past can not be changed and the pain undone. The Challenge Model asserts that life can be satisfying and productive even with the scars of the past.

Keeping Children Safe

As children spend more time away from home and parents, going to and from school or to friends' homes, parents become concerned about their safety. They want to help children be independent and safe in the world, yet they do not want to frighten them and make them afraid of strangers and new experiences. Grace Hechinger, an educational consultant, has interviewed police officials, school safety officials, individuals involved in neighborhood safety programs, and people who have been victims of crime and assaults.[84] From this research she has organized information to help parents prepare their children to be safe as they spend more time on their own.

Fostering children's awareness of danger, caution, and preparedness for unsafe situations does not mean making children live in fear. Children can learn that even though most people in the world are good and helpful and most situations are safe,

284

CHAPTER 9
Parenting at
Times of
Change and
Trauma

◆

BOX 9-3
SOME "WHAT IF" QUESTIONS FOR YOUNG CHILDREN

Parents ask children what they would do if the following situations happened. If children give the wrong answers, parents can calmly tell them more practical alternative responses.

1. We are separated in a shopping center, in the movies, at the beach?
2. You are lost in a department store, in the park, at a parade?
3. A stranger offered you candy or presents to leave the playground?
4. A stranger wanted you to get into his car?
5. A stranger started fussing with your clothing?
6. Your friends wanted to play with matches?
7. Someone you did not know asked your name and phone number?

Grace Hechinger, *How to Raise a Street-Smart Child* (New York: Ballantine, 1984), p. 59.

---

some small number of people and experiences are not, and everyone must learn to protect himself or herself from dangers that arise. It is helpful if parents can put this knowledge in some kind of perspective for children. Life has always involved danger of some sort, and many objects or experiences that are positive also have dangerous aspects. Cars are useful—they get us to work, to stores, to hospitals. We need them, but they can be dangerous if they hit us while we are crossing the street. The answer lies not in eliminating cars, because before we had cars, there were dangers from horses and horse-drawn vehicles. The solution is to take precautions to minimize dangers and enjoy the benefits.

Families need to develop a set of instructions for major dangerous situations, to be discussed and revised as necessary. A one-time discussion is not enough; periodically, parents must review instructions with children. Children can learn these safety rules gradually—for example, at what hours and where they may go alone, what to do if bothered by someone on the street or in a store, even when parents are nearby. Learning safety rules becomes as natural as learning to brush teeth. The emphasis in teaching is that children are learning skills to master the environment, to make them competent and independent.

Although parents worry that talk of possible fearful events will damage the child, the risks that come with ignorance are much greater. Parents can begin with simple discussions of traffic safety—where, when, how to cross the street. They can move from that topic to others of importance for the child. Television may start a discussion. Hechinger suggests a game, "What If?" Parents ask a variety of questions and give children chances to develop solutions to difficult situations (Box 9-3). Parents should not be upset if their children's initial answers are impractical because children can then learn more reasonable responses.

Parents should have clear safety rules on: (1) behavior for a fire at home, (2) traffic behavior, whether on foot or on a bicycle, (3) boundaries within which the child can

◆

BOX 9-4
STREET SAFETY RULES

1. Walk to and from school with a group of friends.
2. Don't linger in the schoolyard when the rest of your friends have left.
3. Know your school route.
4. If you have any problem after school, go back to find a teacher when there is no one at home.
5. Walk in the middle of the sidewalk; avoid bushes and doorways.
6. Know your neighborhood. Remember safe places to go if you need immediate help—storekeepers, gas stations, a nearby friend, local fire and police stations, the post office.
7. Know the location of public phone booths in your area.
8. Never flash money, bus passes, transistor radios, cameras, or other possessions. Don't tell your classmates you don't know well about the things you have in your locker or at home.

Grace Hechinger, *How to Raise a Street-Smart Child* (New York: Ballantine, 1984), p. 68.

---

come and go freely and outside of which an adult or parent must be present, (4) behavior in public with strangers, (5) behavior at home if strangers telephone or come to the house, (6) behavior when a victim or witness of muggings by peers or adults, (7) behavior when sexual misconduct occurs (Box 9-4).

If children are victimized—a bike is stolen, money taken, a stranger approaches them—parents' reactions can help speed a healing process. When parents listen to children's reactions and help children take any possible action, such as notifying the police, they help children cope. When parents' responses are exaggerated—"This is horrible!"—or detached—"I cannot deal with this"—children get no help in coping with their feelings. If they cannot talk about how they feel, they will find it difficult to work out their feelings. Active listening, sending simple I-messages—"If that happened to me, I'd be really upset"—give children a chance to say what the experience meant to them. Sometimes children need to describe the event several times. Each time more details emerge as well as more feeling. Gradually, after the incident, children will regain self-confidence. If a child's eating, sleeping, or play habits change or there are marked changes in schoolwork or personality that continue for some time, professional help should be sought.

An important step in promoting children's safety is working with people in the community. Developing community awareness and community programs gives everyone a positive feeling of working together that does much to banish fear. Promoting public safety programs with school and police officials, organizing block-watch programs to help children in the neighborhood are useful steps. In Block-Parent Programs, one house in the neighborhood is designated as a house where children may come if they need help or reassurance when no one is home.

286

CHAPTER 9
Parenting at
Times of
Change and
Trauma

Family members grow stronger when they face problems and work together to deal with them. Sense of community is strengthened when families and agencies cooperate to make the environment safe for children.

MAJOR POINTS OF CHAPTER 9

When parents are unhappily married,

- fathers are frequently more negative with children
- parents view children as being difficult and interfering with their lives
- children frequently develop behavior problems
- children have a rise in hormones reflecting stress, are less able to deal with their feelings, and play with friends less enthusiastically
- many boys are impulsive and poorly controlled years before the divorce

Society has begun to make accommodations to the needs of divorcing families by:

- making it easier for both parents to stay involved with children
- providing court mediation services to aid families in making decisions in the child's best interests
- making it easier for mothers to get financial support from ex-husbands

Children's emotional reactions at the time of divorce:

- include feelings common to children regardless of age, like sadness, anger, fear, confusion, sometimes relief
- do not predict long-term adjustment to divorce

Children's emotional reactions also vary by age:

- preschoolers feel overwhelmed, abandoned, and worried they caused it; they need parents' acceptance of feelings and support
- children five to seven are vulnerable, try to deny intense feelings of sadness and grief; but divorce dominates their thoughts, and they need to talk about feelings
- children nine and older may feel responsible for helping parents and may get benefit from counseling

Parents' emotional reactions:

- are intense and include many of the feelings children feel—anger, sadness, anxiety, depression
- can interfere with their providing care and support for children

Factors affecting adjustment to divorce include:

- amount of conflict among family members
- availability of both parents to children
- nature of relationships in the family
- responsibilities family members take
- defensibility of divorce from child's point of view

Factors that protect children at time of divorce include:

- child's age, sex, intelligence
- child's easygoing temperament
- manageable amounts of stress
- appropriate supports in help from grandparents, other relatives
- child's getting positive feelings from own achievements

Parenting tasks include establishing:

- effective channels of communication
- stable family structure in each parent's home
- reasonable visiting arrangements
- support for children in coping with divorce
- meaningful lives so everyone can get on with life

In telling children of divorce, it is best if parents:

- do it together
- do it before a parent moves out
- tell all the children together
- refuse to ask the child to take sides
- refuse to burden child with either parents' negative view of
  the other

Establishing reasonable visiting arrangements involve:

- working out fair, practical timesharing schedule
- making effort to live up to agreements
- being flexible in trading times
- preparing child calmly to stay with other parent
- not doing business with other parent at time of transfer
- encouraging child to work out problems directly with other parent

When parents remarry, they:

- experience many emotional benefits like closeness, intimacy, and sexual satisfaction
- do not necessarily repeat the mistakes of the first marriage
- experience stress as they integrate everyone into a new family

When parents remarry, children:

- receive less attention from parents, have less communication with them
- have less consistent rules at home
- differ in their reactions with girls' having more and longer lasting difficulty than boys

Stepparenting is more difficult than biological parenting because:

- long-standing emotional ties do not exist among family members
- the family is more complex with more people
- members of the stepfamily may have deep feelings of jealousy and ambivalence
- members have memories of other marriage
- former spouses may use children to attack parent and stepparent
- there are no clear guidelines for stepparenting

When a parent dies, children go through stages of grief:

- protest against death
- pain and despair as child accepts death
- acceptance

Parent's role in helping children is to:

- be truthful in telling child about parent's death
- include child as active participant in funeral/memorial
- offer child many opportunities to express feelings
- accept child's feelings
- provide model of adult who grieves and goes on with life

Sexual child abuse:

- is estimated to be experienced by one in four girls and one in six boys
- affects children in different ways depending on the actual acts
- appears most traumatic when it involves a father or stepfather, involves force or intercourse, is carried out by a male adult as opposed to an adolescent

- results in a wide variety of symptoms in the victims of such abuse
- can result in traumatic sexualization, feelings of betrayal, powerlessness, and stigmatization
- victims require protection from the abuser
- victims can profit from individual, group, and family therapy

Physical child abuse:

- is difficult to define precisely
- often results from a variety of factors including characteristics of the family, the child, and the social system
- is learned in the context of the family
- results in a wide variety of symptoms in the victims
- requires therapy both for the victim and the perpetrator
- may be so severe on a single occasion that the child should not live with that person again

Community violence:

- affects all children but most particularly those in lower socioeconomic areas
- results in many symptoms that hinder children's development
- requires interventions at the community level to decrease the violence and provide support for children who experience such violence
- victims can be helped with individual, group, and family therapy

Challenge Model:

- focuses on strengths people develop to cope with troubled family experiences or other traumas
- identifies seven resiliencies of insight, independence, relationships, insight, creativity, humor, and morality
- presents an optimistic view of people's capacity to create satisfying lives despite the scars of painful experiences
- encourages people to take pride in their strengths and achievements in the face of adversity

Keeping kids safe:

- requires that parents teach children of potential dangers and ways to minimize them
- requires that parents teach children coping techniques for dangerous situations
- means that parents and society as a whole have to work to provide a safer community for everyone

290

CHAPTER 9
Parenting at
Times of
Change and
Trauma

EXERCISES

1. If your friend's parents divorced when he/she was a small child and now your friend fears intimacy and commitment, what could you do to help him/her be less fearful? What advice could you offer your friend to lessen such fears? In a class discussion, share your ideas of what to advise the friend.

2. Imagine that your married brother or sister or friend came to you and said he or she was getting a divorce and wanted help in making arrangements so his/her eight-year-old daughter and six-year-old son would experience the fewest negative effects. What guidelines would you give your relative or friend?

3. Pair off with a classmate, preferably of the same sex. Imagine one of you is eight and the other fifteen years old. You have just learned that one of your parents has married your partner's parent; you are now stepbrothers or stepsisters. How would you feel now that you are going to be living intimately with each other—perhaps sharing a room, having your time with your biological parent reduced so the parent could spend time with this stranger, having the amount of money available to you dependent on needs of these new people? Would being older or younger make a difference in the reactions? Describe what your parents could do to ease the adjustment process.

4. Imagine your close friend told you that her four-year-old daughter had just showed her how a male relative of twenty-five had touched her genitals. The daughter said he told her it was just a secret between them, but she decided she should tell her mother because they did not keep secrets from each other. How would you advise your friend to help her daughter after she has reported the event to authorities? What would you advise her to do to help herself?

5. Divide into groups of four and work as a unit. Describe general information you would choose to include in an eight-session parenting course for men and women who have physically abused their children. Share your group's results with the entire class. What elements are common to all programs? What elements were chosen by only one or two groups? Combine the best information from all the groups and come up with one eight-session program. If possible, compare it with a program offered in your area by Parental Stress or another agency providing help for such parents.

ADDITIONAL READINGS

Adler, Robert E. *Sharing the Children*. Bethesda: Adler & Adler, 1988.

Ahrons, Constance R., and Rodgers, Roy H. *Divorced Families*. New York: W. W. Norton, 1987.

Gardner, Richard. *The Parents' Book about Divorce.* New York: Bantam, 1979.

Wallerstein, Judith S., and Kelly, Joan B. *Surviving the Breakup.* New York: Basic Books, 1980.

Wallerstein, Judith S., and Blakeslee, Sandra. *Second Chances.* New York: Ticknor & Fields, 1989.

Notes

1. United States Bureau of the Census, *Statistical Abstract of the United States: 1991.* 111th ed. (Washington, D.C.: U.S. Government Printing Office, 1991).

2. E. Mavis Hetherington and Kathleen A. Camara, "Families in Transition: The Process of Dissolution and Reconstruction," in *A Review of Child Development Research,* vol. 7, ed. Ross D. Parke (Chicago: University of Chicago Press, 1984), pp. 398–439.

3. John M. Gottman and Lynn Fainsilber Katz, "Effects of Marital Discord on Young Children's Peer Interaction and Health," *Developmental Psychology* 25 (1989): 373–381.

4. M. Ann Easterbrooks and Robert N. Emde, "Marital and Parent-Child Relationships: The Role of Affect in the Family," in *Relationships within Families: Mutual Influences,* ed. Robert A. Hinde and Joan Stevenson-Hinde (Oxford: Clarendon Press, 1988), pp. 83–103.

5. Gene H. Brody, Anthony D. Pellegrini, and Irving E. Sigel, "Marital Quality and Mother-Child and Father-Child Interactions with School-Aged Children," *Developmental Psychology* 22 (1986): 291–296.

6. Jeanne H. Block, Jack Block, and Andrea Morrison, "Parental Disagreement on Child-rearing Orientations and Gender-related Personality Correlates in Children," *Child Development* 52 (1981): 965–974.

7. Brian E. Vaughn, Jeanne H. Block, and Jack Block, "Parental Agreement on Child Rearing during Early Childhood and the Psychological Characteristics of Adolescents," *Child Development* 59 (1988): 1020–1033.

8. Jeanne H. Block, Jack Block, and Per F. Gjerde, "The Personality of Children prior to Divorce: A Prospective Study," *Child Development* 57 (1986): 827–840.

9. Hetherington and Camara, "Families in Transition."

10. U.S. Bureau of the Census: *Statistical Abstract: 1991.*

11. Judith S. Wallerstein and Joan B. Kelly, *Surviving the Breakup* (New York: Basic Books, 1980).

12. Ibid., p. 66.

13. Joan B. Kelly and Judith S. Wallerstein, "Brief Interventions with Children in Divorcing Families," *American Journal of Orthopsychiatry* 47 (1977): 23–39.

14. Wallerstein and Kelly, *Surviving the Breakup.*

15. Judith S. Wallerstein and Sandra Blakeslee, *Second Chances* (New York: Ticknor & Fields, 1989).

16. M. Janice Hogan, Cheryl Buehler, and Beatrice Robinson, "Single Parenting: Transitioning Alone," in *Stress and the Family,* vol. 1, *Coping with Normative Transitions,* ed. Hamilton I. McCubbin and Charles R. Figley (New York: Bruner/Mazel, 1983), pp. 116–132.

17. Hetherington and Camara, "Families in Transition."

18. Wallerstein and Kelly, *Surviving the Breakup.*

19. Hetherington and Camara, "Families in Transition."

20. Ibid.

21. Hetherington and Camara, "Families in Transition"; Wallerstein and Kelly, *Surviving the Breakup.*

22. Ibid.

23. Ibid.

24. Wallerstein and Kelly, *Surviving the Breakup.*

25. E. Mavis Hetherington, "Coping with Family Transitions: Winners, Losers, and Survivors," *Child Development* 60 (1989): 1–14.

26. Wallerstein and Blakeslee, *Second Chances.*

27. Carol E. MacKinnon, "An Observational Investigation of Sibling Interactions in Married and Divorced Families," *Developmental Psychology* 25 (1989): 36–44.

28. Wallerstein and Blakeslee, *Second Chances,* p. 110.

29. Wallerstein and Blakeslee, *Second Chances.*

30. Ibid., p. 286.

31. Ibid.

32. Wallerstein and Blakeslee, *Second Chances*, p. 287.

33. Frances L. Ilg and Louise Bates Ames, *Child Behavior* (New York: Harper & Row, 1955), pp. 334–335.

34. Hetherington, "Coping with Family Transitions."

35. Marsha Klein, Jeanne M. Tschann, Janet R. Johnston, and Judith S. Wallerstein, "Children's Adjustment in Joint and Sole Physical Custody Families," *Developmental Psychology* 25 (1989): 430–438.

36. Wallerstein and Blakeslee, *Second Chances*.

37. Ibid.

38. Hetherington, "Coping with Family Transitions," p. 13.

39. Wallerstein and Blakeslee, *Second Chances*.

40. Monica McGoldrick and Betty Carter, "Forming a Remarried Family," in *The Changing Family Life Cycle* 2d ed., ed. Betty Carter and Monica McGoldrick (New York: Gardner Press, 1988), pp. 399–409.

41. Wallerstein and Blakeslee, *Second Chances*.

42. Wallerstein and Kelly, *Surviving the Breakup*.

43. E. Mavis Hetherington, Margaret Stanley Hagan, and Edward R. Anderson, "Marital Transitions: A Child's Perspective," *American Psychologist* 44 (1989): 309.

44. Hetherington, Hagan, and Anderson, "Marital Transitions."

45. Ibid.

46. Ibid.

47. W. Glenn Clingempeel and Sion Segal, "Stepparent-Stepchild Relationships and the Psychological Adjustment of Children in Stepmother and Stepfather Families," *Child Development* 57 (1986): 474–484.

48. Wallerstein and Kelly, *Surviving the Breakup*.

49. Fitzhugh Dodson, *How to Discipline with Love* (New York: Rawson Associates, 1977).

50. Brenda Maddox, *The Half-Parent* (New York: New American Library, 1975), p. 167.

51. Earl Grollman, "Prologue," in *Explaining Death to Children*, ed. Earl A. Grollman (Boston: Beacon Press, 1967), p. 15.

52. Harriet Schiff Sarnoff, *The Bereaved Parent* (New York: Penguin, 1978).

53. John Bowlby, "Childhood Mourning and Its Implications for Psychiatry," *American Journal of Psychiatry* 118 (1961): 481–498.

54. Grollman, "Prologue."

55. Thomas Gordon with Judith Gordon Sands, *P.E.T. in Action* (New York: Bantam, 1978).

56. Grollman, "Prologue," p. 27.

57. Sally Zierler, "Studies Confirm Long-Term Consequences of Childhood Sexual Abuse," *The Brown University Child and Adolescent Behavior Newsletter 8*, November 1992, p. 3.

58. Ibid.

59. Diana E. H. Russell, "The Incidence and Prevalence of Intrafamilial and Extrafamilial Sexual Abuse of Female Children," in *Handbook on Sexual Abuse of Children*, ed. Leonore E. Auerbach Walker (New York: Springer, 1988), pp. 19–36.

60. Karin C. Meiselman, *Resolving the Trauma of Incest* (San Francisco: Jossey-Bass, 1990).

61. Diana Everstine and Louis Everstine, *Sexual Trauma in Children and Adolescents* (New York: Bruner/Mazel, 1989).

62. David Finkelhor and Angela Browne, "Assessing the Long-Term Impact of Child Sexual Abuse: A Review and Conceptualization," in *Handbook on Sexual Abuse of Children*, ed. Walker, p. 62.

63. Ibid., pp. 62–63.

64. Angela Browne and David Finkelhor, "Impact of Child Sexual Abuse: A Review of Research," *Psychological Bulletin* 99 (1986): 66–77.

65. Leonore E. A. Walker and Mary Ann Bolkovatz, "Play Therapy with Children Who Have Experienced Sexual Assault," in *Handbook on Sexual Abuse of Children*, ed. Walker, pp. 249–269.

66. Robert E. Emery, "Family Violence," *American Psychologist* 44 (1989): 321–328.

67. David A. Hamburg, *Today's Children* (New York: Times Books, 1992).

68. "Reports of Increase in Child Abuse Deaths," *The Brown University Child and Adolescent Behavior Newsletter 8*, August 1992, p. 4.

69. James Garbarino and Deborah Sherman, "High-Risk Neighborhoods and High-Risk Families: The Human Ecology of Child Maltreatment," *Child Development* 51 (1980): 188–198.

70. Ross D. Parke and Ronald G. Slaby, "The Development of Aggression," in *Handbook of Child Psychology*, eds. Paul H. Mussen and E. Mavis Hetherington, vol. 4, *Socialization, Personality and Social Development*, 4th ed. (New York: John Wiley, 1983), pp. 547–641.

71. Jay Belsky, "Child Maltreatment: An Ecological Integration," *American Psychologist* 35 (1980): 320–335.

72. Emery, "Family Violence."

73. Ibid.

74. Ibid.

75. Ibid.
76. Richard J. Gelles, "Abandon Reunification Goal for Abusive Families and Replace with Child Protection," *The Brown University Child and Adolescent Behavior Newsletter 8,* June 1992, p. 1.
77. James Garbarino et al., *Children in Danger* (San Francisco: Jossey-Bass, 1992).
78. Lenore Terr, *Too Scared To Cry* (New York: Harper & Row, 1990).
79. Garbarino et al., *Children in Danger.*
80. Ibid.
81. Terr, *Too Scared To Cry.*
82. Steven J. Wolin and Sybil Wolin, *The Resilient Self* (New York: Villard Books, 1993).
83. Ibid., pp. 5–6.
84. Grace Hechinger, *How to Raise a Street-Smart Child* (New York: Ballantine Books, 1984).

SUPPORTS FOR PARENTS
AND CHILDREN

C H A P T E R   10

We have looked at different aspects of parenting—understanding children's needs, forming relationships with them, setting limits, responding to problem behaviors, stimulating positive growth. Focus so far has been on what parents can do to accomplish these formidable tasks. The parent-child relationship is nested in a social context which can hinder or help parents as they strive to achieve their childrearing goals. Certainly we have seen that parents have many demands on them—demands from children, demands from spouses and other family members, demands from work. How then can society help parents do their job? What might we in the United States learn from the Europeans who offer far more help to parents via governmental support?

What support is available for parents in the United States? What family rituals and traditions help foster the child's sense of belonging? What individuals within and outside the extended family contribute to a child's development and a parent's sense of well-being? What community resources are currently available and what kinds of programs are proposed to help children develop and to assist parents with their task? Parents can take comfort in knowing they don't have to do the job alone. Taking advantage of supports for parents and children can make the job easier, the parenting more successful.

SOCIAL SUPPORTS

Social supports are conceived as those people, activities, organizations, and environmental resources that provide *emotional, instrumental,* and *informational* benefits to children and parents. *Emotional benefits* include feeling cared for, valued, encouraged, understood, validated as a person. *Instrumental benefits* include help with certain tasks like housework, specific aid like money or childcare. *Informational benefits* include advice about childcare, referral to resources, specific guidance about tasks.[1]

Children and adults have different roles and activities in life; nevertheless, the same general categories of support are useful to both. Supports are divided into those within the family and those outside the family. Further, we can talk about *people* who are supports—relatives, nonrelatives like neighbors, friends; *activities* that are supports—hobbies, recreations; *organizations*—work, churches, government. Finally, we talk about the *environment,* a composite of people, activities, and organizations such as neighborhoods, that are supportive.

What will be most supportive to individuals may vary with the age and the stage of life experience. For example, as we shall see, activities with adult relatives are most supportive to young children, but adult nonrelatives may be most supportive to adolescents as they move away from the family. Single mothers who work may get most support from nonrelatives at the workplace; nonemployed single mothers may get most support from relatives.[2]

We like to think that *all* parents and children have equal access to social supports and that only personal initiative and effort are required to get support. Yet research suggests this is not so.[3] There are constraints on access to social supports. People who have education, employment, income, and congenial neighborhoods receive more supports.[4] Approximately 40 to 50 percent of nonrelative support is affected by these variables. More than any other variable, education determines the number of social contacts a person has and the depth and breadth of the social support network. Education appears to increase confidence and skills in social interaction as well as opportunities for meeting new people.[5] Income provides money for activities as well as for a stable lifestyle in a safe neighborhood. When people live in lower socioeconomic areas that are not safe, they socialize with neighbors less often. So, schooling, income, and neighborhood are interacting factors that influence the amount and kind of support people get.

Though these social constraints exist, people are "biologically wired" for social relationships and seek others out.[6] The exact nature of the social networks is related to cultural, ethnic, socioeconomic, and gender-related factors.[7] Still supportive social ties operate generally to improve children's social-emotional functioning[8] and their academic work,[9] and to increase parents' self-confidence and well-being and to enhance their perceptions of their children.[10] Let us look more specifically at the different kinds of support available.

SUPPORTS WITHIN THE FAMILY

The family environment is the most immediate source of support for both children and parents. So let us look first at people within the family, then at family rituals.

Supportive Family Members

Siblings We have talked about the positive relationships that can develop between siblings. The older sibling may be a model for the younger one, stimulating more advanced play and verbalization, increasing the younger child's empathy and understanding of others. The younger child gives the older a chance to be a protective caregiver. So parents have allies in siblings.

Emmy Werner and Ruth Smith[11] point to the strong role siblings play in helping children overcome the effects of family instability and turmoil. Many of the resilient adults in their study mentioned sibling relationships as an important positive feature of their childhood years. The emotional closeness and shared activities with siblings helped compensate for other difficulties.

Even in well-ordered families, close sibling relationships begun in childhood are maintained and valued in middle and old age even when there is little contact. Sibling relationships appear to gain their power by giving people a sense of intimacy, closeness, and security. "Contact with siblings in late adulthood provides not necessarily deep intimacy, but a sense of belonging, security, attachment to a family."[12]

Grandparents As psychologists turn their attention to important people outside the child's nuclear family, they focus attention on grandparents. In a review article, Barbara Tinsley and Ross Parke summarize the limited work available and state that grandparents exert influence in direct and indirect ways.[13] They influence grandchildren directly when they serve as caregivers, playmates, and family historians who pass on information that solidifies a sense of generational continuity. They are a direct influence when they act as mentors to their grandchildren and when they negotiate between parent and child. They influence grandchildren indirectly when they provide both psychological and material support to parents, who then have more resources for parenting.

More information on the role of grandparents in minority families is available because these families are more often extended ones. For example, in 1984, 31 percent of Afro-American children lived in extended families with one or both parents.[14] The extended family often includes one or both grandparents. Grandmothers are resources that help families nurture and care for children in a less structured, more spontaneous way than is possible when there are only two generations. Grandparents' role depends on whether one or both parents live in the home. Grandmothers are less involved in parenting when both parents are present.[15]

There is limited current information on what percent of grandparents are involved with grandchildren and in what capacity they relate to them when they do not all live together. Research does suggest that family members in the home and in close proximity are positive forces in a variety of situations—at times of added parental responsibility with a sick child, at times of family transitions, at times of sudden individual crises for parents. No research as yet indicates that grandparents per se, as opposed to any positive support, are crucial. One can imagine, however, that there is something very special about a grandparent who combines the roles of playmate, caregiver, emotional confidant, family historian, and mentor for a child.

Other Relatives Other relatives include aunts, uncles, cousins, in-laws. Support from these relatives appears especially helpful to parents in their parenting role. Relatives babysit, give advice, provide financial help, and are available for emotional support. Such support increases parents' positive view of their children and their view of themselves as parents. As noted, such support also related to children's improved school performance.[16]

INTERVIEW
with Steven Wolin

Dr. Steven Wolin is clinical professor of psychiatry at George Washington University and a researcher at the Center for Family Research. He has published several articles on the importance of rituals, and with his wife, psychologist Dr. Sybil Wolin, is co-author of The Resilient Self.

I have read about your belief in the importance of rituals in family life and their protective value when families experience chronic problems. How did you get on to the importance of rituals?

I am a psychiatrist, and I have a long-standing interest in research on families. I was a clinical associate at St. Elizabeth's hospital on a unit studying alcoholism back in 1970. A colleague and I were examining interactions in marriages in which one partner was an alcoholic. We looked at how family processes were altered by alcoholism. I was mainly interested in ways family life was destroyed by alcohol and was, at that time, what I now call "a damage model" thinker.

I got a grant from the Institute on Alcohol Abuse and Alcoholism to study the transmission of alcoholism across generations. I decided to use family rituals as the variable for study. I have always been interested in culture as a powerful factor in family life with family members expressing their shared beliefs through their rituals. I learned a lot about rituals from anthropology and hired a young anthropologist, Linda Bennett, who became my co-investigator. I had the hypothesis that those families whose regular rituals were destroyed by alcohol would have a greater likelihood of transmitting alcoholism to their children.

We compared those families who had two generations of alcoholics (transmitters) with families who only had a parent who was an alcoholic (non-transmitters). The severity of the alcoholic parent was the same in both kinds of families in terms of years of drinking, hospitalizations, etc. We then systematically compared the most important rituals in these two kinds of families. We looked at holiday celebrations, traditions (like family vacations or visits to extended family members), and routines (like dinner-time rituals, greeting rituals, parties). Sure enough, we demonstrated that when alcoholism destroyed the family rituals, then transmission of alcoholism to a child occurred more frequently.

At this point I became more interested in those families that did *not* transmit alcoholism and, for the first time in my life, asked a strength-based question: "How did you do this thing that succeeded? How did you prevent transmission from occurring?" And families were in fact doing something very deliberate. Non-transmitters were protecting their cherished, non-alcoholic rituals. For example, they made certain that Christmas was protected from the alcohol abuse of a parent. They determined that certain of their routines persisted in the face of trouble, and they kept their healthy holidays alive. Non-transmitter families actually were working to keep their families healthy, in spite of the chronic illness process of the alcoholism.

The second project focused on couples from this type of troubled background. How did they negotiate the construction of rituals of the new generation? Since they come from such troubled families, we know that many of the rituals of the family were destroyed or taken over

continued

INTERVIEW with Steven Wolin   *continued*

by the alcohol or substance abuse. How do they decide what is the family of heritage in the new generation?

We selected a group of 68 couples, all of whom had one alcoholic parent. The couples were around 30 years of age and often had young children themselves. We did extensive interviews regarding the ritual process in the couple as well as the rituals in each of the families they had come from. Coders did not know whether the adult children became alcoholics themselves. In half the couples, alcoholism was transmitted to the second generation, and in half not. Sure enough, once again a clear pattern emerged. When rituals were protected in the family of origin and carefully selected in the present generation, alcoholism was not passed on to the children. Couples used a process we came to call deliberateness—the careful planning and carrying out of plans for ritual maintenance and rejection.

I became more interested in the notion that individuals acted in a resilient way to prevent themselves from repeating the past even if they are at risk. When you look at the children-of-alcoholics literature, it is not all so bleak. Sometimes people worry a lot and are afraid they are going to repeat the past. In fact, they often do not. Most children of alcoholics do not become alcoholics.

We are now describing resilience in general, and the ways individuals and couples remain strong in the face of an at-risk past situation. We did a third project that looked at little children; we examined families in which there was an alcoholic parent or grandparent in the previous generation and the adult children who may or may not have gotten into trouble. We looked at their children. Those couples who acted most deliberately, who used this careful planning and carrying out of plans, and who were most conscious and aware of what the task was in the new generation, did the best, and their children did the best. They are grandchildren of alcoholics, and they are often doing well. Like Emmy Werner's sample of resilient children, they have mastered the problems of the previous generation.

While relatives are support sources, they can also add stress when their comments to parents are negative and critical. Still, despite the stress from criticism and advice, parents do better with relatives' support.[17] Single mothers appear less likely to have the support of relatives but can increase such support when they feel more confident and reach out for help.[18]

For children, extended family members are like grandparents who convey a sense that the child is special, important, and capable. Joint activities with relatives—like washing cars or gardening—predicted better performance in school. Outings with adult male relatives (but not with nonrelative adults) were especially helpful for boys living in single-mother homes.[19]

Family Rituals

Steven Wolin and Linda Bennett[20] describe the positive force of family rituals in everyday life and in the long-term development of children. They divide rituals into three categories—(1) **family celebrations** (like Thanksgiving, Christmas), (2) **family**

What helps couples act in a deliberate way?

They practice healthy styles of communication. They are aware of the task in front of them. A lot of couples talk about knowing exactly what to do in the new generation because it is exactly the opposite of what happened when they were kids. Healthy families will have flexibility; they can be chaotic for a while without damaging a child. But the family that is fragmented and has problems really needs healthy rituals.

Would you say the dinner rituals are most important?

We studied dinner and holiday rituals because they are so different. We found dinner rituals disappear first in the alcoholic family. We felt that holiday rituals were the most important because when they went, the family seemed to be in the most trouble. Those families who could not carry out Thanksgiving and Christmas had their identity as a family destroyed by the alcohol. Perhaps mother was so drunk she could not come down for dinner or she lit the tree on fire or there was no money left for gifts. Although holidays are less frequent, they have positive importance and are the more highly valued rituals because everyone in the culture celebrates them. Family traditions like birthdays are more individual; the family defines itself by the way it does the tradition—how much importance it gives to birthdays or vacations.

Our current work is taking kids who are partially resilient and strengthening those clusters of strengths in them. We want to focus on their strengths, and apply the strengths to the areas that are not so strong. For example, if a child happens to use initiative and becomes a good problem solver, but has poor peer relationships, then the child has to learn to apply those same skills to relationship-building that he uses to solve problems.

Similarly, children have to learn to do things differently from their parents. They have to see that what their parents did is not necessarily what they have to do. By recruiting "parent substitutes," children can help themselves have new kinds of relationships so they avoid the past. They will see the various hurdles in front of them as challenges and use initiative to continue to work at their problems.

traditions (like vacations, birthday activities), and (3) **patterned family interactions** (like dinner, bedtime). They believe these rituals provide a sense of rhythm and continuity to life that increases children's feelings of security and their capacity to communicate with adults.

Rituals provide stability by insuring predictability in family life—no matter what else happens, the family eats dinner together, decorates a Christmas tree, has special foods on birthdays. Rituals also provide stability by linking the present family with the past and the future. Families carry on certain traditions from grandparents, and children grow up planning to carry out the same activities with their children.

The drama and excitement of rituals and traditions encourage communication among family members. Family members are more affectionate and more involved with each other at celebrations and holidays. In addition, rituals reduce the gap between parents and children because everyone engages in the rituals as equals—everyone in the family hangs up Christmas stockings and decorates the tree, everyone gets stuffed at Thanksgiving meals.

Family rituals like dinners and holiday celebrations give members feelings of security.

Bennett and Wolin[21] and their co-workers find that children who grow up in alcoholic families which nevertheless maintain their family celebrations and rituals are less likely to become alcoholics themselves than children who grow up with an equally severe alcoholic parent who does not maintain traditions. The rituals serve as protective, positive forces at times of stress, giving children added feelings of security and closeness to others.

SUPPORT OUTSIDE THE FAMILY

Support outside the family includes people like friends, co-workers, as well as organizations like churches, community organizations, and the government.

People Outside the Family

A variety of individuals are available as supports to children and to parents. Often supportive individuals for children, like teachers, serve as supports for parents as well, conveying information and guidelines on caring for children. Parents' supports indirectly affect children when they help parents feel better about themselves and encourage a more positive view of the children.

Teachers Almost all of us can recall a teacher who played a positive role in our school years. The teacher may have identified a special talent or skill and encouraged its development or directed us to an area of study that proved important or motivated us to achieve our very best.

Systematic research also has identified teachers as major sources of support to children and to parents. Werner and Smith write,

> During adolescence, a caring teacher was an important protective factor for boys and girls who succeeded against the odds. This teacher served not only as an academic instructor but also as a confidant and an important role model with whom a student could identify.[22]

Even teachers of very young children have lasting positive impact on children. Innovative research documented the long-lasting impact of an acknowledged effective first-grade teacher.[23] Not only were the achievement scores of her students higher in first and second grades, but their achievement as adults (25 years later) was rated much higher than that of students from other classes involved in the study. Statistical analysis revealed that the teacher's influence was stronger than any other background factor—including father's occupation, family economic situation, number of children—in predicting adult status of her students. Pupils described the attention, kindness, and confidence she gave to them. "Her secret of success was summarized by one of her colleagues this way: 'How did she teach? With a lot of love!'"[24]

School organization and atmosphere have a positive impact on children too. Michael Rutter and his co-workers identified schools that served as protective factors against the development of delinquency.[25] These schools had structured classrooms, emphasized homework, preparation, and competence, and encouraged students to take responsibility for their behavior.

Other Nonrelatives This group includes neighbors, co-workers at the workplace, people in the community. Parents and children are most likely to reach out to neighbors when neighborhoods are safe. Neighbors can and do provide many of the benefits of relatives for families who have little support from relatives. They babysit, give advice, lend or provide material resources. Mothers who work are especially likely to reach out to co-workers as additional sources of support.

While children get more support from adult relatives, adolescents appear to get support from nonrelatives. Adolescent males who interact with adult nonrelatives generally perform better in school.[26]

Programs Outside the Family

Organizations and agencies provide formal and informal support for parents and children.

Parenting Programs As family members are no longer as easily available for advice, parents are seeking support from other parents. They form or join parenting groups often organized around a particular theme—parents of infants and toddlers, parents of adolescents, parents of hyperactive children, parents of children with learning disabilities—or continue parent groups begun during pregnancy.

Carolyn Cowan and Philip Cowan found that parenting groups for mothers and fathers, beginning in the last trimester of the pregnancy, provide ongoing support for parents as they create new families.[27] In their study, six groups of four couples each met for six months. Couples discussed the stresses of adjusting to parenthood and found reassurance in learning that others have similar problems. The parents discussed what reduces stress and what produces well-being and closeness between parents. In following the families over a five-year period, the Cowans found that all the couples who were in the parenting groups were still together when the child was three years old whereas 15 percent of couples who had not been in groups were divorced. When children were five years old, the divorce rate was the same for the two groups of parents.

The Cowans were impressed that the six-month groups had an effect for three years. They have begun a new intervention study offering parent groups at the time of the child's entrance into elementary school. They hope to increase parents' coping skills and their satisfaction in their marriages.

Organized parenting programs are available to parents as well. These usually last from six to twelve weeks and consist of two-hour sessions geared toward giving parents new skills and new approaches to parenting. Thomas Gordon has organized Parent Effectiveness Training sessions lasting from three to six months. Bruce Cedar and Ronald Levant,[28] reviewing studies of PET groups, found that only 26 of the 60 studies reviewed had adequate research design. A meta-analysis of the 26 studies reveals that PET has a large effect on parents' knowledge of the course material, and a small to moderate effect on parenting attitudes and behavior toward children and on children's self-esteem.

A review of 21 studies of Dreikurs' method and the STEP (Systematic Training for Effective Parenting) program reveals that parents' attitudes change.[29] They are less strict and less intrusive with children; they listen more and encourage children more; they are more supportive and trusting of the child. There was slight evidence that children's behavior improved as well.

Anthony Graziano and David Diament reviewed 155 studies of parent behavioral training to determine its effectiveness in helping parents.[30] They found that such training had its greatest success in decreasing problem behaviors such as enuresis, bedtime fears, infant crying, and noncompliant behavior. Parents learn specific management skills. Active modeling and parents' role-playing increases the effects of parents' training.

Gerald Patterson and Carla Narrett point out that the benefits of behavioral training for parents are greatest with young, oppositional children and are limited with older, more severely disturbed adolescents.[31] Even when oppositional children improve at home, the benefits of the training do not always generalize to the school setting where children continue to have difficulty. Patterson and Narrett consider children's behavioral change to be the most important marker for parent effectiveness. Parents report overall improvement at home even when the child's specific behavior has not changed.

The parenting courses just described can last from six weeks to several months. A recent study found, however, that even a brief intervention with parents can be useful to parents and baby.[32] First-time parents attending childbirth classes were

Providing quality programs
for young children
strengthens families.

routinely assigned to one of two groups. During pregnancy, one group received four-session behavioral training in helping their newborn develop healthy sleep patterns. The control group had equal discussion time with instructors but no behavioral training. When infants were six to nine weeks, investigators collected six measures of sleep patterns over several weeks. Infants of trained parents had longer sleep episodes, fewer night awakenings, fewer night feedings. Trained parents experienced less difficulty with their babies than nontrained parents who reported a greater number of hassles caring for their infants. Trained parents felt more competent and confident in managing babies' sleep patterns.

So, informal parent groups can be helpful in providing support to new parents. Specific training in parenting skills has dual advantages in promoting positive child behaviors and increasing parental competence and confidence. Training can be short and focused on a single important area, and still have broad effects on parents.

Work Place Supports for Parents

As noted in Chapter 8, work places can ease the pressures of parenting.[33] First, they can make it possible for parents to take time to be with children in the early years of children's lives. Extended parental leave at birth or adoption of a child can help parents bond with the child and provide sensitive caregiving that enhances the child's development. A combination of paid/unpaid leave can be used. At present, many mothers get disability at the time of the birth and that covers only the first six weeks of the baby's life. Recent national legislation permits the mother to take up to 12 weeks of unpaid leave. Employer-sponsored day care enables working parents to be with their children at the work place. This can be especially useful when mothers are nursing infants. With older infants, such care cuts down on the time that parents take getting to and from the baby-sitter's. It also permits parents to spend time with children during the day at breaks and at lunchtime.

Having flexible work schedules (flextime or four-day work weeks) or permitting parents to work at home when possible are ways that businesses can make it easier for parents to incorporate work into their lives as parents. Having supervisors who are sensitive to the demands of family life helps parents.

GOVERNMENTAL SUPPORTS FOR PARENTS

Edward Zigler and Mary Lang[34] emphasize that government supports are not available for all U.S. families as they are in Europe and many parts of the world. All families in Canada, for example, receive a family allowance based on the number of children under eighteen in the family. France provides many services for parents. For example, a young child allowance begins in the fifth month of pregnancy and lasts for nine months. An additional tax-free allowance is available when a family has subsequent children provided the mother gets prenatal care and the infant gets regular medical care. Low income families receive additional aid. France also provides low-cost day care for infants and toddlers. Child caregivers are trained and licensed and included in the social security system.[35]

In the United States, one must be sick, handicapped, or poor to qualify for the services available through local, state, and federal agencies. David Hamburg describes the variety of programs available for children and parents in *Today's Children*. Initially, many programs are available in conjunction with the health-care system. Some private and public hospitals, for example, offer prenatal care, supplementary nutrition for women and children, and home visits by nurses to demonstrate well-baby care and healthy parenting practices. Nurses can identify high-risk parents who need more services either because of a baby's medical condition or other difficulties in the family.

States provide income to single mothers and to families who demonstrate financial need. The amounts vary from state to state. Even with the largest state payment, a family receives less than the amount considered adequate to exceed the poverty level.

Several intervention programs have targeted the period of infancy. For example, federal funds instituted the Parent Child Development Centers to involve the family from the birth of the child to age three. This program encompassed several features: it included information for parents on home management and child-rearing techniques; it included preschool education for children; it connected families with services for health care, nutrition, employment. It provided an array of needed services for low-income families of different ethnic backgrounds. Assessments of children and parents over an eight-year period showed that children were more advanced in intellectual and social behavior, and parents and children were more positive toward each other, more affectionate, and better able to work out problems. This program ended because of lack of funds.

Federal funds support early childhood education for low-income children through Head Start programs that offer health care, nutrition, and programs for parents. Only a small percentage of children eligible for the program are able to participate because funds are limited.

As children approach early adolescence, government programs exist for discouraging early pregnancies and increasing school attendance and academic performance.

Summarizing programs necessary to promote children's healthy growth, David Hamburg writes,

> The approach taken here has been to recommend fostering early interventions that offer support similar to that of the traditional family. The pivotal institutions are schools, churches, community organizations, the media, and the health-care systems. A developmental sequence of interventions starts with prenatal care and goes to preventive pediatric care, parent education, social supports for young families, high-quality child care, preschool education, a constructive transition to elementary school, a reformulated middle school. Beyond that lies the possibility of further growth in high school in the transition to work and to higher education, drawing on the principles elucidated here.[37]

Hamburg believes coordinated health- and growth-fostering programs might well be cheaper to finance than all the programs geared to problems once they have occurred. For example, universal prenatal care is most likely cheaper than variable care followed by compromised babies who require expensive neonatal care and prolonged programs of compensatory care.

Edward Zigler's comprehensive plan for childcare in this country illustrates the kind of coordinated program Hamburg envisions. Zigler's plan can be implemented in modules or as separate programs, depending on the needs and resources of the individual community. Zigler, the first director of the Office of Child Development and Chief of the Children's Bureau from 1970 to 1972, outlines seven basic principles for childcare in this country:[38]

1. *all* children must have access to high-quality childcare when needed

2. the caregiver is the single most important determinant of the quality of the childcare—caregivers must have adequate training and supervision so they perceive and attend to the child's needs

3. childcare must meet the child's needs in all areas of development—health, nutrition, education—so children's physical, social, emotional, and intellectual growth flourishes

4. childcare should be well integrated with other social systems like health and education and must involve parents as active participants

5. childcare programs must offer options to the great variety of children and families in society—parents should have a role in evaluating different programs

6. quality childcare requires a permanent commitment of resources to children and families

7. a childcare system must be responsive to larger social demands as these change—e.g., the childcare system must support healthy growth that permits individuals to contribute to society

Zigler centers his program at local schools because the school system is a permanent part of our social fabric, and schools are dispersed throughout communities. As a result, they can be sensitive to local preferences, and parents need not go far to get services. All proposed programs are optional for parents; no one is required to participate.

He proposes that after-school and vacation care for the many unsupervised children six to eleven be available at school sites. Parents pay, on a sliding scale, for the hiring of additional personnel who use the school facilities before and after regular school hours. A second proposed program at the school site would provide year-round, all-day care for preschoolers from three to five years of age. This program would promote all aspects of the child's development. Parents again would pay a sliding-scale fee, and local private and public agencies could contribute to its funding.

Zigler suggests that schools serve as a central network for neighborhood family day care providers who care for infants and toddlers in that area. Schools can provide caregiver training and supervision, and make the providers part of the larger community network. Schools would also serve as a resource and referral system directing parents to needed community services and could be the sites of such services as well.

Schools would also provide a base for outreach services to parents beginning in the last trimester of pregnancy. Parent education programs can be offered as well as screening programs to be sure parents and children get the care they require.

Zigler has outlined funding for such programs as well. He also believes it may be cheaper to provide preventive services than to pay for problems that develop when families do not have the supports they need.

Community Programs Here we detail programs that serve as examples of what communities can do to provide support to parents and children.

Communities provide opportunities for all youth to develop skills and abilities in athletic, recreational, artistic programs. Communities also provide support for parents in parenting classes, special programs that meet parents' needs—after-school day care, summer day-long programs for children when parents work.

Community leaders serve as mentors for youth. They are role models in intellectual, social, or athletic activities or they participate in activities as in Big Brother or Big Sister programs. In these activities, they can serve to model for parents ways to relate to children.

David Hamburg describes a national survey of programs for parents of adolescents.[39] A major thrust of helping parents is to connect them with other parents of adolescents in groups so parents can be of mutual help in solving problems with their teenagers. Many of these parent programs are operated through voluntary community organizations such as the Parent-Teacher Associations or Four-H Clubs.

INTERVIEW
with Elaine Blechman

Dr. Elaine Blechman is professor of psychology at the University of Colorado. Her clinical research focuses on training families in communication and problem-solving and treating socially and academically high-risk children. She is the author of numerous articles and chapters as well as Solving Child Behavior Problems At Home And At School.*

I read your book, Emotions and the Family, *and your chapter, "Effective Communication: Enabling Multiproblem Families to Change." Many people believe that teaching communication techniques has limited use when families have realistic problems like lack of money, lack of work. And yet, you found it worked well in multiproblem families.*

You have to be careful about what "it" is. My work has been evolving and has broadened to include various ways of working with multiproblem families and most recently families with seriously aggressive children. Currently I believe the most effective way is to begin with the children at school when they are quite young and identifiable by teachers and parents as having problems and creating difficulties for adults.

I introduce a school-based early intervention that connects the home and the school—a home-note system described in *Solving Child Behavior Problems At Home And At School*. The teacher sends home a good-news note when the child's achievement in a targeted subject meets or exceeds the child's goal for that subject. The note reinforces the child for good behavior and achievement in the class *and* at the same time hooks up with parents who ordinarily only get very negative messages from the school.

After the home-note system is in place, I introduce the school-based component—peer-communication training. The most aggressive children in the class are paired with the most competent children who are not aggressive and have good communication skills. The children are matched for sex and ethnic background. The aggressive children learn the skills of the most competent children and break into the social network of competent children.

When the child has been involved in the home-note system and the peer component, then is the prime time to start to intervene with the family.

Now, it used to be thought that all you needed to do was go in and teach some skills to these families and show them how to use them, then the child's behavior would change. Behavioral parent-training began with the parents of autistic children. These middle-class parents had done a good job of dealing with most problems in their lives, including getting a treatment program for their children. They were already able to learn skills; their whole lives revealed their ability to learn on their own.

As behavioral parent training became more popular, it became more available to people who were not learning things on their own. Most of us have had the supports and guidance to master many skills in childhood, adolescence, or young adulthood, before we have children. We are able to learn new skills on our own and integrate the new experiences involved in child-rearing. Parents in multiproblem families often have not mastered basic skills of daily living before they have children.

continued

INTERVIEW with Elaine Blechman   *continued*

So how do you go about what would amount to a crash course in daily life? For example, you have a single mother, poorly educated, maybe estranged from her own family, dependent on welfare, maybe has a substance-abuse problem, maybe has chronic problems with depression, maybe has an accompanying medical or health problem. She can't pay for treatment, so the treatment has to be quick and help her do things differently in many areas of her life. Her child rearing problems may not be her biggest problems. She may be living in a shelter or going from one friend to another with her children, without having money.

So my approach has changed dramatically over the years. I first started out to change behavior. My earliest work was teaching families problem-solving skills. I would teach the parent to sit down and write out a contract with the child about changing behavior at home. I was able to help them do business in a different way.

But later, I said, there's more to it than problem-solving because this parent and child don't listen to each other. So before we try to get them to influence each other, maybe we ought to get an information exchange. That was the beginning of my training families in communication skills. I needed to get them to exchange information before they tried to solve problems.

Before we start skill-training with a family, however, we first provide crisis intervention as needed and requested by the family. We hook them up with a treatment team that can respond almost immediately to the parent's (usually the mother's but sometimes the father's) urgent request for help. Multiproblem families have many crises. They could not focus on my skills training because there were many other important things that had come up during the week. So, I now start with a crisis management team. If they are well trained in communication, they are able to listen and to teach by example and by involvement the very communication skills that allow people in crisis to calm down, think what is going on, make some decisions about whether it is a crisis, what to do about it, how to avert an even bigger crisis.

I want to respond to the needs of the family, to the immediate experience—I've lost a job, my teenage daughter is pregnant, the landlord is going to throw us out—not so much in terms of doing something because you can't do much, but first form a trusting relationship with the parent, and secondly, to get the parent to appraise information, react differently in many different situations, not just with the child.

Having engaged the family in a crisis management approach, then we involve the family in a network with other families in the neighborhood so they become part of a family support group. The typical place for this to happen is the neighborhood school attended by the younger children. The other families will include families who want help with their children but are managing other areas of their lives and can serve as competent role models for the new families. In some indigent neighborhoods, there are single mothers who are very strong individuals themselves but whose children are having problems. They have strengths, and we don't provide the full range of services to them. We help around the children and provide a support group that is very beneficial to them and to others. We don't want to form a conventional psychotherapy group of troubled people who get more depressed by each other's problems.

The family support group becomes a second place for parents to learn better communication, particularly information exchange. The first time a group of families get together and swap problems or experiences, they all want to give advice to each other just as they want to give advice to their kids. We want them to learn, and we try very hard to promote an atmosphere in which they learn how to listen, how to appreciate somebody else's experience—not jump to the conclusion they have had the same experience you have had or that what they tried works better or worse than what you tried, but just to appreciate the similarities and differences. Show an interest, ask questions, paraphrase what the person has said.

What happens here is the same communication strategies families experienced in the crisis group are used with other people. That allows several things to happen. They learn this is how people make friends with each other—they appreciate one another. Second, it is a great tension reducer to be listened to, and sometimes it makes you feel better to listen to someone else. It is aggravating to give people advice they don't take; it is calming, ennobling to listen to someone else who then appreciates your listening. It is very difficult for adults who are very preoccupied with their own views to listen, ask questions, and take in and focus on what others experience.

A lot of other things happen. Families help each other out. Families together can bring about change in the schools and the neighborhood. Ideally, these groups become self-perpetuating so professionals aren't always missionaries imposing their values on people.

In the last chapter of your book, you talked about the importance of optimism and optimistic feelings.

I think we kindle optimism in other people in very simple ways—so simple, they often escape us. The social skills of people working with the families are critical. My secretary smiles no matter what goes on. That makes people around her feel good. They feel no matter what happens, the roof is not going to cave in. There is a kind of gloomy affect that is associated with a lot of our mental health interventions. I think a lot more enjoyment of other people, pride of making people feel good about their accomplishments is the thing to do. When families are having problems, focus on what they are doing well.

* Research on peer-coping skills training with aggressive children was carried out in collaboration with Ron Prinz, University of South Carolina, Columbia, and Jean Dumas, Purdue University, and was supported by grant number R18-MH 48018 from the National Institute of Mental Health.

Adolescents can be involved in community programs and serve as supports for each other in peer counseling or tutoring programs.[40] Such activities benefit both the person who receives the counseling or tutoring and the adolescent who counsels or tutors. Peer counselors often undergo special training that sensitizes them to the needs of their peers and teaches skills they can use in many other situations. Such counseling provides the "client" with a counselor who really understands the life and stresses of an adolescent. Tutoring benefits the tutor, who often learns the material better in the course of teaching, and benefits the tutee, as the tutor recently learned the material himself or herself and perhaps better understands what is involved in learning it.

As with peer counseling and tutoring, adults who engage in community service frequently learn and receive more than they give.

Church Supports

In their study of resilient children who overcame the odds, Emmy Werner and Ruth Smith point to the importance of faith. They write,

A potent protective factor among high-risk individuals who grew into successful adulthood was a faith that life made sense, that the odds could be overcome. This faith was tied to active involvement in church activities, whether Buddhist, Catholic, mainstream Protestant, or fundamentalist.[41]

When parents attend church themselves, it is easy to incorporate the children in that religious life. If parents have no religious affiliation, they may wonder what to do.

One such father of a young child wrote to Joan Beck, author of *Effective Parenting*, to ask for her advice.[42] He could not pretend a belief he did not have in God, but he wanted his daughter to have the freedom to make her own decision as she matured.

Beck's response is summarized as follows. First, each family must find its own answer. Parents have three alternatives: (1) ignore the whole question, (2) send children for religious instruction without their participation, and (3) develop an inquiring attitude about religion that can be shared with the children as they grow.

Church attendance is relatively low, and so it is increasingly easy to raise a child without religious training. Children, however, will then have many questions that remain unanswered: Who is God? What happens when we die? Will God punish me? As children see the involvement of grandparents and of other families with religion, as they encounter religious references in reading, they may feel a void in their own experiences. This void may be intensified if they lack a source of comfort or solace when a painful loss occurs.

Sending a child for instruction without parental participation, however, seems hypocritical. The most reasonable alternative for some parents is to develop an individual belief system that they share with children as they grow. Parents can explore different conceptions of God, convey to children what they accept and do not accept in each conception, discuss the meanings of rituals and symbols and why others may find them important. In investigating the ideas of different churches, parents may discover a group they can join wholeheartedly, rediscover the religion of their parents, or find they want to join a group that is devoted to social action rather than worship. The process of searching for an agreed-upon code can enrich the entire family.

In fostering children's faith, parents have a natural ally in children themselves. Robert Coles reviewed his interactions and interviews with children concerning crises in their lives and their moral and political views of life. He concluded that the area he ignored for too many years of his professional life was children's intense engagement in religious concerns—the meaning of life, the purpose of their individual lives, their goodness and/or badness, their duties and obligations to themselves, to their families, and to others.[43]

Seeking to understand their spiritual lives, Coles interviewed children around the world about their conceptions of God and the meaning of God in their lives. His recent book, *The Spiritual Life of Children*, summarizes numerous poignant interviews and conversations with children, individually and in groups. Religious concerns are not dry intellectual matters to many children, but emotionally intense concerns that are strongly integrated into their personalities and understanding of themselves and life. Coles stated,

> I began to realize that psychologically God can take almost any shape for children. He can be a friend or a potential enemy; an admirer or a critic; an ally or an interference; a source

of encouragement or a source of anxiety; fear, or even panic ... Often, children whose sternly Christian, Jewish, or Moslem parents don't hesitate to threaten them with the most severe of religious strictures (and thus who do likewise with respect to themselves) can construct in their thoughts or dreams a God who is exemplary yet lenient, forgiving, encouraging, capable of confessing a moment's weakness or exhaustion now and then.[44]

Like Werner and Smith, Coles finds that religious beliefs give children a feeling of security that life is predictable and understandable—God knows and understands and controls all. In conversations with God, children experience an emotional closeness—God is "a companion who won't leave."[45] God provides strength and help as needed though how and when are often questions of lengthy consideration. With benefits come obligations of moral behavior in interactions with others. Children's conceptions of God sometimes add security to life by providing fallible parents with a backup expert who helps them. "God is my parents' parent and mine too," stated one girl.

Church programs help both parents and children. Many churches offer general parenting classes and classes in teaching values. Churches also provide recreational and family activities that bring pleasure and feelings of belonging and security to all family members.

A Catholic Church leadership project in Harlem illustrates the powerful support church activities can be for adolescent boys.[46] Twenty-five years ago, the church selected fourteen boys on the basis of academic and personal potential for participation in a two-year program. The boys attended cultural events, listened to speakers, went on weekend retreats that combined fun and discussion of serious issues. Though program designers hoped to recruit some boys for the priesthood, almost all married, some became fathers, and only one became a priest. In large part, they are professional men.

In looking back at what they gained from the experience, the men made such comments as, "My whole life I owe to it. It made me realize my self-worth. Growing up where I did, you never saw the outside world for what it was. I learned that you can be successful by giving it your all." "It was taking this bunch of energy and this bunch of mouth and channeling it into something positive. It helped me stand up and formulate some thoughts in an intelligent way." This project is now open to boys and girls.

THE POWER OF A SINGLE INDIVIDUAL

All the programs mentioned outside the family have involved large organizations. It seems fitting to conclude a discussion of supports with an example of what a single person with a clear goal can accomplish when she gathers community resources to provide support for children and parents.

Dr. Barbara Barlow, a pediatric surgeon at Harlem Hospital in New York, became concerned at the growing number of preventable injuries she was treating. Children fell from open windows, were hit by automobiles while playing in the street, or were victims of violence.[47]

In 1988, she started Harlem Hospital's Injury Prevention Program (IPP) with a grant from the Robert Wood Johnson Foundation. With a staff of three, she worked to rebuild playgrounds and parks in the community because there were no safe places for children to play. She photographed all the parks and playgrounds and took the information to the Parks Department and the Board of Education. The Parks department has since made nearly all the parks in the area safe. Private funding was sought for playgrounds, and with the suggestions of teachers and students of the schools, two new playgrounds have been built and six more are underway.

The Injury Prevention Program has expanded to include activities that foster children's competence. An in-hospital art program, begun so patients could express their feelings about illness and hospitalization, has expanded. Children have exhibited and sold their work with half the profits going to the children and half to the art program. The IPP also sponsors a dance program serving about 200 children, baseball teams, a soccer team, and a greening program in which children have a chance to grow flowers and vegetables.

Major injuries to children in Harlem have decreased by 37 percent. Motor vehicle accidents have decreased by 50 percent, and fewer children fall from windows. In addition, dancers, athletes, artists, and gardeners develop skills they would not have had without the programs.

The increase in violent injuries to children has led Dr. Barlow to start the Anti-Violence Project that contains several specific programs for (1) teaching children how to stay safe, (2) helping children deal with violence after they experience it, and (3) teaching children, their parents, and educators conflict resolution techniques and other ways to avoid violence.

Funding for these programs comes from individuals, corporations, foundations, and from fees from Dr. Barlow's speaking engagements. She concludes,

> You have to give to get in this world, and we give a lot. We put in lots of hard work, but it's immensely satisfying. There is no such thing as not being able to make things better. In any community, every individual can make a tremendous difference if they truly care, if they look around to see what needs to be done.[48]

MAJOR POINTS OF CHAPTER 10

Social supports:

- provide emotional, instrumental, and informational benefits to children and parents
- are divided into people, activities, organizations, and environments
- vary with the individual's age and stage of life
- are constrained by socioeconomic, cultural, ethnic, and gender-related factors

Supportive family members:

- include siblings, grandparents, aunts, uncles, cousins
- increase feelings of emotional closeness and belonging

- serve as companions in activities
- can help carry out parenting activities and nourishing and protecting children
- teach children new skills

Family rituals:

- provide stability by insuring predictability in family life
- encourage communication among family members
- link family members with the past and the future
- serve as a protective factor in times of difficulty

Teachers:

- serve as models
- provide encouragement
- encourage responsibility and competence in children

Nonrelatives:

- provide help, advice, resources for parents
- help children adjust to world outside family
- serve as mentors and models

Parenting programs:

- can provide support groups for parents
- teach specific skills to parents
- enable parents to promote positive behavior in children
- enable parents to reduce children's behavioral difficulties
- reduce stress of parenting
- increase parents' self-confidence and feelings of competence

Work place supports for parents:

- enable parents to spend more time with children
- can provide quality care for children
- help parents incorporate work into the demands of family life

Government programs supportive of parents:

- are not available for all parents, only for those with some special difficulty
- often have too limited funding to help all who are eligible

- can be operated in conjunction with the health-care and educational systems
- may be cheaper when funded to prevent rather than treat problems
- can, according to Zigler, be operated through schools and provide quality care for children of all ages

Community programs:

- serve parents' and children's needs
- enable parents and children to have active, helping roles

Churches are supportive to children:

- because they help make sense of life
- provide a sense of security
- provide emotional closeness with a special figure who focuses attention on the child
- provide guidelines for daily conduct
- give children a sense that parents have a parent they can rely on for security
- provide programs that help children develop competence

Individuals:

- can mobilize resources to support parents and children
- can make an enormous difference in lives of children and parents

EXERCISES

1. List activities, people, organizations that provided you with positive support when you were growing up. Looking back, what do you think were the factors that gave your parents support when they were raising you?

2. Describe family traditions in your family of origin, the feelings these traditions created in family members, and how you will incorporate these traditions in your family of creation.

3. What positive supports did your school provide for you? for your parents? Were there teachers who gave you special encouragement? Were there life-long interests that you developed at that time?

4. Investigate the supports a large company in your area provides its employees. Do they have on-site day care? flex time? family-leave policies?

5. What services does your community provide for parents and children? Parenting programs? recreational programs? summer day programs for children? joint parent-child activities? How friendly is your community to families and young children?

ADDITIONAL READINGS

Coles, Robert. *The Spiritual Life of Children*. Boston: Houghton Mifflin Company, 1990.

Hamburg, David A. *Today's Children*. New York: Times Books, 1992.

Werner, Emmy E. and Smith, Ruth S. *Overcoming the Odds*. Ithaca: Cornell University Press, 1992.

Wolin, Steven J. and Wolin, Sybil. *The Resilient Self*. New York: Villard, 1993.

Zigler, Edward F. and Lang, Mary E. *Child Care Choices*. New York: The Free Press, 1991.

Notes

1. Moncrieff Cochran, "Parenting and Personal Social Networks," in *Parenting: An Ecological Perspective,* eds. Tom Luster and Lynn Okagaki (Hillsdale, N.J.: Lawrence Erlbaum, 1993), pp. 149–178.

2. Ibid.

3. Moncrieff Cochran et al., "Personal Networks and Public Policy," in *Extending Families: The Social Networks of Parents and Their Children,* eds. Moncrieff Cochran et al. (Cambridge: Cambridge University Press, 1990), pp. 307–314.

4. Ibid.

5. Moncrieff Cochran, "Factors Influencing Personal Social Initiative," in *Extending Families,* eds. Cochran et al., pp. 297–306.

6. Ibid., p. 297.

7. Cochran, "Parenting and Personal Social Networks."

8. Brenda K. Bryant, *The Neighborhood Walks: Sources of Support in Middle Childhood,* Monographs of the Society for Research in Child Development *50* (1985) Whole Number 210.

9. Moncrieff Cochran and David Riley, "The Social Networks of Six-Year-Olds: Context, Content, and Consequence," in *Extending Families,* eds. Cochran et al., pp. 154–177.

10. Cochran, "Parenting and Personal Social Networks."

11. Emmy E. Werner and Ruth S. Smith, *Overcoming the Odds* (Ithaca: Cornell University Press, 1992).

12. Judy Dunn, *Sisters and Brothers* (Cambridge University Press, 1985), p. 163.

13. Barbara R. Tinsley and Ross D. Parke, "Grandparents as Support and Socialization Agents," in *Beyond The Dyad,* ed. Michael Lewis (New York: Plenum, 1984), pp. 161–194.

14. Timothy F. J. Tolson and Melvin N. Wilson, "The Impact of Two- and Three-Generational Family Structure on Perceived Family Style," *Child Development* 61 (1990): 416–428.

15. Jane L. Pearson, Andrea G. Hunter, Margaret E. Ensminger, and Sheppard G. Killam, "Black Grandmothers in Multigenerational Households: Diversity in Family Structures on Parenting in the Woodlawn Community," *Child Development* 61 (1990): 434–442.

16. Cochran, "Parenting and Personal Social Networks."

17. Moncrieff Cochran and Charles R. Henderson, Jr., "Formal Supports and Informal Social Ties: A Case Study," in *Extending Families,* eds. Cochran et al., pp. 230–261.

18. Cochran, "Parenting and Personal Social Networks."

19. Cochran and Riley, "The Social Networks of Six-Year-Olds."

20. Steven J. Wolin and Linda A. Bennett, "Family Rituals," *Family Process* 23 (1984): 401–420.

21. Linda A. Bennett et al., "Couples at Risk for Transmission of Alcoholism: Protective Influences," *Family Process* 26 (1987): 111–129.

22. Werner and Smith, *Overcoming the Odds,* p. 178.

23. Eigel Pedersen, Theresa Annette Faucher with William W. Eaton, "A New Perspective on the Effects of First-Grade Teachers on Children's Subsequent Adult Status," *Harvard Educational Review* 48 (1978): 1–31.

24. Ibid., p. 20.

25. Michael Rutter et al., *Fifteen Thousand Hours: Secondary Schools and Their Effects on Children* (New York: Cambridge University Press, 1979).

26. Cochran, "Parenting and Personal Networks."

27. Carolyn Pape Cowan and Philip A. Cowan, *When Partners Become Parents* (New York: Basic Books, 1992).

28. Bruce Cedar and Ronald F. Levant, "A Meta-Analysis of the Effects of Parent Effectiveness Training," *The American Journal of Family Therapy 18* (1990): 373–384.

29. Paul C. Burnett, "Evaluation of Adlerian Parenting Programs," *Individual Psychology 44* (1988): 63–76.

30. Anthony M. Graziano and David M. Diament, "Parent Behavior Training: An Examination of the Paradigm," *Behavior Modification 16* (1992): 3–39.

31. G. R. Patterson and Carla M. Narrett, "The Development of a Reliable and Valid Treatment Program for Aggressive Young Children," *International Journal of Mental Health 19* (1990): 19–26.

32. Amy Wolfson, Patricia Lacks, and Andrew Futterman, "Effects of Parent Training on Infant Sleeping Patterns, Parents' Stress, and Perceived Parental Competence," *Journal of Consulting and Clinical Psychology 60* (1992): 41–48.

33. Deborah Stipek and Jacquelyn McCrosky, "Investing in Children: Government and Workplace Policies for Parents," *American Psychologist 44* (1989): 416–423.

34. Edward A. Zigler and Mary E. Lang, *Child Care Choices* (New York: The Free Press, 1991).

35. Ibid.

36. David A. Hamburg, *Today's Children* (New York: Times Books, 1992).

37. Ibid., p. 331.

38. Zigler and Lang, *Child Care Choices*.

39. Hamburg, *Today's Children*.

40. Ibid.

41. Werner and Smith, *Overcoming the Odds*, p. 177.

42. Joan Beck, *Effective Parenting* (New York: Simon & Schuster, 1976).

43. Robert Coles, *The Spiritual Life of Children* (Boston: Houghton Mifflin Company, 1990).

44. Ibid., pp. 119–120.

45. Ibid., p. 127.

46. Felicia R. Lee, "Memories of Youths in Harlem: *The New York Times*, July 10, 1993, p. 16.

47. Amy Arner Sgarro, "A Surgeon and Her Community," *Vassar Quarterly*, Spring 1993, pp. 10–13.

48. Ibid., p. 13.

Index